Practices of Dialogue in the Roman Catholic Church

Practices of Dialogue in the Roman Catholic Church

Aims and Obstacles, Lessons and Laments

Bradford E. Hinze

NEW YORK • LONDON

2006
The Continuum International Publishing Group Inc
80 Maiden Lane, New York, NY 10038

The Continuum International Publishing Group Inc
The Tower Building, 11 York Road, SE1 7NX

Chapter 4, "A New Way of Teaching with Authority," is a revised version of an essay that appeared in *Unfailing Patience and Sound Teaching: Reflections on Episcopal Ministry in Honor of Rembert G. Weakland, O.S.B.*, edited by David Stosur and published by Liturgical Press, Collegeville, Minn. Copyright 2003 by the Order of St. Benedict, Collegeville, Minn.

Continuum Publishing is committed to preserving ancient forests and natural resources. We have elected to print this title on 30% postconsumer waste recycled paper. As a result, this book has saved:
5 trees
247 lbs of solid waste
1,920 gallons of water
4 million BTUs
463 lbs of greenhouse gases
Continuum is a member of Green Press Initiative, a nonprofit program dedicated to supporting publishers in their efforts to reduce their use of fiber obtained from endangered forests. For more information, go to www.greenpressinitiative.org.

Library of Congress Cataloging-in-Publication Data

Hinze, Bradford E., 1954-
Practices of dialogue in the Roman Catholic Church : aims and obstacles, lessons and laments / Bradford E. Hinze.
p. cm.
Includes bibliographical references and index.
ISBN-13: 978-0-8264-1721-3 (hardcover : alk. paper)
ISBN-10: 0-8264-1721-3 (hardcover : alk. paper)
1. Dialogue—Religious aspects—Catholic Church. I. Title.
BX1795.D53H56 2006
282.09'045—dc22

2005031726

Contents

Preface

This project began during a sabbatical in the summer of 2002 and was completed in 2005, during the celebration of the fortieth anniversary of the end of Vatican II and the last year of the pontificate of John Paul II. My original plan was to write a chapter describing key examples of dialogical practices in the post–Vatican II church to illustrate the shift to a dialogical understanding of the church that is currently under way. My larger aim was to construct a theological argument about the dialogical and communicative character of the church that would engage diverse and at times contentious philosophical, social-theoretical, and theological resources. As I researched several key examples of dialogical practice in the U.S. Catholic Church, I was reminded of other examples that merited closer study as well. Over the course of several months I became convinced that the voices of the actual practitioners of dialogue in the church were at least as important to heed as those of philosophers, social theorists, and theologians who have addressed the topic of dialogue and communication. What began as a chapter soon became several chapters in part 1, and eventually a book.

Letting the practitioners of dialogue at every level of the life of the church tell of their everyday accomplishments and struggles, their triumphs and tragedies, and scrutinizing their reflections on their achievements and frustrations in their labor has proven immensely valuable. Although I offer some of my own reflections on these practices at the end of this study, my own more extensive theological responses will be developed elsewhere. It has been more important to listen first to the testimonies of these practitioners and to make their accomplishments and struggles more widely known. Their efforts are an important part of the drama of Vatican II and its ongoing reception, and their stories are worthy of widespread attention and discussion at all levels of the church.

Over the course of researching and writing this book I have tried to follow the practices of those about whom I have been writing. As I have conducted my research, I have consulted widely with practitioners of dialogue through e-mail, phone conversations, and face-to-face meetings. Each chapter has been read and responded to by one, two, and sometimes more people who have been involved in these efforts or who have written on particular practices. In all cases I have incorporated some of the recommendations offered, and in many cases I have followed up by exploring new avenues of analysis. Often I rewrote chapters and submitted them again to those who had offered me particularly helpful input or to other people with special experience and expertise. Further amendments were often made in light of subsequent comments.

For taking part in this dialogical dynamic, one I regard as intrinsic to the *habitus* of theology, I wish to express my gratitude to some of the many people whose testimony and contributions have made this work richer and more accurate: Tom Best, John Borelli, Helen Marie Burns, RSM, Francis J. Butler, David Coffey, Bernard Cooke, James Coriden, Paul Crow, Jr., Charles E. Curran, Barbara Anne Cusack, Dan Daley, Michael Fahey, SJ, Mark Fischer, Nadine Foley, OP, Bryan Froehle, Richard R. Gaillardetz, Walter Grazer, Jeffrey Gros, FSC, Ashley Hall, Bryan Hehir, Robert Heineman, Jane Wolford Hughes, Dolores Leckey, Daniel J. Murray, David O'Brien, Virginia O'Reilly, OP, Catherine H. Patten, RSHM, Paul Philibert, OP, Anthony Pogorelc, SS, Archbishop John R. Quinn, Maria Riley, OP, David M. Ross, Thomas Schellabarger, Thomas Sweetser, SJ, Donald Thimm, John A. Vaughan, SS, Judith Schaefer, OP, Anne Riggs, Lynn Ann Reesman, Patricia Walter, OP, Archbishop Rembert Weakland, OSB, and Susan Wood, SCL. I owe a special debt of thanks to Roger Haight, SJ, Judith Schaefer, OP, and Michele Saracino for offering their comments on large parts of this manuscript, and above all to John Thiel, Christine Firer Hinze, and Frank Oveis for their comments on the entire manuscript.

Dialogue with a number of colleagues has enriched my thinking on these subjects over the years: Bernd Jochen Hilberath, Matthias Scharer, M. Shawn Copeland, and Siegfried Wiedenhofer. I am also most grateful for the support of my colleagues at Marquette University, especially Deirdre Dempsey, Michael Fahey, SJ, and Irfan Omar.

My work on this project began in earnest in the summer of 2002, thanks to a Marquette University Summer Fellowship, and the major portion of my research was made possible by the generosity of the 2002–2003 Marquette University Sabbatical Fellowship.

I was assisted by archivists at the Catholic University of America, the University of Notre Dame, the Archdiocese of Detroit, the Archdiocese of Milwaukee, the Adrian Dominican Sisters, as well as by chancellors and archivists in various dioceses across the United States.

The undergraduate students in my class at Marquette University in the spring term of 2004 entitled Theology of the Church offered constructive criticisms of an earlier draft of this text: Alexandria Ahrens, Thomas Andreasen, John Dunn III, Eric Fredell, Jessica Gazzola, Magdalisse Gonzalez, Erica Kowalski, Bruce Lanser, Rebecca Rasiarmos, Kyle Schreiner, Melissa Senftle, Christopher Stolpa, Ryan Wiesman, and Michael Wolf.

I also want to thank the various circles of people with whom I have practiced dialogue during this period of my life. I thank the priests, pastoral ministers, and parishioners of St. Margaret Mary Parish in Milwaukee, especially choir members and musicians. I am particularly grateful to Archbishop Rembert Weakland, OSB, for the invitation to participate in the Archbishop's Consultation on Theological Issues, and for the opportunity to work with Bishop Richard Sklba and Archbishop Timothy Dolan and my theological colleagues across the Milwaukee archdiocese. Thanks to Paul Lakeland and Serene Jones for the invitation to participate in the exciting and challenging conversations that take place in the Workgroup on Constructive Christian Theology. More personally, I wish to express my gratitude for support over the years from members of the Mustard Seed Christian Life Community, a faith-sharing group in the tradition of Ignatius of Loyola: Tom and Bernie Bausch, Ralph Del Colle and Lee Coppernoll, Judith Longdin and Steve Goldzwig, Amy Richter and Joe Pagano, and Joseph Mueller, SJ. The support of George and Nadine Didier, Marcie Paul and Steve Kaplan, Fred Gustafson, Carol Ann Smith, SHCJ, David Shields, SJ, John Schwantes, SJ, and to Donald and Rosemary Firer and all the Hinze and Firer siblings and spouses, nieces and nephews, has also been deeply appreciated.

In my inner dialogue circle, I want to thank my sons, Paul and Karl, for the many conversations we have shared, and for all of their encouragement and technical support throughout this project. I dedicate this book to Christine Firer Hinze, dialogue partner par excellence.

Introduction

Over the last forty years a great deal of time and energy has been devoted to developing a dialogical approach to the identity and mission of the church. This has been on the agenda of virtually all Christians. In a special way, however, Roman Catholics since the Second Vatican Council have struggled to move from a strictly hierarchical approach to the church's activities of teaching, administering the sacraments, governing, pastoral care, and work for justice, to a more dialogical approach in which all the members of the church are actively participating. This is a project that is still very much under way. Yet some Catholics fear that this effort is doomed to fail. Some believe that the exercise of hierarchical and clerical authority by popes, bishops, and priests is jeopardizing and destroying the legitimate and inspired use of dialogue in the church. Others complain that practices of dialogue threaten to undermine the rightful authority of the hierarchy and the content of faith. The future of dialogue in the church is by no means clear.

This book offers an invitation to reflect on the contemporary practices of dialogue in the Catholic Church, especially in the United States. Attention will be given both to internal dialogue in the church among members with different roles and responsibilities at different institutional levels in the church, and to external dialogue between individuals in the Catholic Church and people in other churches, other religions, and in the broader society. Ancient, traditional practices of dialogue, which have been recently recovered and reformed, such as synods, councils, and chapters, will be examined. Likewise, experiments with newer practices, such as national episcopal conferences, Call To Action, the Catholic Common Ground Initiative, and ecumenical and interreligious dialogues will be studied. These are among the most important examples of dialogue in the church.

As this work proceeds, and as each of the practices of dialogue is described and analyzed, two questions will be kept in mind. What are the aims of each form of dialogue? And what are the obstacles? The responses to these questions will in the end lead to two further questions. What is being learned about the use of dialogue in the church from these practices? And what is being learned by the struggles, failures, and breakdowns of dialogue?

My overall objective and commitment in this work are to advance the ongoing development of a dialogical ecclesiology. Here I stand with all those in local communities around the world and at every organizational level in the Catholic Church who believe that the future of the Catholic Church and the church universal depends on the further cultivation of dialogical skills and the necessary reforms in practices in the church and potential revisions of the doctrine of the church entailed therein. But I also believe it is important to understand the struggles involved in these practices of dialogue in the church and to ponder the criticisms and frustrations voiced by the detractors and defenders of dialogue. Exploring everyday practices of the church in dialogue is a starting point that must eventually be accompanied by other forms of critical reflection on these practices in light of basic Christian beliefs and specific theories about dialogue and communication deriving from theology, philosophy, and social theory. Still, this project makes one very important point clear: voices of actual practitioners of dialogue in the church are at least as important to heed as those of philosophers, social theorists, theologians, and pastoral leaders, and ultimately any theology of dialogue in the church must be judged by its ability to account for the richness and complexity of these practices.

THE SHIFT TO A DIALOGICAL UNDERSTANDING OF THE CHURCH

The Second Vatican Council marked a turning point in the development of a dialogical approach to the Catholic Church. Bishops and theologians who participated in the council laid the theological groundwork and identified the reform of key practices necessary for building a dialogical church. A design for a dialogical church emerged in the council's teachings on two levels, like two overlapping sheets in an architect's plan. On one level, the four doctrinal constitutions laid the theological cornerstones and groundwork by articulating the communicative character of God's revelation, the liturgy of the church, the nature and mission of church, and the church's relation to the world. On a second level, the decrees and declarations set forth specific recommendations for a range of dialogical practices pertaining to the offices of bishops and priests, to religious life, laity, missionary activity, ecumenical and interrelgious relations, education, mass media, and civil society. The practices described in this book reveal the initial phases in the construction of this new design.

What is the older style of church that this newer design is intended to modify or replace? The older design is characterized by a certain understanding of human relations, decision making, and communication in the church. This older style of church took shape in direct response to the Protestant Reformation in the sixteenth and seventeenth centuries and the rise of modern science and liberal ideology in the eighteenth and nineteenth centuries. A post-Reformation and modern phenomenon, this older church design is sometimes called Tridentine because of its genesis in the aftermath of the Council of Trent (1545–1563), but this formation reached its high point at the end of the nineteenth and the beginning of the twentieth centuries following Vatican Council I (1869–1870). The pattern of relations and practices that emerged over these centuries was intended to affirm and maintain the sacramental and institutional mediation of faith. Central to this effort was an apologetic and polemical approach to the identity and mission of the church advanced by means of papal, episcopal, and clerical authority. The result was a paternalistic and frequently defensive and protective approach to communication. Internally, the church's organizational structure emphasized a one-way mode of communication. Information and directives flowed from centralized and higher levels of authority, from Rome to local churches, from bishops to clergy, and from clergy to laity. The pope, bishops, and priests were viewed as the teaching church, the trusted fathers who delivered God's clear message as the active representatives of Christ to the laity. The laity, on the other hand, were the docile children, the learning and obedient church. In significant ways the church's external communication defined the Catholic Church over against the reformed churches and modern ideas and practices. The church was not engaged in dialogue with outsiders, but rather was poised to attack and counterattack, to show others where they were wrong and, in the process, to shore up the Catholic Church's distinctive identity and mission in the world.

The four doctrinal constitutions of Vatican II were groundbreaking insofar as they provided the theological foundation for a dialogical approach to the Catholic Church in both its internal and external relations. Of utmost importance, they offered a theological framework and set of principles for a dialogical approach to the exercise of authority in teaching and governance in the Church's internal relations, but not strictly speaking in terms of "dialogue" as such. Rather, the council promoted "collegiality" among bishops in its teaching and through its practices; it fostered "collaboration" between bishops and theologians through its practices, though nothing was said about this collaboration in its teaching; and it laid the theological groundwork for greater "consultation" between bishops and laity, but with very limited practical experience of such consultation contributing to their statements. The term "dialogue" itself was introduced in the documents of Vatican II when treating the relations of Catholics with those outside the Catholic Church: with other Christians, with members of non-Christian religions, with those who hold nonreligious worldviews, and in general terms with "the world."

In principle, then, Vatican II laid the groundwork for a dialogical approach to the church's internal and external relations. Dialogue between official representatives and agents of the Catholic Church with those outside the church thus became a frequent topic in official teachings. Collaboration, shared responsibility, and consultation, that is, creating structures of participation within the church to promote good working relations between people at different hierarchical levels, was encouraged at the council and has been since—but not in terms of dialogue, at least with rare exceptions, and always with restrictions indicating that consultation and participation at all levels of the church have no canonical bearing on the exercise of hierarchical authority in governance and teaching.[1] In other words, open communication is advised, but no canonical requirement for dialogue within the church among bishops, theologians, priests, and laity has been specified up front, and no accountability for following through on the judgments and decisions that derive from such dialogue has been established.[2]

One crucial complicating factor must be kept in mind when considering the older paternalistic, polemical approach to the communicative character of the church in relation to the newer dialogical approach. This problematic issue concerns the basic structure of the Catholic Church, with its dynamic relations between holders of ordained offices and nonordained members of the faithful, especially pertaining to the exercise of various kinds of leadership and authority. This structure is often completely identified for contemporary readers with what is here called the older paternalistic and polemical church design. This structure, however, in various versions, has a much longer history and doctrinal rationale that reaches all the way back to nascent Christianity. Some may wish to speak of any church structure of ordained and nonordained in any period of Christian history in terms of hierarchy. This usage is in principle and semantically legitimate, but it runs the risk of imposing on earlier periods a later theology and particular practices of ordained leadership and ecclesial decision making (for instance, late-medieval, post-Reformation, or early modern). In reality, the structures and practices of the church as they pertain to the relation of ordained and nonordained members have a history that one ought not confuse.

In the pre–Vatican II era, this structure of ordained and nonordained came to be instantiated in paternalistic and polemical hierarchical modes of relation and communication. Equally important, this particular pre–Vatican II design has remained to some degree intact, even as the newer dialogical design has been sketched and practices have been retrieved and reformed, or newer experiments have taken place. After four decades, the outstanding question remains whether and, if so, how the two structures, like two architectural styles, can be integrated without one being violated. The frustration felt by many is that dialogical approaches to teaching, governance, liturgy, and service that the council promised have not been realized. The fear is that they will not and cannot be realized. The various chapters of this book will give plenty of evidence for both the frustration and the fear. But in the process there may be a deeper hope born of wisdom that something is emerging here and that the reception of Vatican II is still very much a work in progress.

The reader will have to decide what kind of stories these are, not only each of the episodes of practices narrated in the individual chapters but the overarching drama of the book. Are these tragedies, which narrate the promise and failure of dialogue at so many different levels of the church?

Or are these plots better identified with the literary genre called *Bildungsroman*, which tells of a circuitous and arduous journey that combines occasions of learning and unlearning in a long process of growing in wisdom and character? The moments of tragedy in the chapters are real and recurring, and I will insist that grievances and laments be given full voice. Tragedy could very well be the last word. But in the end, I argue that these stories can be and ought to be sources of deeper learning, more radical conversion, and new possibilities in the ongoing development of dialogical practices in the church.

THE SHIFT TO A TRINITARIAN ECCLESIOLOGY

Besides initiating a transition to a dialogical understanding of the church, Vatican II also reconsidered the church's identity and mission in relation to the deepest Christian convictions about the identity and mission of God. As has been said, the pre–Vatican II church emphasized one-way hierarchical communication within the church and polemical communication with those outside it. This approach was theologically justified by a christocentric ecclesiology that stressed the divine character of Jesus Christ, the Word made flesh, as the warrant for the Catholic Church's hierarchy, institution, and supremacy. Vatican II continued to affirm Jesus' divine character and its significance for the nature and mission of the church. But it promoted a revolutionary enlargement of vision.

On one level, during the time immediately before and during the council, there began to take place a deeper reflection on the identity of Jesus Christ that sought to incorporate a much fuller appreciation of the humanity of Jesus alongside the affirmation of Jesus' divinity. This expansion was triggered in part by theological reflections commemorating the fifteen-hundredth anniversary of the Council of Chalcedon, as well as by the biblical and liturgical movements, which fostered a return to the original sources of Christianity. As a result doors opened to a deeper exploration of the diversity of christologies in the New Testament and in the history of Christianity. As scholars and believers recovered and newly recognized the diverse biblical portraits of Jesus, the humanity of Jesus, the Jewishness of Jesus, the social and political dimensions of Jesus, the complex personal, social, and institutional dynamics resulting in the passion and death of Jesus, more light was shed on the church's christological character, and the dimensions of an enlarged ecclesiology came into view.

On a second level, Vatican II signaled a renewed attention to the role of the Holy Spirit in the church and the world. Previously, the doctrine of the Holy Spirit had worked on two parallel tracks. One was an ecclesiological track, in which the Spirit inspired the ordained leaders in exercising their leadership roles; on another track the Spirit fostered the sanctification of all Christians through the work of grace. This approach to the Holy Spirit could, and often did, lead to the conclusion that the Spirit assisted the bishops and priests in teaching and guarding the truth with authority, and aided the faithful in obeying the bishops and priests in their communication of the faith. Vatican II, in its theology of baptism and in its theology of the threefold anointings of Jesus Christ as priest, prophet, and king, began to bring into focus the ecclesiological significance of the reception of the Spirit at baptism for all Christians. Through the gift of the Spirit, everyone is called to participate fully in the life of liturgy and to share in the responsibilities of the church in the world. Moreover, through the gift of the Spirit, everyone is called to holiness. Through the gift of the Spirit, everyone has a mission and many have a ministry in the church. Through the gift of the Spirit, one has a sense of faith (*sensus fidei*), and thus the ability to perceive, recognize, receive, and appropriate the truth of faith. By this sense of faith (*sensus fidei*) one participates in and is informed by the sense of the faithful (*sensus fidelium*), which together serve as the basis for the personal and collective reception of the doctrines of faith and the role of all the faithful as guardians and witnesses of faith.[3]

On a third level, the council reflected on the church's origins, identity, and mission in relation to the drama of the relations of the Triune God in eternity and throughout the history of the world. Relationality and communion were recognized as the central categories for understanding God's identity and mission in the world, and the church was being called upon to be a sacrament, an icon, a sign and instrument of this trinitarian mystery of relationality and communion in the world. What is noteworthy is that the council documents emphasized the unity or communion of the three persons of the Trinity as the crucial point for the church's identity, whereas since the council more attention has been given to the mystery of the diverse persons in communion.

Far more attention needs to be given to the ways in which God enters into the dialogue of the church, but these questions will need to be set aside in this present study. It must suffice to note that in these efforts at dialogue one witnesses more attention to a fuller christology, more attention to the role of the Spirit, and more attention to the trinitarian character of the church. The simultaneous emergence of a dialogical and trinitarian approach to the church is not accidental.

TOWARD A WORKING DEFINITION OF DIALOGUE WITHIN THE LARGER FIELD OF COMMUNICATION

Dialogue is a word that can have a wide variety of meanings when it is used to describe communication in the church. This is likewise the case when the term is used in virtually any personal and social context. The distinctive dynamic feature of dialogue, common among the many specific meanings given to the word, is the back-and-forth movement in communication between individuals in which people are acting both as speakers and as listeners and there is an exchange of messages that provide the condition for possible common understandings, judgments, decisions, and actions. Through this exchange people can gain insight into their personal and communal identity and into the world; horizons expand, minds and hearts change, conversions occur. Such a dynamic supplies the necessary ingredients in the formation of bonds of relationship, bonds that may withstand varieties of hostility, or elicit uneasy tolerance, but that also provide the condition for the possibility of the deepest forms of sociality, friendship, and love.

Usually when one thinks of dialogue one imagines a mutual exchange of messages between two individual people. In other words, dialogue often connotes a dyad. This would be its narrowest meaning. The term is often extended, however, to characterize not only the exchange between two individuals but also similar exchanges among a group of people. Some prefer to specify such collective forms of communication as conversation and not speak of this mode of discourse as dialogue at all. So one finds the word *colloquium* used in Latin, *Gespräch* in German, and *palaver* in French to designate a discussion between a group of people, sometimes people of diverse social strata. But in this book *dialogue* and *conversation* will be used as synonyms. In every chapter attention will be given to small groups of people exchanging their opinions about common topics.

In this investigation the term *dialogue* will be further extended to include a variety of other modes of communicative practice. These will be identified as dialogical because they are premised on an exchange between speakers and listeners striving for mutual understandings, judgments, decisions, and actions, even though the form of this dynamic action may not operate in the same way as the intimate give-and-take between individuals or the lively exchange of a small group. One example of such extended usage would be the format of a hearing, modeled on a legislative hearing common in governmental settings, which is sometimes employed in consultation. In such settings certain officials hear (and sometimes read) the spoken (and often also written transcripts or prepared) testimony of individuals with particular kinds of experience or expertise. Those who are the official listeners in these sessions are also frequently questioners, and they may offer observations as well, which can and often do in turn evoke responses from those giving testimony. In other words, dialogical exchanges between official listeners and presenters is not uncommon. Beyond that, official listeners also become "speakers" in a more formal sense often when they prepare a document or develop a course of action to be followed drawing on the wisdom provided by those giving testimony. And there are times, though rare, when additional responses are invited and received from those who have previously given testimony to the speakers.

Plenary sessions at meetings of diocesan synods, episcopal conferences, or synods of bishops, as well as in larger ecumenical and interreligious gatherings provide yet wider extensions of the dialogical term. These gatherings will likewise be called dialogical because these larger groups meet to discuss and deliberate while aiming at common understandings, judgments, decisions, and courses of action, often articulated in a public declaration or text of one kind or another. It is important to note that every one of the larger plenary meetings treated in this book is a part of a process that includes smaller group modes of dialogue, groups often composed of eight to fifteen to twenty-five or more members, as a necessary condition for the larger plenary session to be possible and effective.

There are further necessary extensions of the word *dialogue* in this book.

Dialogue or *conversation* is used to name the to-and-fro movement of a reader and a text. This is a motif developed to great effect by the German philosopher Hans Georg Gadamer and by Catholic theologian David Tracy.[4] Again, the specific dynamism of dialogue identified in this study is being affirmed here: a back-and-forth exchange (of some sort) between two communicators (reader and text). Clearly, the interchange between reader and text is a dialogue or a conversation only by analogy; a text can only respond to the questions of readers and address questions to readers in the imagination and intellect of the reader as a gift and achievement of discernment.[5] This important qualification notwithstanding, the term *dialogue* will be used in this book to characterize a certain mode of relation between readers and texts. When people learn how to read and meditate upon the scriptures or participate in liturgy a crucial part of this process of initiation is learning how to enter into the world opened up by these texts, whether characters portrayed or arguments constructed to address specific life situations, and in this process people participate in a living dialogue with these characters and arguments.

Since at least the tradition of Plato, it has been postulated that people enter into dialogue with the self: this is how the process of thinking and conscience was frequently described. More recently there has been a critique of a unitary view of consciousness and the corresponding stable sense of self-identity associated with classical and modern theories. This has been accompanied by the belief that people experience themselves as composed of (or fragmented by) a plurality of self-identities that are vocal within the self. A person may identify with one of these interior voices (identity postures) at different times or must adjudicate and choose between them. Accordingly, the self can be described as a dialogue of inner voices through which a plurality of possibilities, needs, wishes, motivations, and ideas are expressed. One is challenged to balance or integrate the various inner voices in order to develop a unitary sense of self by postulating a self who takes the lead in relation to the variety of individual voices in the "inner group" in order to establish one's identity in plurality.[6] This experience of an inner dialogue with a range of possible selves offers one way of describing the lifelong process of identity formation (individuation), from the early phases of experimentation in childhood and teenage years with different personas and egos, to the life transitions and sometimes course corrections that occur in middle and later life, all of which take place through dialogue with the voices of possible selves or dimensions of the self (as well as the dialogue that takes place in the web of relationships with family, friends, and associates). For Christian theology, this offers as well one way of thinking about the lifelong process of discerning vocation and personal mission in life.

These experiences of the internal dialogue with multiple selves or with multiple voices within the self appear to be distinct from, and yet related to, the internal struggles that take place with "psychological complexes." Carl Gustav Jung in his 1934 essay on complex theory wrote of the experience of personal trauma or shock that causes a conflict within the self and results in a splitting of the personality in which each fragment of the personality has its own character and memory and even autonomy. Jung spoke of these complexes as "little people" who are a part of our inner experience. They have the power to destroy not only individuals but also families and communities.[7] For Jung these little people can manifest themselves in one's daily conscious life as dark forces and unconscious slips, but these complexes are also the architects of dreams, and the pathway to the unconscious. The Christian tradition has long acknowledged destructive forces that can possess people and destroy them. Likewise the ancient tradition of the seven deadly sins has been reconsidered in terms of unconscious or half-conscious psychological complexes, not simply conscious moral depravity.

All the uses of dialogue that have been mentioned, the encounter and engagement that take place between individuals, in small groups, and larger collectivities, with books and liturgical rituals, and throughout the inner dialogue with the self are undergirded by and culminate in the individual's and community's dialogue with God. Although the question of how God enters the conversation that we are will only indirectly be considered, we will leave room for the notion that God does seek to enter into the conversation that we are through all the levels of dialogical discernment that are explored in this book. That God "speaks" through the scriptures and liturgy, and through other individuals and communities is a theological claim worthy of pondering and probing that, strictly speaking, moves beyond the confines of this work. But for believers it is a working assumption that indeed God is not only speaking but also listening and responding. Though advancing a proper theological case for God's communication must be considered elsewhere, that God is the source of dialogue and that God seeks to enter into dialogue constitute deep convictions that are shared by many if not all of the participants in the practices of dialogue that are considered in this work. How precisely God is speaking and listening, how exactly God is entering the conversation that distinguishes our very identity, and how best to discern what God is communicating are topics about which there are different views and strong disagreements.

In this work I will speak of the practices of dialogue. I will say more about practices in the next section, but at a most basic level it is important to note that this formulation assumes that beliefs and practices are intertwined. Moreover, it implies that one can learn the skills and cultivate the habits of dialogue.

Dialogue is only one form of communication; there are others. How is one to understand dialogue in relation to the larger field of communication? This issue cannot be adequately addressed in this volume; however, it is important to acknowledge that there are forms of communication that are not based on the back-and-forth dynamism between individuals or within groups. The philosopher Vilém Flusser has contrasted a dialogical mode of communication, in which messages oscillate between participants, and discursive modes, in which a message flows from sender to receiver.[8] Lecture halls, theaters, movies, and television provide examples of this kind of discursive, one-way communication. Speakers are not required to listen and listeners are not required to speak. There is no open-ended mutuality, no chance for all parties to learn, for participants to be influenced by each other leading to mutual growth. One often thinks of nondialogical communication in terms of passing on information. And while there is an important truth in this distinction that merits further reflection, in cases of communication that do not have the clear traits of dialogue, I am asking the reader to consider that even in discursive modes (such as a public reading or an address as in teaching and in liturgy) there may be dialogue-like dynamics at work.

Symbols, rituals, and sacraments are also important forms of communication, especially in Catholic practice and theology, that may not seem dialogical. Water and oil, fire and incense, bread and wine provide symbolic modes of communication where not one, but multiple meanings are conveyed sometimes simultaneously. Assembled people, musicians, lectors, communion distributors, and priests are all actively involved in proclaiming the gospel, celebrating the sacrament, and communicating with God and with each other in the work of worship. In sacraments, meaning is conveyed by things, gestures, and actions, and together they are combined with liturgical words and biblical stories in a complex hybrid mode of communication. These cannot be reduced to discursive instruments of a one-way communication: from God or from priests or ministers to congregations who become all ears. Rather, they are a part of a much more complex mode of communication that includes dialogical dynamics but is not reducible to dialogue.

A WORD ABOUT METHOD

This book invites readers to attend to the practices of dialogue in the church. By doing so, it follows the method advanced by Latin American theologian Gustavo Gutiérrez, who proposed that theology should start with historical praxis. By historical praxis he means the committed spiritual and pastoral action of Christians in the church and the world. If one begins by attending to praxis, theology can be understood, he proposed, as critical reflection on this praxis in light of the Word of God.[9] Gutiérrez's approach to theology does not follow a classical method that starts with sources and beliefs and constructs a coherent Christian worldview, from which, by following procedures of application (a hermeneutics of application), are deduced the proper responses to contemporary situations and problems that occupy the everyday practices of people. Nor does it adopt a modern approach to theology that seeks to correlate the human situation or human experience with Christian texts and traditions (a hermeneutics of correlation), which runs the risk of compromising the challenges posed by praxis and by sacred texts and traditions.[10] Gutiérrez's alternative is to start with everyday Christian praxis. Here praxis and beliefs are already intertwined and mutually informing. By attending to praxis first, Gutiérrez believes that one discovers the deeper aspirations and desires of people, but also one is forced to confront their suffering and struggles. Praxis, personally and collectively, says a great deal about who one is, one's deepest convictions, and who one is striving to become.

To speak of practices also evokes the ancient philosophical tradition of Aristotle, which understands virtues as habituated practices. This

Aristotelian legacy was further developed by Thomas Aquinas in his theological interpretation of the cooperation of God's grace with human freedom in the cultivation of virtuous human beings and communities. More recently, Aristotle's contribution has been retrieved and reworked by philosopher Alisdair MacIntyre. MacIntyre makes the case that social practices, in particular virtues, are united within and constitutive of narrative traditions (e.g., Greek, Roman, Jewish, and Christian epics, tragedies, and other genres), which shape and guide the lives of individuals and communities. MacIntyre defines practice as "any coherent and complex form of socially established cooperative human activity through which goods internal to that form of activity are realized in the course of trying to achieve those standards of excellence which are appropriate to, and partially definitive of, that form of activity."[11] As a result, individuals flourish and excel, but there occur at the same time a growing understanding and realization of the ends and goods involved in these social practices. Such practices are realized through the cultivation of virtues, which are "acquired human qualit[ies] the possession and exercise of which tend to enable us to achieve those goods which are internal to practices and the lack of which effectively prevents us from achieving any such goods."[12] What will become clearer as this study proceeds is that the last forty years have been a time to foster the growth of the social practices, the skills, the habits—in short, the virtues—necessary for honest, generous, and fair dialogue in the interest of advancing the identity and mission of the church, the goods and ends which the church collectively seeks. The cumulative evidence will show that while the virtues of dialogue have been cultivated, they have neither reached maturation nor been widely or well taught.

What can also be appreciated in light of MacIntyre's contribution is that Vatican II began to develop a larger narrative and ritual framework in its four foundational documents for the particular social practices and virtues needed to develop a genuinely dialogical church. By developing such a narrative and promoting these social practices there can be realized the very notion of a living tradition, which MacIntyre espouses, "as an historically extended, socially embodied argument [or in the terms of this book, a historically extended, socially embodied dialogue or conversation], and an argument precisely in part about the goods which constitute that tradition. Within a tradition the pursuit of goods extends through generations, sometimes through many generations."[13] But such a tradition, specifically as reflected in the dialogical practices examined here, can "decay, disintegrate and disappear" and so additional questions must be asked: "What sustains and strengthens traditions? What weakens and destroys them?"[14]

Throughout my investigation, I have worked with the implicit assumption and growing conviction that it is not enough to think with Gutiérrez and MacIntyre, because there is a need to account for more than committed praxis and disciplined practices. There is a need to face head-on the struggles and contestations caused by the unconscious, by bias, by ideologies, by power dynamics, by patterns of exclusion, by how people deal with the abject in their own lives or in social life, by the human traffic that takes place between the borders and boundaries of persons and groups, whether porous or transgressive, hospitable or hostile, all of which regularly emerge in the practices of dialogues. Here the work of social theorist Pierre Bourdieu on practice provides a helpful resource as this work proceeds.[15] What is particularly important about Bourdieu's work for my purpose is that he is especially alert to the power of *habitus* as a set of dispositions that orient people to act and react in certain ways and which are a product of history and social conditions that integrate past experiences and serve as "a matrix of perceptions, appreciations, and actions" in the interest of historical continuity and social harmony. In other words, practices reflect habits that affect how people personally and collectively think, feel, act, order their world, and orient themselves over time. Moreover, and important for this study, Bourdieu's concept of *habitus* recognizes the power of the "unconscious" and the unsaid as ingredients in the generative logic of practice as well.[16] Because of the unintentional and unconscious dimensions of personal and social life, there is a need in the midst of practices for "a critique which brings the undiscussed into discussion, the unformulated into formulation," and as a result can contribute to transformations or revolutions.[17] Bourdieu's decisive contribution for our investigation of practices of dialogue is his insistence that "practice has a logic which is not that of the logician." One cannot "wring incoherences out of [practice] or . . . thrust coherence upon it."[18] What one discovers in the logic of practices is generative principles that provide a coherence, organization, and integration; but at the same time this logic has a "fuzziness," that can bear "irregularities and incoherences" in the interest of addressing, avoiding, and negotiating the complexities of social life.

Each chapter identifies the aims of specific dialogical practices. In this, I follow in the tradition of older approaches, such as that of Alfred Schutz, who sought to investigate the phenomenology of the social world employing a version of intentional analysis associated with Edmund Husserl.[19] Here one is reminded of the important earlier work of Edward Farley, drawing on Husserl and Schutz, as well as Bernard Lonergan's own influential approach to intentional analysis.[20] Indebted to this phenomenological tradition, each chapter of this book searches for the intentions of those engaged in dialogical practices. What were their aims, their aspirations, their desires? This endeavor is not simply or strictly phenomenological, as if one could intuit or perceive directly the intention of a group of actors in a complex social world and field. Rather there is a need for a hermeneutical approach to this phenomenological endeavor, one that seeks to identify and interpret the expressed aims of given practices of dialogue by the practitioners, but also to examine the textual evidence of these various communities as they have named and narrated and at times sought to explain their intentions and goals. Here my thinking has been influenced by Paul Ricoeur and David Tracy, as they have helped me wrestle with and understand the philosophical legacy of Martin Heidegger and Hans Georg Gadamer.[21]

The problem one must face in each and every chapter is that there is more than intentionality at stake, more than "willed types" in written discourse, to use E. D. Hirsch's expression, in the practices of dialogue.[22] There are obstacles, and these obstacles merit our close attention because they not only are a burden in dialogue, but they also are disclosive of unresolved issues, of a surplus of meaning, of diversions, slippage, and unaddressed power dynamics of exclusion and control that can and often do cause harm and even bring ruin. Yet these obstacles are also the wellspring of innovations and discoveries and the doorway to personal and communal growth. Struggling with obstacles in dialogue can be the way that individuals and communities confront the residues of idolatory and of false or distorted construals of the self and the community. My own efforts here are similar to the attention given to disturbances in communication in the communicative theology espoused by Jochen Hilberath and Matthias Scharer, and they also have been enriched and made fittingly more complex by the contributions of M. Shawn Copeland, Mary McClintock Fulkerson, and Kathryn Tanner.[23] I share with these various thinkers a commitment to a hermeneutics of difference that destablizes any too-easy hermeneutics of application and correlation or coherence, not in the interest of advancing a program of deconstruction or pragmatism but in order to be receptive and responsive to the transgressive power of God's mercy and compassion and to be resistant to destructive powers operative in the trenches of practices.

In the end, the methodological approach I am espousing is a hybrid version of phenomenology and hermeneutics that concedes certain claims advanced by postmodern cultural anthropology (like the position advanced by Pierre Bourdieu) in order to describe the complexity and conflict inherent in the practices of dialogue.[24]

What kind of theology is being offered here? As previously indicated, my ultimate interest is in developing a dialogical approach to the church. The contours of a fundamental theology of the church will emerge from these historical studies of local, contextual practices, which in turn have implications for the universal church. A variety of critical and disputed issues will surface during these investigations, concerning, for example, the roles of the laity and theologians in authoritative decision making in the church, the trinitarian character of the church, and obedience. These and other related topics merit a more comprehensive theological response, the kind of response historically identified with systematic theology as well as fundamental theology. But this will be developed elsewhere. Motivated by the impulses to advance a dialogical ecclesiology, the immediate task here is to attend to what the practitioners of dialogue in the church have done in their dialogical practices and what they have said about their work of dialogue, especially during the last forty years. This hybrid method of phenomenology, hermeneutics, and a postmodern approach to culture can be understood as combining historical theology and practical theology in the service of fundamental and systematic theology.

These chapters provide a gallery of portraits of instances of dialogue in the church, descriptive historical interpretations and interrogations of practices over the last forty years. Each study in this collection, as in a gallery containing various distinct portraits, makes sense on its own. However the parts also come together to provide a rich mosaic of the last four decades in the Catholic Church. This investigation begins with dialogical practices in parish settings, especially parish pastoral councils, and moves to larger and more complex forums—diocesan synods, the deliberative assembly of chapters as used by women religious, synods of bishops, and ecumenical and interreligious dialogues. Also important are the dialogical processes initiated by the U.S. bishops in the Call To Action assembly in Detroit in 1976, the work of the U.S. Episcopal Conference in preparing its pastoral letters on war and peace and on the U.S. economy, and the failed effort to address women's issues, as well as the Catholic Common Ground Initiative. As will become clear as this study proceeds, there are important connections between the diocesan synod held in Detroit in 1969, the chapter of renewal held by the Adrian Dominicans between 1969 and 1971, and the Call To Action in 1976. Likewise, the method used at the Call To Action had an impact on the dialogical method used by the U.S. bishops in generating pastoral letters in the 1980s. Important connections between the Call To Action conference and the Catholic Common Ground Initiative will also surface. One will notice harmonic resonances and dissonant soundings in the interventions of curial offices in the U.S. Call To Action, in the U.S. Episcopal Conference, in gathering U.S. women religious, and even in the international synods of bishops. In order to do justice to the church's efforts at dialogue over the last forty years, it will be necessary to move beyond the U.S. church experience to consider the international synod of bishops and ecumenical and interreligious dialogues, all of which underscore certain dynamics in the preceding chapters but also disclose distinctive challenges and opportunities.

This study closes by reflecting on the following questions: What does one learn from these practitioners of dialogue in the church? And what is one to lament based on what these practitioners of dialogue have suffered and lost in their work and in their failures? I am urging a genuine expression of lamentation in the face of obstacles to and opponents of dialogue, especially in light of the suffering and anguish evoked by the ambiguities and aporias involved in dialogical situations. To lament is to draw near to God in pain and darkness and loss, but it is also to find deeper pathways of discovery, transformation, and resistance in the absence of apparently fruitful dialogue. This leads us finally to articulate the practical, theoretical, and theological challenges that have surfaced over the course of our investigation.

1

The Matrix of Dialogue in the Church

The Life of the Parish and the Pastoral Council

The parish is the communicative matrix of Catholic Christianity. For every Catholic it is the source and context within which the communication of faith occurs. Of the many forms of communication in the parish, three of the most basic do not seem to be dialogical at all: liturgies, homilies, and religious education. These have often appeared and been described as vehicles for one-way communication: a transmission of a divinely given message (revelation, doctrines, moral codes, catechism) from a sender (God) through intermediaries (bishops and priests) to a receiver (the faithful). Such a unidirectional explanation of communication in Christianity reflects an older understanding of revelation, the church, liturgy, and religious education that stressed the role of the hierarchy and clergy as the primary official speakers in the church and the laity as obedient receivers. Dialogue in parish life among clergy and laity was not really sanctioned or considered in this earlier approach.

Vatican II marked a major step beyond this viewpoint by advancing an enlargement in the Catholic Church's articulation of the communicative character of revelation, the liturgy, and the church. At the same time, the older understanding of communication in the church has been widely judged as offering a truncated and fundamentally flawed view of the process of communication in the church. Even though the older approach had certain sound insights, partial truths, and legitimate concerns, a more comprehensive approach to communication in the church, including the central role of dialogue, was advanced by theologians and pastoral leaders surrounding Vatican II. This has resulted in the reclamation of traditional convictions and ancient practices pertaining to prayer, liturgy, mission, and ministry, appreciated anew and reoriented as exercises in dialogue. Even though the summons to dialogue at all levels of the church has been widely acknowledged as among the most important achievements advanced by the council, the implementation of dialogue in the parish setting has been neither consistent nor well executed, and at times it has been challenged and unrealized.

Thomas Sweetser, SJ, and Paul Wilkes recently published books that identify what it takes for a parish to be successful or excellent.[1] Of all the contributing ingredients they discovered, the role of dialogue stands out by implication as a decisive criterion: a parish is successful or excels to the extent that it is energized by and thrives on the dynamism of dialogue. The basic ingredients of a vibrant parish life include a culture of hospitality and catholicity; a palpable sense of communion expressed in bonds of affection, belonging, and mutual concern; a place that promotes a real-life sense of holiness born of a genuine spirituality and embodied in everyday lives committed to social service and work for social justice; and a community known for its apostolic rootedness in the gospel message of the scriptures, the liturgy, and the creed. For these dimensions to flourish in a parish requires the cultivation of practices of dialogue in the hybrid modes of communication in the liturgy, preaching, religious education, and service,[2] and in the explicitly dialogical forums provided by the parish pastoral council. A parish is not successful and does not excel when dialogical practices within the various spheres are diminished, under attack, or not functioning.

DIALOGUE IN THE HYBRID COMMUNICATIVE ACTION OF LITURGY, WITNESS, AND SERVICE

The very first work completed at Vatican II, the Constitution on the Sacred Liturgy (*Sacrosanctum Concilium*), was devoted to the reform of the liturgy. The overriding objective was to promote the full and active participation of the entire church community in the liturgy. As illustrated in the retrieval of the ancient rite of Christian initiation and the reforms of the eucharistic liturgy, this requires self-giving responses to recurring invitations to join in the dialogical character of the liturgy.[3] Priest and lectors may seem to be talking at their congregations during Sunday masses, using a one-way mode of communication, but in fact their ministerial role is to initiate a spiritual dialogue in the worshiping community. Cantors, choirs, and musicians likewise contribute to the dynamic of dialogue in the liturgy. The *Missa dialogata,* developed in light of the council's teaching, established a ritualized dialogue between the celebrant and the entire congregation, not just the servers, to foster full and active participation in the mysteries of faith. But regularly the conversation of liturgy falls flat. The choice and enactment of ritual words, gestures, environment, and music are judged as not conducive to communication but rather as breeding boredom, frustration, and contempt.

Preaching is one particular form of Christian witness and proclamation that is too often experienced among Catholics as a unidirectional and unsuccessful form of communication. Preaching at its best, however, engages what can be called the threefold dialogical dimensions of the homily: the dialogue of everyday life, the dialogue of scripture, and the dialogue of the liturgy.[4] First of all, the preacher's mandate is to heed the everyday dialogues in the lives of community members, where the joys and sorrows, the conflicts and the peacemaking of parishioners are found. The preacher's attentiveness to the everyday psychic rhythms and ruptures of community members should inform the topics, tenors, and tones of the homily. In the second place, homilies are to draw community members into a living dialogue in the imagination with the many voices and characters and contentions of the scriptures in the range of stories and genres offered by the lectionary. The challenge is to help community members wrestle with the dynamics of the dialogue of everyday life in terms of the dialogical dynamics disclosed in the scriptures. In the third place, homilies should draw people at the crossroad of the dialogue of life and the dialogue of the scriptures into the ritual dialogue of the liturgy. The preacher should bring the conversations of life and scripture back to the conversations of Jesus and the disciples around bread and wine, around the painful toll of love, around betrayal and breakdown of dialogue enacted as breakthrough to newer dimensions of life and love, wholeness and healing, compassion and mercy, always returning to repentance and gratitude. The interaction between these dialogical networks of life, scripture, and liturgy is the preacher's and presider's province. The possibilities for dialogical encounter occasioned by the preached word abound, but the general state of preaching in Catholic parishes is woefully deficient. So much more could be done.

Catechesis, understood here as the Catholic form of religious education, is another form of Christian witness that has developed a distinctively dialogical pedagogy over the twentieth century. But it has been a circuitous journey on a rocky road. Catechesis developed in reaction to the neoscholastic approach to religious education that gained ascendance in the last quarter of the nineteenth century and first half of the twentieth century. That form of religious instruction emphasized rote memory of doctrinal propositions as a system of dogmatic truths, moral precepts, a code of rules, and a set of rituals, tasks, and duties requiring strict adherence. In the United States, neoscholastic pedagogy was concretized in the *Baltimore Catechism*, published in 1885 (after the First Vatican Council in 1869) and revised in 1941, a text that dominated religious instruction with a pseudo-dialogue of 421 questions and answers in the older version, and 515 in the revised edition. The problem with this older approach was that one could learn the answers but not wrestle with deeper questions raised by the information dutifully learned.

Over the course of the twentieth century several approaches to catechesis were developed to address the deficiencies of the neoscholastic paradigm. The three most noteworthy models incorporated a dialogical pedagogy: kerygmatic, anthropological, and praxis-oriented.[5] Each of these three approaches advocated a particular kind of dialogical method for catechetics. The first promoted a kerygmatic dialogue with the scriptures and liturgy and thus with the doctrinal heritage of Christianity within the narrative framework provided by salvation history. The second fostered an anthropological dialogue about the range of experiences in everyday life. The third promoted a praxis-based dialogue attuned to the social and political realities of people in a suffering world.

These three newer approaches to catechesis were implemented in parishes. In the process, the depth and breadth of insight of the original architects were frequently lost or diminished. Each model was subsequently criticized for having limitations that fostered a fragmented approach to catechesis (one approach criticizing another) and restricted the dialogical parameters. The kergymatic approach framed in terms of salvation history was judged harshly for repeating the problem of the neoscholastic model—too much information without personal experience-based engagement, or for distorting or diminishing certain characters in the biblical narratives, for example, the role of Jews and women. The anthropological approach was criticized for fostering a new wave of experientialism associated with progressive and liberal models of secular education. Critical thinking about one's experiences took precedence over learning through the use of memory and classical skills, resulting in a generation of religious illiterates—lacking knowledge or memory of basic stories and traditions of belief and practice, and with an underdeveloped dialogical imagination to enter into these traditions of belief and practice. The praxis-oriented approach was accused of unleashing a wave of activists with no sense of spirituality, promoting secularism without mystical and liturgical wellsprings and moorings.

These criticisms reflect the boisterous theological debates that have been going on over the last forty years. Certainly they suggest legitimate concerns that merit attention. Nevertheless, each of the three approaches to catechesis reflects genuine insight and important judgments that are both true to the depth of the gospel message and that should contribute to the dialogue of the church.[6] Unfortunately, these contributions are rarely integrated and implemented and the state of religious education in parishes and local churches is widely viewed as disgracefully poor, or at least very uneven. There is much room for grieving here about unrealized possibilities.

In addition to liturgy, preaching, and catechesis, the development of small faith-sharing groups called small Christian communities or base Christian communities has been one of the most important practices of dialogue introduced into many parishes during the postconciliar period, for example in the U.S. parish-based program begun in 1976 called Renew, and in various forms around the world.[7] These faith-sharing groups are often composed of relatively small numbers of people, often no more than six to twelve. There are three basic dialogical ingredients in these group meetings: meditation on the dialogue of biblical stories read aloud together; faith sharing, in which the members converse about their personal search for God in everyday life in light of the biblical stories; and extemporaneous spoken prayer. These small-group experiences have provided one of the most important forms of dialogue to be experimented with during the postconciliar period. For precisely in these faith-sharing groups parishioners learn about spiritual discernment, about making decisions about one's personal and collective life in light of assessing the presence and hiddenness of God in daily experiences. The major difficulty with these new forms of dialogue is that these experiences are too infrequently offered in parishes and local churches; too few people get involved, or the programs are introduced but not continued.

This discussion of dialogue in hybrid forms of communication in the parish culminates with a word about service, ministry, and mission. Over the last forty years there has been a renewed appreciation of the call of each baptized Christian to share in the apostolic mission of the church both in terms of ecclesial ministries around the altar and in the parish, and in wider forms of service and work for justice. All forms of ministry and mission are rooted in the dialogical process of identity formation. People respond to a call to serve those in need voiced by other community members or by hearing the voices of people in need in their own parish and in the world around them. The cries and aspirations of human beings are heard and echo in the human heart and elicit a response. The major difficulty here is that too often parishes are not helping members hear and respond to these invitations to service.

In acts of service and the promotion of justice and peace, dialogue is a crucial ingredient. Consider, for example, parishioners who visit people in hospitals or prisons, people who spend time with those grieving the death of a loved one, or with victims of domestic abuse or urban violence. The most important form of service these people render is to communicate God's presence and compassion by entering into an attentive receptive posture of dialogue. The great charism and virtue in all of these is the ministry of listening.[8] Although dialogue with the needy may not seem to be a crucial element in the collection of needed clothing or food items, or in the preparation and distribution of food in meal programs, dialogue is the added dimension that conveys care and concern. In work for justice, whether in efforts to promote structural changes in the social, political, or economic arenas, or in attempts at promoting reconciliation in communities torn apart by conflict and violence, dialogue is the medium of social healing and reconstruction. The call to witness to the gospel, as a constitutive ingredient in the baptismal call of all Christians, is realized through dialogue. The challenge is to cultivate lasting and productive practices of dialogue in the diverse ministerial settings.

The conclusion I have drawn from the work of Sweetser and Wilkes is that a parish is successful or excels to the extent that it is energized by and thrives on the dynamism of dialogue in the areas of liturgy, preaching, catechesis, service, and work for justice. The catholicity, unity, holiness, and apostolicity of the parish depend on genuine, effective communication made possible through the grace and hard work of dialogue. But the sad fact of the matter is that there are many parishes that are not successful and do not excel because dialogue within these various spheres of hybrid modes of communication have not been cultivated. Ultimately, the responsibility for the vitality of dialogue in the parish and the burden of its faltering and failure falls upon the pastor working collaboratively with the parish pastoral council. Consequently, pastoral councils offer the most important dialogical practice of leadership in the parish setting.

PARISH PASTORAL COUNCILS

In the parish setting, dialogue is the privileged mode of communication in pastoral councils, finance councils, parish staff meetings, and the various committees that are formed to address issues of worship, religious formation and education, social outreach, community life, and the administration of the parish. The dialogical approach employed in all of these groups is similar and their purposes are interrelated. The formation of pastoral councils at the parish and diocesan levels as an instrument to promote the life and work of the local church was encouraged but not mandated by the teachings of Vatican II and the new Code of Canon Law issued in 1983.[9] I will concentrate on parish pastoral councils in the remainder of this chapter and will comment on diocesan pastoral councils in the next.

Since Vatican II, parish councils have steadily grown in number and often in maturity. The number has increased from about half of the U.S. parishes in 1970 (about ten thousand) to three-quarters in 1976 and again in 1986, to as high as 79 percent in 1994, which amounts to roughly 17,000 councils in the 18,764 U.S. parishes and missions in existence at the time.[10] As of 2004, "close to two-thirds of bishops mandate the establishment of parish pastoral councils . . . in their diocese or eparchy."[11] (Eparchy is the equivalent of a diocese in Eastern canon law and applies to Eastern rites of the Catholic Church.) The dramatic increase from no parish pastoral councils to fifty, seventy-five, and higher percentages in the decades that followed Vatican II, raises a question about why all parishes are not required to form pastoral councils. More important are questions about the composition, structure, aims, and effectiveness of these councils, and about what impact these have on the identity and role of the priest and the laity in the life of the church.

The central concern here, however, is more narrowly focused on the cultivation and role of dialogical practices in these meetings. In the strict sense, the term *dialogue* was not introduced and recommended for pastoral councils as the means of participating in shared responsibility and collective deliberation in either the documents of Vatican II or in the new Code of Canon Law.[12] However, dialogue was implicitly recommended. The Decree on the Apostolate of Lay People (hereafter abbreviated Decree on Lay People) advocated cooperation between people in the congregation and the priests by means of surfacing, examining, and solving problems through "general discussion" (10), which is the translation of the Latin term *consiliis*—based on the word for council, meaning to take counsel. Likewise, the Decree on the Ministry and Life of Priests urged priests "to listen to lay people, give brotherly consideration to their wishes, and recognize their experience and competence in the different fields of human activity. In this way [priests] will be able to recognize with them the signs of the times" (9).[13] For the priest to take counsel from and listen to parishioners does not fully reflect the mutual dynamic of dialogue, but rather suggests passing on information, personal testimonies, and opinions, which the pastor can use as he sees fit. Consultation, then, remained all that was recommended for parish pastoral councils. However, these directives opened the door for genuinely dialogical procedures aimed at collective discernment and decision making. Three areas provide evidence of development in dialogical procedures in pastoral councils.

The first example concerns the process for selecting parishioners for the council. When councils were first formed during the 1960s and 1970s, council members were either hand-picked by the pastor, selected through a parish election, or elected to represent a particular parish committee. Unfortunately, these approaches did not guarantee that the people selected had the practical wisdom and skills associated with dialogical discernment or the inclination to develop them. Nor were these members necessarily representative of the various sectors of the parish: ethnic, racial, neighborhoods, social and professional groups, and apostolates.[14] Often the election process was a popularity contest or a choice among those few parishioners expressing a willingness to serve.

Beginning in the late 1970s there developed a discernment model of selection, which was advanced by Mary Benet McKinney, OSB, in her widely used book *Sharing Wisdom: A Process for Group Decision Making*. This requires a longer group deliberation process during a series of assemblies to which all parishioners are invited. At these meetings, there is a description offered of the purpose and work of the parish council, the strengths of the parish and those areas that need attention, and a discussion of the qualifications of a good councillor. Nominations are accepted and a conversation takes place among those participating in these assemblies concerning what the nominated people can bring to the council. This process culminates in a prayerful discernment in which the participants assembled elect the councillors, possibly by ballots.[15] While this kind of model is used far less than the open parishwide election process, it still reflects a growing trend and is recommended by many.

A second area of growth pertains to the more explicit attention given to faith sharing in the pastoral council meeting. The components of faith sharing—reflection on one's daily life in light of the scriptures and extemporaneous prayer—foster a spirituality that is attuned to Christian identity formation and mission in general, and to discernment about the pastoral mission and ministries undertaken by the parish council in particular. During the 1980s and 1990s increasing attention was given to establishing a prayerful context for the work of the council and even of encouraging days of recollection and retreats. Greater care was also given to recognizing the value and importance of members giving personal testimony or witnessing in the context of the meetings to how they did or did not encounter God in parish activities, and of attentive listening to the testimony of others.

The third area of maturation, and clearly the most important, involves the cultivation of dialogical discernment skills. Some critics of earlier efforts at councils suggest that during the 1960s and 1970s pastoral councils imitated political and business models. Like representative democratic governments (e.g., local city councils), parish councils used dialogue in the interest of achieving majority rule. Council members used dialogue to build coalitions, with the interests of the pastor sometimes in tension with those of the elected officials, and representative members sometimes pitted against one another, where there were winners and losers. Like business models using corporate business management techniques, pastors or council presidents fostered dialogue seeking compromise and negotiated settlements, sometimes while exercising leadership with a heavy hand.[16] These earlier democratic and business approaches to dialogical procedure regularly resulted in tension and sometimes conflict between power blocs, and between the pastor and the council. Participants were often bruised in the process. A parliamentary procedure, like *Robert's Rules of Order*, was associated with this earlier (democratic or business) model and continues to be a widely relied-upon method for decision making.

In the 1980s, however, again reflecting the influence of Mary Benet McKinney's work, there emerged a new trend to develop group processes, that is, dialogical formats that seek to discuss each agenda item and to reach a consensus, a group decision, that reflects the convictions and the unity among those in the council, including the pastor, in a manner that avoids polarization by seeking the good of the entire parish.[17] Council members were invited to set individual topics within a larger framework and to think more broadly about the collective journey of the parish in terms of the parish's strengths and weaknesses, and envisioning its future. Personal sharing as well as exchanging information about the parish contributes to a collaborative process of discernment about where the parish is and needs to grow in its pastoral mission and activity.[18]

There are several ingredients that contribute to the development of collective discernment. First, council members are called upon to be in active relation with the parish at large, the pastor, and the pastoral staff, and thus have personal knowledge of the larger community. Although each member represents a certain sector of the parish, everyone on the council must strive to be attentive to the various sectors of the parish so as to determine the range of concerns, needs, and problems. In many parishes there are regular opportunities, yearly, semi-annually, or quarterly, where all parish members are invited and encouraged to attend an open-ended discussion with the pastor, the pastoral staff, and the pastoral council about the life and mission of the parish.

A second ingredient for group discernment concerns the specific practices at the meetings: participants share responsibility by listening and through contributing one's point of view by speaking up. The council serves its purpose well if there is honest conversation about the parish's agendas and goals, and about parish programs and personnel, based on reflective judgments. Being diplomatic, kind, and generous in one's interpretation of another in conversation, must be combined with an ability to be honest and, at times, blunt. Being forthright and standing by one's convictions must be matched by an ability to see various aspects of a problem and an ability to search for consensus and find compromises. Shared responsibility in the context of parish councils requires the ability to make judgments and decisions, sometimes through voting. This is a spiritual discernment process, not simply because it is based on the prayerful attitude of the participants, but because it reflects the effort to make judgments and decisions based on an orienting pastoral, theological vision of the parish.

Mark Fischer, drawing on his considerable research, has captured well the fact that the dialogical method of the council corresponds to the need for the council to exercise practical wisdom about contingent matters, like Aristotle's *phronesis* and Thomas Aquinas's *prudentia*, through dialogical deliberation.[19] The challenge is to identify councillors who have dialogical skills.

> Prudent people can deliberate well, take counsel, inquire, and judge shrewdly. How can we discern who they are in a parish? The only way is to watch parishioners using their gifts in dialogue. They are the ones who express their opinions well. They listen attentively to the opinions of others. They are able to synthesize their opinions, clarifying them and making sound recommendations. They exercise self-control, preserving their ability to judge what is good. These are the people, in short, who are able to get at the knowledge of contingent things.[20]

Dialogue is a practice that demands certain skills that need to be developed through exercise. Fischer speaks of them in terms of appreciative inquiry, guided by questioning that does not dominate but searches for larger truths and inclusive goods through collective discernment.

The most important questions being discerned by parish pastoral councils, and a frequent source of confusion and frustration, concern their aim(s). In other words, what topics of conversation are appropriate and should be given priority at the parish council meetings? There is confusion about which of the three principal agenda items that emerged during the postconciliar period were the proper or primary aim of the council. First, there was the daily administration of the parish—money issues, building maintenance, the so-called temporal affairs. Second, there was the coordination of the apostolic ministries in the parish, fostering collaboration between those in religious education and youth ministry, the Rite of Christian Initiation for Adults and liturgy, social justice outreach, and social service ministries. Third, there was the larger task of evaluating and exploring the pastoral mission and activities of the parish.

The documents from Vatican II contributed to the confusion about objectives. The Decree on Lay People proposed that diocesan and parish councils are "to assist the Church's apostolic work." "These councils can take care of the mutual coordinating of the various lay associations and undertakings, the autonomy and particular nature of each remaining untouched" (26).[21] Moving in what was widely perceived as a different direction, the Decree on the Pastoral Office of Bishops in the Church (hereafter abbreviated Decree on Bishops) commended the importance of diocesan pastoral councils which have as their aim or function "to investigate and consider matters relating to pastoral activity and to formulate practical conclusions concerning them" (27). Diocesan pastoral councils provided a model for parish pastoral councils.

Following these diverging leads from Vatican II, councils were formed with distinctive or combined purposes: administering money matters, coordinating apostolic ministries, and developing pastoral plans. The new Code of Canon Law required the formation of finance committees in all parishes to address the administration of financial matters, which meant that financial matters were removed from the pastoral council's agenda or reduced in the attention they received. At the same time the Code specified the aim of parish councils as properly to foster pastoral action, further developing the position advanced in the Decree on Bishops, while not ruling out the apostolic purpose of coordinating ministries in the parish, which was mentioned in the Decree on Lay People.

When the U.S. bishops were surveyed in 2004, they emphasized overwhelmingly that parish pastoral councils should concern themselves with pastoral planning (95%), consulting with parishioners about "their hopes and concerns for the community" (88%), and "empowering parishioners to carry out plan objectives" (73%).[22] This survey revealed that U.S. bishops set pastoral planning as the most important aim of the parish pastoral council, but it did not offer any data about the variety of topics actually treated by councils and their effectiveness in addressing them. Other studies indicated that while pastoral planning is certainly one of the most important aims of the council, others issues, such as coordinating ministries, often receive considerable attention.[23] These findings revealed a few of the general aims being pursued in local parish settings, but they did not provide sufficient data to shed light on the struggles experienced by councils to weigh and balance aims, priorities, and conflicting agendas in the life of parishes.

FRUSTRATIONS AND FAILINGS

Parish pastoral councils provide a pivotal practice of dialogue in the life of the parish, which has the proven ability to influence every area of ministry and mission in the parish: liturgy, spiritual formation, religious education, social service, and work for justice. This practice provides a direct way for the pastor and parishioners to share responsibility and collaborate in advancing the apostolic life of the parish. The vitality of the parish community depends on the parish pastoral council's functioning well. But in fact there are many kinds of obstacles.

How do conversations in parish pastoral councils struggle or fail? Councils falter because members have not cultivated the practical wisdom associated with dialogical skills. There are three basic skills required: listening well, speaking well, and being able to move the conversation toward a collective decision and action. Some people are not good listeners. They struggle to hear, not in the physical sense but in the sense that they cannot really understand or accurately interpret the concerns and judgments of other individuals, subgroups, and the wider community. Others are not able to speak their minds and share their wisdom about the issue at hand with clarity and directness of expression. They cannot stay on topic; they cannot helpfully draw on their own experience and expertise; they dominate the conversation; they do not know when to stop talking and when not to start. Some are unable to move the conversation forward by advancing proposals, identifying assets and deficiencies in the proposals being considered, revising proposals in light of the contributions of council members, clarifying areas of agreement and disagreement, and modifying proposals where possible to incorporate the concerns of dissenting voices and minority positions. Any lack of dialogical skills among the members takes its toll and jeopardizes the efforts of the group to deliberate about their aims.

Another reason why councils are unable to enter into a productive discerning dialogue is that the members do not have an adequate understanding of the identity and mission of the parish. As a matter of principle, a parish council is called upon to consider the identity and mission of the parish, its pastoral activities, and the ministries involved, and to envision and discern the ongoing realization of this identity and mission. This requires an honest appraisal of assets and deficiencies in every area of the parish's life: cultivating the spiritual life and liturgical worship of the parish, advancing the community's knowledge of the scriptures and traditions and Christian identity formation through religious education, serving community members who are sick, in need, or grieving, as well as working for social justice and reaching out to those who are marginalized, alienated, and outcast. The parish council falls short if the members have a selective understanding of what is included in the identity and mission of the parish and so are not sufficiently informed about the many dimensions of the topics that need to be discussed. The council falls short if there is an inability to affirm the genuine gifts of a parish community and to voice honestly the weaknesses in personnel, in the programs, and in the coordination of programs.

Council dialogues struggle and fail when the majority do not make room in their conversation for the voices of those who are minorities, dissenters, and those who feel excluded. When the pastoral mission of the parish is being discussed, are there members on the council who represent, consult with, and speak for young people, ethnic or racial minorities, people who are living together as partners without being married, those who are divorced and remarried, and gay individuals and couples? A council is faltering in its mandate to promote catholicity and hospitality in the parish if it does not converse about the needs and concerns of all the members of the community, including those struggling at the margins of the parish.

Councils also falter because they are unable to discuss controversial subjects. There are many different kinds of difficult topics. Deficiencies in parish programs and the need for professional growth among parish staff members are difficult to discuss. Parishes have been notorious in the past for not addressing changing racial and ethnic demographics, and today the question can still be raised: How can parish councils help the parish community address the problems of racism and ethnocentrism and create a hospitable community for all kinds of people?[24] Are there other taboo topics, for example, alcoholism and other forms of substance abuse, as well as abusive relations, that should be addressed in the parish but that rarely, if ever, are found on the parish agenda? More generally, is the parish council able to facilitate discussion in the parish about and provide resources for addressing the range of life issues: unwanted pregnancies, criminal justice and capital punishment, war, as well as local, regional, and international social-justice issues? Equally challenging, is the parish council able to foster discernment in the parish community about the impact of broader and chronic cultural currents on individuals, families, and the parish: violence and sexual exploitation in everyday life and in the music, movie, and television industries, the issues raised by economic hardship, crime, and materialism? Also pertinent are certain topics of church teaching and discipline that apparently have no direct bearing on the work of the council: for example, the male and celibate requirements for ordained ministry, the practice of birth control, divorce and remarriage, and homosexuality. Even though the council has not been commissioned to address these issues, is the council able to speak openly about parish programs that touch upon people in these life situations? Is it possible for councils, for instance, to discuss and discern matters surrounding the shortage of priests and not raise questions about the requirements for priesthood? The pastoral priorities of the parish will inevitably touch upon many, if not all, of these issues, and a parish council that is not open to discussing them in constructive ways fails in its mission.

One of the most contested reasons why the dialogical work of parish councils is undermined and threatened is that the new 1983 Code of Canon Law legislated that parish pastoral councils are to be consultative only and not genuinely deliberative (canon 536).[25] The Catholic Church has attempted since Vatican II to foster shared responsibility, active participation, and collaboration among all the members of the church in the interests of promoting the gift and task of collegiality and communion in the church, while still holding firmly, some would say stubbornly, to the hierarchical character of all ecclesial relationships, where bishops and by extension priests retain the binding canonical power to judge and decide in matters of church teaching and governance within their own distinct spheres of authority. One of the major, recurring complaints about the nature of the dialogical processes in which the nonordained and ordained are involved, at all levels of the church (it will surface again in the treatment of diocesan synods, Call To Action, and synods of bishops), and in particular in pastoral councils, is that they are, according to church teaching and canon law, to be consultative or advisory only, and not deliberative.[26] Many believe this undermines and frustrates the dialogical practices of the pastoral council, and they therefore criticize the consultative-only canon. Others maintain that this canon clarifies the council's aims and limits, and they urge the wider reception of the power of consultation recommended by the council while reserving decision making to the priest. The issue is complicated by the fact that various people have interpreted the consultative-only canon quite differently, resulting in contrary implementations. Let us examine the range of interpretations, before discussing the critics and their alternative views.

Based on his own study of numerous pastoral council guidelines, Mark Fischer shows that consultation has a variety of meanings and modes of implementation. The first meaning adheres strictly to a legal approach that defends the council as only consultative by emphasizing what it is not—in the words of one bishop, "not a policy-making, decree-issuing, statute-formulating body."[27] The pastor is not bound by the council's recommendations. Councils that want "real power" to exercise authority and the power of leadership need to be put in check. The second formulation stresses that councils "may not have the final say" but that they exercise genuine authority and leadership and wield real power and influence by giving advice. A third meaning construes the aim of consultation as consensus by means of group processes, thereby avoiding pitting the authority of the council against the authority of the pastor, or of the majority against the minority. The fourth meaning of consultation builds on a consensus approach and adds that the pastor is the one who ratifies the discernment process of the council. The pastor has the pastoral role of detecting consensus in the council. "If the council remains divided, and if consensus is not possible, the pastor must acknowledge that he cannot accept the majority's recommendations." The pastor "is the one who, for the sake of consensus, grants or withholds ratification." Consensus and ratification are linked. Fischer believes that "many pastors see themselves precisely that way in relation to their councils" and that this approach combines the best insights of canon law and consensus.[28] The fifth meaning given to consultation is that of policy making. The key assumption here is that if consensus is reached between the pastoral council and pastor, then together they make policy. Just as bishops delegate authority to pastors, so do pastors delegate authority to parish councillors.

Fischer has demonstrated that the consultative-only clause is in fact interpreted in a wide variety of ways. Based on his analysis, it is clear that the clause as it now stands in canon law is able to function with the older pre–Vatican II ecclesiology that was paternalistic and associated with clericalism and authoritarianism, but that it can also be interpreted as allowing communal discernment and decision making by parish pastoral councils.

A number of pastoral ministers and practical theologians have criticized the consultative-only clause as subverting the emerging dialogical practices of collective discernment and decision making developing in the postconciliar church. William Rademacher has been one of the most outspoken critics.[29] Thomas Sweetser has developed an alternative to the consultative-only formula. In the early 1970s he founded the Parish Evaluation Project, which examined the practices of decision making in many parishes and listened to many pastors, pastoral councillors, and parishioners discuss their frustrations, anger, and sense of achievements in these matters. With codirector Patricia Forster, Sweetser identified five levels of decision making:

1. The nitty-gritty level of concrete ministries. In these authors' view, pastors and pastoral councils often exceed their expertise and authority and meddle in minsters' work. "Let the person in charge of [a certain] area of ministry make the decisions."[30]
2. Voting about small matters by voice or hand in order to show support for a person or committee offering recommendations and to express preferences.
3. Consensus concerns larger issues and requires going through a process of exploring alternatives and discussing reactions to various options.
4. Problem-solving concerns concrete difficulties that need to be addressed: leaking roofs, flooding basements, budget crises, inadequate facilities, insufficient teachers.
5. Discernment process concerns larger issues that pertain to the identity and mission of the parish and affect the entire parish, such as renovation projects, closing or starting a school or program, chang-

ing mass schedules. This process of discernment begins by focusing problems, identifying tentative solutions, naming vested interests, invoking openness to the Spirit working in the deliberations of the group.

Once a proposal has been developed, parishioners are invited to voice reasons for opposition to the proposal, then reasons in favor of the proposal. The council needs to be alert to possible new alternatives and revised proposals can be developed. Once a revised proposal has been developed, the next step is to seek the response of the parish and, if the response is positive, celebrate the consensus; if there is a groundswell of discontent, the proposal can be reformulated.

In view of these findings Sweetser argued that the pastoral council must move toward a process of communal discernment and decision making. This process has three phases: consultation, decision making, and informing the parish. The council with the pastor must recognize that "when any decision comes up, the distinction must be made between those who are the actual deciders, those who are being consulted before the decision is made and those who should be informed after it is decided but before the decision is implemented."[31] Sweetser believes that council members must be able to exercise their authority by setting the agenda, as well as participating in the group discernment and decision-making process about who is to be consulted, who is to decide, and who is to inform. Sharing in this responsibility does not mean that every decision is made by the parish pastoral council. There may be some areas where it is agreed upon that a holder of a certain pastoral position (director of religious education, director of liturgy, or pastor) is the most well suited to decide this matter. However, this decision making is ultimately an extension of the parish pastoral council.

Is the consultative-only clause an asset or a detriment for parish pastoral councils? The clause does commend the importance of consultation by means of dialogue within the church, but it simultaneously affirms without limiting hierarchical and clerical authority. Thus, the clause symbolizes the asymmetrical combination of dialogical and hierarchical styles of ecclesiology at Vatican II and in its aftermath. It has functioned to promote internal dialogue in the church, but it has also limited and enfeebled it.

For parishes to fulfill their apostolic mandate, hybrid modes of communication and above all the practices of dialogue must thrive. As this chapter has indicated, there are two institutional reasons why the work of dialogue is constrained in the parish: (1) pastoral councils are not required and (2) the consultative-only clause restricts collective discernment and decision making in the parish. But there are countless local personal reasons why dialogue is frustrated or fails in the parish because the virtues of dialogue are lacking. The outstanding question is whether the church can learn from the experiments and struggles during the last forty years and move to the next level of maturity in parish life and ministry, or whether it is condemned to remain stuck in its current ruts. God's saving self-communication is freely given and unmerited, but human cooperation and institutional mediation in this work of communication cannot be denied.

2

Discerning the Mission of the Local Church

The Bishop and the Diocesan Synod

The ordinary of the local church, identified here as bishop, although he may be an archbishop or a cardinal, was encouraged to establish certain dialogical practices, usually designated structures of participation and consultation, by Vatican II and by the new Code of Canon Law. Two institutional forms—diocesan pastoral councils and diocesan synods—merit special attention because they invite representative participation of the laity, religious, and priests in a process of dialogical deliberation with the bishop about Catholic identity and the pastoral mission of the local church. Taking the long view of history, we can say that these two forms offer genuinely hopeful signs of renewal and reform in the church. However, the sad reality is that many bishops have not yet implemented or effectively utilized these two forms of collective discernment, and this represents a monumental failure to implement the teachings of Vatican II. Not surprisingly, most Catholic parishioners do not know of the existence of diocesan pastoral councils and diocesan synods or that these structures are strongly recommended. Still, a significant and growing percentage of dioceses have developed these new forms of dialogue with the bishop, and ongoing efforts are being made by the United States Conference of Catholic Bishops (USCCB) to advance them.

The bishop's working relations with diocesan pastoral councils and diocesan synods need to be set within a larger network of relationships. There has been a long-standing requirement, which the new code reaffirmed, for the bishop to work together with the diocesan curia, now identified as the episcopal council, composed of vicars general and episcopal vicars. The new code called for a groundbreaking, innovative set of practices of collective diocesan discernment. A diocesan finance council was to be established, composed of at least three experts in financial matters and a financial administrator, to work with the bishop in the development of the budget and to monitor its administration. A presbyteral council must be formed, composed of a group of priests chosen to represent the presbyterium of the diocese, out of which there is to be chosen a smaller college of consultors to advise the bishop. The code also recommended, but did not mandate, the formation of a diocesan pastoral council and, when deemed apt, the convocation of a diocesan synod, both of which are to be composed of priests, religious, and laypersons. Individual theologians have regularly served as consultants to bishops and offices of local churches. A council of theologians, however, composed of representatives from diocesan universities, colleges, seminaries, and pastoral settings to meet with the local ordinary on a regular basis to discuss theological issues has neither been mandated nor recommended, although it has been attempted in some dioceses since the council.[1]

These various levels of administrative collaboration with the bishop supplement the work of regular staff members of various diocesan offices, often headed by people with considerable knowledge about local parishes, Catholic schools, outreach programs, diocesan and regional networks, ecumenical groups and other religious communities, as well as local history, cultures, and customs. The bishop's ongoing working relations with these various councils and diocesan offices provide the possibility and prospect of intersecting circles of dialogical discernment in the life of the local church. So it is all the more deplorable that these councils and organizational groups often work in isolation and have not been given sufficient opportunities together to develop with the bishop practices and a culture of exchanging the wisdom of the different groups vital for collective discernment.[2]

Although the focus here will be on diocesan synods, a few remarks about diocesan pastoral councils are warranted since they are among the most important forms of participation with the bishop in the life of local churches. Diocesan pastoral councils have developed at a slower rate than parish pastoral councils and still lag significantly behind. During the first period after Vatican II, there were about eight or nine diocesan pastoral councils established each year since 1966. In 1972 there were reports of 57 arch/diocesan pastoral councils among the 166 U.S. dioceses, or 34 percent.[3] By 1984 there were 89 arch/diocesan pastoral councils in the 170 dioceses at the time, or 52 percent (in comparison with approximately 75 percent with parish pastoral councils at the time).[4] In 1997 there were recorded 91 out of 175 dioceses (again 52 percent) with pastoral councils, with 23 more planning on forming or reactivating a pastoral council, and 29 stating that a diocesan council had never existed.[5] The numbers in the 2004 survey were roughly the same.[6] One conclusion to be drawn from these reports is that a central obstacle to the promotion of collaborative practices of discernment in dioceses is the absence of a diocesan pastoral council, and the burden of responsibility for this failure rests solely upon the bishop.

The diocesan pastoral council constitutes a new dialogical structure in the local church. It is an experiment establishing a new pattern of relationship and a new practice of shared responsibility in discernment and decision making concerning the pastoral mission of the local church. The required participation of laypeople and religious is a crucial development. Equally important, the code stated that the members are "to be selected in such a way that the council truly reflects the entire portion of the people of God which constitutes the diocese, taking account of the different regions of the diocese, of social conditions and professions, and of the part played in the apostolate by the members whether individually or in association with others" (canon 512). In the United States there has been a reduction in the median size of diocesan pastoral councils between 1984 and 1997 from thirty-three to twenty-five in an effort to assure "quality group process and decision-making."[7] The average appointment of members is for one three-year term that is renewable once. The average group meets four times a year over a weekend. A significant percentage of councils periodically ask members to evaluate the work of the council.

Diocesan pastoral councils operate with the same dialogical method as parish pastoral councils and pursue similar purposes; they also encounter many of the same obstacles. They sometimes struggle because of lack of direction or confusion pertaining to the possible purposes of the council—study particular pastoral issues, discuss and develop pastoral vision or long-term plans for the local church, develop concrete recommendations, or serve as administrative coordinators. They can falter because individual members have deficient knowledge and formation in various areas—Catholic identity and mission, diocesan issues and policies, larger social and church issues, and local and practical matters—all necessary to discuss productively the issues being addressed. There may be insufficient representation on the council of certain sectors of the diocese and respectable theological and pastoral viewpoints. Individuals can also have limited pastoral wisdom or lack the communication skills needed to participate actively, attentively, and helpfully in the ongoing process of deliberation. There can also be struggles because the bishop, like the pastor, is resistant to the exercise of collective discernment and consensus reached in these conversations. Bishops with diocesan pastoral councils have overwhelmingly reported that they are receptive to the work of the council, but in keeping with the consultative-only clause, do they recognize any sense of obligation to heed and adhere to the council's discernment and deliberation? Are there any mechanisms for discussing the bishop's accountability in this web of relationship and shared responsibility?[8]

The bishop and the diocesan pastoral council working alongside of, and hopefully with, the other councils—presbyteral, finance, episcopal—can sometimes fail to listen to voices at the margins and in the hinterlands, but also at times to the silent majority of parishioners in the diocese about the challenges and opportunities facing the local church. The bishops working with the diocesan pastoral council are invited to be prophetic, priestly, and pastoral in their receptivity and responsiveness to the aspirations and sufferings of the entire local church and especially to those marginalized in their midst.

One way that the unfulfilled longings and pressing needs in the diocese can be identified, and programmatic responses developed, is through a diocesan synod. Diocesan synods provide a special structure that optimally builds on these councils; such synods offer unique occasions for dialogical discernment involving a larger and wider spectrum of people from across the diocese. Since diocesan synods can play such an important role in the life of the local church, they merit special attention.

DIOCESAN SYNODS IN HISTORICAL PERSPECTIVE

The term *synod* comes from two Greek roots: *syn* means "to come together with," and *od* refers to "the movement forward on a path." The word *synod* thus conveys the assembly of a people on a common journey. A synod brings together representatives of the church for collective discernment about the identity and mission of the church and specific areas of concern that need attention for the good of the community. The term originally applied to local, regional, national, and universal (designated ecumenical) assemblies and so was synonymous with *council.* But according to the new Code of Canon Law, *synod* is restricted to designating diocesan synods and synods of bishops–two structures that are distinct from ecumenical councils, consistories of the college of cardinals, regional councils, and episcopal conferences (canons 342–48).

Synods of bishops, which will be treated in a later chapter, assemble representative bishops, along with certain leaders of religious institutes, and occasionally lay members of the church with the pope. Diocesan synods invite various representatives of the diocese–priests, deacons, religious, and laity–to meet with the bishop to discuss matters pertaining to the good of the entire diocese.

Diocesan synods go back at least to the sixth century. The Council of Trent mandated that bishops hold synods yearly. The 1917 Code of Canon Law required that bishops convene synods every ten years. Dioceses rarely met these time requirements. The new code stated that the bishop convokes the synod at opportune times as he sees fit in consultation with the priests' council, yet it does not require or even recommend consultation with the diocesan pastoral council.[9]

The single most important change brought about by the reconstitution of the diocesan synod by the new Code of Canon Law is the required involvement of a significant number of laypeople. This reinstates older practices of the church, which came to an end in the eleventh century under increased exercise of centralized ecclesial authority.[10] The change in canon law was profound: in the 1917 code diocesan synods were a clerical institute treated in the section entitled "De clericis in specie" under the power of the bishop; in the new code they are dealt with in the section on the people of God devoted to "the internal ordering of particular churches."[11] Between Vatican II and the promulgation of the new code, some bishops followed the older clerical paradigm, whereas others sought to implement Vatican II by allowing widespread lay participation.[12]

Diocesan synods provide the most comprehensive interaction of members representing various sectors and groups of the local church. There are to be representatives of all of the councils—episcopal, presbyteral, and, if in existence, the diocesan pastoral council. A priest from each vicariate is to be elected by fellow priests, while superiors of religious institutes with residence in the diocese are to be elected to represent their societies and are joined by other individual dignitaries (e.g., canons of the cathedral church, major seminary rectors, priests who serve as deans of the vicariate). The bishop is permitted to invite other priests, religious, or laypersons to participate as he sees appropriate, in consultation with his councils if he chooses. It is common practice for a diocesan synod committee, led by an individual priest, to make sure that there is representation from diverse groups in the diocese: geographical, socioeconomic, racial, and ethnic. Frequently, all members of the diocese are invited to participate in the synod in some way: by responding to a survey or through discussion of selected topics at meetings held in the parish or in parish clusters. There is a movement from widespread discussion to smaller regional forums, which lead to the final general assembly of the diocesan synod. Often each parish is asked to elect a small number of parishioners to join their pastor in representing their parish at the general assembly. The diverse voices and viewpoints are here brought together to listen to one another and to ponder the pastoral mission of the local church.

The hallmark of the synod is free discussion of all the topics being addressed. Because synods include a greater diversity of participants, with far more laypeople involved, there is a greater possibility of not only divergent viewpoints but also tensions. Beyond general discussion of these matters, voting can be used to determine the opinions of those present and so capture the "degree of concurrence among the synodal members with regard to a given synodal proposal."[13] But as with the parish council, the majority vote is not binding on the bishop; the bishop is the sole legislator issuing declarations and decrees. Canons 465–66 use language we have seen in the treatment of parish councils: participants other than the bishop "possess only a consultative vote," not a deliberative one.

Diocesan synods have traditionally had a certain set of possible aims: implementing universal norms, communicating the decisions and decrees of provincial councils, correcting diocesan abuses, and fostering reforms.[14] Since Vatican II, the Vatican Congregation for Bishops has reaffirmed these aims. However, there has been a growing appreciation, especially at the 1985 Extraordinary Synod of Bishops, of the important role diocesan synods play in the process of promoting greater understanding, reception, and implementation of the church's teachings, such as those of Vatican II.[15] There has also been a new awareness that synods are vehicles for collectively discerning the pastoral mission of the local church and as instruments of spiritual renewal in the local church.[16] The 1997 "Instruction on Diocesan Synods," prepared by the Congregations for Bishops and for the Evangelization of Peoples, summarized this larger vision when it stated that the canonical aim and final object of diocesan synods to pursue the "good of the whole diocesan community" should be understood in terms of "communion and mission, both indispensable aspects of the church's pastoral activities."[17]

There have been over 650 diocesan synods in the course of the history of the U.S. Catholic Church. Of the roughly 176 dioceses in the United States,[18] fifteen synods took place between Vatican II and the appearance of the new Code of Canon Law in 1983. Between 1983 and the end of 2004 there have been approximately forty-two.[19] Eight took place in the second half of the 1960s; four in the '70s; twenty-five in the '80s, nine in the '90s; nine already in the first decade of the new millennium. There is a high correlation between dioceses that have diocesan pastoral councils and those that have held diocesan synods.[20] But it is alarming that such a low percentage of dioceses (approximately 33 percent) have held synods since the council. As in the case of diocesan pastoral councils, structures of dialogical discernment are not being utilized sufficiently.

Two diocesan synods will be treated in more detail here, one that took place shortly after Vatican II and before the new code, the Detroit Diocesan Synod of 1969, and one held after the new code was issued in 1983, the Milwaukee Diocesan Synod of 1987. This will be followed by observations about several diocesan synods held in the last several years.

THE DETROIT DIOCESAN SYNOD OF 1969

The dialogical procedure pioneered in preparation for the diocesan synod that took place in the Archdiocese of Detroit, Michigan, in 1969 merits special attention for two reasons. It provided a prototype that was studied by many dioceses across the United States preparing their own synods, in part because it was developed under the leadership of one of the most influential U.S. bishops, John F. Dearden, who was the founder and became the first president of the National Conference of Catholic Bishops (now the U.S. Conference of Catholic Bishops). The second reason is that its dialogical method was used by the U.S. bishops' ad hoc committee preparing a bicentennial celebration, which culminated in the Call To Action meeting held in Detroit in 1976 (to be examined in the next chapter).

The Second Vatican Council formally ended on December 8, 1965. Less than four months later, on April 1, 1966, John F. Dearden, archbishop of Detroit (named cardinal in 1969) appointed a Synod Preparatory Commission to plan a diocesan synod with the purpose of evaluating and planning the future of the archdiocese in accordance with the teachings of Vatican II. At the request of the archbishop in the summer of 1967 the Archdiocesan Institute for Continuing Education, under the leadership of Jane Wolford Hughes, developed the Parish Participation Plan to involve priests, religious, and laity in the work of the synod. Dearden's decision to give an extensive role in the synod to the laity reflects the influence of Vatican II on his own thinking. The agenda of this Parish Plan in its simplest form was to identify the needs and concerns of the archdiocese and to offer proposals to address them. Three groups of three topic areas were established. Three focused on the people of God: clergy, religious, and laity; three treated the work and relationships of the people of God: worship, education, administration; and three concentrated on the people of God in their relationships with the world: ecumenical affairs, community affairs, and missionary activity. Television programs were prepared for each of the three major groups. These introduced people to the principles of Vatican II and provided some background for applying these principles to the various areas.

The original Parish Participation Program was launched in a booklet sent out to the parishes. On its cover was a picture of Archbishop Dearden and these words: "I will be guided by the thinking of the majority of our people . . . especially in those areas where I have the authority to act and where it is humanly and responsibly possible to do so." This line was taken from one of Dearden's letters describing the synod. The full letter was included on the first full page of the booklet and evokes the spirit of synodal participation through dialogue. The sentiment is later repeated a third time in the document with the addition: "Archbishop Dearden has promised to be guided by the thinking of the majority of the Catholics who make up the Archdiocese of Detroit." Dearden's "promise," however, was never intended to be at the expense of the archbishop's authority, as was clearly indicated by the beginning of the sentence from which the quotation was taken: "Even though it is my responsibility to make the final decisions for the Synod. . . ." What is the overall impression? The front cover: the archbishop will be guided by the thinking of the majority of the people; the inside page: the bishop makes the final decision. The front cover promotes open dialogue; the inside page indicates that the bishop's relation to the conversation is complex. This double message symbolizes the reality of a diocesan synod.

The twelve-page document goes on to describe the idea of a synod, as revised by the teachings of Vatican II, and issues the challenge that Vatican II would remain just words "unless it is translated into action . . . unless its spirit breathes into the lives of the people who make up the Church." The diocese was being called upon to ponder one of the central teachings of the Dogmatic Constitution on the Church (*Lumen Gentium*), that is, that all the baptized are the people of God. "The Church is Pope, Prelates, Priests, Religious and Laity *together* . . . all who have been united to Christ by faith and baptism. We together constitute the People of God. *We are the Church*."[21] If the synod is designed to plan together the collective future of the church in Detroit, "how do we get so many people to speak their minds, to open their hearts, to express their hopes?"

Any parish members who wanted to participate in the synod process were to list their preferences from among the nine topic areas. Each parish organized Speak-Up sessions. Interested parishioners were divided into groups of six to fifteen people who met in private homes or parish school classrooms for six consecutive weeks to discuss the designated topic. Each group had a discussion leader who made sure that all participants "spoke up" and offered their point of view, and each group had a recorder. Each parish had at least nine groups, one for each topic. Each person participating in the sessions received six pamphlets, one per week, exploring the principles and problems related to that particular topic and providing a basis for discussion. The pamphlets urged participants to come ready to "speak up" on the topic and to foster the development of proposals on this particular aspect of the topic. At the end of the week these proposals were collected. The results were published on three consecutive Sundays "in such a way that all the members of a parish [could] vote upon them." Voting on the proposals that were developed through dialogical procedures was a crucial step in the process. The booklet invoked civil democratic and ecclesial conciliar precedents: "It is no easy task to get a bill through Congress with 100 senators and 435 representatives. It is no easier to get a declaration through the II Vatican Council, with well over 2000 bishops." It is an "enormous undertaking" in congress and the council and all the more so when one is trying to tap into the experience and knowledge of a million and a half Catholics in a diocese. The results were tabulated and sent to regional centers for compiling the parish votes and refining the proposals by eliminating duplication.

Nine synod commissions were established, one per topic area. The commissions reviewed the proposals submitted, evaluated them in terms of the doctrinal standards of Vatican II, and determined the number of people who supported them. On the basis of their findings the commissions developed a set of recommendations: statements, principles, and guidelines. These sharpened recommendations, and the original list of proposals from the parishes was then submitted to the archbishop. The booklet explained the work of the synod commissions: "The nine Commissions are meant to be reflective more than creative. They are responsible not for creating their own rules and regulations but for reflecting the thinking of the one and a half million Catholics in the Archdiocese."

The written documents sent to those involved in the synod assembly clearly indicated that all recommendations and proposals were sent to the archbishop and emphasized that he had a "genuine desire to know the thinking of the Catholics in Detroit." But it also spelled out that not all proposals and recommendations would be enacted. Some might be contradictory. Others could be beyond the archbishop's authority. "He does not, for example, have the power of changing the laws regarding priestly celibacy or birth control. But even in questions such as these, the Archbishop needs to receive your thinking. More important, however, are those areas in which he, as Archbishop, can make decisions and enact them." These lines are noteworthy. He invited people to speak up not only about the assigned topic areas, but about any church doctrine or discipline that they felt strongly about so that he could receive their thinking on these matters. He wanted to hear people on any issues they felt should be voiced, but there were only certain issues where the final decision concerning a course of action rested with Archbishop Dearden. Still, this did not mean that the bishop could disregard the position of the majority. "Pope John and Pope Paul did not over-ride the mind and will of the two thousand bishops at the II Vatican Council. They listened to the Holy Spirit speaking through these bishops. Neither will Archbishop Dearden over-ride the mind and will of the more than one and a half million Catholics of the Archdiocese of Detroit. He will listen to the Holy Spirit speaking through you."

Between September 1967 and January 1968, approximately 80,000 adults participated in 7,200 Speak-Up groups. There were 335 participating parishes and 65,000 proposals were recorded. During the same period of time 110,000 high school students also discussed the topics and formulated their own proposals, which were submitted to their youth leaders. The 65,000 proposals were then discussed, revised, and refined at three levels: regional, deanery, and archdiocesan. The regional phase involved 3,000 elected representatives from the parish Speak-Up groups who distilled the proposals down to 23,708. There were 1,100 deanery delegates who further consolidated proposals down to 13,223. There were 115 representatives at a two-day archdiocesan level meeting in May 1968 who narrowed the proposals down to 3,639, and there were members elected to serve on the various pre-synodal commissions. During the summer of 1968, the nine commissions met to develop documents for the synod discussions. A final version of the draft document was prepared in January 1969, which was in turn discussed and agreed upon by the 1,100 deanery delegates of the Parish Participation Plan at Cobo Hall on February 15, 1969. One and a half months later, on March 30, 1969 (exactly three years from the date of his original announcement, April 1, 1966) the archbishop promulgated the documents from the diocesan synod, offering a decree that they take effect and that they be accepted throughout the archdiocese and that the archdiocese be guided by them.

The Detroit Diocesan Synod of 1969 offered an opportunity to discuss the pastoral concerns and problems of the diocese and to develop proposals for addressing them. But in a larger sense it afforded an opportunity for the archdiocese to reflect on and implement the teachings of Vatican II. One can speak of this as a form of pastoral planning, what in business might be called strategic planning. But the documents offer more than a plan of implementation; they serve first as the expression of a genuine diocesan-wide process of reception of the teachings of Vatican II. Each set of recommendations in the nine areas corresponds to specific documents from Vatican II. Each articulates with conviction and substance the teachings from the Vatican II documents. The recommendations and the particular statutes that were approved reflect this agenda. Hortatory statements are interwoven with programmatic recommendations and sometimes followed by specific changes in the diocesan statutes. Statutes were proposed forming new diocesan offices for the laity, religious, and clergy; new diocesan departments for worship, formation, and service; and a commission for ecumenism. Also proposed were structural changes, most noteworthy, the establishment of a priests' senate and councils at parish, vicariate, and diocesan levels. There is no indication in the final document of any discussion of controversial subjects raised at the Speak-Up sessions, although it seems likely that such topics were discussed. Indeed there is no mention of these topics in the final documents: nothing on birth control and the ordination of married men, topics that were raised at the original meetings. There is no record that women's issues or homosexuality surfaced at any level of the discussions. One controversial topic, however, did make its way into the final document on the laity. A significant confession was made. While affirming that various ethnic groups have been well served by ordained ministers, the document admits that

> the Church has not . . . developed the same kind of ministry to the black community. This is a situation which must be regretted. Because of the dearth of black priests and religious, black laymen have a unique responsibility to bring the presence and witness of the Church to the entire black community. To achieve this purpose they must be representative of that community. They must have an effective voice in the design of the apostolate to the black community at archdiocesan, regional and parish levels.

This one example testifies that at least on this topic an honest exchange took place and that through this conversation people in the diocese were called to a deeper conversion.

How is one to assess this synod? The Archdiocese of Detroit can be credited with developing an impressive pedagogical and discerning process that involved a significant number of people in a discussion of the situation in the archdiocese in light of Vatican II teachings with the aim of developing practical pastoral proposals for this local church. The leitmotif sounded from the very start of the process—that the archbishop desired to hear from all the sectors of the diocese and that his own decisions would be guided by the majority opinion—engendered widespread involvement and fostered not only a desire among the participants to contribute actively to the process but also a willingness to learn from each other and the archbishop. Whether the particular pastoral judgments and decisions, or the follow-up implementation of these conclusions, were received and withstood the test of time is a harder question to answer, but it merits attention. Detroit has not had a diocesan synod since 1969.

THE MILWAUKEE DIOCESAN SYNOD OF 1987

The synod held in the Archdiocese of Milwaukee was formally announced in a pastoral letter by Archbishop Rembert Weakland, OSB, in August 1984, six months after the new Code of Canon Law was promulgated.[22] Like Archbishop Dearden in announcing the Detroit synod, Weakland underscored in this letter that "all Synods today on a diocesan level must be a furthering of the work of the Second Vatican Council. . . . The renewal begun by Vatican II is far from achieved; the application and working out of its insights on the local level have only begun." Thus, pastoral planning played a defining role for this synod: "we must ask what crucial problems face us as church and how we should plan for the future." The archbishop invited everyone to raise their own concerns, but he drew attention to two areas: ministry and education. The topic of ministry was framed in terms of Vatican II's teaching that by baptism all are called to share responsibility for the mission of the church and the decline in vocations to the priesthood and religious life. The topic of education demanded special attention because of the challenges of maintaining large parish-based school systems and the need to address the church's special commitment to educate the poor, as well as black, Hispanic, and Laotian children, those with special needs, and the handicapped.

The Milwaukee synod process began with a survey, "Setting the Synod Agenda." Mailed to all the Catholic homes in the diocese, the survey listed eight possible themes: future of education; future of lay, religious, and clergy in ministry; worship and sacramental practice; spreading the gospel; family life; role of women in the church; social concerns; and parish life and organization. People were to rank their importance (of no importance to me, . . . little . . . , somewhat . . . , important . . . , very important . . .), and space was provided for identifying unmentioned themes. Then people were asked to identify which of the six to eleven issues listed under each of the eight topics were important and to select the top three issues for that topic. Six synod themes were chosen from among those raised on the survey. As in the Detroit model, there were parish and regional meetings before the general assembly, but no deanery meetings as such. These assemblies were called parish synods, regional synods, and the general archdiocesan synod. Parish/community synods in September 1986 discussed the first three themes and developed recommendations, which were discussed and revised at regional synods involving 1,800 delegates in December 1986. Parish/community synods were held in February 1987 to discuss the three final themes and to develop recommendations, which were discussed and revised at the regional synods in May. The general synod was held August 28–30, 1987 (three years after the original announcement), and Archbishop Weakland published his plans for implementation of the synod recommendations on November 29, 1987. Final recommendations were ranked according to the voting done at the regional and general synods. Between twelve and seventeen recommendations were approved in six areas: Prayer and Worship, Christian Education, Ministry, Needs of the Family, Racial and Cultural Concerns, and Justice and Human Dignity. So, for instance, "Promote Quality Preaching" was the top recommendation in the Prayer and Worship area. The document reads: "We recommend that . . . [various diocesan institutions] develop a program of ongoing enrichment and evaluation for all those with preaching faculties. Establish a formation program to prepare quality laity to share and exercise the preaching ministry." This is followed by: "We make this recommendation for the following reasons . . . ," which offers rationales (1) from scriptural sources and tradition, (2) from the survey, regional synod votes, and general synod votes, and (3) practical reasons.

The Milwaukee synod illuminates well what has become increasingly true of every synod, that in all its phases each participant is invited to cultivate three distinct kinds of dialogical practices. First, participants are invited into prayerful dialogue with God as a central dimension of the discerning process, both personally and communally, during solitary times of preparation, and in small groups, and liturgical settings.[23] Second, participants are called upon to enter into active dialogical engagement with the scriptures, liturgy, creed, and the tradition of doctrinal and moral teachings of the church.[24] Third, and most distinctively, synods create a free and honest communal dialogue among the various sectors of the diocese about the chosen topics of the synod for the greater good of the diocese. All of these levels of dialogue can provide opportunities for conversion, deeper insight and conviction, change of perception, and new courses of action.

About this third level, communal dialogue, it is noteworthy that Archbishop Weakland consulted with the Archdiocesan Council of Priests as well as the Archdiocesan Pastoral Council at the beginning about the advisability of the synod at this time in the history of the diocese. He also discussed with them the initial survey results, and the two councils gathered for a joint meeting (for the first time) to discuss the selection of the themes. They also served as a "test group" and "evaluators" for the work of the various commissions before the materials were published and presented at parish, regional, or general synods. Council members were encouraged to raise missing perspectives or issues. The archbishop consulted with the two councils to discuss ways to implement the results of the synod. These councils were also charged to do these tasks within the context of prayerful dialogue with God and a dialogue with the scriptures and traditions of faith. The archbishop's interaction with these two councils throughout the diocesan synod process, from its genesis to its implementation, reflects a multilevel and intersecting discernment process at work.

When the six synod commissions were chosen, with groups of nine people who worked through the surveys and proposals on each topic, one can detect in the criteria for selection that the leaders were seeking to identify people who were wise practitioners of the threefold dialogue. First, one needs a "persistent prayerful attitude toward the task." Second, one should be thoroughly conversant with the gospel, the documents of Vatican II, and other relevant church teachings and documents. Third, the practical skills of group dialogue are specified: "An openness to different points of view; Ability to listen in a variety of ways; Ability to analyze, synthesize and discern; Ability to differentiate between what is a popularly expressed need and what is a Spirit-led need; Ability to formulate recommendations that are clear, concise and achievable; . . . A willingness to seek out the experiences of those who are separated from the Church."

Like the Detroit synod, which emphasized the archbishop's promise to be guided by the voice of the majority, the Milwaukee synod was designed so that the archbishop (and the archdiocesan councils and staff) could be receptive and responsive to the cumulative wisdom that emerged from the grassroots, parish-centered, consultative process of collaboration. At the same time, the Milwaukee synod did not stress being guided by the voice of the majority as the Detroit synod had emphasized. Rather, as one of the initial goals stated, the synod should "open the Church to marginalized people," or as it was put in the foundational principles developed by the Synod Coordinating Committee, "it was important to remain open to the 'prophetic' voice which is not always contained in the loudest voice or greatest number of people."[25] At the regional synods, small groups were encouraged to bring up "prophetic recommendations" in the midst of the multitude of voices, a task that was difficult for participants to understand.[26] At one of the most basic levels this need to cultivate habits of listening to prophetic voices, whether within or against the majority, was translated into the need to train group leaders for the meetings at all levels so that certain voices would not dominate and drown out other voices, and that those that are quiet and reserved would be invited and encouraged to speak up. There was likewise an effort to make sure the youth were not ignored but were actively involved in the dialogue. Moreover, group leaders were "to challenge and assist people in listening to differences."[27] At the structural level there was a desire to promote inclusiveness in the synod commissions and deliberations. The archbishop with the Synod Coordinating Committee made efforts to elicit feedback on the themes and proposals from the Hispanic Commission, the Office of Black Catholic Concerns, and the Native American Center at numerous points along the way. Difficult decisions had to be made. Professional or personal expertise in a particular theme was the primary criterion used to choose members for commissions. "Representation by gender, ethnicity, occupation, state in life, or geography were considered when possible."[28] There were insufficient numbers of people from diverse ethnic and racial sectors. The Racial and Cultural Concerns Commission was the only group that was self-consciously diverse in composition.[29]

One of the great obstacles to getting people involved and invested in the process was the attitude that "they won't listen anyway."[30] This complaint was assumed to be directed at the archbishop or the diocesan staff, but in fact it may reflect a larger suspicion of the desire or willingness of hierarchical authorities and bureaucracies to listen and to be receptive and responsive, indeed accountable, for what they have heard. Many people voiced frustration and anger at not feeling heard. The challenge was to create a process whereby people could be heard, their concerns registered, and for the bishop to respond in ways that could be understood. To achieve credibility like this takes time and must be cultivated through habituation of practices. In the words of David Ross, "If the recommendations by the participants are not respected or, in most cases, followed, the result could be apathy and disillusion at best. The experience of some diocesan pastoral councils may attest to this. Even though the synodal members recognize the consultative character of the assembly, if they devote significant time and talent to the endeavor, many will expect to be more than heard."[31]

But a difficult question remains: even though the bishop and the pastoral and priests' councils seek to receive and act upon the recommendations approved, what can be done when sensitive issues are raised that cannot be openly discussed (e.g., those concerning the shortage of priests and the need to examine the requirements of an all-celibate male clergy)? Is silence on such subjects a constructive option? Can and should certain topics be "received" and "recorded" and "acknowledged" as of vital importance for this local church by the bishop even though the local church does not have the authority to address or remedy these situations?

There are also large issues of group dynamics involved. How does the diocese foster widespread involvement in an effort to clarify the consensus of the group but also recognize the need to hear the quiet prophetic voices in the midst of the process? How does one promote inclusion of ethnic diversity of diocesan membership in the process, and along the way teach people to listen and learn from difference? How does one deal with excessively outspoken personalities and power struggles? The "Instruction on Diocesan Synods" writes of "the danger of pressure groups—oftentimes a regrettable reality." Bishops are instructed that they should "always avoid creating unjustified expectations with regard to the effective acceptance of their [advocacy groups] proposals."[32]

Some have suggested that the great danger of diocesan synods is that communal dialogue threatens the dialogue of prayer and the dialogue with scripture and tradition that leads to obedience. The church is not a democracy, so the argument goes, and the synod is not a political convention. The people of God is not a sociological or political reality, but one that uncovers its true identity in the Eucharist. Consultation is not a diminution of the community's role in the process but a genuine expression of coresponsibility. The question must be raised: to what extent are such reductionistic views of the synod process operative among any sectors of the diocese?[33]

Archbishop Weakland wrote frequently about the dynamics of the diocesan synod. In his opening pastoral letter we read:

> The preparation for the Synod is most important, perhaps in some respects as important as the conclusions reached. During that period of preparation we must be listening to the needs of our "traveling companions," we must be sensitive to the issues people are struggling with, we must be free to articulate dreams and visions and concerns. In other words, we must be church. What is significant about a Synod, however, is not just the listening process but the conclusions reached. Not all points of view can be equally "victorious," as some will be voted down; but I count on the goodwill and spirit of cooperation of all in working towards equitable solutions to the questions and problems raised. Christians do not attend such meetings as if such gatherings were just any kind of political or social rally. They come together to pray and discern what God wants of them today. Discerning his will must be more important than winning or losing. (August 1986)

In his columns in the diocesan paper, the *Catholic Herald*, Weakland made numerous attempts to describe the nature of the diocesan synod process. Early on he explained that the process is "consultative" and that the bishop is the sole legislator.

> A consultative process is not well understood by Americans: we want to restrict the Holy Spirit to a majority vote. Consultative to us means the legislator can do as he or she pleases, and so it seems like a waste of time. We fail to realize that a consultative process is, first of all, a listening one. One single voice might be the one responding to the Spirit and, thus, the one that must be heard by all. It is true that after much reflection and discussion one should be able to rely on the wisdom and insights of the vast majority as being the most valid course to follow. It would be wrong, however, to dismiss the minority voice as unimportant, as it, too, might be saying something quite significant for all to hear and profit from, even if it is not the course here and now selected. A Synod is, therefore, formative as well as consultative. It forms the mind and conscience of the legislator; it forms the thinking of all in the church, not just the members of the Synod. (*Catholic Herald*, May 8, 1986)

Weakland contrasted diocesan synods with normal democratic assemblies. The point of the synod is to discern God's will. "It is not a question of doing what would please most of the people, but discerning what will serve the most, especially the most in need, in the best way possible" (*Catholic Herald,* August 14, 1986). Even if one feels that one's voice has not been heard because one's favorite resolution is not in the final selection, Weakland argued that each one's contribution remains important (*Catholic Herald,* July 23, 1987).

On the other hand, in response to the criticism that the synod was trying to make the church a democracy, when, as the argument goes, "everyone knows it is a monarchy–willed so by Jesus Christ," Weakland rejected the claims that the church is either a democracy or a monarchy:

> If by democracy one means that the majority vote of the people rules, then the church is not a democracy. The Holy Spirit will never be tied to 51 percent of those voting. Nor can revealed truth and morality be determined by popular majority vote. God's revelation of the inner divine life, of how we are saved and can participate in that life, of the action of the Holy Spirit among us—these are truths revealed to us and not subject to a vote of majority determination.
>
> But there are elements in the church that could well be called "democratic," and we do injustice to the church and its history if we do not recognize them. (*Catholic Herald,* August 13, 1987)

The church needs to acknowledge the historical role of the community involved in discernment processes.[34] The Holy Spirit resides in the church in all the baptized and confirmed, and the church needs the gifts of the Spirit given to all. Through baptism all share in the responsibilities of the mission of the church. And the church acknowledges the "*sensus fidelium,* the sense of the faithful"—"an inner consciousness on the part of the faithful that a teaching is a part of what the faithful have always accepted as being contained in the revealed truth" (*Catholic Herald,* August 13, 1987).

RECENT DIOCESAN SYNODS AND THE ADVENT OF THE INTERNET

Although dialogue provides the creative impulse and the guiding medium in the diocesan synod, there are other forms of communication that are indispensable. Bishops and synod coordinating committees have tried to use every form of communication at their disposal to lead the members of the diocese through the process. The Institute for Continuing Education helped produce for the Detroit synod an introductory booklet and numerous leaflets on topics for distribution throughout the diocese as the process progressed, and Archbishop Dearden talked about the synod on a television show. The Milwaukee synod had a Communication Committee, a public relations consultant, and staff that helped the director of the synod and the Synod Coordinating Committee. Their media included: twelve single-sheet parish bulletin inserts over a two-year period; parish bulletins and synod artwork; articles and numerous columns in the archdiocesan newspaper by the archbishop on the synod; press releases to weekly and daily secular newspapers throughout the diocese; discussions on local radio and television programs; two thirty-minute television programs before the two major parish/community synods; advertising in all public venues; synod folder; synod posters; banners; photography; video; opening video for the general synod; synod memorabilia; prayer cards; press kits and press room for the general synod; and a published final report for distribution throughout the diocese.[35]

With the dawn of the Internet and its increasing use since the mid–1990s, dioceses have created Web sites, which are commonly being used to advance the work of diocesan synods. The Los Angeles synod, which ended in 2003, and the Omaha synod and the Sacramento synod, both completed in 2004, illustrate how diocesan Web sites are now being used as major communication vehicles in the synod process. The Web sites for these three dioceses posted information that was written by the local ordinary and by other important leaders and facilitators in the synod processes for the diocesan Catholic newspapers. Beyond that, the Web site provided valuable information about the meaning, motivation, and guiding principles of a synod, as well as a description of the stages involved in the process, who was involved, and how synod proposals were to be developed, assessed, revised, and finalized. In addition, the Los Angeles Web site provided visitors to the Web site with the means to contact a member of the Office of the Synod, which was subsequently replaced by the Office of Synod Implementation, which allowed visitors to comment on any of the main topics addressed by the synod. In addition, the Sacramento synod used its Web site as one means for communicating with synod delegates, requesting responses via e-mail.

These Web sites provide valuable vehicles for communicating information about the synod and can provide opportunities for reactions and suggestions, even though this information continues to be made available by other means. However, dioceses have not yet experimented with interactive forums on the Internet that are dialogical in character, such as setting up chat rooms to discuss synod topics, discussion boards, instant messaging, and Web logs or *blogs*. This seems inevitable, but these venues will never provide a substitute for the face-to-face dialogical forms provided by parish, regional, and general assemblies utilized in diocesan synods.

PRACTICAL PROBLEMS, REASONABLE EXPECTATIONS

Diocesan synods, as reformed in light of Vatican II, offer an important vehicle for fostering far greater involvement of members throughout the diocese in the process of collective discernment about the identity and mission of the local church. People across the diocese are offered an opportunity and a challenge to reflect on each aspect of the local church's life: liturgy, religious formation and education, social service and work for justice, and the development of lay, consecrated, and ordained ministries. The promise and achievements of diocesan synods, as well as the difficulties, can be fully understood only when considered in relation to the network of diocesan councils—pastoral, presbyteral, finance, and episcopal—as well as the contribution of the diocesan staff. Together these dialogical circles of discernment reposition the person and role of the bishop within the diocese and reconstitute episcopal credibility, power, authority, leadership, and accountability within a relational understanding of the bishop's office and his exercise of his ministry. The bishop fulfills his office and his vocation to the degree that he cultivates the dialogical skills needed to work within such a reconstituted practice of episcopacy, one that invites the ongoing development of the theology of episcopacy and the local church.

A host of practical concerns pertains to the communicative and dialogical character of diocesan synods. It is important that the intended goals of the diocesan synod are clearly enunciated as the synod unfolds. The bishop and the coordinating synod committee need to be clear in their original objectives and in the selection of the theme and topics. Widespread consultation in the selection of topics through surveys and parish meetings far exceeds pre–Vatican II practices and must continue to be enhanced.[36]

There must also be an attempt to clarify, as the process goes forward, what is coming into focus and the various options that are available for the participants in terms of proposals and recommendations. There should be special attention devoted to sharpening and fine-tuning communication throughout the process in order to foster dialogical exchanges at parish, regional, and general synods and in the various commissions. During the various stages of the Milwaukee synod people were given a chance to evaluate surveys, input, forms, discussion formats, and so on, and the coordinating synod committee did receive a great number of reactions. Forms were confusing; options not clearly differentiated; efforts to surface prophetic recommendations in the small-group discussions were confusing; prayer was not well integrated; large-group process needed clarification. Discussion questions and procedures can all be revised in response to such input.

What particular results are coming into focus throughout the process? Pastoral goals and vision statements, diocesan legislation, program directives, resolutions, suggestions? In orienting participants toward intended, specific results, there must be an effort to be clear, concrete, specific, precise, and easily understandable. "Declarations and decrees" are crucial products of the process that will "extend beyond the memories of the participants."[37] Developing a pastoral vision of the diocesan mission and practical planning goals are important. It is not enough, however, to articulate the goals and specify intended results. The vision and goals will be forgotten or ignored if they are not practical and realizable. Since the time of Vatican II it has become increasingly clear that the diocesan synod is not to be judged simply in terms of whether the dialogical process appeared effective when it culminated in a vision statement and a general plan, but in terms of concrete pastoral recommendations and their subsequent implementation. Consequently, there is a need to formulate an implementation process and time lines for realizing the synod goals and recommendations.[38]

Are any topics and particular proposals raised by participants at the parish and regional levels filtered out of the diocesan synod process by diocesan commissions along the way? If so, on what basis? Is there a majority rule at work? Are minority concerns and targeted missionary foci able to find expression in the final documents? These are important questions that must be addressed by each diocese as it runs a synod. Archbishop

Dearden indicated in a straightforward manner at the outset in 1967 that he wanted people to feel free to speak up about any topics, even ones that were controversial and were outside his ability to address formally, for example, priestly celibacy and birth control. Perhaps input on such controversial topics was evident in the recommendations made and voted upon at the parish, regional, and general synod levels, but it was not attested to in the final report.

These kinds of controversial issues were evident in the ranked and approved Milwaukee Synod Recommendations. The third recommendation in the area of ministry was "promote dialogue on change in ordination policy" (which was ranked very high in over half of the 228 parishes responding); the fifth recommendation was "promote women in leadership in ministry." In the area of Needs of the Family, "examine current church policy on family planning and its pastoral implications" was ranked seventh. While each set of recommendations in a given topic area raises many interesting questions, the point that people are allowed to discuss and offer recommendations on controversial topics that are not filtered out and suppressed is very important. It should be added that nothing on homosexuality is apparent in the recommendations; the recommendations on life issues do not contain any mention of capital punishment or just war.

In the closing statement on the synod, "One in Heart and Mind: Implementing the Archdiocesan Synod of 1987," Archbishop Weakland did not address any of the controversial issues raised in the recommendations. They remained on record, however. With this in mind, it is important to point out that the Vatican "Instruction on Diocesan Synods" states clearly, "the bishop has the duty to exclude from the synodal discussions theses or positions—as well as proposals submitted to the synod with the mere intention of transmitting to the Holy See 'polls' in their regard—discordant with the perennial doctrine of the church or the magisterium or concerning material reserved to supreme ecclesiastical authority or to other ecclesiastical authorities."[39] It is difficult to know how to assess this statement in relation to the fact that the Code of Canon Law mandates free discussion at synods and voting is allowed, if not encouraged.

Some would argue that synod participants have no competency to address these matters of church teaching and church discipline and so should not waste their time talking about them and trying to work up recommendations to address them. Only the pope and the bishops, and the theologians whose views are drawn upon by these episcopal teachers, it is argued, have the sanctioned authority to address them. This position asserts that the local church has no competence based on practical everyday living, and that no teaching authority is invested in the laity, religious, and clergy by virtue of their baptism and the gift of faith they have received. This argument concludes: avoid frustrating participants in diocesan synods by not allowing these subjects to be discussed.

By contrast, I would agree with those who argue that the pastoral mission of the church is jeopardized or at least at issue because of the church's stance on these practical issues: celibacy requirements, women's ordination, birth control, the prohibition against receiving the sacraments after divorce and remarriage, and the prohibition against homosexual behavior and committed relations are the most common examples. This is why people feel obliged and conscience-bound to raise these in the setting of the diocesan synod, even though the vast majority will recognize that the bishop has no authority to address these controversial issues. How else will the local ordinary and indirectly Roman offices come to hear the voices of the faithful on these matters if they are not allowed to record their voices and votes? The diocesan synod is the place established in the practice of the local church where free discussion of issues facing the church is to take place. Any effort to cut off this discussion and disallow voting on these subjects violates the dialogical character of the synod and calls into question the authority and authenticity of its final recommendations.

It is one thing for proposals to be introduced that are contrary to current church discipline (ordaining women or married men, changing the teaching on birth control, etc.). It is a far different approach to claim, as did the Milwaukee synod statements, that there needs to be further open discussion and deliberation about celibacy requirements, the role of women in ministry, and family planning sensitive to the pastoral needs and concerns of the entire people of God. No doubt, these issues can be politicized. However, the question might be asked, Under what conditions might conflict in the discourse of the diocesan synod be helpful for the local process or for deliberations beyond individual dioceses, and when might it in fact undermine the process?[40]

The consultative and not deliberative nature of pastoral councils, which was introduced in the previous chapter, arises in the context of synods as well. It should be noted that Archbishop Dearden drew the distinction differently. In the final synod document he stated that "these pages represent months and even years of dialogue and deliberation between bishops, priests, religious, and laity of every station and age of life." Or again, "Together we have considered and made decisions about the most important areas of our life in Christ." Deliberative, yes, but not strictly speaking legislative. However, it is interesting that Dearden "promises" to be guided by the deliberations of the synod and in fact encourages others to make a kind of covenantal promise to this dialogical process. "Indeed, if we could insist on only one point it would be that all of us in this Archdiocese continue in a state of Synodal co-responsibility, of constant searching both to identify and clarify what our Christian concerns should be and to find new and better ways to satisfy them." There is some sort of mutual bond established between the bishop and all the members of the diocese and a mutual accountability is implied, although not specified. Participatory decision making and mutual accountability among laity, religious, and clergy are specifically mentioned in the section of the final synod document devoted to the visible structure of the church. Two canon lawyers have commented on these issues. J. Alesandro indicates that deliberative process exceeds simple advice and "implies mutual responsibilities on the part of all the people of God gathered together in synod." Tom Green asks "in a time of such significant pastoral change, might not a synod be an appropriate vehicle specifying long range diocesan objectives, to be implemented concretely by the diocesan pastoral council and other diocesan institutions? Although the bishop is said to be the only legislator . . . , what would prevent his committing himself as a general rule to sanctioning the determinations of a body such as a synod?"[41]

The development of participatory forms of collective discernment is necessary to advance the pastoral mission of the local church. The theology, spirituality, credibility, and authority of the bishop of a local church depend on the development of diocesan pastoral councils to work together with the episcopal, finance, and presbyteral councils, as well as with the diocesan staff in developing cycles of pastoral planning and implementation. But in this cyclical process of renewal and reform, there is a need for the wider consultation provided by diocesan synods. Based on the current statistics, it is by no means clear whether diocesan pastoral councils will increasingly be formed and will develop the kind of dialogical expertise needed to foster collective wisdom and accountability. There is even greater reason for doubt about the future of diocesan synods. These are causes for lament and anger because they are clear signs that the reception of Vatican II is incomplete and in jeopardy. There is also evidence, however, that diocesan pastoral councils and diocesan synods are new institutional signs of promise and hope in the church that are taking root. The Los Angeles synod of 2003 is a case in point. In its pastoral initiative devoted to structures for participation and accountability it states: "If all the baptized are to share in the Church's mission, then the structures of Church life and governance must be renewed, and some new structures established, to allow for the greatest degree of participation on the part of the greatest number of the baptized. . . . The Church must evaluate and revitalize present structures and devise new ones to provide for increased participation, collaboration, and accountability in mission and ministry." As a result, five pastoral regions were identified in the archdiocese and a charter for developing regional pastoral councils in each of the five areas was set forth in fall 2003. The members of a newly reconstituted archdiocesan pastoral council will be taken from the regional pastoral councils.

3

An Overwhelming Response to a U.S. Bishops' Invitation

The Call To Action

One of the most important experiments in dialogue during the postconciliar period was initiated by the U.S. Conference of Catholic Bishops (USCCB).[1] In preparation for the national celebration of the bicentennial, the bishops in 1973 launched two years of consultations across the country on the role of Catholicism in the United States, which culminated in the national assembly given the name Call To Action (CTA), held in Detroit, October 21–23, 1976.[2] Though never replicated, this experiment has been profoundly influential.[3]

The National Conference of Catholic Bishops (now the United States Conference of Catholic Bishops) will be examined more fully in the next chapter. Here it is important to recall that this organizational structure, which had an antecedent form in the U.S. church, was refashioned in response to teachings of Vatican II and provided the bishops with opportunities to gather to deliberate about matters pertaining to the apostolic mission of the church in the United States. In addition to their semiannual general assembly, the NCCB comprised a variety of different committees, composed of bishops, staff members, and experts, on such topics as doctrine, liturgy, education, and missions, as well as on social development and world peace. The United States Catholic Conference (USCC) was formed during the same period as the NCCB as a distinct organization designed to promote the work of the U.S. bishops and as a nonprofit social service organization devoted "principally [to] affairs involving the general public, including social concerns, education, and communications."[4] As of July 1, 2001, the USCC and the NCCB were restructured and combined as the United States Conference of Catholic Bishops (USCCB).

The idea for a conference on justice was initially introduced by Sr. Marie Augusta Neal, SNDdeN, of Emmanuel College. She was a member of the advisory council of the NCCB, which was considering the feasibility of a National Pastoral Council. Neal proposed a preliminary experiment in shared responsibility that would foster a discussion among Catholics, that is, an extracanonical, national consultation about recent official teachings on justice, both Paul VI's "call to action" in *Octogesima Adveniens* (1971) and the statement from the 1971 synod of bishops on justice in the world. The advisory council advanced the idea and the NCCB approved it.[5] Bishop James S. Rausch, the general secretary of the NCCB/USCC at the time, was the episcopal inspiration and tireless advocate of the national Call To Action convention.[6] A special Committee for the Bicentennial was formed and John Cardinal Dearden was chosen to chair the committee. Three subcommittees were established: one to write about the role of the Catholic Church in the history of the United States, one to prepare liturgical resources for parishes to commemorate the bicentennial, and a third to plan a nation-wide conference on justice issues.

DEVELOPING A PLAN FOR A CUMULATIVE PROCESS OF DELIBERATION

J. Bryan Hehir, a priest of the Boston archdiocese and director of the USCC division of International Justice and Peace, wrote a letter on July 17, 1973, to Bishop Rausch proposing a three-phase process for the national conference on justice: First, he suggested, explore the concept of justice in its various meanings and applications—political, strategic, economic, and then specific topics such as trade, arms, and human rights. Second, hold regional conferences on these topics and involve the local churches in "a period of listening" as a process of education in justice in preparation for a national event. Third, hold a national conference in which papers would be prepared, presented, revised through dialogical exchanges, and expanded by quality resource people on these various topics. This format was initially adopted.

A significant revision of the plan took place during meetings of the justice subcommittee, especially on March 22 and April 5, 1974. Members decided to move away from a didactic process, aiming at policy statements on key domestic and international church–state issues, to a dialogical process with a consultative format. In this shift to a more open-ended dialogical approach increasing attention was given to the issues of justice in the church. Various people contributed to this change. Hehir's proposed regional conferences, his second phase, were to provide those in attendance a "period of listening" to experts lecturing on various topics. But this was modified in response to a suggestion made by Francis Butler, the executive director of the Bishops' Committee for the Bicentennial, that the regional conferences employ a "hearing model" similar to investigative legislative hearings on Capitol Hill, which would have a town hall format for collectively discerning the signs of the times by providing a forum for bishops and all participating members to listen to diverse people's experiences. This new format offered the occasion to hear about situations of injustice and struggle in the wider society, but, as numerous religious women, among others, were urging, also in the church.[7]

The first phase of Hehir's original proposal was devoted to exploring the various meanings of the concept of justice and its application. The shift to a more open, consultative approach in the second phase led to a revision of this first phase as well. Parish and local community discussions about justice issues in society and in the church were developed across the country as a helpful complement to and preparation for the regional hearings. The major impetus for these grassroots conversations was Msgr. Jack Egan, a diocesan priest from Chicago. Egan was well known for community organizing. He had established the first Office of Urban Affairs in the Archdiocese of Chicago and had formed the Catholic Committee on Urban Ministry (CCUM) in 1967, which included Msgr. Geno Baroni, the head of the Center for Urban Ethnic Affairs, as one of its founding members. Baroni came to play a key role in crafting the format for the regional hearings.[8] On September 20–21, 1974, the justice subcommittee met in Washington, D.C. Presiding over the meeting was Archbishop Joseph Bernardin, who was the chair of this subcommittee at the time. Egan and Baroni were present, as were representatives of about fifty organizations. Egan led one of the discussions. A main task at this meeting was to consider what topics should be included in the parish discussion guide.

Egan proposed that the bicentennial justice subcommittee convene in

Arlington, Virginia, with diocesan justice and peace coordinators, many of whom were connected to CCUM. This meeting took place in December of 1974 with Cardinal Dearden in attendance. Ninety-two diocesan coordinators who were present urged grassroots participation in the program. This profoundly influenced the parish and local community phase of the program. These coordinators formed an ad hoc steering group, which met on February 6 and April 28, 1975, to plan the grassroots community discussions. This alliance of diocesan justice and peace groups and the network of people involved in creating the program in these earlier phases proved to be a crucial ingredient in the cumulative process that resulted.

It is important to ask about the kind of dialogue associated with Egan's brand of community organizing, which ultimately influenced the understanding of dialogue in each phase of the bicentennial program. In 1954 the Catholic philosopher Jacques Maritain introduced Egan to his friend, Saul Alinsky, the premier U.S. advocate of social change through organizing grassroots communities.[9] In 1957 Egan became Alinsky's first priest intern in organizational skills. Alinsky trained leaders to become organizers who would mobilize local communities on controversial issues. Alinsky espoused a confrontational brand of dialogue between civic and business leaders and members of grassroots communities. His organizers were to empower marginalized people to come together and speak up for themselves and exert collective pressure on power elites that would educe cooperation for their collective goals. Public demonstrations and confrontations were used to make demands and hold powerful people in the community accountable for their actions. This model of communication, which highlights disparity in power relations and the important role of conflict and confrontation, has been viewed by some as clashing with Catholic predilections for harmony and cooperation, and by others as a corrective insight.[10]

Egan was significantly influenced by Alinsky. Like Alinsky, Egan was a sober realist about power dynamics involved in social structures, including church structures. Like Alinksy, Egan wanted marginalized people to make their own voices heard for their own sake and for the sake of the larger good of the community. But Egan was not Alinsky and, reflective of his Catholic convictions, he took a less conflictual and confrontational approach to dialogue and promoted the cultivation of long-term social relations. Egan's larger vision reflected his close association with the Christian Family Movement (CFM), which subscribed to the see–judge–act model of French Catholic Action, and in particular his close friendship with the CFM leaders Patty and Patrick Crowley. The Crowleys had been influential members of Pope Paul VI's commission on birth control and were deeply disillusioned when the majority opinion of the commission was rejected in the encyclical *Humanae Vitae* in 1967.[11] Patty Crowley, who was a member of the writing team for the preparatory documents for Call To Action, along with Egan, urgently desired to promote ways for the U.S. hierarchy to listen to expressions of the lived experience of the Catholic faithful, which had been too often ignored, discredited, and dismissed.

The various phases of the bicentennial project—local, regional, and national—were ultimately organized into an overarching program around eight topics. This schema followed neither Hehir's original division of the concept of justice and its subdivisions, applications, and topics nor Alinsky's strategy of identifying a burning issue and organizing a group around it in order to demand change from power elites. Michael Novak, a member of the justice subcommittee, suggested that the focus be not on specific social issues but on social "organisms": family, neighborhood, ethnic and racial groups, personhood, humankind, and church. He also suggested the name that was chosen as the title of the resource book. *Liberty and Justice for All: A Discussion Guide* was the work of a commissioned group of scholars and was published for use during Lent 1975 to foster reflection on the eight themes in parishes and dioceses. Francis Butler was the general editor of the volume, which was originally published in January 1975. Jane Wolford Hughes, who was asked by Cardinal Dearden to serve as the local coordinator of the project for Detroit, took the guidebook and tested it in the Archdiocese of Detroit. On the basis of these tests, she advised other local coordinators from across the country at a meeting held in Detroit on April 28, 1975, on how to use the discussion guide. She recalled Dearden proposing the 1969 Detroit synod "speak up" model as a valuable prototype for the Call To Action process. Her own leadership role in designing the Detroit synod process informed her testing of the bicentennial discussion guide and her advice to the other coordinators on its usage. The call for strong local community involvement by Egan and Baroni may have allowed for more confrontational participants in principle, but their own emphasis on open dialogue, which Butler came to advocate on the justice subcommittee, blended well with the Detroit synod model of group discernment.

An active process of dialogue thus became the main vehicle for an exercise in shared responsibility, one that enabled people to "speak up" and fostered the practice of episcopal listening.[12] Feedback sheets were included in the guidebook, raising questions about the topics in each section. These enabled local groups to record in their own language the major issues that they decided merited attention and to identify up to five courses of actions to address them. These books aimed to nurture dialogue in parish settings in preparation for the six regional hearings. Cardinal Dearden introduced the guidebook by stating the intention of the bishops' bicentennial committee: "Our goal is to arrive at both a Catholic expression of the meaning of liberty and justice for all and a collective commitment to a common course of action in the years ahead. . . . The discussion guide . . . will play a major role in this process. Through its use the Catholic community can begin to focus on common concerns, and also voice its aspirations for the future course of the Church."[13] The bishops of the United States were inviting parishioners to participate in a dialogue and to share responsibility for the promotion of justice in everyday life in the spirit of the Gospel of Jesus Christ and Christian discipleship. The dialogue was to take shape in numerous forms.

THE PLAN BECOMES REALITY

The first phase of dialogue took place at the parish and diocesan level. Groups gathered in parish halls and schools to discuss the themes in the guidebook. "79 of the nation's 162 dioceses submitted feedback sheets to the national offices. These provided opinions from over 800,000 participants."[14] About seventy dioceses, twenty-eight of which had not participated in the parish phase as designed, sent reports on bicentennial conventions and results from hearings that took place in their local communities. In all, about 107 dioceses had some level of involvement, which was an impressive return for such a new experiment. However, the results also showed the lack of experience with such a process. National Catholic organizations and religious communities were able to participate in these earlier phases, but few did.

The second phase was regional hearings. These built on the experience of the parish programs. They became one of the key dialogical innovations of the bicentennial program. As Cardinal Dearden himself said, "the process of the hearings might prove the most lasting contribution of the bicentennial program."[15] Strictly speaking the hearing process was not dialogical in the way that the local and national meetings were, both of which incorporated small-group and large-group discussion processes. By contrast, at the hearings, bishops and church leaders came to listen to expert testimony and the witness of Catholics struggling to promote justice in their everyday lives, sometimes against seemingly insurmountable obstacles. Questions were posed by the bishops or other panelists to those who were giving testimony, and brief dialogical exchanges occurred. Overall, the hearing process contributed to the various dialogical structures being utilized: listening to and recording testimonies and dialogical exchanges from the hearings provided an important source for the development of proposals that were discussed and deliberated upon at later phases in the process.

Six meetings took place on domestic issues, with a seventh devoted to international matters: the first topic was humankind, but special attention was given to justice in the church and the role of women in the church (Washington, D.C., February 3–5, 1975); the second topic was nationhood, and the concerns of Spanish-speaking populations were prominent (San Antonio, Texas, April 3–5); the third topic was land, and attention was given to rural life issues, Native Americans, and again justice in the church (St. Paul, June 12–14); the fourth topic was family (Atlanta, August 7–9); the fifth topic was work (Sacramento, October 2–4); the sixth topic was racism and ethnicity (Newark, December 4–6); and the seventh special session was devoted to global issues (Maryknoll, New York, July 14, 1976).[16] These hearings were intended to provide open, public forums; however, they could not accommodate all those who wanted to be heard. After the first hearing, which seemed formal and stodgy, there was "a good deal of criticism, some of which suggested that the entire program, with its promise of openness, consultation, and honest listening, was in fact 'stacked,' not with ordinary people but with experts and people cosy with the bishops."[17] In response to such frustrations, efforts were made to broaden participation so that the bishops would hear from a variety of groups and individuals from across the spectrum of opinions in the church.

Msgr. Geno Baroni from the Center for Urban Ethnic Affairs influenced the second, more open and dramatic set of hearings, which took place in San Antonio, Texas. Like Egan, and in the spirit of their common mentor, Alinsky, Baroni vigorously emphasized the need for grassroots community involvement in order for the process to be credible. Baroni especially urged the involvement of ethnic Americans. Through Baroni and Father John Yanta, a friend of Baroni's who led a Hispanic parish in San Antonio, contacts were made with the Communities Organized for Public Service (COPS), which provided a list of participants for the San Antonio hearing. COPS, which was funded by the Campaign for Human Development, was started in 1973 by Ernesto Cortes, Jr., another Catholic who had been trained in community organizing at Saul Alinsky's Industrial Areas Foundation. Following in the Alinsky tradition, COPS wanted to empower local people to address social problems. But Cortes and COPS developed a strategy that was different from Alinsky's. Unlike Alinsky, they did not shy away from religious convictions and concentrated on promoting personal commitments to the community. Instead of a leader identifying an issue that people could rally around, COPS developed "relational organizing." "Specific plans for action emerged out of conversations at the bottom, rather than issues identified by activists at the top. Relational organizing worked to bring community leaders together to find common ground for action and to develop the capacity to act in the interests of the broader community."[18] Instead of Alinsky's strategic and tactical advances on particular issues through confrontation and power alliances, COPS fostered building wider communal relations, including interracial bonds, in the promotion of a broader consensus with greater longevity for community development. The COPS approach to relational organizing left its mark on Call To Action.

Beginning in San Antonio, each part of the hearings featured an expert or academic—someone with name recognition—and a local person. Msgr. George Higgins, one of the architects of the program format, attended each of the hearings and sat by the bishop chairing the sessions as the panel heard testimony and asked questions of the presenters. The stories of local people, sugar cane workers and farm workers, illegal migrants, textile mill workers, Native Americans, were regularly very moving and instructive, but so too were some of the experts: Dorothy Day, César Chávez, Bayard Rustin, Peggy and Peter Steinfels, Charles Rangel, Walter Mondale, Sheila Cassidy, Bishop Donal Lamont, and many more.

These hearings generated a great deal of excitement and energy. People came to feel invested in the dialogical process. The bishops were well aware of what was transpiring. As David O'Brien observes, "The drama of the hearings was provided by the bishops' assumption of a posture of listening to their people as they responded to the invitation to speak up. The very process of speaking and listening became more and more central to the program."[19] The official record of the hearings remained opened for a month so that additional written testimony by those who were unable to contribute at the public event could be added. The record from each hearing was then printed and distributed to dioceses, libraries, and any individual who requested a copy. Seven volumes of testimony were compiled and made available across the country.[20]

Call To Action was the name given to the national phase of the bicentennial dialogue process, following the suggestion of Francis Butler to use the phrase from Pope Paul VI's 1971 apostolic letter, *Octogesima Adveniens*: "It is to all Christians that we address a fresh and insistent call to action" (48). Maria Riley, OP, a member of the Adrian Dominican Congregation, designed the Detroit Call To Action program at the request of Frank Butler and with the help of Jeanne O'Laughlin, OP, also an Adrian Dominican. Their overriding concern in developing the process was that everyone—bishops, clergy, laity, and women and men religious—would be fully participating "as equal partners in dialogue in framing the recommendations and resolutions of the meeting."[21] Instead of parent–child or teacher–student relationships, the working assumption was the adulthood of all participants. The design of the program reflected the dialogical consensus processes developed by the Adrian Dominican Congregation, like other communities of women religious, especially in their general chapter of renewal, which took place shortly after Vatican II. The experience of women religious in North America, and the Adrian Dominicans in particular, will be examined more closely in a subsequent chapter. Their guiding conviction was that all participants were to be given a chance to name their own realities and influence the agendas. Based on their experience of chapters, Riley and O'Laughlin believed it was crucial to build in opportunities for small-group dialogues and larger-group discussions. The small groups gave everyone a chance to be actively involved. Both the smaller and larger formats were to foster free, open discussion, not controlled in any substantial way. At the same time, the conversations needed to be focused and to aim at reaching a consensus. Consequently, it was decided that the groups would have discussion leaders trained in moving the dialogue forward, clarifying disputed issues, and advancing the group toward reaching a judgment. Margaret Cafferty, PBVM, was chosen to train Catholic Charities directors to serve as discussion leaders for the Call To Action conference. And following the design of chapters and diocesan synods, all the participants were to be given an opportunity to vote on the final resolutions. It was Riley's role to convince Cardinal Dearden, Bishop Rausch, and Archbishop Peter Gerety that this process would work.

The next step was the formation of eight writing committees to prepare working statements on the eight themes. These committees summarized the feedback received from phase one, the parish and diocesan discussions, and the testimonies from the hearings, and prepared draft recommendations, which would be discussed, revised, and voted on at the national conference. Each group had between eight and fifteen members, was chaired by a bishop, and included scholars, activists, and pastoral ministers. In light of subsequent criticisms leveled at the recommendations proposed and approved at the Call To Action conference, it is important to stress the composition of these groups and the leadership role played by bishops in each. These were not groups of radicals. Their task was difficult. They worked with a wide variety of materials voicing a wide range of opinions. The groups strove to honor the desires of those who were involved in the previous levels of discussion. The organizers of Call To Action never claimed that these reports offered a representative scientific survey of U.S. Catholic opinion.

Each of the eight reports introduced its theme in the context of Catholic tradition and experience.[22] Then a summary of the results of the consultations was provided with some interpretation of the theological significance of the findings in light of Catholic teaching and its practical importance for contemporary American Catholic life. The reports concluded with three or four recommendations for action. Nine criteria guided the committee in preparing draft resolutions. Several merit attention: "1. Each resolution should have some intrinsic relationship to the program theme of freedom and justice. 2. It should grow from reflection on the scripture and the teaching of the church. . . . 4. Except in very unusual circumstances, it should find significant support in the materials from the consultation and the hearings."[23] The resolutions for each topic thus emerged from within what could be analogously described as two sets of dialogical relationships: with the scriptures and teaching of the church, on the one hand, and the consultations, on the other. The recommendations were addressed to different levels of church authority—parish, school, diocese, NCCB—and to church members, depending on the nature of the recommendation.

Between April and June of 1976, training workshops were held around the country for the 1,340 delegates who would be attending Call To Action. These workshops prepared participants to know what to expect at the convention, the steps and goals of the process, and how each member could enter into the conversation during the convention.

By the time people started arriving for the Call To Action convention on Wednesday afternoon, October 20, 1976, in Cobo Hall in Detroit, Michigan, the organizing committee had wrestled with basic questions about what had been unleashed by their process and about how this event might possibly move it forward. What were the expectations of those participating? Could they reasonably be met? Could the issues themselves be addressed in a satisfactory way? Would the organizers be able to respond to objections raised along the way? What options were available to the bishops, who had said all along that they would respond? In the end the conference was directed toward three objectives: (1) Develop an orderly way to treat a large amount of material on substantive issues. (2) Create a process that would enable all participants wishing to do so to voice their opinions on issues about which they had strong convictions. (3) Plan time for prayer, worship, relaxation.[24]

There were 1,340 voting delegates and approximately 1,500 observers in attendance at the assembly. The bishop of each diocese was asked to appoint nine delegates and one additional delegate for every 100,000 Catholics over one million in their diocese: one-third of the delegates from each diocese were to be from diocesan leadership, a third from parishes, and a third from people who had suffered injustice in the diocese. Delegates from dioceses numbered 1,100; 91 Catholic organizations sent one delegate, and approximately 159 were from the USCC Advisory Council and the NCCB/USCC committees.

Cardinal Dearden began the convention on Thursday morning with the only public address. He portrayed the convention as a continuation of the renewal of the church initiated at Vatican II. "People today, rich and poor, are often studied by scholars and pollsters. . . . Only rarely are they asked directly to speak up and be heard; so rarely, in fact, that many greet the invitation with understandable skepticism. Yet this is what we have tried to do, in our perhaps inefficient way. We are left with an enormous sense of responsibility and an equally strong feeling that there is great power in the spirit and faith of the people who appear before us." People have expressed their desire "to work closely with their priests and bishops, and they want their leaders to trust them and be accountable to them for the use of Church resources." "Many Catholics have become skeptical of the ability of Church leaders to take them seriously. Again and again the listeners heard people say that while they would speak up, they were doubtful anyone would really listen and would really respond." In one of the most moving passages, Dearden spoke about the bishops' sense of excitement and challenge living in the aftermath of Vatican II, as well as the sense of frustration and anger at the recognition of their own mistakes and weaknesses.

> Most of all we have all wished there were some way we could relate more directly and intimately with our people, share their burdens and have them share ours, know their anguish and let them know our own. If nothing else has happened to those of us who took part in this process, we at least learned this: that when we take the risk of listening and being open to our people, they demonstrate almost without exception a sensitivity to our feelings and a willingness to share our problems with us, if we will only let them.[25]

After Dearden's speech, the delegates gathered for the rest of the morning into the eight section groups of about 165 delegates each to clarify their tasks and to address questions to the writing committees who had prepared the reports on this topic. These section groups then broke into three or four smaller groups with about thirty to forty delegates in each to clarify troublesome and contentious issues. Then, over two hundred small groups were formed, each charged with working on a few lines of the recommendations, and discussing, debating, and revising the resolutions. In these small groups people communicated their convictions about the topics, and honest, sometimes heated, discussion took place. Open discussion was fostered in these groups, and the facilitators strove to be sensitive and flexible and to encourage everyone to participate in the deliberative process. Revised texts were subsequently typed and copied for the next day's work, which began early the following morning in the eight large section groups.

The level of discussion was more formal in these larger section meetings. With less time for wider participation, people had to focus on specific revisions in the proposed text. The process of debate and revision continued through Friday morning until 1:00 P.M. The plenary session began at 3:30 when delegates reconvened with second revised drafts (beginning with family life and neighborhood and the others following) and worked straight through until 6:00 P.M. passing three resolutions on family life, family ministry, and divorce. In plenary sessions, only formal motions or votes were allowed, so that discussion would not get out of hand. Each recommendation was read and the question was posed: "Shall this amendment be considered?" A voice vote was taken. If the outcome was in doubt, people would raise their hands to vote. Most amendments were voted down, and some evoked lively debate. "Almost all the many amendments offered by the outnumbered conservatives were defeated."[26]

The tempo of the plenary sessions was especially fast; each of the eight sections received an hour and fifteen minutes for voting. Some people, including a bishop on at least one occasion, were cut off in the process of making a point in order to move the agenda along. This contributed to the sense of frustration on the part of some people and might have led to suspicions that some opinions were not being taken seriously or were being too easily dismissed. After the noisy deliberations of Friday afternoon, there was a rich, contemplative liturgical celebration in the evening. Saturday's meeting began at 8:15 and the delegates worked throughout the day without a break. In the end, each amendment was voted up or down and then the final document on the section was voted on. At 5:00 P.M. Dearden brought the assembly to a close.

The results of the three days of deliberation were the approval of twenty-nine general recommendations, with 218 parts (a total of 182 recommendations were subsequently identified by the bishops). Seventeen amendments from the personhood document were tabled because of lack of time; and many amendments were rejected.[27] Statements in all eight topic areas were improved. Many statements offered a strong affirmation of the basic beliefs and institutional practices of Catholics concerning the religious calling of all people and their need for vibrant church communities. Much attention was given to the importance of building church communities of character and forming individuals through the sacraments and religious education in "the gospel," in the teachings of the church, in spirituality, and in the Christian moral life. Moreover, the documents expressed affectionate support for bishops and priests, for official ordained ministers and ministries in the church, even as they encouraged the diversity of ecclesial charisms and lay ministries. The documents affirmed basic Catholic teachings about the dignity and sacredness of life and supported pro-life activities as well as pastoral ministries to the aging, the handicapped, and the poor and marginalized. Marriage and family life received considerable attention, with the basic goods of marriage, as passed on in Catholic tradition, affirmed. Important positions on worker justice and on racial and ethnic equality were addressed, as were a larger set of issues about the power of the economy on the lives of Americans and those who were influenced by the U.S. economy.

At the same time, the central disputed issues of the postconciliar period appeared in high relief: birth control, women's issues, homosexuality, male and celibate priesthood, divorce and remarriage, laicization of priests, and priests' ability to remain in active ministry.[28] Concern for the promotion of justice nationally and internationally in the family, neighborhoods, and workplaces framed the treatment of all these issues.[29]

The hope for this event to serve as a pedagogical process (a "consciousness-raising event" as it was called at the time) was fulfilled on certain issues and in unplanned directions. Through the dialogical exchanges, bishops learned about how widespread certain opinions were in the American church. Many learned about the issues of Hispanic, black, and Native American Catholics. More progressive Catholics heard the concerns of conservatives and vice versa. But at a very fundamental level, this event abundantly testified to the significance of the Catholic community, its practices, and its institutions in the lives of those participating.

The advocacy of ongoing dialogue in the church as a structured communal practice became a major recommendation at the convention. In other words, the process became a part of the product. Numerous recommendations promoted participatory forms of governance and teaching in the church through dialogical discernment and decision making. The very first recommendation in the section on justice in the church was that the formation of parish and diocesan pastoral councils would enable laity and religious to work with bishops and priests in shared responsibility concerning financial policies and pastoral practices. The second recommendation was about due process in the church. And the third concerned "the continued development of shared responsibility in the church" in two areas: policy making (in response to the question, What should the church be doing?) and administration (answering How do we do it?). Participatory decision making was advocated in all of the recommendations offered. In the section devoted to the nation is found the following recommendation:

> That the process of consultation (listening, responding, implementing) become a regular element of U.S. Catholic life, especially initiating, encouraging, enabling pastoral programs relating the ministry of the church to the broader community, the nation and the world. That this process of consultation be continued as a normal process structured into diocesan and parish life. [And] that there be established local structures to enable people to participate in the decision-making processes so that trust can grow between: the bishop and the people, the pastor and the people, and the powerful and the powerless.

It is also noteworthy that there was a special summons to ongoing dialogue among all members of the church about sexual identity and practices, and among people of diverse races and ethnic identities.

THE CRITICAL RESPONSES OF ANDREW GREELEY AND JOSEPH BERNARDIN

Call To Action was met with a firestorm of criticism. As the various kinds of criticism leveled at this entire process are recalled, one needs to be especially alert to what can be learned about the promise and perils of dialogue in light of this experience.

From early on, Andrew Greeley, the well-known, outspoken priest sociologist who headed the National Opinion Research Center at the University of Chicago, expressed sharp disagreements with all facets of the bicentennial program: the process, the methods, the people involved, and the results.[30] He launched his critical evaluation of the guidebook and the process in the *National Catholic Reporter*.[31] Contrasting the "old-style" social action of labor schools and labor priests John A. Ryan, George Higgins, Jack Egan, and Geno Baroni, with the "new" social action of the anti–Vietnam War movement, liberation theology, social activist analysis, and the protests of the Berrigan brothers, Greeley identified the majority of the guidebook essays with the latter and faulted them for not appreciating the achievements of America.[32] He was especially critical of the involvement of Peter Henriot, a Jesuit from the Center for Concern, who combined attention to the problems of the third world with a critique of American political economy.[33] Greeley suggested that the entire program showed that the USCC bureaucracy had been taken over by radicals, "peace and justice activists who were influenced by liberation theologies."[34] The guidebook was to be the basis for discussion involving all sides, but Greeley argued that it would fail to generate this discussion: "the authors know the answers; they are calling the rest of us to admit our guilt and convert. That is hardly a basis for dialogue. Nor does it sound like a 'listening' book. It preaches, it does not listen." Greeley elaborated:

> You can't dialogue with those who are convinced that their mission is to convert you to "concern" and to draw from you a self-abasing admission of guilt in the face of your moral superiors. You can't dialogue with those who substitute moral fervor for professional competence. You can't dialogue with those who commit the idolatry of identifying the gospel with very contingent social policies or positions. You cannot dialogue with those who worry about the mote in another's eyes and ignore the beam in their own. You cannot dialogue with those who hate their own country and do not even understand its heritage. You can't dialogue with those whose idea of listening is to arrange a rigged conference in which they are both witness and jury. You cannot dialogue with those who think conversion is a substitute for the difficulty of coalition building. You cannot dialogue with those who are so unaware of their own people that they produce an educational tool that will certainly be counterproductive. You can only dialogue with those who want to. And the "new" social action does not want to. It wants you to get off the golf course and abandon your sinful ways.[35]

After the justice conference was over, Greeley leveled a bitter assault on the final convention: A "very small minority" of Catholics gathered in Detroit, "a ragtag assembly of kooks, crazies, flakes, militants, lesbians, homosexuals, ex-priests, incompetents, castrating witches, would-be messiahs, sickies, and other assorted malcontents." He argued that the bishops need "to reassert their control over what goes on in the church."[36] Greeley had complaints and concerns that merit consideration, but his vitriol had destructive repercussions.

Two questions are raised by Greeley's venomous polemic. What impact, if any, did his critique have on the dialogical process as it proceeded? Did it influence the reception of the Call To Action, how it was framed, interpreted, and evaluated by various sectors of the church, and how it was portrayed in the Catholic and secular press? It stands to reason that Greeley's assault discouraged some people from getting involved who might otherwise have been inclined to respond generously to their bishops' invitation. Moreover, Greeley's high-profile attack put the bishops in a defensive posture concerning the exercise of their own authority, since this was their own project. His critique contributed to bishops' sense of obligation to distance themselves from Call To Action and exercise damage control. Greeley's rant distorted the objectives, the intentions, and the complexity of this multifaceted dialogical process. People with cooler heads and discriminating judgment would be needed to make sure the wheat was not thrown out with the chaff.

It was clear from the initial response to Greeley's diatribe that his assessment was viewed by some as extremist. Msgr. George Higgins, the well-respected spokesman and activist for labor rights, and a good friend of Greeley, who was himself actively involved in the planning and chaired the hearings, took Greeley to task in his column "The Yardstick" for the week of April 14, 1975. He acknowledged that Greeley's criticism was valid "up to a point—but only up to a point," but judged that he ended up indulging in "polemical overkill."

> The tone of his criticism has become increasingly shrill and abusive and, worse than that, extremely intolerant of other legitimate points of view. Moreover he is violating his own commendably high professional standards as social scientist. [H]e makes apodictical statements about a process which he has never personally examined and, so far as I can tell, knows about only on the basis of second- or third-hand information. . . . He has written them [the participants] off permanently and definitely as utterly hopeless charlatans—and that's the end of the matter so far as he is concerned. I think that's a serious and highly unprofessional mistake on Greeley's part.[37]

David O'Brien countered Greeley's criticism in the *National Catholic Reporter* by claiming that the church needed representatives of the "old" and the "new" forms of social activism to enter into a constructive and honest dialogue with each other to sort out the various concerns that unite them, their different modes of analysis, and the divergent modes of active response. This dialogue among activists is needed for the good of the church's pastoral mission. O'Brien closed by saying that Greeley's own contribution was important and his participation needed. The invitation fell on deaf ears. If Greeley had accepted O'Brien's invitation, he might have come to share Higgins's conclusion, which he expressed in his column after the session held in San Antonio, Texas: "While I disagree with some of [the members of the subcommittee] in certain respects and have told them so directly, I find them willing to engage in courteous dialogue about our differences of opinion and willing also to revise their opinions in the process of the dialogue."[38]

The most influential episcopal interpreter of the Call To Action became Archbishop Joseph Bernardin, who was at the time the president of the NCCB. Before his election to that post in 1974, he had been the chair of the subcommittee of the bishops' bicentennial project devoted to the justice conference (this passed over to Archbishop Peter Gerety of Newark when Bernardin was elected). On the eve of the Call To Action convention, Bernardin chose not to be a voting delegate so as to convey his detachment and impartiality. Immediately after the convention, he expressed publicly serious reservations about what had transpired. He identified two basic deficiencies. The first was that "too much was attempted." One topic would have been enough; eight "overwhelmed the conference. The result was haste and a determination to formulate recommendations on complex matters without adequate reflection, discussion and consideration of points of view." The second concern was that "special interest groups advocating particular causes . . . dominated the conference as a whole. The result was a process and a number of recommendations which were not representative of the church in this country and which paid too little attention to other legitimate interests and concerns." His second concern can be divided into two: the influence of special interest groups, and the fact that delegates did not represent the breadth of the American church.[39] Bernardin in his capacity as president of the NCCB said that the bishops would need to "take a very careful approach" in evaluating the recommendations. He gave an initial list of criteria for evaluating these recommendations, which began with "the teachings of the church; its laws and disciplines," and ended with "the opinions of others with expertise in the many different fields involved and sensitivity to other legitimate points of view." Officials in Rome were very pleased with Bernardin's response.[40]

In the year that followed the Call To Action convention Bernardin drew the conclusion that "polarization" in the Catholic Church was a crucial problem operative in and exacerbated by the Call To Action. It is interesting that the word polarization became the key word Bernardin used to describe the main problem motivating his establishment of the Catholic Common Ground Initiative in 1996, which will be analyzed in a subsequent chapter. But the question should be raised: Did Bernardin discover polarization at this event, or did he himself create it, or did he contribute in a significant way to a polarized reception of the work of the Call To Action convention by overemphasizing the influence of special interest groups on the fruits of its labor?[41] He stated in his opening address to the NCCB on May 3, 1977: "the Call To Action conference . . . has tended to increase polarization and factionalism in certain quarters of the church. Whether we like it or not, this places us under some unusual pressures."[42] The criticisms of Greeley and Bernardin had the net effect of portraying the participants in the Call To Action as radical and marginal to the everyday life of the vast majority of American Catholics. One might reasonably ask to what extent these responses contributed to the unnecessary radicalization of those who had invested in the process initiated by their own bishops in the years that followed.

THE FORMAL RESPONSE OF THE U.S. BISHOPS

At their May meeting in 1977 the bishops decided to respond to the resolutions at the Call To Action by having a committee do two things: prepare for approval of the bishops "a pastoral statement on some of the more controversial resolutions, and design a chart assigning each resolution to the appropriate committees of the bishops' conference for study, evaluation, and action."[43] The pastoral statement read in part:

> The process of consultation was imperfect and there are some conclusions which are problematical and in some cases untenable.... We are grateful to all who shared their insights with us. We reaffirm our commitment to the principle of shared responsibility in the contemporary church, and we assert our intention to improve consultation with our people in the future.[44]

The report produced by the bishops' committee proposed that the entire bicentennial program should be understood in terms of the conciliar vision of the church set forth in *Lumen Gentium* as the people of God and the hierarchy. Within that context they spoke of their own understanding of their role as bishops.

> As pastors who are teachers we are called both to listen and learn from our people and also to respond to what we hear by announcing the Good News in all its implications, unfolding its riches and applying it to contemporary circumstances. In any process of dialogue in the church we listen, as all Christians do, for the voice of the Spirit in the church and the world; we also exercise the charism of judgments and discernment in the church in a special way. For bishops are "authentic teachers, that is, teachers endowed with the authority of Christ, who preach the faith to the people assigned to them, the faith which is destined to inform their thinking and direct their conduct." ... We have to be both pastors who can listen and teachers who can speak.... The particular process of consultation ... cannot be the sole factor in determining the pastoral agenda of the church. It is our task to assess those proposals in the context of God's plan as revealed in and through Christ.[45]

The intentionality of the bishops in inviting the dialogue is underscored: "the bicentennial program was initiated by us to clarify and specify the implications for the church in the United States of a social ministry at the service of the justice of God." And in certain ways, to the extent that the conversation stayed on the topic the bishops had specified, they affirmed its outcome. The bishops even accepted and embraced the recommendation of Call To Action that advocated "the further development of both structures and practices of consultation and shared responsibility at every level of the church."[46] They stressed the importance of parish councils and diocesan pastoral councils, and they supported in principle a wide variety of specific recommendations about parishes, religious education, and neighborhoods. But, as previously noted, the bishops regarded a number of conclusions as "problematical and in some cases untenable." The dialogue had taken on a life of its own, as people spoke about justice in the church when the bishops had not asked to talk about that and did not want to talk about that, and the Call To Action group had reached consensus judgments about some controversial issues. The bishops ruled these topics to be illegitimate subjects for further conversation: the ordination of women and married men and women, birth control, homosexuality, and separated and divorced Catholics. Their justification: "As bishops we cannot compromise Catholic teaching."[47]

Archbishop John Roach of St. Paul-Minneapolis was selected to head an ad hoc committee established by the U.S. bishops to formulate a response to the two-year Call To Action program and to oversee its implementation. In Roach's September 1977 progress report he reiterated the intentions of the bishops: "to clarify and specify the implications for the church in the United States of a social ministry at the service of the justice of God," which provides a framework and basis for evaluating the results of the Call To Action. The bishops' intentions for the topic of the conversation provided a basis for dismissing certain topics: "for, as you know, some of the recommendations of the Detroit assembly have only the most tenuous connection to the social order."[48] Again, the conclusion was drawn: the conversation and conclusions had gone off subject; the dialogue had digressed from what the bishops wanted to discuss. The bishops would need to reassert their rightful authority.

> Our assignment does not entail the implementation of the resolutions of the Call To Action conference itself, but rather the development of a broad-based plan of action taking into account what we have heard from the bicentennial consultation and the Call To Action conference. The distinction, while obvious to this body [of bishops], is not altogether that clear to the public. . . . [T]he perception and expectation in some quarters at least is that we are engaged in a process of moving the NCCB and USCC into most of the directions and areas addressed in the Detroit resolutions.

The people who took this occasion to raise vital questions were, in essence, told that they did not understand the church's teaching and their contributions to the dialogue were not discussed further. The judgments and discernment exercised by the bishops were set over the judgments and discernment of the people who had spoken out on disputed issues, and no attempt was made either to address this conflict or to move the discussion forward.

This conflict brings into clear relief the difficulty identified in the treatment of pastoral councils and diocesan synods in the previous chapters: the nature of a dialogical process within a hierarchical church as consultative, not deliberative. All are invited and called to share responsibility, to participate, to contribute, but only the ordained, and in this case, bishops, have the authority to make final judgments and decisions about the matters they decide are important, or relevant, or on topic. There is no attempt to identify the means whereby those bishops making judgments and decisions can and must be held accountable for being receptive and genuinely responsive to the consensus reached by lay, religious, or clergy participants in a process of discernment, and accountable for the positions they themselves maintain. As Donald Cozzens states the issue, "Especially in hierarchical institutions like the church, accountability is, for the most part, upward: the priest is accountable to his bishop, his bishop is accountable to the pope, and the pope is accountable to God. The idea of accountability to one's hierarchical inferiors is simply dismissed out of hand."[49]

On May 4, 1978, the U.S. bishops approved a five-year plan for the social mission of the church as the official response to the two-year consultation on social justice that culminated in the Call To Action convention.

> This consultation, in which the bishops listened to the voices of many groups and individuals, was intended to help us formulate a plan to establish goals and programs in the area of social justice over the next five years. As bishops we were called both to listen and to exercise judgment in teaching an extremely vital part of the Gospel of Jesus pertaining to the mission on behalf of social justice. Through this process of structured public dialogue, we learned much about the needs of our own people and about the problems of justice and peace which they face in their own lives and communities.[50]

The topics treated in this document are (1) education for justice; (2) family life; (3) the church: people, parishes, and communities; (4) economic justice; (5) human rights; and (6) world hunger. This text demonstrates that many issues raised by the Call To Action recommendations had been received and were being acted upon.[51] However, the document also gives abundant witness by its silence that many issues raised throughout the bicentennial program—about justice in the church, about advancing dialogue and shared responsibility on financial affairs and pastoral ministry, about dealing with contested issues concerning sexual ethics, divorce and remarriage, and the role of women and married men in ordained and nonordained ministry—were not being addressed. On these matters, dialogue was being discontinued. These subjects had become taboo.

The May 1978 statement by the U.S. bishops was the formal conclusion of the bicentennial program. In the aftermath of the Detroit Call To Action, a Chicago Call To Action organization was established in 1978. None of the original leadership from the bicentennial program was involved. The founder of this organization, the lay Catholic Chicagoan Dan Daley, had no connection with the NCCB program and was not at the initial Call To Action conference. One should recall that John Cardinal Cody, who became the archbishop of Chicago in 1968, had a record of contentious relations with social justice activists in the archdiocese. During his first year in the archdiocese, Cody closed the Office of Urban Affairs, which had been established by Msgr. Jack Egan. Cody refused to participate in the NCCB's bicentennial program; his was a home-grown version of polarization that had nothing directly to do with either Greeley's or Bernardin's reaction to the original Call To Action process.[52] A variety of groups of nuns, priests, Catholic school teachers, and laity from the Chicago archdiocese were motivated to join forces to address this situation. They identified their group as the Chicago Call To Action and decided to use the CTA logo without permission from the NCCB. To initiate this new group, they held a conference in October 1978 that was attended by four hundred people. Local issues and a confrontation about the autocratic decision-making style and policies in the Chicago archdiocese dominated the initial assembly.

Following its inaugural convention in 1978 the Chicago Call To Action organization sponsored yearly meetings.[53] It quickly drew a larger group of people from across the country, including many involved in the original U.S. bishops' program. The Chicago Call To Action, launched by an anti-Cody agenda, further heightened polarities and tensions with the hierarchy beyond those arising from the response of the U.S. bishops to the original Call To Action convention. This further complicated efforts to alleviate the conflicts and divisions.

This new organization initiated and produced *Churchwatch* and *CTA News*, a journal and a newsletter on church reform and justice issues. Members of the Chicago Call To Action were well aware of the fact that the U.S. bishops' pastoral letters on war and peace ("The Challenge of Peace: God's Promise and Our Response," 1983) and on the economy ("Economic Justice for All," 1986) were taking up recommendations made at the original Detroit Call To Action conference (and, in fact, drew inspiration from its dialogical mode of teaching from the bicentennial program as will be explored in the next chapter). In response, Chicago Call To Action developed multimedia resources and a performing arts ministry, Peaceworks and Between the Times, on the topics of the U.S. bishops' pastoral letters. These resources and pastoral ministries were used on over five hundred occasions, often in parish settings, to educate local communities about the pastoral letters, and in the late 1980s Call To Action received a Vatican World Communications Day Award in recognition of its contributions in this area.[54]

In 1990 Chicago Call To Action issued a public statement, "Call to Reform," which was signed by twenty-thousand persons. This statement called upon church officials to incorporate women at all levels of ministry and decision making; to revoke mandatory priestly celibacy; to open priesthood to women and married men, including resigned priests; to engage in extensive consultation with Catholic people to develop the church's teaching on human sexuality; to involve laity, religious, and clergy in selection of local bishops; and for academic freedom, due process, and financial openness and accountability. After this document Chicago Call To Action was further marginalized by the U.S. bishops, and members in many dioceses were told that they could no longer exercise their education and performing arts ministries.

DANGLING CONVERSATIONS

Many who were involved in the original Call To Action convention lamented that it did not result in a pastoral plan of action for the U.S. church. No priorities were set. No plan of implementation was endorsed. And many bishops distanced themselves from the process and its proposals immediately after the event. Reactions, receptions, and results must be sorted out. Dearden, in his report to the NCCB shortly after the conference, stressed that the bishops had sought "to initiate a *process* of dialogue and consultation. From the beginning it has been clear that the program was to produce *advisory* recommendations which would form the basis of a pastoral plan on justice. This process of consultation and dialogue has given new hope to many who had grown skeptical of sharing responsibility in their church. It has allowed many persons and groups long excluded from having an effective voice to be heard at last. . . . As a process of consultation and dialogue, the program has been successful." The deficiencies in the process of decision making and deliberation were real—overly ambitious, time frame too short, insufficient research and study about complex issues. "Yet, even these flaws," Dearden insisted, "can be exaggerated." "The experimental nature" of this endeavor must be kept in mind when evaluating it.[55]

Many of those who participated in the Call To Action said they were inspired and renewed in their commitment to their faith and the Catholic Church by what had transpired, even if it had been difficult and frustrating. All who participated were challenged to listen to contrasting points of view, reform-minded and traditionalist, and to some voices in the church never, or at least rarely, heard before: homosexuals, disgruntled women, blacks, Hispanics, Native Americans. These conversations served as a pedagogical process, a raising of consciousness, an expanding of individual and collective horizons to envision a larger understanding of the reality of the church. This entailed a measure of conflict and confrontation that has always been unavoidable in church matters but has rarely been discussed and encouraged as a crucial ingredient in the process of church deliberation or in the theology of the church. The criticisms leveled against the meeting, and the focus in the religious and secular press on the approved recommendations that were at odds with official teachings, put the bishops on the spot. They were in some sense responsible for the messy process and the controversial results of this conversation that they themselves had initiated. They were not able to view the elements of honest and open discussion and conflict on controversial issues as a net gain. Bernardin's detached and critical initial response set the tone and framed the larger discussion, interpretation, and reception of the Call To Action in the years ahead. By ignoring, dismissing, or criticizing the more controversial issues in the final recommendations, the U.S. bishops distanced themselves from, disrespected, and really stifled some of the most important living dialogue that went on throughout the entire bicentennial process. By so doing they ended up fostering the "radicalization" of the Call To Action process, which contributed to the polarization that crescendoed in the aftermath of this event. Those many participants who wanted honest discussion about the need for genuine church reform were portrayed as radical opponents of the bishops and as in some way radically unfaithful to the church. But in fact, the vast majority of those involved in Call To Action were and remained faithful Catholics responding generously and in good faith to the U.S. bishops' invitation. The conversation that had been initiated by the bishops was cut short by them as well. In the end, the response of the U.S. bishops was not entirely negative or dismissive, but ambiguous and ambivalent. Significantly, they did not in the final analysis repudiate the dialogical experiment, but indicated that within certain limits these experiments should continue. One should not lose sight of these important dangling conversations in the midst of the stormy aftermath of the Call To Action, even though there are many who remain convinced that the limitations placed on these dialogues will eventually need to be lifted in order for the church fully to realize its identity and mission.

4

A New Way of Teaching with Authority

The Pastoral Letters of the U.S. Episcopal Conference

Collegiality is the term used at Vatican II to describe the proper relationship of bishops as successors of the college of the apostles. So understood, collegiality concerns the human characteristics and institutional structures that promote constructive episcopal interaction. By promoting collegiality bishops assist one another in furthering the apostolic mission of local churches and, more broadly, the common good and communion of local churches and likewise of the universal church. In the process bishops develop a deeper appreciation of the catholicity of the church, the contributions of diverse manifestations of the one church of Christ in the world.[1]

Various forms of councils—provincial, plenary, ecumenical—provide the most widely recognized collegial structures in the history of the church.[2] Two additional structures received special attention at Vatican II: synods of bishops and episcopal conferences. The council retrieved the tradition of synods of bishops, in which representative bishops from around the world or from specific continents are convened to deliberate about matters of pastoral urgency. That topic will be examined in chapter 7 below. National and regional episcopal conferences, which came into existence during the late nineteenth and early twentieth centuries with more than forty established prior to the beginning of Vatican II, were strongly recommended by the council.[3] Ever since, the council conferences have developed around the world and have become effective institutions, generating pastoral teaching and public declarations on social and political issues and pastoral concerns, and rendering church policy decisions.

This chapter offers an analysis of a new, more explicitly dialogical approach to generating church teaching, pioneered by the U.S. Episcopal Conference during the 1980s and 1990s in the preparation of three pastoral letters: "The Challenge of Peace" issued in 1983, "Economic Justice for All" in 1986, and the document originally entitled "Partners in the Mystery of Redemption: A Pastoral Response to Women's Concerns for Church and Society," which was finally abandoned, voted down by the bishops in 1992. This chapter examines the process employed in generating these letters, not their content. To an unprecedented extent, these efforts promoted a public forum that combined the collegial activity of bishops, the bishops' collaboration with theologians, and broad-based, open consultation with representatives of the people of God in a genuinely deliberative process of discernment about the church's position on particular pastoral issues.

The U.S. bishops demonstrated through this dialogic process that the effectiveness and credibility of the exercise of episcopal teaching authority is correlative to their development of teaching within the triadic relations of the people of God, theologians, and bishops.[4] However, in the aftermath of the debacle of the pastoral on women, the use of a wider dialogical method of generating teaching instead of being expanded by the bishops has been curtailed and, in a strict sense, stopped entirely. This development receives attention at the end of this chapter.

The preparation process designed for these three documents by the bishops was distinctive; however, it was not without precedent. The story of these recent letters constitutes a significant episode in the remarkable history of pastoral letters issued by the U.S. Catholic bishops.[5] The practice of U.S. bishops issuing pastoral letters to communicate to priests and laity can be traced back to the first U.S. bishop, John Carroll, after the first American diocesan synod was held in Baltimore, Maryland, in 1791. This practice became standard as letters were issued following the seven provincial councils of Baltimore (1829–1849), the three plenary councils (1852, 1866, 1884), and again in 1919 in conjunction with the release of the Bishops' Program of Social Reconstruction.[6] Both the provincial councils of Baltimore, which in effect served as proto-national assemblies of bishops, and the subsequent plenary councils, were, according to canon law, aimed at bishops reaching legislative judgments and decisions about pastoral matters. Abiding by developed practices and canon law, bishops were joined in these efforts by canon lawyers and theologians as consultative participants, and some bishops, like John England (1786–1842), promoted the involvement of priests and lay persons in these councils.[7] Even though the earlier assemblies were often more narrowly focused on legislative deliberations, when one considers the U.S. bishops' collegiality with one another, their collaboration with theologians, and their wide consultation with the people of God on these three recent letters, this early history of provincial and plenary councils must be recognized as the prototype.

The formation of the U.S. bishops' conference also provides important information about the practices of generating pastoral letters. The U.S. bishops established in 1919 a new institutional structure to promote regular collegial discussion of pressing national issues concerning social justice, education, and the promotion of peace. This new structure, the National Catholic Welfare Council, initiated annual meetings of the U.S. bishops, the formation of a national administrative office, and subsequently the formation of committees devoted to specific pastoral and social issues. This institution was renamed the National Catholic Welfare Conference in 1922. The word conference came into usage to underscore the fact that the group was consultative in character, and not in any way advancing a canonical approach that might envision councils as deliberative and legislative. Participation of bishops was voluntary, and the decisions of those bishops in attendance had "no formal canonical status."[8] Therefore, individual bishops could dissent from the positions taken by the national assembly.

The National Catholic Welfare Conference was reorganized by the U.S. bishops after Vatican II. In 1966 the National Conference of Catholic Bishops (NCCB) became the organizational structure bringing the U.S. bishops together in their capacity as chief pastors and official teachers to deliberate about the life of the church in the nation. The constitution of this group as a canonical entity developed in response to the Second Vatican Council's endorsement of the formation of national episcopal conferences that would promote greater collegiality among bishops at the national level.[9] As mentioned in chapter 3, the NCCB is composed of a variety of committees, including those on doctrine, liturgy, education, and missions, as well as social development and world peace. These committees comprise bishops, a staff, and experts, sometimes lay persons, who serve as active members of these committees or are readily available to them. The United States Catholic Conference (USCC) was established during the same period as a nonprofit social service organization dedicated to addressing issues in the public realm, including social concerns and education.[10] The USCC also had committees and staffs that differed from those of the NCCB. The U.S. bishops composed the membership of both organizations, the NCCB and the USCC, and they had the same officers.[11] The NCCB and the USCC generated various kinds of statements: national liturgical norms, pastoral letters on teachings of the universal church as they applied to the local situation, and formal statements on a variety of political and social issues. In July 2001, the USCC and the NCCB were joined together to form the United States Conference of Catholic Bishops (USCCB).

DEVELOPING A MORE DIALOGICAL METHOD OF TEACHING

Since its inception in the late 1960s there has been a standard procedure used to generate joint pastoral teachings by the committees of the NCCB. There are two versions of this standard process.[12] The most commonly used form follows this pattern: pastoral teaching statements are written by the staff of a given committee, often with informal input from individuals or a small circle of theological, moral, biblical, or public policy experts as needed. Once a draft has been prepared it is sent to the bishops on that committee and sometimes to specific theologians or policy experts for reactions, written or oral. These responses become the basis for amendments to the drafted policy statements, which when completed are brought before the NCCB for discussion, possible revision, and final approval by a two-thirds majority vote of the full body of bishops. In a second version of the standard procedure an ad hoc committee is formed to generate the working document. The "Pastoral Letter on Marxist Communism" (1980) was developed by such an ad hoc committee and approved by a wide margin.

After the successful completion of the statement on Marxism, two new ad hoc committees were formed in 1980 and given the charge to develop pastoral teachings: one on war and peace in the age of nuclear warfare and another on capitalism. In 1982 the bishops also decided to write a pastoral on the role of women, which was to build upon the work of a previous ad hoc committee established by the bishops in 1972 on the role of women in society and the church. In each of these committees there was a group of bishops (war and peace, 5; economics, 5; women, 6); consultants (war and peace, 3; economics, 6; women, 6), and staff members (war and peace,

2; economics, 5; women, 2). All of this reflected the standard procedure for ad hoc committees commissioned to prepare pastoral statements.

During the preparation of the pastoral on war and peace, however, a number of significant innovations in the process of generating church teaching were introduced. This pastoral was slated by the executive committee of the NCCB to be addressed by the entire assembly of bishops before the economic pastoral. The standard procedure for developing pastoral letters as it had been previously employed by ad hoc committees was initially operative. But this soon changed when people from various sectors—from diverse spheres of the Catholic community, people from other Christian churches and faiths, and spokespersons from governmental, political, and public policy groups—became quite interested in the document and wanted to voice their views on the matters under consideration. In the case of the war and peace pastoral, what originally was expected to require four to six meetings before the first draft could be prepared, took fourteen meetings (between July 1981 and June 1982). "The witnesses were selected to provide the committee with a spectrum of views and diverse forms of professional and pastoral experience."[13] Thus, the first innovation from the bishops' standard procedure was that a much wider consultation took place. In each case, the initial consultations were followed by the drafting of a written document, usually with preliminary drafts circulated among the ad hoc committee members first before an official draft was released for a larger audience.

It is important to note that the ad hoc committee on women conducted far more extensive consultations than either of the other two committees. The bishops made an effort from the beginning to maximize the voices of women in the process. In the previous economic pastoral, direct attention in the text to the voices of the poor had been absent, as was noted by commentators.[14] The bishops did not want to repeat that pattern here by speaking about women and not letting them speak for themselves. As Bishop Joseph Imesch, the chair of the committee on the women's pastoral when the first draft was made public, stated: "This letter is written in a different style than the other pastoral letters. It is written in response to the consultations held in 100 dioceses, 60 college campuses and 45 military bases. The text contains a number of quotations from women who participated in these consultations." This "style," which offered a further development of the dialogical approach being pioneered by the bishops, was subsequently criticized by some, including members of the Roman curia, and was significantly curtailed in subsequent drafts.[15]

The second innovation emerged initially as a breach of standard operations: once the first formal draft on war and peace was approved by the committee it was marked "confidential" for distribution only to the bishops and to selected theological and policy experts, but in this case it was "leaked" to the secular and religious press.[16] Subsequently, each of the approved first drafts was made public by being published in *Origins: NC Documentary Service*. These documents were thus widely available, discussed, and debated in the public realm, not only among Catholics, but at a variety of levels of society. The provisional drafts became a crucial ingredient in a public dialogue. The first wave of consultations contributed to the generation of an official draft text, which was widely read, and people offered a variety of responses. A back-and-forth dynamic of speaking and listening and responding had been introduced into the teaching procedure.

In a third innovation, written and oral reactions to the first draft were welcomed and encouraged, and responses were taken into consideration during the preparation of the next draft. This was an unprecedented breakthrough and marks a genuinely dialogical teaching procedure: the initial receptions and responses to a draft document were heard and reflected upon by the bishops and contributed to their process of revising the document. The responses to each of the initial drafts exceeded expectations.[17] This meant that greater reflection on the reactions was needed and the revising took longer. The war and peace ad hoc committee had to postpone the next discussion at the NCCB by six months. Once reactions from the bishops and the other participants were heard and read by the committee, a second revised draft was written and received the committee's approval to be made public. Making public the second draft was the fourth innovation. This led to the repetition of the previous procedure, as written and oral responses were considered in the preparation of the third draft. The third draft was then discussed by the bishops at one of their biannual meetings, where final revisions were formulated and the bishops approved the final document by a two-thirds majority vote.

Each of the pastoral letters has its own history, but a basic pattern of operation was the same for all three documents: open dialogue among the bishops, theologians, and consultants from the Catholic community and the wider society in the preparation of the documents, public disclosure and discussion of the drafted texts, and revisions of the documents in light of these discussions. In the cases of the war and peace and economic pastorals, the preparation of the first draft, including time for consultations, took two or more years. The time for written and oral reactions between the first and second draft was approximately one year. The time for reactions between the second and third draft was approximately six months. Each step of the document on women took longer: the preparation of the first draft (four years), the time between the first and second draft (two years), the time between the second and third draft (two years), and the time between the third and fourth drafts (six months).[18]

A NEW DIALOGICAL METHOD OR AN ELABORATION OF A U.S. TRADITION?

Unprecedented. Inspired. Brilliant. These are the words that come to mind when thinking about the development of this open consultative process. There were, however, earlier precedents, and the events that led to this procedure suggest that it was the work of pragmatic reasoning in response to a dynamic set of circumstances rather than an idea generated with considerable forethought. Simply put, this new consultative process was the result of a self-conscious attempt to give all who so desired the opportunity to have their voices heard. At the time it did not seem groundbreaking, but rather a spontaneous and practical adjustment of the established process of deliberation.[19] More time was consequently needed to digest the many written responses sent, to allow concerned parties to address the committee, and to debate, prayerfully reflect, and discern.[20]

As previously noted, these three pastoral letters have their more remote antecedents in the nineteenth- and early twentieth-century history of provincial and plenary councils in the United States and the early history of the National Conference of Catholic Bishops. Shortly after the council, the U.S. bishops' conference began to promote consultation with the laity in the exercise of their own pastoral office in an effort to implement one of Vatican II's teachings.[21] Following this policy yielded two more recent and more directly influential prototypes for the kind of broad-based consultation and public discussion the U.S. bishops subsequently utilized for the three pastoral letters.

The most important and immediate precursor consisted in the regional "hearings" on social problems, spoken of as a national consultation, initiated by the committee for the bicentennial in 1973, examined in the previous chapter. The second and related antecedent is provided by the 1976 Call To Action conference itself. Some of the same key figures were involved in both the bicentennial program and the war and peace pastoral. The most important of these was Bryan Hehir, who had supported regional and national meetings in preparation of pastoral teaching by the U.S. bishops. Frank Butler had proposed the model of the legislative hearings for the bicentennial program. And Cardinal Bernardin was involved in these early deliberations of the bicentennial committee, before he was elected president of NCCB. Any concerns and misgivings Bernardin had about the dialogical procedure introduced in the bicentennial program and the Call To Action conference did not keep him from utilizing the hearings model as he chaired the committee preparing the war and peace pastoral letter. Bernardin did not repudiate the method of dialogue pioneered by the bicentennial committee. His complaint about too many topics being discussed at the Call To Action was here remedied by the focus on one particular topic at a time. In order to protect against special interest groups exerting undue pressure, as was alleged of the Call To Action proceedings, there was a concerted effort to let the various sides of the argument on these contested issues have an opportunity to speak and be heard by all involved, especially by the bishops, and for the bishops to exercise their individual and collective leadership roles of discernment and judgment in teaching. Certainly no voting on the part of the various audiences was involved, but for the purposes of this study the question is whether this offered a process of consultation that was simply advisory, or whether this experiment sought to fashion a consultative dialogical process that was also more genuinely deliberative. Could a hybrid model of decision making be emerging from this experiment that combines consultation and a broader process of communal deliberation?

Ultimately the dialogical procedure experimented with by the U.S. bishops must be traced back to an antecedent that is more pervasive and diffuse, yet also more significant. Within the national ethos of the United States one finds a great awareness of the benefits (and frustrations) of public processes of deliberation based on representative governance. Without denying the hypocrisy revealed in the ways U.S. citizens of European ancestry treated Native Americans, Africans, and eventually Latin Americans and Asians, those who arrived in America after the new nation was formed came to be a part of the American experiment in democracy, sharing neither ethnic bloodline nor language, but only a belief and hope in the dignity and freedom of human beings—the bedrock of democratic societies. These aspects of the U.S. character were formed over generations by the influence of democratic practices, themselves shaped by a singular historical combination of traditions—republican, liberal, and biblical.[22] Herein lies a national charism, the fruit of a shared history in the exercise of freedom and the practice of democratic institutions. It is these national cultural impulses for collective participation and shared responsibility that the pastorals came to embody.[23]

In 1986, with the "Challenge of Peace" approved, the second draft of the economic pastoral distributed, and the committee on the women's pastoral established and meeting regularly, the president of the NCCB that year, Bishop James Malone, articulated the achievement of the U.S. bishops this way:

> Together as a national hierarchy, we have found a new and collegial method of teaching. For centuries, hierarchies have been publishing pastoral letters, but for the first time the people of God have been involved in the formation in a more intense manner. For the first time, the church has taught not simply through a finished product, but through the process that led to the finished document. Teaching is not a unilateral activity. One is only teaching if someone is being taught. Teaching and learning are mutually conditional.[24]

The two pastoral letters on war and peace and on the economy were widely appreciated for both the process that was used and the product that resulted. Because of this dialogical procedure, the documents that were prepared were more widely read and received, and the arguments in the documents were strengthened. The open process had engaged an audience in a dialogical process. As a result the authority of these documents was increased by the way the teaching was generated. This is not to say that everyone agreed with every aspect of the documents; but there was a discriminating reception, and the areas of agreement and disagreement were more clearly focused. To be sure, some critics were suspicious of the entire process. Among these, Vatican officials were the most powerful and persistent.

THE RESISTANCE OF THE ROMAN CURIA TO A DIALOGICAL METHOD OF TEACHING

Vatican officials in the Roman curia repeatedly voiced concerns and grave reservations about the open and consultative processes used by the NCCB in drafting the pastoral letters under consideration.[25] These concerns were articulated both in formal meetings with delegates of the U.S. bishops and in a variety of statements made during the years the consultation process was being utilized. Questions were posed concerning what precise level of teaching authority should be attributed to these documents, the mixed public audience intended by these documents, and the particular issues of content addressed. These curial efforts to clarify the precise nature of the teaching developed in these pastoral letters provided the context in which nettlesome issues about a dialogical process of teaching were explored.

The pastoral letters on war and peace and on women precipitated official discussions with Roman officials and representative ordinaries from other nations: Western European in the case of the letter on war and peace and global responses in the case of the women's pastoral. On January 18–19, 1983, a meeting was held in Rome, called by curial offices, between the U.S. committee on the war and peace pastoral, and representatives of the curia and of episcopal conferences throughout Western Europe. According to a Vatican communiqué, "this common dialogue" among bishops was recognized as "an expression of episcopal collegiality and by reason of the interdependence of nations and churches in these grave matters, it is normal that a great communion of thought should be established between the episcopal conferences and with the Holy See in order to provide guidance along the path to peace for the people of God and all people of good will."[26] Jan Schotte, who was at that time a monsignor (later cardinal) and the secretary of the Pontifical Commission for Justice and Peace (later the secretary of the Council of the General Secretariat of the Synod of Bishops), wrote the official Roman synthesis (interpretation) of the meeting, which was dated March 21, 1983. A major question kept resurfacing in these exchanges about the teaching authority of the U.S. Episcopal Conference and how it functions. One way the issue was framed directly bears on the dialogical process of teaching. "Should a pastoral letter be limited to proposing only the teaching that is binding? Or should it also contribute elements to encourage a debate?" Certain "ecclesiological problems" were detected that pertain to the teaching mission of bishops and the nature or form their pronouncements should take.[27] One particular formulation states the issue sharply:

> When bishops propose the doctrine of the church, the faithful are bound in conscience to assent. . . . The concluding pages of the draft [on war and peace] seem ambiguous when they refer to pluralism of opinions on the matters touched upon in the pastoral and at the same time urge substantial consensus. Substantial consensus must be based on doctrine and does not flow from debate. It is wrong to propose the teaching of the bishops merely as a basis for debate; the teaching ministry of the bishops means that they lead the people of God and therefore their teaching should not be obscured or reduced to one element among several in a free debate.[28]

One of the central concerns voiced by Schotte's synthesis was that the faithful will probably be confused by entering into a dialogue or debate about episcopal teachings where different levels of authority are intertwined. As a result each bishop's teaching authority might be wrongly applied and its credibility obscured. Schotte states clearly that the episcopal conference per se as a collectivity has no *mandatum docendi.*

Six years later, on March 8–11, 1989, a special meeting was held between the pope and thirty-five U.S. metropolitans (cardinals and archbishops), along with twenty-five members of the curia, on the theme of evangelization. That the U.S. bishops' new way of teaching was a part of the conversation is reflected in several statements.[29] Before the meeting Cardinal Bernardin delivered an address describing what was distinctive about the United States. Some of the elements Bernardin mentioned had noticeably contributed to the U.S. bishops' experiment with a new way of teaching: cherished freedoms and democratic traditions, communication-oriented society, and government in the open with maximum participation of governors and governed.

At the meeting, Cardinal Joseph Ratzinger, prefect of the Vatican Congregation for the Doctrine of the Faith, delivered a brief lecture on "The Bishop as Teacher of Faith," and gave the following comments about the importance of the role of the bishops as shepherds in light of a passage from *Lumen Gentium* (20), which states: "This sacred synod teaches that by divine institution bishops have succeeded to the place of the apostles as shepherds of the church, and he who hears them, hears Christ." Ratzinger comments:

> The pastoral ministry, the shepherd's office, is explained through the notion of hearing. One is a shepherd according to the mind of Jesus Christ, then, inasmuch as he brings people to the hearing of Christ. In the background here the words of the prologue of John's Gospel calling Christ the *Logos* can be heard; resonant too is the ancient Christian idea that it is precisely the *Logos* who is the shepherd of men, guiding us sheep who have gone astray to the pastures of truth and giving us there the water of life. To be shepherds, then, means to give voice to the *Logos*, voice to the redeeming Word.[30]

Ratzinger goes on to point out that a particular danger in the postconciliar exercise of episcopacy is a diminishment of the ancient role of the Christian bishops to one similar to that of the *mebaqqer* of the Qumran community who acted as pastoral "supervisors." Instead of preaching the redeeming word with decisiveness, the contemporary bishop reflects the Qumran spiritual administrator who is being pressured "to avoid polarizations, to appear as a moderator acting within the plurality of existing opinions, but he himself is not to become 'partisan' in any substantive way." "Why to so large an extent have we bishops acquiesced in this reduction of our office to the inspector, the moderator, the *mebaqqer*? Why have we gone back to Qumran when it comes to this essential point of the New Testament?"[31]

The postconference statement of Archbishop John May, then president of the NCCB, indicates that the process of generating U.S. episcopal teaching was at issue:

> Clearly, there were some differences of perspective in the room . . . , but these differences have to do with approach and not with doctrine. The church's teaching is universal; the bishops of the United States work to support, defend and promote the teaching as do the curia officials in Rome. Many of the factors that make America distinctive are the ones that make her great—the freedom of thought and expression, the pluralism of cultures and religions, the democratic spirit which values the opinion of each individual. America is a "marketplace society," where ideas have to sell themselves on their own intrinsic merit. That this would conflict at times with the hierarc

> hical nature of the church is not surprising. What we came to Rome to say (and it was received calmly and well) was that this spirit of America must influence our own approach in the States. Though the teaching of the church is one and universal, our approach to presenting this teaching must be custom-fitted to the United States.[32]

One year after this meeting in Rome, the Congregation for the Doctrine of the Faith again expressed apprehensions in a written response to the U.S. bishops after the second draft of the proposed pastoral letter on women's issues appeared in April 1990. And on May 28–29, 1991, the third time in three years that the "ecclesiological problems" concerning the U.S. bishops' teaching procedure received attention, the Roman curia convened an international consultation to discuss the second draft of the women's document with representatives of the U.S. hierarchy and two U.S. women (Sara Butler, MSBT, and Mariella Frye, MHSH) involved in the development of the pastoral. Also participating were representatives of various dicasteries of the Roman curia (Cardinals Joseph Ratzinger, Alberto Bovone, Angelo Sodano), and eighteen bishops from around the world.[33] The first issue raised pertained to "the precise nature of the document and the related question of methodology."[34] Cardinal Ratzinger's opening address at this gathering echoed the misgivings voiced previously to the U.S. bishops by the Congregation for the Doctrine of the Faith when the second draft appeared.[35] Besides surfacing the concern about confusing the faithful by not distinguishing levels of authority in the text, which was also discussed during the preparation of the pastoral on war and peace, there was a special worry that this text allowed diverse voices from the community to be represented without clearly indicating the bishops' own voice. The voices of women were more conspicuous than the collective voice of the bishops.

The issues raised by Roman officials consistently pertained to the teaching authority of bishops, specifically in terms of the authority of the universal and ordinary magisterium in relation to episcopal conferences. There were a number of facets involved. One of the major problems concerned whether national episcopal conferences, as an institution promoting collegiality, have a collective *mandatum docendi*. Following the teachings of Vatican II, bishops, are exhorted to cultivate closer collegial relations (*collegialis affectus*) among bishops, and they are also to develop the practices of collegial decision making in councils and synods (*collegialis effectus*). But it has been disputed whether the episcopal conference is solely a manifestation of the collegial spirit or whether it can also render collegial acts, that is, reach collective judgments and decisions that have binding authority. This has a direct bearing on the precise nature of the teaching authority of episcopal conferences and whether it has a *mandatum docendi*.[36] Representatives of the curia have argued that the U.S. bishops' conference and other national and regional conferences are a reflection of the collegial spirit, but that they do not have a mandate to teach and to render collegial acts to the full extent, as found in ecumenical councils.

One of the major arguments advanced by the U.S. bishops in defense of their dialogical methodology underscored a distinction between unchanging or more stable doctrines on the one hand and practical applications in national contexts on the other. The bishops have maintained that in their deliberative processes in preparing these pastoral letters the door has not been opened to disagreements about dogmas and dogmatic principles, the province of the universal and ordinary magisterium. Yet there must be room for wide-ranging discussions and debates in a process of collective discernment about how to apply these dogmatic principles in practical living. This kind of communal dialogical process, the U.S. bishops contended, does not undermine the deepest convictions of faith but in fact can affirm and bolster them.

The consternation among Roman officials ultimately bore upon larger questions of methodology: How does the hierarchy teach? And do open conversations about church teachings have any role in this process? The 1991 meeting on the women's pastoral illuminated a genuine conflict between two approaches to episcopal teaching. The Roman approach emphasizes the teaching authority of the universal magisterium as established by official Roman Catholic teaching and practice, and the derivative authority of individual bishops and bishops' conferences. This Roman approach to the exercise of episcopal authority is viewed as incompatible with public discussion and wide consultation. The approach being experimented with by the U.S. bishops was not intended to call into question the official Catholic position at the level of principle, but rather to create a context for the members of the church—bishops, theologians, and representatives of the entire people of God—to gather to speak and think with one another about a certain teaching so as to learn from one another and thus strengthen the church's teaching. Both the Roman and the U.S.

approaches are intent on preserving and strengthening the authority of the church's teaching and even the exercise of hierarchical authority. The conflict centers on the way in which episcopal authority is bestowed, generated, and best exercised.

A triadic structure of the church as a community of dialogue and communication—bishops, theologians, and the entire people of God cooperating in dynamic interrelationships of learning and teaching—has been developed and exemplified by the U.S. bishops' conference in the process of generating these three pastoral letters.[37] Collegiality, collaboration, consultation are the terms used here to name these three modes of acting in relationships—collegiality among bishops, collaboration between bishops and theologians, consultation between bishops, theologians, and the entire people of God. Together these modes of ecclesial interaction are intended to denote the inclusive and open, participatory form of learning and teaching that Vatican II symbolizes and began to articulate.[38] The critical reaction of the Roman curia to these pastoral letters was ultimately not only about the authority of episcopal conferences, nor about the specific positions taken in these letters, but in significant ways about how the U.S. bishops were receiving and implementing the teachings of Vatican II about the exercise of authority.

CONTESTED ISSUES AT HOME

U.S. bishops faced other forms of resistance besides that of curial officials. During the generation of the peace pastoral and the economic pastoral, officials of the Reagan administration and conservative Catholics became outspoken critics of the positions that were emerging. These conservative policy makers and Catholic intellectuals sought first to change the bishops' minds by taking part in the open public debate, and then, when it became clear that such an effort would not work, they sought to challenge, undermine, and discredit the results and the deliberative process employed by the U.S. bishops. With tenacity and clarity of purpose, the bishops followed through on their process, listened to their conservative critics, and conceded some points in revised documents, while holding to positions previously arrived at through their multi-faceted deliberative process.[39]

There were likewise critics among more progressive Catholics, but on the peace and economic pastorals their grievances were usually about strengthening individual positions advanced by the bishops' documents rather than seeking a consensus between two opposing trajectories of thought, and certainly not about the public deliberative process. On the process, there was widespread support for the pioneering effort of the bishops. This support among progressive Catholics began to deteriorate, however, with the release of the first draft of the women's pastoral in April 1988. While generally appreciative of the widespread consultation with women and the use of women's voices in the document, progressives called for a document that more strongly promoted women's rights in society and changes in the church, especially by addressing the pope's and Roman reticence to open up discussion on the ordination of women to priesthood. When the second draft appeared in April 1990, which introduced major changes in style (fewer women quoted in the text) and substance (including mention of the "distinctive embodiments" of men and women reflective of the theology of gender complementarity espoused by John Paul II in his 1988 apostolic letter *Mulieris Dignitatem*), serious reservations were voiced by increasing numbers of progressive Catholics. Throughout the summer and into the fall numerous individuals and organizations, including Center of Concern, the Leadership Conference of Women Religious, and the Women's Ordination Conference, called for the bishops to scrap the proposed letter. Soon after the second draft appeared, Archbishop Rembert Weakland argued that the second draft document had a "strident, negative, judgmental tone" and was "preachy" and "not inspired" and that the process should not be continued. Other bishops joined Weakland and voiced negative verdicts on the document.[40] On November 18, 1992, the U.S. bishops voted on the proposed pastoral. The vote of 137 in favor and 110 against failed to reach the two-thirds majority needed to adopt the pastoral letter.[41]

The demise of the pastoral on women's issues merits further reflection. The ad hoc committee that prepared this document had in fact held the most extensive dialogues to date in a variety of settings and had creatively experimented with incorporating the voices of women participants from these dialogues into the text being prepared. These moves were viewed by many as positive advances. Why then did the pastoral letter on women's issues fail? A number of reasons have been offered. Some argue that this effort fostered a premature discussion of certain contested issues in theological anthropology, while others maintain that it was a discussion long overdue and now frustrated. One recurring reason given for its failure was that certain topics, and specifically women's ordination, were considered taboo subjects for open discussion based on the statement by the Congregation for the Doctrine of the Faith, *Inter Insigniores* (1976). This was exacerbated by the contentions concerning gender complementarity presented in John Paul II's 1988 apostolic letter on women, *Mulieris Dignitatem*. Two years after the women's pastoral failed, John Paul II imposed an official silence on the question of women's ordination by his 1994 apostolic letter *Ordinatio Sacerdotalis*, which was reaffirmed in the Congregation for the Doctrine of the Faith, *Response to the Dubium concerning the Ordination of Women* (1995). On December 6, 1992, after the pastoral on women's issues failed and before the apostolic letter and CDF response just mentioned were issued, Archbishop Rembert Weakland published an editorial in the *New York Times* in which he identified two options on the discussion of women's issues.

> The first is to close the doors to all discussion on the ordination issue and accept the consequences. That means, first all, preparing to live in a church of reduced size, for many women and men would say goodbye to a church they feel is out of touch with the world. The church also would have to stop telling society to increase signs of respect for women and how to use women's abilities to the fullest: it would be seen as hypocritical.
>
> The other option is to keep the doors open to further discussion and continue the important, even if painful, dialogue between the church's tradition and modern insights. This dialogue involves listening to all voices, especially the wisdom of the laity, and, with prayer and reflection, seeing what God wants of the church today. For some of us, too much is unclear, and too much is at stake to close the doors now.

The official declarations by the Roman curia in 1994 and 1995 reflect the first option. During the 1992 meeting at which the women's pastoral was rejected, Bishop Joseph Imesch, chair of the ad hoc committee that had prepared the document, addressed the assembly of bishops: "As a bishop I challenge you—and challenge myself—to reexamine the role of women in our dioceses, *to hear more than we allowed ourselves to hear*, and to cross a bridge from word to action."[42]

THE AFTERMATH OF AN EXPERIMENT

After the failure of the women's pastoral, the U.S. bishops abandoned the practice of using the more open dialogical process that they had experimented with during 1980s in the creation of the pastoral letters on peace, the economy, and women. This process was distinguished by an expanded consultation process, the public release of draft documents, and the use of a feedback loop in which bishops invited oral and written responses to draft documents and then revised these documents based on their deliberations on the responses. Instead of dedicating themselves to continuing this particular kind of practice, and even expanding its usage to other social issues (racism, for example) or to extend it to internal church matters (religious education, for instance), the bishops returned to their older standard procedure. The disuse of this method could be viewed as one more example of the tragic failure of dialogue in the postconciliar church.

However, since the demise of the women's pastoral, the U.S. bishops have not abandoned dialogical methods altogether. They still collaborate with selected theologians and consult with representatives of the people of God. They have continued to experiment with different models of dialogical practices, but in a dramatically curtailed manner by comparison with the experimental procedures used in the preparation of the three pastoral letters.[43] Their use of different, smaller-scale dialogical methods, conducted with either much less or no public and open procedures, could be judged as practical decisions made by the bishops tailored to particular new issues and situations, though it could mean a return to an older approach to exercising episcopal authority. The main conclusion is the same: the distinctive features of the experimental method—the publicly released drafts and the use of a feedback loop in which the bishops invited reactions to the drafts and then revised the drafts in light of these reactions—have not been in evidence since the women's pastoral.

Why were the specific methods used for these three pastoral letters curtailed? One plausible, but debatable, explanation is that the U.S. bishops finally, or at least for the time being, capitulated to the insistence of Cardinal Ratzinger and other representatives of the curia that this was no way to exercise the teaching office of the bishop and episcopal conferences. It is also reasonable to conclude that the bishops themselves came to have serious reservations about the amount of time spent on these efforts, the energy invested by the bishops and their staffs, and the expenditure of money needed to sustain these grandiose national processes.

How can these efforts be assessed? A case could be made that the processes generated substantive documents with long-term significance and applicability, even though they continue to be debated. Certainly Catholic and national elites were engaged by these processes and documents developed by the bishops, and they have continued to be, evidenced by articles in journals and on Web sites, even though the process is less expansive and less public and open. However, there has been an ongoing struggle to promote a wider discussion and reception of these documents and other pastoral letters by the bishops among the Catholic faithful in the United States.

What is clear is that the bishops have no inclination to raise controversial topics about the church's teachings and practices on internal matters, such as women's ordination or the role of women in decision making in the church, even though many continue to believe that these issues were precisely the ones that needed to be talked through in a collective, mutually receptive, and accountable manner. Here the bishops dutifully adhered to the silence on the issue imposed by current papal teaching and the restrictions placed on the bishops by the Roman curia. Open-ended public discussions of other controversial taboo subjects in church teaching, like birth control and homosexuality, are unlikely to be broached in this climate.

There also appeared to be no interest among the bishops in advancing public discussions about the identity and pastoral mission of the Catholic Church in the United States on social and political issues, with the bishops set in the role of not simply teachers but also learners. On the one hand, this reflects a shift away from the attention given to public policy issues that engaged a wide public during the 1980s, like war and peace and the economy, toward more pastoral internal church issues, like evangelization (1990), stewardship (1992), and liturgy (concerning the guidelines on the Roman Missal in 2000 and the Eucharist in 2003), many of which reflected the implementation of papal initiatives. On the other hand, even when important public policy issues were raised, often by the Department of Social Development and World Peace, there were no public pastoral letters issued but rather public statements of policy decisions, which did not require two-thirds approval of the U.S. bishops. It may be that the bishops could not identify issues that might generate as much public interest as the debates on war and economics. The question can be raised, however, whether the U.S. bishops could have served an important role in the broader U.S. context by sponsoring a public discussion of issues like immigration, multicultural diversity, racism, environmental issues, and the U.S. policy toward the peoples and nations of Africa, all of which received attention by the bishops, but not widespread consultative and collective deliberation. Such deliberation could have raised consciousness for many U.S. Catholics and policy makers, politicians, and for the general public interested in Catholic convictions on these matters. On the one issue that galvanized the vast majority of U.S. bishops, especially during election year cycles, the bishops' pro-life position on abortion, euthanasia, and more recently, the death penalty, the bishops chose to issue statements rather than generate a pastoral letter that used the same kind of open public forum to promote discussion. Is this because in these instances it was deemed that dialogue would serve no useful purpose?

There have been instances since the demise of the women's pastoral when the bishops have promoted dialogue in the U.S. church nationally, regionally, and at the parochial level. But in these cases, they have been promoting a pastoral dialogue among church members, not a dialogue between the bishops and other interested people within and outside the church about teachings and policy statements. The bishops' call for dialogue in the church during this period is most clearly evident in the series of documents surrounding multicultural diversity generated at the threshold of the new millennium, including the pastoral letter "Strangers among Us: Unity in Diversity" (2000) and the program "Encuentro 2000: Many Faces in God's House," which advanced multicultural dialogue.[44] But no open forum with the bishops and no feedback loop were used in generating these pastoral initiatives.

Certain departments and committees of the USCCB have continued throughout this period to be inclined to utilize widespread consultative methods. This is most clearly evident in the work of the Committee on the Laity, a division of the Secretariat of Family, Laity, Women, and Youth, and the Department on Social Development and World Peace. The Committee on Ecumenical and Interreligious Dialogue must also be recognized for promoting bilateral and multilateral forms of dialogue with other

Christian communions and other religious traditions, but as always with selected committees and groups.

The Committee on Laity employed surveys and widespread consultations in the generation of the report "Lay Ecclesial Ministry: The State of the Question," issued in 1999 and the reports on Diocesan/Eparchial Pastoral Councils and Parish Pastoral Councils in 1997 and 2004. But in these cases there were no corresponding public processes seeking reactions to drafts, which could influence the bishops' revisions. In June 2005 the Committee on Marriage and Family Life, also a division of the Secretariat of Family, Laity, Women, and Youth, initiated a new multiyear national pastoral initiative on the institution and sacrament of marriage. Discussions by focus groups surrounding various stages of married life and particular pastoral and sacramental issues are designed to offer bishops input as they prepare a pastoral letter on marriage. Beyond their involvement in these focus groups, it remains to be seen whether and, if so, how married couples will be invited to participate in the genesis and revision of the draft document and whether and, if so, how controversial topics will be addressed.

Extensive consultations have likewise been advanced by the Department of Social Development and World Peace in the drafting of public statements on justice issues in preparation for the new millennium and in organizing the National Catholic Celebration of Justice meeting in 1999. This department has long been known for promoting consultation since they were the major catalyst for the peace and economics pastoral letters and the earlier bicentennial program that culminated in the Call To Action convention. It stands to reason that they remain committed to using dialogical methods in generating some larger documents, even though, once again, the distinctive feedback loop of issuing draft documents, eliciting reactions, and revising the documents in response to reactions has not been in evidence.

The U.S. bishops have chosen not to expand the experiment with the dialogical pedagogical process of learning and teaching with wider participation of members of the Catholic Church and with those in other religious communities and in the broader society. This raises several questions. Are there topics where such a wider dialogical approach would more effectively advance the pastoral mission of the U.S. church? The larger question is whether the U.S. bishops can reclaim their use of a more public and open dialogical process in the generation of pastoral letters—

releasing draft documents and using the feedback loop in the revision of these documents. If a more widespread investment of all sectors in the church in the learning and teaching process were promoted, would it not strengthen the teaching of the church and the authority and credibility of the bishops and the Catholic Church in the United States?

It was not until the clergy sex abuse scandal broke publicly in the new millennium that the U.S. bishops once again held hearings in local dioceses, regionally, and nationally on the extent of the crisis and listened to testimonials given by victims and advice by experts. This crisis gave the bishops an opportunity to relearn the insight into how to restore credibility to episcopal authority through collegiality, collaboration, and widespread consultation. The U.S. bishops came to a collective legislative decision at their assembly in June 2002 to establish review boards at diocesan, provincial, and national levels, composed predominantly of laywomen and men to advise bishops about specific allegations of sexual abuse of minors by clergy, about pertinent policies, and about the fitness of candidates for ministry, which implied a measure of deliberative authority. The Roman curia required changes in the language of the norms to underscore the consultative character of the review boards and to rule out any decision-making role, which would violate the juridical authority of the bishops.[45]

5

Placating Polarizations or Making Them Productive?

The Catholic Common Ground Initiative

Called to Be Catholic: Church in a Time of Peril was a brief document released by Cardinal Joseph Bernardin on August 12, 1996, at the formal announcement of the inauguration of the Catholic Common Ground Initiative (hereafter called the Initiative).[1] This effort had its origins in conversations that took place between Bernardin and Philip Murnion, priest of the Archdiocese of New York and director of the National Pastoral Life Center, about a document Bernardin wrote in 1992, *The Parish in the Contemporary Church*, which he sent to his parishes in Chicago. Bernardin and Murnion discussed how the pastoral concerns about worship, religious education, the church's social and pastoral ministry, the declining number of priests and religious, and the role of young people raised by Bernardin's paper "were often obscured by increasing polarization among individuals, groups, and organizations in the church."[2] They subsequently formed a discussion group of a few bishops, priests in both pastoral and academic work, sisters, and laypeople, some of whom were involved in church ministries and some not; the group met twice a year between 1992 and 1996. Over time this group came to the conclusion that their concerns were widely shared and that a public statement on these matters was warranted.

The document they issued, *Called to Be Catholic*, described the current situation in the church as one beleaguered by polarizing and centrifugal forces that keep people from addressing directly the pressing pastoral issues of the day. Instead of engaging in polemics or refusing to discuss difficult issues, the challenge was to foster an honest dialogue about these matters. Rather than establishing a self-selective group based on a given vision of the church or particular positions on disputed issues, the challenge was to create an inclusive group of Catholics. The "invitation to a revitalized Catholic common ground should not be limited to those who agree in every respect on an orientation for the church, but encompass all—whether centrists, moderates, liberals, radicals, conservatives, or neo-conservatives—who are willing to reaffirm basic truths and to pursue their disagreements in a renewed spirit of dialogue. Chief among those truths is that our discussion must be accountable to the Catholic tradition and to the Spirit-filled living church that brings to us the revelation of God in Jesus."[3] The model of accountability espoused here does not imply a rigid institutional model of authority and obedience, but it requires a clear recognition that the dialogue about Catholic identity takes place within boundaries, even though the boundaries themselves will be tested and debated.

The document proposed that disagreements in the church be addressed in a renewed spirit of dialogue guided by the following seven principles of dialogue (also described by members as the rules of dialogue):

1. We should recognize that no single group or viewpoint in the church has a complete monopoly on the truth. While the bishops united with the Pope have been specifically endowed by God with the power to preserve the true faith, they too exercise their office by taking counsel with one another and with the experience of the whole church, past and present. Solutions to the church's problems will almost inevitably emerge from a variety of sources.
2. We should not envision ourselves or any one part of the church a saving remnant. No group within the church should judge itself alone to be possessed of enlightenment or spurn the mass of Catholics, their leaders, or their institutions as unfaithful.
3. We should test all proposals for their pastoral realism and potential impact on living individuals as well as for their theological truth. Pastoral effectiveness is a responsibility of leadership.
4. We should presume that those with whom we differ are acting in good faith. They deserve civility, charity, and a good-faith effort to understand their concerns. We should not substitute labels, abstractions, or blanketing terms—"radical feminism," "the hierarchy," "the Vatican"—for living, complicated realities.
5. We should put the best possible construction on differing positions,

addressing their strongest points rather than seizing upon the most vulnerable aspects in order to discredit them. We should detect the valid insights and legitimate worries that may underlie even questionable arguments.

6. We should be cautious in ascribing motives. We should not impugn another's love of the church and loyalty to it. We should not rush to interpret disagreements as conflicts of starkly opposing principles rather than as differences in degree or in prudential pastoral judgments about the relevant facts.
7. We should bring the church to engage the realities of contemporary culture, not simply by defiance or naive acquiescence, but acknowledging, in the fashion of *Gaudium et Spes*, both our culture's valid achievements and real dangers.[4]

These principles do not offer a theory of dialogue, nor even a practical structure of the process of dialogue, nor do they identify specific goals of dialogue. Rather they offer an ethic of dialogue, not in terms of specific acts or means, but by addressing problematic attitudes and fostering certain dispositions. As the Initiative gathered together in dialogue at their conferences and as they fostered dialogue in parish settings, these principles were set forth as criteria for evaluating concrete experiences of dialogical practice.

CRITICAL REACTIONS AND REJOINDERS

There were unusually strong negative reactions to *Called to Be Catholic* by four cardinals and two theologians. In various ways these cardinals expressed concerns that dialogue would undermine the authority of tradition and the exercise of authority. Is not a dialogical approach to Christian faith and truth being proposed that is opposed to a hierarchical understanding of the church and the articulation and defense of truths of faith by the magisterium and the obedient response of the faithful? Cardinal Bernard Law claimed that "the fundamental flaw of [the Initiative's founding document] is its appeal for 'dialogue' as a path to 'common ground.'" "Dialogue as a pastoral effort to assist in a fuller appropriation of the truth is laudable. Dialogue as a way to mediate between the truth and dissent is mutual deception."[5] "Conflict cannot be dialogued away."

Cardinal Anthony Bevilacqua feared that talk of common ground would cause confusion among Catholics and that it would promote a "lowest common denominator" mentality. "A polite debate or a respectful exchange of divergent views about what would be the most commonly acceptable Catholic teaching is not sufficient to adequately address and heal the differences which exist among the faithful. Rather, what is needed is that common vision illuminated through prayer to see Jesus as he himself asked to be seen: the way, the truth, and the life."[6] "The strongest support the faithful have in successfully responding to the challenge to be holier, to be better Catholics, is the person of Jesus Christ and his church's teachings."[7] Cardinal Adam Maida feared that the statement would confuse by suggesting that "Catholic teaching is open to dialogue and debate." "We do not 'dialogue' about membership in the church any more than we would discuss our status in our family. Dialogue is a helpful tool and step in a larger process, but of itself it cannot solve religious differences." Genuine dialogue must be based on scripture and church teaching. "The way to peace among nations and religions, and the way to unity within our church itself, is not so much through dialogue, but rather through conversion which is the result of prayer and fasting."[8] Cardinal James Hickey voiced concerns about the status of scripture and tradition and feared the authority of the magisterium would be undermined by dialogue, "accommodating those who dissent from church teaching."[9]

Cardinal Bernardin and Archbishop Oscar H. Lipscomb responded to these criticisms by defending the dialogical model of the Initiative. They argued that a dialogical approach need not be viewed as antithetical to the Catholic understanding of the authority of the scriptures and tradition and of a hierarchical church. Bernardin admitted that,

> the idea of dialogue has sometimes been cheapened by turning it into a tool of single-minded advocacy. It is also true that dialogue is not in every case or at every moment the universal solution. Nevertheless . . . dialogue is a critical need. The church is built up, not brought down, by genuine dialogue anchored in our fundamental teachings. . . . It is essential that we offer these faithful people guidelines and models of dialogue. We do not seek "least common denominator Catholicism." Rather we seek to help the faithful move beyond the often unnecessary and unhelpful polarization in our community and to refocus on the fundamental principles and pastoral needs of the church.[10]

He divided the cardinals' criticisms into three areas: "First, that it [the *Called to Be Catholic* statement] does not adequately acknowledge Scripture and tradition as the actual common ground of the Catholic Church and reduces the magisterium to just one more voice in a chorus of debate. Second, that it places dissent on the same level as truth and seems ready to accept compromise on the truth. Third, that it insufficiently acknowledges the centrality of Jesus."[11] Bernardin responded to his fellow cardinals by pointing out that *Called to Be Catholic* unequivocally affirmed that scripture and tradition are the foundational sources, the "basis" of any common ground, and that there must be "accountability" to the Catholic tradition and attentiveness to the living magisterium of the bishops and the pope. Second, the document did not legitimate dissent or give it equal footing with the truth, but spoke of limits and boundaries and stated that tradition cannot be dismissed with an appeal to experience or inclusivity. However, there must be room for questions and disagreements about important substantive issues, and "the question of dissent in the church and whether it is ever justified is a complicated and theologically technical one," which the document did not address.[12] Third, the centrality of Jesus Christ, as encountered in scriptures and sacrament, as "the measure and not what is measured," is the cornerstone of the document. He also noted that "some people hoped, and others feared, that this initiative would aim ambitiously at resolving all the church's major conflicts in our nation. Some seemed to imagine that the project planned to bring contending sides, like labor-management negotiations, to a bargaining table and somehow hammer out a new consensus on contentious issues within the church."[13] This is a misunderstanding of the Initiative's intentions. "The call for dialogue has too often become routine, a gambit in the wars of image-making, a tactic in reopening or prolonging bureaucratic negotiations."[14] But dialogue is a real achievement of Vatican II and the teachings of the popes. "In dialogue we affirm, examine, deepen, and rectify our own defining beliefs in relationship to another person. That relationship involves opposition but also sincere respect, trust, and expectation of mutual enrichment."[15]

Jesuit theologian Avery Dulles, both before and after becoming cardinal in February 2001, entered into the debate about dialogue in the church, which the founding document initiated, once as outside critic and twice as invited lecturer. Whereas Dulles in his previous written work had concentrated on symbolic communication in the church, the Initiative provided the occasion for him to address the dialogical character of the church. In a lecture delivered at Fordham University on November 19, 1996, he contrasted a traditional approach to dialogue, which he associated with Plato, Augustine, and personalist philosophies, and which has been utilized by John Paul II and Joseph Ratzinger, with "prevailing conceptions of dialogue," such as the dialogue theory in comparative approaches to religions, like that of Paul Knitter and John Hick, and democratic political theory, that is, liberalism, which espouses a proceduralist approach to dialogue that is relativist.[16] He identified the benefits, limitations, and disciplines of ecumenical and interreligious dialogue and admitted that dialogue within the church is "always in order if the purpose is to understand church teaching better, to present it more persuasively, and to implement it in a pastorally sensitive way." But it always must be based on the conditions of obedience to ecclesiastical authority, rather than on independence and criticism. "Authentic dialogue, even at its best, has limits. It cannot appropriately replace every other form of communication."[17] He concluded that "dialogue, properly understood, is an excellent thing, whether carried on within the Church or between the different Christian churches or different religions. But it needs to be kept in mind that authentic dialogue is premised on truth, and is directed to an increment of truth. Where the conditions are not met, true dialogue cannot occur."[18]

David Schindler, following up on Dulles's concerns, voiced grave reservations about the governing liberal assumptions and the prevailing liberal cultural context of reception for the Initiative's invitation to ecclesial dialogue. Indebted to Hans Urs von Balthasar's theology, Schindler concentrated on "the normative place of Jesus Christ and the living Catholic tradition in the dialogue being called for." The perceived problem concerns the treatment of dialogue in the foundational documents "in its *ordering and integration* of these christological-ecclesiological principles: it is precisely the lack of this proper ordering and integration that distorts already at the beginning the model of dialogue appealed to by the document."[19] "All dialogues among Catholics and between Catholics and non-Catholics must be measured intrinsically by this christological dialogue which is extended in a unique way through the sacramental *communio* of the Church." Specifically, "in Jesus Christ and through the hierarchical-sacramental Church, an objective revelation of the truth of God" is transmitted, which provides the basis and conditions for the church's understanding of inclusive love and solidarity.[20] For Schindler, one cannot in such forums enter into dialogue intending to settle disputes about christology and ecclesiology, for to do so betrays the influence of hidden liberal assumptions. Instead, one needs a dialogical process and method that seek to confirm and clarify the demands of Catholic doctrinal truth.

Schindler concludes that the approach to dialogue espoused by the Catholic Common Ground Initiative reveals a model of dialogue indebted to conventional liberalism, wherein an open process of dialogue undermines the substance and truth of doctrine, and common ground implies formal and shallow agreements about peripheral matters. Schindler in effect identified the Initiative's alternative to his own approach to dialogue with a liberal paradigm that is reductionistic and works with a sociological and contractual view of dialogue insufficiently shaped by the means of grace and the judgments of doctrine.

The essay by Schindler forces readers to conclude that either one subscribes to his own christocentric ecclesiology or to a reductionistic, sociological, liberal approach to dialogue in the church. This is the same kind of choice Dulles offers. There are entertained no mediating theological positions that legitimately promote wider dialogue about a diversity of positions. If you do not agree, you are subscribing to the alternative liberal viewpoint, and failing to appreciate the reality of personal sin and the need for conversion.[21] Any discussion about polarization in the church is judged illegitimate unless it subscribes to Schindler's approach to the substance of Catholic doctrinal truth. Breakdowns in communication can only be addressed in terms of "the divine trinitarian *communio* revealed in Jesus Christ and present sacramentally-hierarchically in the Church. The Church is an icon of the trinitarian *communio*."[22]

Archbishop Oscar Lipscomb identified three kinds of criticisms: those based on perceptions (the cardinals), implications (Dulles), and those that identified what the text failed to say (Schindler). He acknowledged the seriousness of these criticisms, but he insisted that the Initiative was not antithetical to the official teaching of the church on dialogue. Its approach to dialogue was based on "the conviction that there is an 'objectivity' and 'out-thereness' which is the proper subject matter of theological reflection: An objectivity that is received and not created." Dialogue does not create objectivity, but "pursued in the context of community" it can help the human subject "overcome alienation and despair."[23]

CREATING A CATHOLIC CULTURE OF DIALOGUE

The Initiative sought from its inception not only to promote dialogue among polarized factions in the church's national elites, but also among a cross section of local church leaders—episcopal, pastoral, and theological—by discussing grassroots issues of pastoral life that are contentious: worship, religious education, the exercise of authority, public policy issues, the struggles and aspirations of young adults, and the participation of all the faithful in the life of the church. The underlying hope has been that by modeling this kind of dialogue among representatives of a spectrum of opinions in the church it might stimulate similar dialogues at various levels: in parishes, in dioceses, and in academic settings.

The yearly convention of the Initiative has provided one exercise in dialogue and has served as a means of experimentation with methods and models of dialogue. This event brings together the established committee of the Initiative (approximately twenty-five members) and invited speakers and participants (a total of forty members, speakers, and participants attended the first conference, and subsequent meetings have drawn usually between fifty and sixty—so, roughly half committee members and half invited guests). The first Cardinal Bernardin Conference of the Initiative was held in 1997 on the topic "The United States Culture and the Challenge of Discipleship." Since then, there have been yearly conferences, each devoted to a different topic: church authority in American culture (1998), Eucharist (1999), Catholics in the public arena (2000), young adults (2001), participation in the church (2002), priesthood (2003), sexual ethics (2004), religion, law, and politics in light of the 2004 national election (2005).[24]

The original Catholic Common Ground Initiative committee and the first group of conference participants were composed of carefully selected people representing contrasting viewpoints in the church. Often the participants had never met one another, even though their written works and positions were known, and sometimes a participant had criticized another participant's position in print. The conferences were designed to bring these people together for a weekend (Friday evening, Saturday all day, and Sunday morning) to meet one another in a nonhostile environment, to identify the shared loves and deep convictions that distinguish Catholics, and to discuss contentious issues in the church in an effort to move the conversation forward. This required setting up the conditions for participants with contrasting points of view to get to know one another in the context of liturgical prayer, informal conversations during social times and especially at meals, and in more formal dialogue sessions where each participant would have the opportunity to speak one's mind and to hear the others out in various formats (panel discussions, small-group meetings, and large-group discussions). The basic requirement was that participants agree to abide by the principles of dialogue.

Fostering such a dialogue takes planning. For the first conference, a subgroup of the Initiative committee worked together on a topic proposal with Philip Murnion and Sr. Catherine Patten, RSHM, who has been on the staff of the National Pastoral Life Center and collaborated closely with Murnion on the Initiative, and who has subsequently become the director of this project. A program committee refined the overarching topic, decided whom to invite, selected those who would write the papers to be distributed beforehand, and designed the dialogical process, that is, the individual subtopics and questions for each part of the conference (panel and small- and large-group discussions). The participants received beforehand a conference proposal that described the topic, the assumed contrasting positions on the topic, and the papers prepared by representatives of those contrasting positions.

The first evening of the conference regularly begins with a prayer and a panel discussion among those who have written the papers. The writers are given an opportunity to underscore certain facets of their papers in light of the other papers and also to raise questions and criticisms of the other papers. Often the conversation is opened to the entire group. The second day is composed of a variety of panel presentations, small-group, and large-group discussions. The panels always contain representatives of contrasting viewpoints, but there have been occasions when one panel is composed of bishops, another of theologians, and a third of pastoral ministers, all modeling dialogue. The composition of the small groups is carefully arranged, and people are given questions to structure their conversation. Over the course of these exchanges, there is regularly an attempt to move the conversation to a deeper level, beyond ideas and positions to the underlying hopes and fears and personal experiences that have given rise to and motivate the positions and ideas held. "What do you most fear if your position isn't heeded?" On the closing morning there is sometimes an effort to have observers summarize what they perceive has transpired: points of agreement, neuralgic points, and topics that have not been addressed. The participants are invited to evaluate the time together.

These conferences have modeled dialogue by offering an orderly process whereby participants' differing points of view can be voiced and heard by cultivating an environment and an ethos for genuine, honest exchange about the most important matters of Catholic faith and living. Initially there were concerns raised about the category "common ground." Some thought that this category implied "dialoguing away" differences or a search for the "least common denominator." But as Lipscomb noted, the hope animating their efforts is that they can gain a clearer understanding of the objective reality that constitutes the common ground of their faith, what has been commonly "received" as gift and recognized as the deepest convictions and shared loves that define the faith. The conferences have demonstrated again and again that those across the spectrum of positions have far more in common than not, and this commonality extends to the basic ingredients and practices of the faith, the recognition of the need for authority, specifically the rightful authority of both the pope and the curia in relation to the authority of episcopal conferences and local bishops, and the need for radical discipleship and prophetic witness in the midst of complex and sometimes pernicious economic and cultural forces.

There have been real differences of opinion nonetheless, and there were initial concerns that participants would be too polite to state their disagreements directly. As greater trust was engendered among the participants, these disagreements frequently came into focus. The task has been neither to avoid nor to overcome differences in the interest of promoting the common faith, but, from within a common faith, to make the differences fruitful for the good of the church, where debates can move the dialogical momentum forward. The differences have not always been between the so-called right and left, conservatives and liberals (the perceived basis for polarization that launched the initiative), but also between academics with their technical terms and abstract theories and pastoral leaders with their straight talk about concrete situations and problems that require clear practical solutions and not fancy, coherent, speculations.

There have been, in practice, some limits on the inclusivity of the participant pool. There was a self-conscious effort to bring together a group of people who would be able to enter into a constructive conversation with one another. As a result, representatives of the "extreme right and left" were not invited, which a number of participants believed made genuine conversation and movement possible, without unbridled polemics and rancor or apocalyptic black and white thinking. (One cannot help but think of the concerns raised by Bernardin about polarization and special interests at the Call To Action convention fifteen years earlier.) But at what price were the "extreme right and left" excluded? Who was not asked and why? Did the belief that their absence makes a conversation possible express a prejudice without effort or evidence? Even if the working assumption was reasonable and prudent to get the initiative started, can the boundaries of acceptable participants be expanded? Difficult is not the same as impossible and unnecessary.

Philip Murnion admitted that involving conservatives in the initiative was more difficult than finding willing progressives. There have also been a desire and a commitment from early on to have women and representatives of diverse ethnic and racial groups actively involved in the conferences to better reflect the realities of the U.S. church. On another front, often conspicuously missing from the committee and conferences were representatives of generations X (young people between 20 and 40) and the so-called millennium generation (13 to 19), the generations born after Vatican II. These younger Catholics are not invested in the debates surrounding the interpretations and outcomes of Vatican II, but they do have a combination of religious aspirations and anxieties, a deep desire for life meaning, direction, and community, a hunger both for mystical practices and to work for justice and in social ministries, and an impatience with boring liturgy, vacuous catechesis, and unintelligible moral teachings about sexuality and the requirements for priestly ordination. There may be few representatives of this group actively involved in the Initiative, but the need for more participation of younger Catholics is a recurring topic of conversation at the conferences.

Philip Murnion explained that the committee wanted "to both illuminate a particular issue and identify methods and models of dialogue that could enhance discussion of issues in any forum."[25] They wanted their conference behavior to offer an example of their principles, providing an opportunity to habituate the practices of generous, honest, and fair dialogue. At the end of the first conference, the following list of advice was compiled:

> [1] Take the time necessary to build trust. [2] Attend to the experience which underlay different perspectives. [3] Establish clear ground rules for the discussion. [4] Clarify the common goal; work for common ground. They wanted to lower the decibel level in debate and they made great efforts to listen, to be gracious, to be hospitable to one another. [5] Ask no one to give up his or her view, but ask all to be self-critical and open to conversion.[26]

At the second conference, participants were asked to "identify conditions that foster dialogue and develop models of dialogue to share with others."[27] In response, many participants claimed that "gathering the group itself—Catholics who manifest love for the church and who command the respect of one another—was one of the strengths of the conference." The desire and commitment to search for common ground "generated inspiration and hope." The effort to make sure that people socialized and dined with people from differing circles and with differing viewpoints was judged very important. Praying together has proven important. "Bridging the interests and perspectives of theologians, those who are engaged in pastoral work, and the layperson 'in the pews' remains a challenge." As much as the participants wanted to "gather the fruits of such a conference for the wider church," it has been a challenging, if not unrealistic, goal "to write statement of agreements in a weekend."[28]

After several years of experience Murnion confessed:

> We . . . still find it difficult in the short time of a weekend to move beyond the airing of differences to clarifying the foundations of those differences, and broadening the ground of agreement. Yet, the civil conversation, the mutual respect, and the shared worship—just being together as fellow Catholics—continue to make it clear that we are at home with one another. We do better at strengthening the relationships in the family than deepening the dialogue of ideas and contributing to the debates in the church. Maybe there's a lesson as well as consolation in that.[29]

The model and method of dialogue espoused by the Initiative is most clearly articulated in the principles of dialogue and exemplified by their conferences.[30] It has also served as the basis for several symposia sponsored by the Inititiative: one on women's issues in the church and society, a second on liturgy and church architecture, and a third on restoring moral credibility to the church in the aftermath of the clergy sex abuse crisis.[31] Based on these documents and these expanding efforts at dialogue, a program was developed to introduce the CCGI and the principles of dialogue through videos and a resource workbook for small-group discussions. Their workbook describes the CCGI in a number of ways: "A way of exploring differences (dialogue and conversation). A spirit and ethic of dialogue (working principles and rules of conversation). A space of trust set within boundaries (Scripture, Tradition, accountability). A place of respect where we can explore differences (issues and concerns)." Three aims are specified: (1) to address vital questions about Catholicism in the United States; (2) to learn how to make differences among Catholics fruitful; and (3) to foster greater effectiveness in pastoral mission. Two tasks are named: (1) to make conflicts constructive; and (2) to come to a deeper understanding of the meaning of discipleship in Jesus Christ, which can then be articulated for the world.[32]

Leonard Swidler's definition of dialogue was offered as a starting point in the workbook: "Dialogue is a conversation on a common subject between two or more persons with differing views, the primary purpose of which is for each participant to learn from the other so that he or she can change and grow."[33] David Tracy's rules for conversation were also invoked: "Say only what you mean; say it as accurately as you can; listen to and respect what the other says, however different or other; be willing to correct or defend your opinions, if challenged . . . ; be willing to argue if necessary, to confront if demanded, to endure necessary conflict, to change your mind if the evidence suggests it."[34] These materials provide practical advice for small-group dialogues. Participants are encouraged to identify and prioritize together the pressing issues the church faces today, focusing on their parish experience. This process begins by watching videos and reading materials that encourage people to attend to their responses (feelings, thoughts) and reactions (reinforced beliefs or points of disagreement). They are encouraged to name and articulate honestly in the group their own religious positions, beliefs, and commitments, but also to cultivate active listening to someone with whom they disagree. Deeper questions are raised about the significance of diversity in the church and about the problems of relativism (epistemological, moral, and religious). But the goal of the initial set of dialogue encounters is to identify three pressing areas of concern (e.g., worship, evangelization, the poor, polarization in the parish) that each one would personally like to discuss in order to identify areas of general agreement or more pressing concern.

Dialogical practices have also been modeled in a video series, sponsored by the Initiative. The videos feature two professors from the University of Notre Dame—church historian Scott Appleby and Cathleen Kaveny, with degrees in law and theology—leading a discussion with panelists representing differing points of view on a variety of topics: Sunday worship, faith formation, sin and forgiveness, the death penalty, poverty and responsibility, generation X, and lay ministry. These videos offer a starting point for small groups seeking to foster dialogue on these specific issues.

These various kinds of efforts to promote dialogue at diverse levels of the church indicate that for the Initiative the basic substantive issues and the quest for common ground take precedence over teaching a dialogical process. In other words, the content of the dialogue is more important than the method of dialogue. Still, there has been an attempt to introduce a wide variety of resources on the topic of dialogue, especially in the quarterly newsletter *Catholic Common Ground Initiative: Initiative Reports,* edited by Catherine Patten, with numerous reports written by her as well. The *Initiative Reports* have offered reflections on promoting dialogue in diverse church settings: in the parish, by Katarina Schuth, OSF; in ecumenical and interreligious encounters, by Eugene Fischer and Leonard Swidler; in situations of racial conflict and healing, by Richard K. Taylor with LaVonne France; in the exercise of authority, by Frank Hartmann; and Robert Schreiter on the healing power of listening in situations of abuse and conflict.[35]

Since 1999, the Initiative has sponsored an annual lecture promoting a deeper understanding of dialogue in the church. Each lecturer has had a distinctive contribution to make to this collective effort.[36] Let me offer two illustrations that combine theological acumen with pastoral sensitivities. Cardinal Walter Kasper claimed that in order to address the problems arising from the plurality of local churches within the one universal church, the church must search for a Trinitarian approach to church unity. "The church should develop means of communicating and undertaking dialogue which correspond better to its *communio*-structure; . . . the church should be a house and a school of *communio*. Thus church leadership must look for a means of communication, consensus-building and reception and for the widest ranging participation. There should be public opinion, open discussion and debate in the church."[37] Joseph Komonchak reviewed various "bipolar" interpretations of Vatican II and postconciliar theologies that pit conservatives against progressives. As an alternative, he developed the thesis that a Thomistic orientation and an Augustinian orientation distinguished influential groups of theologians at the council. The former searched for correlations between the Christian classics and a particular culture; the latter presented and defended the wisdom and beauty of the gospel and Catholic tradition. What Komonchak found most noteworthy and worthy of emulation is that, at the council, theologians and bishops representing these two orientations cultivated practices of collaboration for the good of the Catholic Church. What the council can still teach is the "basic method and structure followed. . . . It provided ample room for discussion, debate, for disagreement, and, as often as not, these were dealt with by conciliation and compromise for the sake of as broad a consensus as possible."[38] In their respective lectures, both Kasper and Komonchak articulated the deepest theological and pastoral aspirations of the Initiative.

SOLID GROUND AND FAULT LINES

The Initiative dialogue has been self-described by its leaders in terms of the following characteristics: above all it is pastoral in orientation, engages a spectrum of views, follows its own rules of dialogue, and espouses an inclusive view of church that is set within the boundaries of the living tradition of the church; it aims at pastoral action, fosters unity in the church, and searches for the points of agreement, while recognizing the legitimacy of genuine disagreements.[39] The great aspiration and self-conscious intention of the Initiative continues to be its attempt to move beyond polarization by keeping the focus of dialogue in the church on the most basic ingredients of the faith and practice of the church. By so doing, it also draws attention to the dialogical character of prayer, liturgy, religious education, Christian discipleship, and friendship among adults and generations born after Vatican II, and the pastoral ministries of the church both in the church and in the world. The conversations have always gone back to parish, pastoral life: the dialogical dimensions of the messy, confusing daily lives of Christians, where individuals and communities are being formed by entering into dialogue with the scriptures, liturgies, traditions, and doctrines. The Initiative has sought to advance the debates going on among religious professionals in the church, but in the process it has returned to illuminating the dialogical journey into the deepest mysteries of Christian faith and life, and to the church's prophetic witness in society. Here it has attempted to keep not only the centrists and liberals engaged in dialogue, but also the conservatives and neoconservatives who are willing to participate. These are among its greatest achievements.

The ongoing struggle of the Initiative has been to find ways to address constructively the contested issues that have defined the postconcilar period. On one level, much time and energy has been spent on the disputed issues concerning sexual ethics, the role of women in the church, the requirements for priesthood, and the process of selection of bishops. But when these issues are framed in terms of dissent and obedience, there seems to be little to no room left for dialogue, and the argument shifts to whether and, if so, how dialogue is related to God's revelation and the divine constitution and mission of the church. Conservative critics both in the United States and in Rome have resisted the various experiments in inner-church dialogue in the United States and around the world. The counterargument has frequently been made that dialogue in this context is unavoidably smitten by liberalism, and any sense of objectivity, truth, and authority is inevitably given up to perspectivalism, relativism, and democracy.

The Initiative has attempted to combat these kinds of either/or choices. They have held on to the belief that there are basic truths that are non-negotiable about divine revelation, tradition, and the magisterium, but have also insisted that there must be discretion and latitude in applying these truths in the pastoral setting, and that in some areas there must be room for a diversity of respected positions. This formulation leaves some dissatisfied. Some have argued, as the four cardinals did initially, that the dialogical model espoused by the Initiative is contrary to scripture and tradition and to their hierarchical interpretation and defense. The Initiative has sought to stake out a claim that one can hold on to both. Avery Dulles argued that the classical and personalist approaches to dialogue that inform the church's official position are in opposition to the liberal assumptions that may be operative in the formation and reception of the Initiative. But Cardinal Kasper and Komonchak have suggested that the postconcilar church is aiming to create structures of a genuinely collegial, collaborative, and consultative practice of dialogue, that is not based on a reductionist liberal model.

These same issues have surfaced during the conferences and lecture series in terms of the relationship of the local churches to the universal church and in terms of the role of the curia: centralizing tendencies and the application of the principle of subsidiarity in the church and inculturation, and how the *sensus fidelium,* communal reception, and experience should be properly understood. Dulles has consistently offered a defense of the official position of Pope John Paul II and Cardinal Ratzinger and of the assumptions about internal dialogue in the church operative in the curia. This approach was in evidence during his lecture at the second conference of the Initiative.[40] In this context, Dulles debated with Judge John T. Noonan, who defended doctrinal discontinuity in official Catholic teachings; with Joseph Komonchak's claim that episcopal conferences have the authority not only to apply doctrinal principles established by the universal magisterium but to generate new doctrines in response to new questions and situations; and also with James Coriden's defense of the legitimacy of discretion in applying disciplinary norms and self-determination, all of which illustrate a fault line that runs throughout the discussions concerning practices of dialogue over the last forty years.[41]

John L. Allen, Jr., in one of the annual lectures, shared the results of a questionnaire he informally sent to colleagues in countries around the world asking whether polarization was a problem and if there were spaces for dialogue among people with different outlooks. The results from this admittedly limited inquiry confirm the reality of polarization as not only a U.S. experience but a global phenomenon. The extent of polarization may not be as extreme as it is perceived by those in and outside of the United States, and the polarization between the rich and the poor often rivals that between conservatives and liberals. More important is Allen's conclusion from his findings: "There seems near-universal despair about the absence of public spaces for conversation among Catholics of different opinions, outlooks and temperaments."[42] Allen then turned his attention to the sobering question: "Why Didn't Common Ground Work?" Admitting the Initiative does important things, he contended that "most observers would probably agree that measured against the aspirations of Cardinal Joseph Bernardin, which were to transform the public conversation in the American church, the Initiative has not had the desired impact. If anything, we are more polarized, more strangers to one another, today than when the project began. So, the tough question: Why?"[43] Allen suggested that one reason may be that things have not gotten bad enough. American Catholics have been content to let things go on in dysfunctional ways rather than face difficult issues. The pain must become bad enough for people to recognize that the status quo will no longer suffice. "In some fashion, . . . Catholics need to be brought to see how their blinders and prejudices, far from safeguarding their faith, actually impede full Catholicity."[44] The solution, Allen concluded, is that Catholics need to cultivate "a spirituality [of dialogue] before a program for dialogue can realize its potential."[45]

Philip Murnion, the dedicated collaborator with Joseph Cardinal Bernardin on the Catholic Common Ground Initiative, died after struggling with cancer, on August 19, 2003, almost seven years after Bernardin himself died of cancer. In his last days, Murnion wrote a letter to the bishops of the United States. In it he spoke of the clergy sex abuse scandal, the ongoing polarization in the church, and the loss of the bishops' credibility. Invoking Pope John Paul II's promotion of "structures of participation" and "a fruitful dialogue between pastors and faithful" at the beginning of the new millennium, Murnion implored the bishops not to set authority and consultation in opposition, but in symbiotic relation.[46]

> [C]onsultation, listening, and dialogue only enhance true authority, because they issue from a lived trust and they serve to increase trust. It is imperative that we work together to restore the trust that has been eroded. If I were to sum up my final plea to you, it would be: "dialogue, dialogue, dialogue!" . . . A spirituality of communion and dialogue is as demanding in its asceticism as a spirituality of the desert or the cloister. . . . Do not be afraid to embrace this spirituality of communion, this "little way" of dialogue with one another, with your priests, with all God's faithful. Doing so, you will touch not only the hearts of your brothers and sisters; you will draw closer to the very heart of Jesus, the Lord and brother of us all.[47]

6

The Church Women Want

What Women Religious Learned in Chapters

Women religious have been special agents in the cultivation of the dialogical practices in the U.S. Catholic Church we have thus far examined. Let us acknowledge some of those involved. Mary Benet McKinney, OSB, advanced a dialogical discernment model for use in parish pastoral councils. Sociologist Marie Augusta Neal, SNDdeN, who served on the advisory council of the U.S. bishops, proposed the nationwide bicentennial discussion on justice issues; Maria Riley, OP, along with Jeanne O'Laughlin, OP, both members of the Adrian Dominican Congregation, designed the deliberative process used at the Detroit Call To Action; Margaret Cafferty, PBVM, trained Catholic charity directors as group discussion leaders for Call To Action; Alice Gallin, OSU, compiled and interpreted all the parish data for the bicentennial program. Juliana Casey, IHM, was a special consultant on the U.S. bishops' peace pastoral, Anne Margaret Cahill, OP, on the economic pastoral, and Sara Butler, MSBT, and Mariella Frye, MHSH, were on the NCCB staff and involved in the ill-fated women's pastoral letter, which strove to involve many women in the process and to give them an active voice in the document. Catherine M. Patten, RSHM, serves as the director of the Catholic Common Ground Initiative; Doris Gottemoeller, RSM, Elizabeth Johnson, CSJ, and Katarina Schuth, OSF, were on the founding Catholic Common Ground Initiative committee and were later joined by Donna Markham, OP, Elizabeth McDonough, OP, Anne E. Patrick, SNJM, and Mary Johnson, SNDdeN.

The contributions of these particular women provide but a small illustrative sample from the much larger history of the role that women religious have played in cultivating the skills of dialogical discernment and decision making in the postconciliar church.[1] I will concentrate on the efforts of women religious in "chapters," a traditional form of communal deliberation used in religious institutes as it came to be practiced after Vatican II, and on the dialogical processes they used to revise their constitutions, especially as they prescribed revised governing practices.

Chapters have their origins in monastic communities in the sixth century, when "a chapter" of the Rule of St. Benedict was read daily with the abbot, who would comment on it. When needed, the abbot took these occasions to ask for the advice of community members on matters that affected them all. Mendicant orders like the Dominicans and the Franciscans, whose mission of preaching spread them out geographically, found it difficult to replicate the monastic experience of daily chapters, and so they came to use this form of communal deliberation far less frequently. When apostolic congregations devoted to the apostolic ministries of teaching, hospital work, and care for the poor and the needy emerged in the nineteenth and twentieth centuries, the practice of convening general chapters became widely utilized.[2]

General chapters came to be the time set aside for members of religious institutes to elect new general superiors or superiors of regions or houses, and to address pressing matters that led to formulation of legislation. Otherwise, executive decisions were made by the centralized authority of superiors: for example, abbot, mother general, provincial, prioress, house superior. Provincial chapters were held prior to general chapters and had as their main items of business to elect delegates and to approve proposals to be considered at the general chapter. House chapters were convened in convents to elect delegates to provincial chapters.[3] After Vatican II these three institutional settings became the arena for more open communal conversations about religious identity and mission.

Vatican II called for general chapters devoted to the renewal of religious congregations, which in turn led to the renewal of this traditional form of communication and decision making. *Perfectae Caritatis*, the Decree on the Up-To-Date Renewal of Religious Life, issued on October 28, 1965, called upon religious congregations to consult with all community members about this renewal and to experiment with adapting patterns of religious life and their constitutions.[4] The specific norms for implementing this decree, Paul VI's *motu proprio Ecclesiae Sanctae* (August 6, 1966), mandated (1) that special chapters be held within two or three years to foster adaptation and renewal of the religious congregation; (2) that all the members be given the sufficient time to be fully and freely consulted in preparation for the chapter, possibly by means of provincial and conventual chapters, establishing commissions, and proposing discussion questions; and (3) that general chapters can revise the constitution as an experiment insofar as such revisions are in keeping with the purpose, nature, and character of the particular religious institute and the sources of Christian life in general. Experimenting with dialogical methods of discernment and decision making was a reasonable response to this document.

At the time of the council there were 181,000 sisters and nuns in the United States in over 500 different religious orders and congregations.[5] Each congregation understood their own efforts at developing dialogical methods as being true to its older traditions, such as the Rule of St. Benedict, Augustine's Rule, or Dominic's directives, and as being in strict accordance with canon law.[6] However, these evolving communal procedures were also significantly informed by their own pastoral experiences of dialogical deliberation in schools, hospitals, and other social agencies.[7] Moreover, they were influenced by studies in psychology, sociology, and other social disciplines. The cultivation of practices of dialogical discernment and decision making by these women religious using a creative combination of older spiritual traditions, pastoral experiences, and diverse social scientific resources was one of their most important contributions to the wider church. These endeavors offer some insight into the church these women want.

In this chapter, special attention will be given to the experience of the women religious of the Adrian Dominican Congregation. The Adrian Dominicans provide a well-documented illustration of a congregation that developed dialogical methods in their chapters, their constitution, and their practice of governance.[8] It is one of the larger communities and happens to be the largest community of Dominican women religious in the U.S. It is beneficial for my analysis that Nadine Foley, OP, who served as general councilor (1974–82), vicaress (1982–86), and prioress (1986–92) of the Adrian Dominican Congregation, was also elected as president of the Leadership Conference of Women Religious (LCWR; 1988–89), a group which has played a very important role during the post-conciliar period in advancing dialogical practices in the church.

CHAPTER OF RENEWAL, 1968–1970

In the weeks, months, and years that followed Vatican II, the members at each convent of Adrian Dominican sisters gathered to discuss the conciliar documents of Vatican II and the challenges involved in updating religious life.[9] Certainly women religious met with their community members in their convents before Vatican II, but now their orienting frame of reference, working assumptions, and expectations were in transition, and their agenda was open in an unprecedented way. The sisters' personal and collective deferential posture during the preconciliar period, cultivated in a hierarchical, centralized, clerical, and patriarchal culture of authority and obedience, was gradually replaced by a new awareness of personal and communal decision making.[10] The government of the Adrian Dominican Sisters was previously highly centralized around the prioress general, who exercised supreme authority; provincial superiors, with their four councillors, who exercised authority over the province; and house superiors, who exercised authority over local convents of various sizes. General chapters and provincial chapters allowed, in principle, for communal deliberation that could result in executive judgments and decisions, but participants played a very limited, passive, supporting role in relation to the authority of the prioress and her council. Here the exercise of "the virtue of obedience as submission . . . explicitly excluded discussion."[11]

In the aftermath of Vatican II, women religious, like the Adrian Dominicans, began to develop an active voice in their communities through dialogue. As one of the first steps, women religious were encouraged to discuss with sisters in their house the documents of Vatican II, articles about the founders and charisms of their community, and the prospects of changes in religious life. More importantly, they were encouraged to offer their own personal reflections on these documents with their community members. So, in 1965, Mother Mary Genevieve Weber, OP, the prioress of the Adrian Dominicans, following the directives of Vatican II, invited the Adrian sisters to reflect upon their Dominican history and charism; and in 1966 they were urged to study and reflect on the conciliar and postconciliar documents. Regular household meetings precipitated self-discovery and a process of personal and collective maturation, what some described as the development of adult consciousness, among a group of women long accustomed to living under paternalistic tutelage. In these meetings individuals were invited to respond to some basic questions: How have I understood my religious vocation and how is it that I am to rededicate myself to this at this new moment and in this new historical context? Likewise, these conversations opened up group processes of deliberation: how should we as a group understand the identity and mission of our congregation? These household meetings provided the seedbed for immense new growth and the cultivation of considerable skills, but the learning process was at times slow and painful.

In keeping with the recommendations to be open to the insights of psychology and sociology in evaluating the shape of religious life given by the Sisters Institute of Spirituality (SIS), the Sisters Formation Conference (SFC), and the Conference for Major Superiors of Women (CMSW), Adrian sisters were offered opportunities during the years after Vatican II and into the 1970s to participate in communication workshops at the Weber Center at their motherhouse in Adrian, Michigan. The topics for these workshops included learning sensitivity training and group dynamics. Here the sisters learned about the importance of listening, trusting, and respecting other speakers with different points of view. They were taught to not dominate the conversation, to recognize who the "gatekeepers" were who made sure everyone had a chance to voice their opinions, and how to promote conflict resolution.

In light of what was learned in these workshops, the experiences of dialogue in individual convents and in small regional networks reflected, on the one hand, what was learned in the psychological method of sensitivity training. As in therapeutic, self-analytic groups, sisters learned about the personal psychological dynamics and goals involved in dialogical situations: the need to establish a safe sphere for a small group of people to communicate with one another, the conditions for building mutual trust, fostering sensitivity, and empathy for one's self and others; community members were encouraged to be authentic and honest, each saying not what superiors or peers wanted to hear, but naming one's own convictions, concerns, questions, and doubts; disagreements were not to be denied, but negotiated with mutual respect. On the other hand, these small-group sessions served as fledgling exercises in group process and small-group dynamics. They provided the opportunity to learn how to move a conversation forward toward communal judgments, decisions, and consensus.

Sisters were trained to attend to process as much as to results: "individual participants were constantly to observe and analyze not only the groups' process toward a specific goal, but more importantly, the process and dynamic of the group, and each member, during group interaction."[12] In some circles, these approaches to small-group encounters were understood in light of authority studies that contrasted authoritarian, coercive bureaucratic institutions with more open dialogical and democratic models, and they resulted in criticisms of the exercise of authority in the church as it impacted women's institutes.[13]

Between 1965 and 1968, in preparation for the chapter of renewal that began in the summer of 1968, the Adrian Dominicans, following the direction of a prechapter commission of sisters, began to discuss in their individual houses the Vatican documents and articles on updating religious life and scripture. By 1967 it was deemed important to give members an opportunity to network with other congregation members regionally, outside of the house and provincial structures. Members were invited to select their own compatible small group of five to eight members from nearby convents and elect a group leader for each session. Some groups merged.[14] Thirteen geographical areas were established for these clusters and each group elected an area representative. These discussions resulted in the generation of questions, proposals, and suggestions, which were prioritized.[15]

The hard work of dialogue at local and regional levels paved the way for the drafting of a revised constitution of the Adrian Dominicans. In the process, new forms of communal discernment and decision making were cultivated, and the older forms of the exercise of authority, the general council and the general chapter, were reevaluated and reconceived. According to the 1961 constitution of the Adrian Dominicans, the general council was composed of the major superior (the prioress) and four councilors, all elected positions, who served as the administrative or executive body for the running of the congregation. The general chapter was convened by the major superior to elect new officers and to address any matters of grave importance and thus provided the highest legislative authority in the community while in session. The general chapter included the prioress, four council members, the ex-prioress, the secretary general, the bursar general, the provincial superiors, five elected delegates from each province, and six elected representatives of the houses not belonging to any province but directly dependent on the prioress. Delegates had active voice if they had taken their perpetual vows. What became increasingly clear was that the powers of the general chapter were not fully appreciated even in the immediate aftermath of Vatican II among many sectors of U.S. women religious. But that would soon change.

In the summer of 1967 representatives of the thirteen regional areas, now called the central committee, convened for six weeks to pray, reflect, and converse. The central committee established a prechapter commission to prepare an agenda and to make sure all the delegates were well educated and invested in the deliberative process. Commission members were to be, above all, communicators who would listen to the responses of the sisters and convey pertinent information from regions to the whole group. Compatible small groups were formed with an elected leader; each gathering was to be at least three hours for study but also for personal reflection on ideal and real values. Half a year was devoted to reflective inquiry into sources, followed by half a year to develop proposed actions for the general chapter and to discuss delegate selection. By spring 1968, 1,046 proposals for the general chapter had been generated.

Session One, June 21 to July 30, 1968

The chapter of renewal convened on June 21, 1968, for its first of three consecutive yearly sessions. There were 133 delegates. The agenda had seven topics: Dominican life, formation, apostolic works of the congregation, government, finances, communications, and constitution and directory. Time was divided between committee work on the seven particular topics and plenary sessions. In the plenary sessions the sisters were seated in straight rows, although in the third session they occasionally broke up into small groups. In subsequent general chapters, plenary sessions took place at circular tables allowing for small-group work. Parliamentary procedures were used throughout the chapter of renewal, but this formal process of communication was dropped in subsequent general chapters. The prioress was the de facto chair of the general chapter, but another chair was chosen to serve as presider, running the plenary sessions.[16] Each committee examined the reports prepared by prechapter subcommittees and proposals submitted by the members in light of the constitutions and other conciliar documents. Each proposal was to be evaluated "in light of collegiality and subsidiarity."[17] By *collegiality,* they understood a style of exercising authority in which leadership is recognized as an attribute of the group since it is based on cooperation and coresponsibility of the community members in collective decision making. *Subsidiarity* was recognized as a principle that prescribes that decisions should be made at the lowest level of community and institutional structure by those affected by and obliged to carry out the decision. These two categories became crucial norms in decision making at all levels of the community. The seven committees were then to prepare recommendations for the full delegation in plenary session. The committee on government recommended that the local communities, using the practice of house chapters, would make decisions about their own communities: policies, house responsibilities, permissions, and finances.

There were 151 enactments at the first session of the chapter of renewal. Some of the most important for our topic are these: monthly local chapters were mandated; there was to be experimentation with electing officials; and a self-study of apostolic commitments and resources was to be commissioned. There was a speedy dissemination of conclusions of the first session. By August, committee explanations were distributed on tape. By September, two-day provincial meetings were held that featured videotaped comments by the general council as well as reports by the provincial and by delegates on committee work, and small-group discussions were convened with delegates. A chapter report of approximately three hundred pages was given to each sister. Delegates visited local communities and study guides were given to individual houses. Each sister was asked to evaluate the implementation of chapter enactments at the local level in house chapters. This work, as described by Patricia Walter, OP, was difficult:

> Many women found house chapters were excruciating; local communities were still formed by assignment and were not always "compatible groups." Assertiveness, negotiation, active listening, honest feedback, and consensual decision making were characteristics and skills not highly valued or developed in preconciliar religious life (nor in most women at that time). Often monthly meetings became exercises in politeness or political action; sometimes they were transmogrified into sensitivity sessions, with individuals leaving no doubt about their needs, their hurts and their hates. For some

> women, emotional development and psychological maturity were the necessary first stages of individual renewal; their instability or immaturity had been far less glaring in structured environments.[18]

To comply with the chapter call for a self-study of apostolic commitments, the firm Nelson Associates was hired in the fall of 1968 to conduct a survey of the 2,323 Adrian Dominican sisters. The survey of forty questions gathered information about formation, current apostolic assignments, apostolic preferences, general opinions on the role of the congregation in certain institutions (elementary and secondary schools, colleges, hospitals, and others), and based on one's acquaintance with specific institutions, whether the Adrian congregation's effort should increase or decrease there in the next ten to fifteen years.[19]

Because the Nelson Associates' questionnaire focused on apostolic commitments, not on internal matters of religious life, it was decided that a second survey would be prepared by a select group of six Adrian sisters. This instrument asked seventy-four questions covering a range of topics and sought information about sisters' feelings and opinions about religious life, community life, spirituality, perceptions of God, friendship, religious superiors, change in religious life, perceptions of other sisters in the community, sense of self in the congregation, practices of prayer and liturgy, religious commitment, the distinctive charisms and practices of the Adrian Dominican Congregation, and vows. The survey, conducted in 1969, attained a 98 percent return rate. Every community member received a copy of the survey results, referred to as the Adrian Synthesis, and was asked to write a response to questions concerning the document posed by regional coordinators, and participate in regional workshops to discuss the written responses. Results from these meetings were compiled and submitted to the general chapter delegates.

Session Two, August 4–22, 1969

This phase of the two-year long chapter meeting was largely shaped by the Adrian Synthesis and the report of the Nelson study. Both studies surfaced an emerging conflict of viewpoints during session one of the general chapter and in subsequent house chapters. Most agreed that change was needed but not about what kind and on what basis.

Sociological, psychological, and theological consultants were invited in to help interpret the results of the Synthesis and the regional workshops. The sociologist William C. McCready found "strong support for the concept that the proper role of the superior is as a facilitator of collegial decisions."[20] The psychologist Sister Mary Grace Davis, SND, found mixed feelings about change: wanting it, yet fearing it. She traced this back to the authoritarian culture of the church, which prized conformity and the approval of superiors and bred a fear of failure.

Theologian Benedict Ashley, OP, identified a growing gap, a polarization between two groups of sisters reflected in the survey: those professed more than thirty-five years (20%) and those professed less than thirty-five years (80%). The former tended to have a post-Tridentine theology and spirituality; the latter, a personalist approach. He believed that change was long overdue, and because gradual change had not taken place, radical changes were now necessary and would be more difficult. He urged dialogue between the two groups:

> These two theologies obviously lead to very different attitudes and emphases. At first sight they appear contradictory, and we might be tempted to say that it is impossible for people holding such different views to live together in the same religious community. However, they are not contradictory, and both exist in the Catholic community. If we are to have a really deep understanding of the faith we must somehow bring these two aspects of truth into dialogue with each other, just as we are now bringing Protestantism and Catholicism into dialogue for a mutual enrichment of theological understanding. Is there any place more fitting for this dialogue than in a religious community where the bonds of charity and the search for truth are supposed to be especially strong? In an age of dialogue what better witness could the Adrian Congregation give than to show an example of such a dialogue?[21]

By the end, those gathered in assembly agreed on the following statement: "The Adrian Dominican Sisters, for the love of Jesus Christ, vow to live together in Him a poor, obedient life in celibate community, sharing His love with one another and with all mankind."[22] Seven policy statements were approved, which included the following: "decisions regarding specific ministries were to be made by individuals in a dialogical process which included both the people they served and congregational leadership."[23] Collegiality and subsidiarity were to be practiced by all members, and each person has a role in her own governance. Sisters were invited to choose to retain, elect, or rotate leadership in local communities, and sisters with temporary vows and promises were to be given voting rights.

Between September 1969 and August 1970 house chapters of Adrian Dominicans devoted attention to experimenting with developing collegial practices and structures of self-governance, and different provinces developed different structures—senates, committees, boards.

Session Three, August 10–17, 1970

The final session of the chapter of renewal developed a policy on the government of the congregation. The decision was reached to strive to balance the contributions of the individual for the life and mission of the entire community and the need for collaboration and coresponsibility among individuals when determining and fulfilling the community's mission. Many decisions were made about the basic structural units in the congregation—five provinces, two vicariates (motherhouse and Adrian Dominican Latin American Missions), and the general council. A commitment to affirm diversity of forms at the local level and subsidiarity in governance meant that numerous questions were left to the lowest possible level of community and governance. Experimentation in governance was encouraged. As stated in the chapter enactments: "In the Dominican tradition officials of the Congregation are first among equals. Elected by their peers and guided by the democratic legislation of the Order, superiors of every rank are bound to collegial patterns of government and accountability to their local, provincial, and general chapters."[24]

It was also agreed on that it was premature to form a constitution committee, but a theological foundation was developed for a provisional constitution. There must be a clear commitment to link the consecration of religious life with mission, especially the mission to communicate the gospel and to witness to Christ to those experiencing social and economic hardship. Moreover, their call to obedience was articulated in terms of dialogue:

> For us a like experience of Christian freedom in mutual obedience to the call of the Lord strengthens our confidence in the realization of God's kingdom

> within ourselves and the communication of its message to our fellow men.... Total sharing of our life in love makes visible the Gospel message, and discloses by means of our patient dialogue the mystery of the Father's will.[25]

To return to the central question: What were the aims and obstacles of the chapter of renewal? The aims were to fulfill the mandate set forth by the council in *Perfectae Caritatis* and by Paul VI's *motu proprio Ecclesiae Sanctae* by reflecting on the charism of their founders, experimenting with aspects of religious life, and by means of a general chapter, which included discussions at local and regional levels, to foster the renewal of the congregations. These were the conscious intentions of the group. The unintended results included the personal and communal growth processes of reevaluating and refocusing members' sense of religious identity and mission and their modes of communication. The consequences could be exhilarating. But they frequently produced anxiety and raised fears about change for those who had been trained in what could be called a controlled and regimented social environment. The policy of the congregation did not impose changes generally, but instead honored a diversity of responses, a tactic intended to mitigate the personal conflicts involved. As much as there was a growing commitment to honor personal self-determination and communal decision making grounded in the dialogical process, there was residual evidence of a high percentage of members having more of an external, rather than internal, locus of control, which "may have been an effect of the centralized authority structure in which these sisters lived throughout their lives."[26]

Were there obstacles? The chapter of renewal was a demanding and risky exercise. Were the experiences and expressions of raw emotion, anxiety, fear, apprehension, deep conviction, and conflicting viewpoints obstacles to dialogue? Often they provided an impetus for conversation and growth. But they could and, in all likelihood in the cases of some individuals and groups, did offer occasions to stumble in the conversation. These hurdles provided occasions for more honest communication not only of needs and fears but also of hostility. They became roadblocks only if not addressed, resulting in withdrawal, frustration and, ultimately, even cynicism. No doubt there were disagreements surrounding the directions taken by the congregation at the chapter of renewal and in the convening years. Some chose to stay within the community to work out their disagreements within, whereas others left the community.[27] In the end, the dedication and hard work of the Dominican sisters in reflecting on their history, gathering data about their community, discussing options, and developing and revising proposals prepared them well for what lay ahead.[28]

THE AFTERMATH OF THE CHAPTER OF RENEWAL: REFINING SKILLS, REFORMING STRUCTURES

The closing of the chapter of renewal was not the end but the beginning of a new phase of renewal and experimentation among the Adrian Dominicans, reflective of the experiences of many communities of women religious in the United States during this period of time. On one level the task was to continue to cultivate the personal and collective dialogical skills necessary to bring into clearer focus the congregation's sense of identity and mission. On another level, the challenge was to experiment with structures of government that were consistent with the principles of decentralization and collegial decision making affirmed at the chapter of renewal.

One research tool became an important part of the life of the community in the years after the chapter of renewal. The Adrian Synthesis, first developed and administered in the fall of 1968, was administered three more times until 1981.[29] This data-gathering and communication instrument provided a pedagogical device that helped community members learn about themselves, about their shared sense of identity and mission, and about their community members. The survey and the tally of responses served as useful conversation starters and as an instrument to monitor the reactions of the women religious to their historical evolution. A sample of the questions, sometimes paraphrased, reveals the depth of reflection they could evoke.[30] Some dealt with the sisters' personal life and relationships.

> Has community life been overall rewarding for you? Do you feel that you will be fulfilled as an Adrian Dominican? Are your talents and skills being used well in the Congregation? Do you feel that the sisters in your community are sensitive to your needs? Are there tensions in your local community about proposed changes, ideas among subgroups, or about the exercise of authority?

Some questions were about one's spirituality and sense of the community's identity and mission.

> What is your concept of religious life? Service to the people of God? Consecration to God? Witness to the Christian community? Dedication of self to the works of the Church? Personal growth in full Christian freedom? Community life centered in Jesus Christ? Continued process of conversion? Following Christ in a radical way?
>
> Does radical commitment characterize religious life? What does radical commitment mean? Service to Jesus Christ? Gospel lifestyle? Preaching? Total dedication to church service? Politically revolutionary lifestyle? Religious lifestyle as set forth by the bishop? Is the congregation renewing or improving quickly enough? Are the congregation's goals and objectives adequately established, in need of further clarification, or in flux and relatively inadequate like anything in society?

Questions were also asked concerning the perceptions and attitudes of members about their relation to the church and its authority and about authority and government structure in the congregation.

> Is service to Jesus Christ and an evangelical lifestyle the same as service to the church? Is it consistent with our role as a religious congregation that at times the Adrian Dominicans may have objectives that conflict with those of the official church hierarchy? What is the best description of the function of leadership? To legitimate and encourage the objectives of the Sisters? Facilitate and implement collegial decisions of the community? Manage temporal affairs? Apply divine approval to a Sister's activity by granting or refusing permission? Provide spiritual direction? What is the formal authority in the local community: appointed superior, elected coordinator, appointed administrator, elected contact person, collegial group with elected coordinator, collegial group with volunteer coordinator, collegial group with no coordinator?

The general chapter of 1974 continued the process of renewal and experimentation.[31] Considerable efforts were made to report and reflect on the sisters' experiences since the previous chapter as well as to ponder the central issues facing the community now: How do the members of the congregation understand the signs of the time and the gospel mandate, especially in terms of justice, community life, responsibility, and the need for more open-ended approaches to mission placement?

In 1975 Nadine Foley addressed the national assembly of the Leadership Conference of Women Religious. Her message reflected the experience of her Adrian congregation at the time. She focused on the call of women religious to be diaconal, service oriented in mission and ministry. This impulse was a catalyst in the realization of the freedom of women religious as they sought to respond to the directives of the council: "The experience was painful, rupturing, having repercussions among all segments of the church. To become collegial, to implement subsidiarity, to scrutinize the signs of the times and interpret them in light of the Gospel, and to adapt ourselves accordingly (LG, 4) were processes fraught with risk. But for those who endured, the effort was life-giving and freeing."[32] She elaborated, "the collegial processes of our chapters set aside our authority structures and allowed the spirit to have voice from the sisters themselves."[33] And as a result of these efforts: "we have found our *maturity* as Christian women and have claimed our prerogative of *co-responsibility*."[34]

The participants at the general chapter of 1978 formulated a mission statement, and a new government structure was subsequently developed and put into place at the general chapter of 1982.[35] It is important to appreciate the connection between these two issues: mission and government structure. The congregation was henceforth to be identified in terms of a mission, and congregation government structures were established to promote interaction among the members (participatory decision making) for the sake of mission. A mission group of fifteen to twenty sisters replaced the house community as the basic unit of government. Fifteen mission groups would constitute a mission chapter, which would each have its own elected prioress and delegate, analogous to provinces. The chapter prioresses and delegates from these fifteen mission groups would form the mission council. The chapter prioress along with the general council, the secretary, and the treasurer made up the leadership council, which was chaired by the prioress of the congregation. The general chapter was revised according to this new plan. Common efforts and congregational goals were coordinated and implemented by these six groups acting as parts of a relational whole. Accountability was exercised at the various strata of groups: mission group to mission council to leadership council to general council. Jeanne Lefebvre viewed this new structure as an institutionalization of practices that had emerged over the decade since the chapter of renewal.[36] The new government structure was implemented following the 1978 general chapter, initiating a further phase of experimentation that proved crucial in the subsequent revision of the constitutions.

THE REVISION OF THE CONSTITUTION AND ROMAN RESISTANCE

The chapters of renewal in congregations of women religious, and their subsequent experiments in participatory forms of decision making, led to significant revisions of their constitutions.[37] The Sacred Congregation for Religious and Secular Institutes (CRIS) of the Roman curia was often critical of some of the revised constitutions insofar as they seemed to undermine the traditional model of personal authority within communities of women religious and did not express sufficient deference to papal, curial, and local episcopal authority.[38]

Selected committees of Adrian Dominicans prepared two provisional constitutions, one before the chapter of renewal in 1967 and one during. Both were judged unacceptable by chapter delegates. During the 1974 general chapter, another constitution committee was formed, which devoted itself to monthly meetings to devise a scheme for a constitution drawing on biblical, theological, ecclesial, and Dominican elements and concentrating on the lived experience of members; however, this committee did not draft a document.

At the 1978 general chapter a new constitution committee was formed and a decade later, in 1988, their work was completed.[39] Rather than initiate a new round of consultations with community members, this committee chose to reflect on the written testimonies of members as reflected in general chapter reports and on a compilation of historical and theological documents as the basis for a draft of the constitutions and statutes. They completed their initial draft in June 1980. They then initiated a two-fold process of communication and feedback. On the one hand, the committee sought to disseminate information and to receive input initiated through meetings with all congregation members to provide: (1) a presentation of the proposal and time for study and discussion; (2) specific training in some of the canonical issues involved; and (3) the initiation of a feedback process. In response, the document received widespread favorable reaction, but there were also numerous questions and concerns about matters of substance. Miriam Mullins, OP, and Nadine Foley, as representatives of the constitution committee, requested a meeting in 1980 with Sister Mary Linscott, SNDdeN, who was the member of CRIS charged with overseeing chapters and constitutions of institutes of women religious. At this meeting Linscott explained the procedures to be followed so that Vatican officials could evaluate and offer revisions on proposed constitutions.

In light of responses from community members, a second draft was prepared and distributed in July 1981 for further discussion and feedback. Carol Johannes, OP, the prioress at the time, requested a meeting with CRIS, which was not required but was designed to discuss the documents and explore possible areas of conflict and concern before the general chapter began in February 1982. In the second half of 1981, the draft was sent to CRIS, and an anonymous consultor prepared comments on the document. While commending its style and treatment of the Dominican charism, the consultor raised numerous, substantive questions about juridical, statutory, and semantic issues. On January 19, 1982, Carol Johannes and Nadine Foley met with four representatives of CRIS, including Mary Linscott.[40] This group reinforced the issues raised by the written evaluation. They asked for more emphasis on religious consecration, and it was urged that some material be dropped as inspirational and not constitutional and canonical in character, for example, the first five articles about the identity of the congregation.

In particular, the members of CRIS wanted a clarification of the proposed article 30 that read: "From the Gospel of Jesus Christ mediated through the Church, the authority of the Adrian Dominican Congregation resides in the communion of its members." What does it mean to say that the authority resides in the communion of its members? How does this authority differ from the personal authority associated with office? After the meeting, one of the CRIS representatives indicated that when the document was formally submitted for approval, they would be looking for a statement about obedience to the pope.[41] The constitution committee revised the draft in light of the issues raised and suggestions given by CRIS, just as they had done in response to the recommendations of the members of the congregation. But on certain issues they decided not to revise the text, for example, on the opening "inspirational" material and on article 30.

In February 1982 at the general chapter, the committee presented a revised text, which was well received by the delegates. They reached unanimous agreement about the majority of materials, especially noteworthy in the areas of authority, obedience, and the relationship of the congregation to the universal church, which was a point of contention with CRIS. They agreed to retain article 30, and agreed that obedience to the pope by reason of the vow of obedience was not consistent with the Dominican theology of that vow. They also agreed to add the following article (no. 48):

> The government of the Adrian Dominican Sisters, with its elective offices and participative structures, is the framework within which the authority of the Congregation functions. This authority is subordinate where applicable to lawful ecclesial authority and those in whom it is vested, according to the norms established for pontifical institutes by the common law of the Church.

This article was intended to affirm the conviction of Dominic that the order reflected the universal mission of the church, but not the monarchical structure of governance. The relationship of the congregation to the universal church and the pope's authority was recognized, while still leaving room for discernment of any such exercise of obedience.[42]

Between 1982 and 1998, the constitution committee continued its dialogue with members of their Dominican Congregation, on the one hand, and through the general council of the congregation with members of CRIS, on the other. Based on these meetings, two revised drafts were created during this time. In June 1982, the approved constitution and statutes were submitted to CRIS along with a substantive commentary delineating the rationale for the retention of certain texts that were criticized at the previous meeting with CRIS. These events were taking place during a momentous period with the promulgation of the new Code of Canon Law in 1983 and various papal initiatives on religious orders, followed by a number of collective responses by U.S. women religious to these Roman edicts and declarations.[43]

Archbishop Jerome Hamer, OP, the new prefect of CRIS, in a seven-page letter to the Adrian congregation sent on November 27, 1984, indicated that CRIS was urging a strictly hierarchical model of authority at odds with the collegial model of discernment and decision making proposed in the Adrian constitutions and statutes. The proposed article 31 read: "Congregation leadership is exercised by the General Chapter, the Prioress of the Congregation and the General Council. We govern ourselves in keeping with the principles of collegiality and subsidiarity at every level of the Congregation so that each sister may exercise co-responsibility." Hamer urged that the term *leadership* be replaced by *authority*, and that the article state that authority is exercised by "the Prioress of the Congregation, *assisted by* the General Council." *Collegiality*, in his judgment, meant that "the superior is bound by the decisions of the group." He recommended saying "Our government respects [or 'takes into account'] the principles of coresponsibility and subsidiarity." CRIS also "directed [furthermore] that the Constitution include a statement to the effect that the Prioress or General Chapter 'may give practical interpretations of the Constitutions,' but the Holy See alone is empowered to render authentic interpretations."[44] On the vow of obedience, CRIS wished to define the term in its narrow meaning as the only pertinent juridical meaning: "complying with the directives of those in positions of authority in all matters which pertain directly or indirectly to the Constitutions and Statutes" is the precise "object of the vow."[45]

The general council requested the assistance of the constitution commission in responding to this missive, and the prioress, Carol Johannes, sent a letter in January 1985 to the entire congregation concerning a response, describing the range of issues it raised. Besides making minor semantic changes that were requested, the constitution committee created a process for education and discussion among the members of the community, consultation with other congregations seeking approval of their constitutions from CRIS, and the development of a set of recommendations for discernment in preparation for the 1986 general chapter.

During the spring of 1985 the question was raised among the Adrian sisters, and by other religious congregations as well, whether they should retain their canonical status.[46] Specifically, attention was drawn by Miriam Mullins to the tension in ecclesiological orientations between a juridical approach that emphasized hierarchical authority in contrast to one that was rooted in a theology of the people of God, baptism, and mission. After examining the range of opinions in the community and the options available, Carol Johannes offered the general council's position on the issue of canonical status: "unwarranted ecclesiastical interference" may occur, but "a formal relationship with the official church was still advantageous."[47] Their apostolic mission was worthy of such a recognition by the official church; all their work of renewal, revision of the constitution, and seeking approbation had been in response to the call of the church to renew their dedication to the gospel and to the Dominican charism; "religious life was evolving and the Congregation had a contribution to make" in that process; and finally, "the priority of the council was the protection of the congregation's legitimate autonomy," which "was best served by avoiding confrontational tactics and win/lose situations."[48]

In August 1985 there was a prechapter conference held for delegates and observers. The constitutional committee provided "a theological framework for dialogue." Nadine Foley contrasted the Adrian congregation's approach to authority and obedience "connected with mission and emerging from the presence of the Spirit within each member and the total group" with a traditional hierarchical approach to authority and obedience as enunciated by Mary Linscott from CRIS.[49] Anneliese Sinnott, OP, drew from the analysis of Margaret Brennan, IHM, who contrasted two approaches to religious life: one consecration oriented and one mission oriented.[50] Miriam Mullins examined official statements on religious life in relation to the formulations in the proposed constitution and identified seven critical areas raised in the exchange with CRIS. Four of the seven issues of concern raised at this assembly were collegial discernment and hierarchical authority, "the relation of the Congregation with the Holy See; the Holy See as the authentic interpreter of the Congregation's documents; obedience to the Pope; the internal governance of the Congregation."[51] Summary papers on these contested issues, which delineated possible courses of action, were distributed to those in attendance. Subsequently, position papers were sent to the entire membership of the community. Members were asked to indicate to the constitution committee whether they agreed with proposed responses to the minor issues, and to discuss each substantive issue in mission groups and reach consensus on the suggested response. Results were compiled by early January 1986. The majority wanted to respond to the concerns raised by CRIS in a way that would maintain the articulation of Adrian Dominican life and self-understanding in the proposed constitution, particularly concerning the congregation's relation to the Holy See and to the universal church relative to the issue of the authentic interpretation of the constitution and the locus of authority as stated in the proposed article 30.

The 1986 general chapter convened from February 14 to 28. They agreed to change the section on ministry to indicate that members exercised their ministry "in union with the whole church and in collaboration with the local bishop."[52] On the locus of authority (previously article 30, now 20), the decision was to retain the substance of the previous text on the crucial issues but to refashion the first part. The revised text read: "From Jesus, proclaimed in the Gospel, the authority of the Adrian Dominican Congregation, mediated and affirmed through the Church, resides in the communion of its members." The descriptions of the roles of congregational offices and of the general chapter were in many, but not all, instances revised in accordance with changes recommended by CRIS. The decision was made, however, to insist on "collaboration rather than subordination between the prioress and the rest of the council" and that the term *collegiality* was maintained as the principle of government, not coresponsibility.[53]

On the disputed issues of obedience to the pope and of a consecration-oriented approach versus a mission-oriented approach to the vows, the general chapter carefully crafted a statement that allowed them to maintain their mission orientation and to affirm obedience to the pope within a larger frame of reference. The approved article 21 reads:

> According to the tradition of the Order of Preachers begun by Dominic the Constitution and the Statutes express the manner in which the mission of the Adrian Dominican Sisters is incorporated into the universal mission of the Church.
>
> The approval of the Constitution by the Holy See unites the Adrian Dominican Congregation in fidelity to papal authority.
>
> The ordinary and practical interpretation of the Congregation is made by the General Chapter of the Congregation, when in session, and at other times by the Prioress of the Congregation.
>
> It may be amended by a two-thirds majority of the General Chapter of the Congregation with the confirmation of the Holy See. The Holy See is also consulted on those matters which require authentic interpretation. . . .
>
> The Constitution and Statutes express the essence of vowed life in the Adrian Dominican Congregation and form the foundation of the profession made by each Sister in the vow statement.

In November 1986, the revised constitution and statutes approved by the general chapter in February were sent by Nadine Foley, the prioress of the congregation at that time, to Archbishop Hamer. Her accompanying letter stated that

> all the members of our Congregation were involved in a comprehensive study of the recommendations under the direction of our Constitution Committee. Careful attention was given to every suggestion. . . . We consider it a special sign of the Holy Spirit's activity among us that we were able to achieve universal assent from our members, and subsequently, from the delegates to our General Chapter.[54]

The congregation was notified in December 1986 that the constitution and statues were being sent to the *congresso*, a review committee, which was the next step in the process of approbation.[55]

Nadine Foley received notification from Mary Linscott on April 13, 1987 "that the *congresso* had approved the constitution contingent upon the incorporation of certain amendments."[56] Archbishop Vincent Fagiolo, secretary of CRIS, sent a list of thirty observations on the text. Seven observations dealt with issues of authority and obedience and addressed previously raised issues on which the Adrian sisters had decided not to change their positions, along with two new points concerning the understanding of obedience. On April 27, 1987, Nadine Foley sent a letter informing the members of the congregation of the conditional approval and delineated five key issues of substantial disagreement with CRIS, two of which pertain to this discussion: "obedience to the pope by virtue of the vow of obedience, . . . and the relationship between authority and communion of the members."[57] On the former issue, Foley stated in her letter that the issue appeared "to be one of insuring that in any case in which a sister might receive a personal directive from the Pope that she would be bound to obey it as a consequence of the vow of obedience," which, she reminded her readers, was a view not in keeping with the Dominican understanding of the vow according to the consensus of the congregation.[58] On the latter issue of authority and communion, she recalled the congregation's agreement that "the authority we exercise in our chapters and in our elections derives from the group. We have felt this to be an important concept. It differs from the way authority is exercised in the appointment of the bishop, for example."[59] She reaffirmed the integrity of the process of discernment and decision making that they had gone through: "I urge you to receive this word . . . in the peace that is ours in knowing that the Spirit of God is working creatively and surely among us. I also ask that you reflect upon the issues prayerfully, alone and with others. We need always to keep our mission before us and to weigh all our options in light of the consequences for our mission among the people of God."[60]

The issues of authority based on communion and obedience to the pope remained sticking points of contention when Miriam Mullins and Anneliese Sinnott, representatives of the constitution committee, Nadine Foley, prioress, and Sharon Weber, OP, vicaress, met with Mary Linscott from CRIS. While in Rome, they also met with Damian Byrne, OP, the master of the order, who concurred that CRIS was proposing an understanding of the vow that was not in keeping with Dominican tradition. The same process was used in addressing the contested issues that had been followed in 1985. In June 1987 the constitution committee prepared documents that were discussed with the leadership council in September, then mailed to members. Again, individuals were asked for their comments on nonsubstantive issues. The substantive issues were to be discussed and discerned in the mission groups: obedience to the pope; local authority; authority residing in members. In May 1988 the results from the deliberations in mission groups were compiled. On two of the three disputed issues of substance, concerning the CRIS formulation of obedience to the pope and authority residing in the communion of its members, over 90 percent of those participating (1,042 valid responses and 981 valid responses, respectively) were in favor of the document as written and approved, and requested that the constitution committee draft a rationale based on Dominican tradition.[61]

In August 1988 Nadine Foley was installed as president of LCWR. During that year, LCWR began a new phase in the inquiry of the 1976 task force studying the identity of women religious.[62] For this project Foley wrote a helpful summary description of some of the central changes among women religious in the United States since Vatican II,

> the process of consulting the members once begun has become a continuing feature of dialogue and decision making within the congregations. It is no longer possible to hold a chapter of a religious institute without the consultation of the members. Consultation, in fact, is built into the forms of governance currently being adopted by increasing numbers of U.S. women's

congregations. . . . Processes of consultation, to draw upon the individual and collective experiences of members of religious institutes, have been employed with great expertise by apostolic women religious in the United States. They have been developed through relying upon the competence of their members who have adapted techniques from the behavioral sciences, and who have reflected upon modes of decision making uniquely appropriate to women for eliciting responses from the members. Such processes honor and respect the individual experiences of women religious in the variety of their ministries and the awareness that has developed in carrying them out.[63]

Foley brought the constitution approved by the Adrian congregation to Rome in January 1989 to hand deliver to CRIS, renamed in 1988 the Congregation for Institutes of Consecrated Life and Societies of Apostolic Life (CICLSAL). Archbishop Fagiolo replied in March 1989 for CICLSAL that the changes were acceptable with the exception of the issue of obedience to the pope and the locus of authority in the communion of its members. Drawing on suggestions proposed by Fagiolo, the constitution committee amended article 21 as follows: "The approval of the Constitution by the Holy See unites the Adrian Dominican Congregation and its members in fidelity to papal authority." Article 20 reads: "From Jesus, proclaimed in the Gospel, the authority of the Adrian Dominican Congregation, mediated and affirmed through the Church, resides in the communion of its members according to their respective roles as given in this Constitution and Statutes." With the addition of one word, "individual" before "members" in article 21, the revisions were deemed acceptable, and final approval was sent out on May 18, 1989, postdated to the feast of St. Catherine, April 29, 1989.

Between 1970 and 1989 the Adrian Dominicans were involved in a long process of discernment and decision making on, among other matters, the structure of governance and the revision of their constitution. These were the clear aims of their deliberative process. They utilized the ancient practice of chapters in this endeavor, guided by Christian convictions about collegiality and about the exercise of authority in communion, but now practiced more self-consciously in terms of dialogical procedures—small-group meetings, surveys of community members, formal procedures for reactions and additional feedback resulting in the development of revisions. The challenges faced in the process were less internal among community members and far more often external, specifically occasioned by the interventions of the Roman curia over the proposed changes in structures and over the proposed constitution's emphasis on collegial deliberation in contrast to hierarchical deliberation. These challenges did not become insurmountable obstacles, but did prove to require further clarification of convictions, discourse, and courses of action. In the end, responses to concerns raised by Roman officials did not constitute either concessions or capitulations, but reasoned nuances on selected issues.

Reflecting back on what the Adrian congregation had achieved, Nadine Foley expressed the conviction that their experience in the chapter of renewal, their subsequent efforts to focus on the primacy of mission, and their development of a new constitution were "remarkably compatible with," and even inspired by, the guiding vision and practices of St. Dominic. But no less important, through their own experiences there arose an inner conviction that

> we were endowed with an "inner authority," evident from reflection upon our history. Within carefully drawn parameters for our apostolic endeavors in fields of education, health care and social service we had exercised an extraordinary degree of self determination and achieved acknowledged success for the mission of the gospel.[64]

Foley extolled the importance of "the principle of consultation" exercised not only with all the members of the congregation but also with CRIS/CICLSAL. But she was also clear that there remained considerable tensions concerning how the charism of religious leadership and canonical-juridical authority were to be exercised in relation to the community. The new organizations for governance embodied now in new constitutions offer attempts to move beyond this tension by developing an understanding of the exercise of authority in relation to the community that is not structured according to hierarchical patterns.[65] These new forms and patterns of governance "offer models of ecclesial organization for local parish and diocesan communities and for the church at large. Clearly, what women religious have been about, and continue to assess and evaluate, has been the revitalizing of external form with the interior driving force of the Holy Spirit of which Pope Paul VI spoke. It has been remarkably freeing."[66] This entire experience has been an ongoing invitation to renewed attentiveness and fidelity to the Holy Spirit, "the author of charism and prophecy," in prayer, ritual celebrations, and in carrying out mission. "For religious life, as we women are experiencing it and hoping for it, is a vital symbol of the ecclesia as community in mission in and for the people of God. Perhaps in time to come we will be judged prophetic for having held on to that conviction."[67]

A LINGERING QUESTION

One question has surfaced in communities of women and men religious, just as it has been raised at parochial, diocesan, national, and international levels. How can Catholics envision and promote the effective exercise of authority and leadership by means of participatory forms of governance, especially in the wake of the relentless critique of the abuses of hierarchical and paternalistic authority, on the one hand, and the resiliency of the U.S. culture of individualism on the other? Since Vatican II, various attempts to develop models of leadership that are collegial and consensus-oriented and that implement the principle of subsidiarity and collective discernment are accompanied by diverse and diffused views of authority that have yet to be fully worked out.

In matters of leadership and authority, it appears that the church women want is at odds with the church men have created. According to Miriam Ukeritis, CSJ, and David Nygren, CM, based on their 1992 study of more than ten thousand religious priests, brothers, and sisters, women religious have favored consensual exercise of authority by far greater margins than male religious, who favor a traditional approach.[68] Male leaders are recognized as outstanding for being initiators of new projects, assertive, outspoken, critical of subordinates, and delegators of authority, whereas outstanding women leaders are known for being consensus builders. Women religious by and large are fairly satisfied with their leadership. But the analysts worry that "the hidden side of the satisfaction is that it may signal complacency among membership who, at the same time, find it difficult to influence the direction of the group."[69] Of course, this is leaving to the side the important fact that some congregations of women religious have maintained and staunchly defended traditional forms of authority.[70]

One way the issue is formulated is that there is a need for strong leaders who can articulate a vision reflective of the mission of the foundress or founder of the community that can unite individuals in the community, and that also can generate strategies for realizing its purpose and mission. The alternative collegial and subsidiary use of consensus models of decision making are viewed as having risks. The Nygren and Ukeritis study reports that there is an "increasingly widespread use of consensual processes and team leadership. The findings indicate that, while potentially effective, such approaches can often lead to mediocre management, representing the least common denominator within an organization. Uninformed implementation of consensual methods often paralyzes the visionary leader."[71] This concern has been raised by curial representatives, such as Mary Linscott, who defended a traditional approach to authority for both theological and practical reasons.[72] But it is also raised by advocates of more collegial approaches to decision making in various congregations who ask whether the prophetic character of exercising personal authority and leadership necessarily suffers in collegial, consensual models of discernment and decision making or whether there are prophetic checks and balances that can be structurally set in place to safeguard against the tyranny of the one or of the lowest common denominator of the group.

It is true that prophetic individuals can be members of prophetic communities and that individuals and groups need to be able to call upon one another to risk more radical and demanding forms of witness and mission in the church and the world. But it is also possible that individuals and groups can be shortsighted, misguided, and can fail, and both individuals and groups must fully participate and be responsible as well as be held accountable in this discernment process over the long haul. In the words of Donna Markham, the current prioress of the Adrian Dominican Congregation,

> Majority rule or absolute consensual agreement are not necessarily decision-making styles that will break open the future any more than will authoritarian or dictatorial modes. Too often, consensus has resulted in cautious, untimely and unimaginative action that arises more from what has been familiar than from the eruption of synergistic surprise. [Effective collaborative] leaders [are called upon] to develop modified consensual strategies that leave the door open for the unexpected.[73]

7

Collegiality and Constraint

The Synod of Bishops

The practice of holding synods, originally synonymous with councils, developed in ancient Christianity in various forms.[1] These meetings provide precedents of dialogical practices of collegiality among bishops, collaboration between bishops and theologians, and the consultation of bishops with representatives of the entire people of God. Since Vatican II, the term *synod* has been reserved for the diocesan synod, the topic of an earlier chapter, and the synod of bishops. The practice of the synod of bishops was retrieved and reshaped in light of teachings on episcopacy, collegiality, and communion at Vatican II, and it was established as a permanent institution by Pope Paul VI in September 1965.[2]

The synod of bishops is designed so that representative bishops from around the world can engage one another in conversation about a theme chosen by the pope that merits attention for the good of the universal church. This provides an opportunity for the pope to receive the bishops' advice on this subject, and the bishops, if called upon by the pope, are asked to reach a collective decision about the matter. In the words of the Code of Canon Law: the synod of bishops is "a group of bishops selected from different parts of the world . . . to foster closer unity between the Roman Pontiff and bishops, . . . to assist the Roman Pontiff with their counsel in the preservation and growth of faith and morals and in the observance and strengthening of ecclesial discipline, and to consider questions pertaining to the activity of the church in the world" (canon 342).[3] Although this is neither required nor encouraged, synods can also offer opportunities for wider consultative processes of bishops' conferences and individual bishops with theologians, and with priests, religious, and laypersons representing the entire people of God.

The synod of bishops serves as a symbol of the collegiality of bishops.

Their collegial effort aims at fostering a deeper sense of communion among the local churches in the advancement of the mission of the universal church. No less important, although less explicitly developed in doctrine and in canon law, the synod fosters a fuller realization of the church's catholicity by cultivating mutual receptivity to the contributions of local churches around the world in their common quest for the good of the universal church. These goals are achieved by means of dialogue: bishops speak and listen to one another, deliberate with one another, and collectively reach some advisory judgments and decisions that are conveyed to the pope. The synod of bishops has been widely recognized as one of the most promising instruments of dialogue in the postconciliar church, but it has also been repeatedly criticized for falling short of its promise because of the constraints that have been placed upon it. This chapter will describe these efforts and assessments, following the lead of Thomas J. Reese, SJ, and John G. Johnson.[4]

Paul VI's *motu proprio Apostolica Sollicitudo* established the synod of bishops as a permanent institution and offered an initial description of the various aspects of the synod, which were later elaborated upon in the *Ordo Synodi Episcoporum Celebrandae*, issued in 1966 and revised in 1969 and 1971. Explanations of these procedures are prepared and revised for each synod, and these fill in for lacunae in the law. The practices of the synod of bishops thus have evolved since the time of Vatican II as the participants have gained experience and struggled with the achievements and the limitations of the procedures being used.

Following these norms, there are several different forms for the synod of bishops. Ordinary synods of bishops have been the most common general assembly since Vatican II. They have been convened approximately every four years to address various issues related to particular groups within the church (priests, religious, laity, families) and pastoral problems such as faith, justice, family life, evangelization, catechesis, penance, and reconciliation.[5] Interestingly, neither theologians as a group in the church nor the task of theology has been chosen as a topic for the church universal to ponder at a synod of bishops. These topics have remained the sole province of the Congregation for the Doctrine of the Faith.

The extraordinary synod of bishops is a general assembly convened to address particularly important and timely issues. Since Vatican II they have been rare, and each one has considered primary issues raised at the council (1969, on the collegiality of bishops with the pope and episcopal conferences; 1985, on the twentieth anniversary of the end of Vatican II; and 2001, on the episcopacy). A special synod of bishops can be convened to consider issues of a particular region or nation. The schedule of ordinary synods every four years was interrupted by John Paul II in order to give time to a series of special synods in preparation for the new millennium: Europe, 1991; Africa, 1994; Lebanon, 1995; America, 1997; Asia, 1998; Oceania, 1998; and a second one held in Europe, 1999.

The process of an ordinary synod of bishops provides the best example for the sake of analysis, but reference will also be made to special regional synods held during the 1990s. We will examine the format of the synod in its more recent form, even though revisions continue.[6]

Who participates in a synod of bishops? In ordinary synods, the following five major groups are in attendance: (1) representatives of the Catholic Church of the Eastern rite as *ex officio* members;[7] (2) a specific number of bishops elected by national conferences;[8] (3) bishops elected by the episcopal conferences composed of several countries that do not have national conferences; (4) ten religious men representing religious institutes elected by the Union of Superiors General; (5) cardinals that serve as the heads of the various departments of the Roman curia as *ex officio* members. The pope can add bishops, religious representatives of religious institutes, and expert ecclesiastics not to exceed 15 percent of the total number of participants of the previous totals. Besides these official members of the synod, there are sometimes priests, religious, or laypeople who are invited to attend as expert witnesses, theological advisors, or observers. These latter participants are able to contribute by addressing the assembly and participating in the small-group sessions, but they have no vote. The formula for selecting participants for an extraordinary synod is only slightly different, while it is markedly different in the case of special synods of bishops.[9]

How many people attend the synod? At the last ordinary synod held during the papacy of John Paul II in 1994 there were 244 members and 75 observers. Of the total number of 4,257 bishops in the world in 1994 (2,415 diocesan bishops and 1,842 titular bishops[10]), the number 244 seems quite small.[11] At the synod assembly in 1994 there were 6 oriental patriarchs, 2 oriental archbishops, 6 oriental metropolitans, 36 bishops from Africa, 45 from all of America (4 from the U.S.), 22 from Asia, 42 from Europe, 3 from Oceania,[12] 10 representatives of religious institutes,

25 cardinals from the dicasteries of the Roman curia; 48 members named by the pope.[13] The representatives from the U.S. Episcopal Conference were Cardinal Joseph Bernardin, Cardinal James Hickey, Archbishop John Quinn, and Archbishop William Henry Keeler. Some delegates, like Bernardin, Quinn, and Archbishop Rembert Weakland, were frequently chosen to represent the U.S. Episcopal Conference.[14] Three representatives from the curia were from the United States: Cardinal William Baum, Cardinal Edmund Szoka, and Archbishop John Foley.

What is the duration of the synod of bishops? The synod is often understood as a thirty-day assembly of elected bishops and invited speakers and observers. But in fact the synod process often lasts more than a year. Regularly this has included consultation of delegated bishops with the body of the episcopal conference, theological experts, and representatives of the entire people of God. There has also been room for the formation of study commissions by means of election of members from the synod if a particular topic needed further study.[15]

The synod process includes many levels and stages of dialogue and communication.[16] I will divide the process into two parts: the preparatory phase and the synod assembly. My main objective is to identify sets of conversations that contribute to the formation of formal synodal documents, nine in all, from the first document, the *lineamenta,* which invites those participating to consider the topic, to the ninth, the post-synodal *apostolic exhortation*, issued by the pope. These documents can serve as official markers that indicate the end of one phase of dialogue and the beginning of another. As important as these markers are in highlighting the culmination of one stage in the process of dialogical discernment and decision making and the beginning of another, I wish to draw more attention to the various kinds of dialogue that take place in the processes that lead to and from these documents. Here one should be alert to the dialogue that occurs in committees (especially the so-called General Secretariat of the Synod of Bishops, and the council of the General Secretariat established for a particular synod, but also the drafting subcommittees), in small groups in the synod assembly process, and in the formal communicative procedures (dialogical by extension) that are utilized in full plenary sessions of the synod. Once one has identified the diverse kinds of dialogue in the synod process, one can ponder assessments of the quality of those dialogues, their achievements, struggles, and obstacles.

PREPARATORY CONVERSATIONS

The synod process begins with the preparatory tasks undertaken by the General Secretariat of the Synod of Bishops, under the leadership of a general secretary. The General Secretariat works in conjunction with the council of the General Secretariat, which has fifteen members—twelve prelates who are elected by the members of the previous synod near the end of their assembly (usually three from each continent: Africa, Asia, Europe, and the Americas; Australia and Pacific Islands are included in Asia, and the Americas are considered one continent) and three chosen by the pope. U.S. cardinals who have served on this council include Cardinals John Krol of Philadelphia (beginning in 1982), Joseph Bernardin of Chicago (beginning in 1984), and James Hickey of Washington (in 1990). The council of the General Secretariat serves from the end of one synod to the convocation of the next synod assembly.

The pope chooses the topic for a synod, after considering the suggestions offered by the bishops attending the previous synod and in consultation with the presidents of episcopal conferences and the general superiors of religious institutes. Topics are chosen based on four criteria: (1) the topic has a universal character and is not simply local or regional; (2) the topic is pastoral in nature with a firm doctrinal basis; (3) the topic is a contemporary issue on which there is a sense of urgency, that has the ability to excite "new energies, and movements in the church towards growth"; and (4) a topic that can be addressed within the allotted time.[17]

Once a synod devoted to a particular topic has been announced, the first set of conversations is initiated by the general secretary of the General Secretariat as he consults with experts, often from Roman universities, about the topic of the upcoming synod. This results in the production of the *lineamenta*, from the Latin term for outline, prepared by the General Secretariat, which is the first document, sometimes about five pages, outlining the topic and posing questions intended to foster discussion and generate responses from bishops' conferences, the Roman curia, and the Union of Superiors General. The council of the General Secretariat is asked to review this document and suggest revisions when needed. The final document is approved by the pope and promulgated.

The second set of conversations follows the reception of the *lineamenta*. Bishops' conferences are invited to develop a written response to be sent to the General Secretariat, but individual bishops can also offer their own responses. Most conferences in Europe offer responses as a conference, while in the United States individual bishops from specific dioceses submit responses. The bishops' conferences and individual bishops are free to and often do consult with experts and members of the community as they see fit, but this is neither mandated nor recommended. Depending on the topic, bishops may choose to consult not only with theologians and philosophers, or researchers and intellectuals in the fields of sociology and history, but also people with expertise in pastoral ministries, priests' councils, pastoral councils, religious education, or seminary formation.[18] Discussion may take place in the Catholic press and theological journals, and pre-synodal symposia are sometimes convened by the curia.

Episcopal conferences or individual bishops prepare written responses to the *lineamenta* that are supposed to be confidential but do not always remain so. Episcopal conferences and individual bishops have a short time (sometimes from six to nine months) to prepare their responses to the *lineamenta*, which determines the amount of time available for bishops to converse among themselves and with their diocesan officials, theologians, and representatives of the faithful. The *lineamenta* have to be translated into foreign languages, which further limits the time for consultation and deliberation, sometimes dramatically.[19] Besides responses from episcopal conferences and individual bishops, there are responses from the Roman curia, the Union of Superiors General, and others who were asked to offer comments.

A third set of conversations takes place between the General Secretariat and the council of the General Secretariat concerning the input received from the various participants. This deliberative process results in the production of the *instrumentum laboris*, the working paper, which is the second document drafted by a group of experts in the General Secretariat. Cardinal Jan Schotte, CICM, who served as general secretary between 1985 and 2004, has described the process. The fifteen-member council is "usually split . . . into three language groups so that they can discuss more openly. Each group returns with a set of observations and proposals that in general assembly we work on together and produce something. In drafting the working papers, we work with some experts in the [General Secretariat's] office, but it is the council who reviews the drafts, makes suggestions, and decides what to change. Then the final draft goes to the Holy Father for approval."[20] This document is intended to promote and sharpen further conversation as the synod process continues. During this phase the experts in the office of the General Secretariat and the council members have a difficult assignment: to read through, comprehend, distill, categorize, select, prioritize, and organize topics from the responses to the *lineamenta* in preparation of the *instrumentum laboris*.

Once the *instrumentum laboris* has been revised by the council and approved by the pope, it is sent to delegates and made public approximately six to nine months before the time of the synod assembly in Rome. This offers the occasion for a fourth set of preparatory conversations among those in bishops' conferences or between bishops and representative theologians and other sectors of the church, usually initiated by the episcopal conferences or individual bishops, but occasionally by theologians and other sectors of the church. As is the case with the *lineamenta,* episcopal conferences or bishops representing an individual diocese are asked for written reports on the *instrumentum laboris*. Once again, most conferences submit a response as a conference, while bishops in the United States have always sent in individual responses.

DIALOGICAL PROCEDURES DURING THE SYNOD ASSEMBLY

The next phase of dialogical discernment and deliberation begins with the convocation of the synod assembly. One bishop (sometimes more than one) is appointed by the pope as president-delegate of the synod who serves as chair during the assembly.[21] Another bishop is chosen and appointed by the pope as the relator, the main reporter, during the synod on the given topic. If there is more than one main topic at a given synod, a second relator is appointed. The relator has the crucial role of being the moderator and facilitator of the synod dialogue, and he is charged with fostering consensus as the synod proceeds. He prepares a third document, which summarizes both the *instrumentum laboris* and the written responses to this document by episcopal conferences and individual bishops and is to be sent out at least thirty days before the synod. When the synod convenes, it begins with the relator summarizing his own report (*Relatio ante Disceptationem*).

The first significant set of communicative actions that occurs during the synod assembly is not dialogical and has frequently been criticized for dissipating the desire for further dialogue during the assembly.[22] During the pontificate of John Paul II, each bishop was allowed, but not required, to address the entire synod assembly for eight minutes on the topic of the synod assembly as representative of an episcopal conference or as an individual bishop, with no follow-up dialogue allowed. These statements had to be oral, and were not to be written and distributed to the assembly, nor publicly released, although some did make their statements available to news organizations. The *Ordo* specifies that delegates express "the common opinion of their brothers in the episcopate on the [synod] topic of discussion. . . . [T]he delegates are to make sure that, after explaining the majority opinion, they also explain to the Assembly the minority opinion held by the members of their Conference."[23] Reese reported that "the number of initial speeches at synods has been steadily increasing: 77 in 1969, 82 in 1971, 86 in 1974, 141 in 1977, 162 in 1980, 177 in 1983, and more than 200 in 1994."[24] The first two weeks of the synod assembly have been devoted to these eight-minute speeches. These practices have recently been slightly modified,[25] but the widespread criticisms of the detrimental effects of these speeches on the advancement of the dialogical dynamic of synods, which will not be examined here, suggests that far more radical alterations are required.[26] After these statements have been given, the relator synthesizes them in a fourth document (*Relatio post Disceptationem*), which is intended to serve as the basis for ongoing discussions.

The first major set of conversations then takes place for approximately one week, in smaller language-group meetings (*circuli minores*), which were introduced into the synod process in 1969. At the 1994 synod there were fourteen groups: "four English, three French, three Spanish-Portuguese, two Italian, one German and one Latin (made up primarily of East Europeans)."[27] The average size of the small groups that year was twenty-three persons. Each group elects a moderator, who conducts and monitors the discussion to make sure that everyone stays on topic, encourages everyone's contribution, and prioritizes topics and limits time, if needed. In addition, prefects of the curia attend each group.[28] In the final week of the synod, each small language-based group prepares the fifth document of the synodal process, which offers proposals or recommendations on the topic, the result of their collective deliberation.

The second major set of conversations during the synod assembly takes place among members of a drafting commission that receives the reports of the small groups. This drafting commission is composed of the president-delegate of the synod, the synod relator, the special secretary of the synod, group relators, and any assistants appointed by the president. Through a process of dialogical deliberation they prepare a sixth document. They select, combine, and edit the propositions, recommendations, and proposals put forward by the small language groups. Some do not survive the scrutiny and are filtered out.[29]

The third major conversation during the synod concerns this sixth document, a set of propositions submitted to the entire assembly for debate, then voted upon: *placet* (yes), *non placet* (no), and *placet iuxta modum* (yes, with amendments or reservation). Two-thirds approval is needed for acceptance. As Reese observes: "Ultimately the quality of the commission's work is judged by whether it can get agreement from the assembly. . . . Consensus is often achieved by dropping controversial recommendations."[30] There is no minority report given; the various *modi*, amendments, and reservations are often dropped by the drafting committee instead of being incorporated into the final document, but these are included in the documentation accessible to the pope when he receives the recommendations.

During the closing days of the synod, the delegates prepare a final document. Initially this took the form of a final report, a seventh synod document. In 1971 two final reports, one on justice and one on priesthood, were prepared. In 1974, the bishops were unable to come to an agreement on a document on evangelization and instead agreed on a list of propositions offering recommendations and proposals that were submitted to the pope. On that basis the pope prepared an apostolic exhortation on evangelization, *Evangelii Nuntiandi*. The 1974 practice of reaching a consensus on a set of propositions as the new seventh document to be submitted to the pope became the standard practice thereafter. The pope is free to use or not to use the materials in the propositions as he chooses (e.g., in 1977, there were thirty-four propositions on catechesis; in 1980, forty-three on family life, 15 percent of which are directly evident in the pope's apostolic exhortation *Familiaris Consortio*).[31] At the 1977 synod, the bishops prepared a Message to the People of God on the theme of their assembly, the eighth synod document, which has likewise become standard practice. Before 1980, the commission to write the Message to the People of God was appointed by the secretary, but since then the commission has been chosen by election among the delegates. (The Extraordinary Synod of 1985 did not follow this pattern; rather, the bishops chose to issue a final report.)

The agreed-upon list of propositions is given to the pope, who issues, about a year after the synod takes place, a ninth synod document, a post-synodal text known as an apostolic exhortation on the topic discussed by the synod. The apostolic exhortations that have been issued after the ordinary synods are as follows: *Evangelii Nuntiandi* (1974), *Catechesi Tradendae* (1977), *Familiaris Consortio* (1980), *Reconciliatio et Paenitentia* (1983), *Christifideles Laici* (1987); *Pastores Dabo Vobis* (1992); *Vita Consecrata* (1996).

IN PRAISE OF SYNODS OF BISHOPS

How is one to assess the dialogical accomplishments of the synod of bishops? It is best to begin by recalling its intended aims and then to evaluate it according to those standards. Although *Lumen Gentium* did not introduce the idea of the synod of bishops, it provides the doctrinal frame of reference on episcopacy for the synod's subsequent establishment. Specifically it speaks of bishops being in communion with other bishops around the world and with the pope, and the need to promote hierarchical communion by acting collaboratively (21, 22). Episcopal collegiality is likewise to be fostered both "in the mutual relations of individual bishops to particular dioceses and to the universal church," and it asserts that the authority of the college of bishops exists in union with the pope (22, 23). Pope Paul VI, in his opening address at the last session of the council, said that he was establishing the synod of bishops for the purpose of consultation and collaboration with the pope when it seems opportune out of concern for the church. Moreover, he acknowledged that it will be helpful for the daily work of the Roman curia.[32] In his *motu proprio Apostolica Sollicitudo,* which established the synod of bishops as a permanent institution, he specified these objectives.

> From its very nature the Synod of Bishops has for its purpose to give information and counsel. It may also have deliberative power when this is given by the Sovereign Pontiff, to whom it shall pertain in such case to ratify the decision of the Synod. 1. The general purposes of the Synod of Bishops are: a) to maintain close union and collaboration between the Sovereign Pontiff and the bishops of the entire world; b) to see that direct and true information be given on situations and questions relative to the internal life of the Church and to the action which the Church should take in the world of today; c) to facilitate the concordance of views, at least on essential points of doctrine and on the modalities of the life of the Church. 2. Its special and proximate purposes are: a) to establish an exchange of useful information; b) to give advice on the questions for which the Synod has been convened.[33]

Based on *Lumen Gentium*, *Apostolica Sollicitudo*, *Christus Dominus* (5), and the 1983 revised Code of Canon Law, the intended goals of the synod are to promote ecclesial communion and collegiality among the bishops, including hierarchical communion with the pope as the bishop of Rome, in the service of the universal church.

The catholicity of the church is not explicitly raised as a criterion with respect to the synod of bishops, but it is no less important than communion in specifying the specific character and requirements of episcopal collegiality. When *Lumen Gentium* asserts that "all the faithful scattered throughout the world are in communion with each other in the Holy Spirit," there is an affirmation of the gifts and riches of the diversity of God's people in the universal church (13). From this assertion it follows that "in virtue of this catholicity, each part contributes its own gifts to other parts and to the entire church, so that the whole and each of the parts are strengthened by the common sharing of all things and by the common effort to achieve fullness in unity" (13). As a result, the diversity of traditions of local churches ought not undermine ecclesial communion, but contribute to it. This is reaffirmed later in the document when it states:

> It has come about through divine providence that, in the course of time, different churches set up in various places by the apostles and their successors joined together in a multiplicity of organically united groups which, while safeguarding the unity of the faith and the unique divine structure of the

> universal church, have their own discipline, enjoy their own liturgical usage and inherit a theological and spiritual patrimony. . . . This multiplicity of local churches, unified in a common effort, shows all the more resplendently the catholicity of the undivided church (23).

It can be concluded that, although catholicity is not mentioned as an aim or norm in the doctrinal and canonical statements devoted to the synod of bishops, it is implied in these same texts when there is specified the need for accurate and reliable information about local churches and for the mutual exchange of such information. What is not addressed are the kinds of learning, the mutual pedagogy, that can take place among the bishops and by the universal church in the synod context based on contributions from local and regional churches to the gift of catholicity.

One of the central challenges and complications involved in evaluating synods of bishops pertains to the basic terms that have been introduced for assessment. There is general agreement that communion and collegiality are two key measurements for evaluating the work of synods of bishops, and that the synod of bishops has as a matter of fact abundant practical and pastoral impact in these regards. However, there are disagreements about how these terms are to be understood and explained theologically and realized in the doctrine and practice of the church. As a result, the question has been raised from the beginning whether the definition of the work of the synod of bishops limits its collegial character and authority in relation to papal authority and in relation to the power of the curia. Are communion and collegiality advanced through honest, and perhaps at times contentious, dialogue on the issues of universal concern and pastoral urgency, or are there subtle and not-so-subtle ways in which compliance with papal and curial interpretations of contested theological issues stifles genuine communion and collegiality born of dialogue? These questions must remain open for discussion, but for purposes here, concentration will be especially on evaluating the quality of the dialogue involved and the limitations and frustrations entailed therein.

Some of the most positive evaluations of the work of the synod of bishops have come from Cardinal Jan Schotte. He has stated unequivocally that through the synod of bishops, "the Holy Spirit generates collaboration, co-responsibility, and *communio* among the bishops with the effect that the whole church is served."[34] The aim of the synod of bishops is "not to devise solutions for regional, national or local problems, but to provide assistance to the Holy Father in the common responsibility for the universal church." This takes place through an exchange of information, which fosters mutual enrichment, but this communication also reflects the mystery of "communion through a diversity in unity, [and] that mystery is the principle governing all its workings. At this level the particular Church meets the universal Church in the mystical yet always fruitful exchange of charity, God's own life of communion."[35] In this work of communion in diversity, the cultural riches of a particular church or national or regional church should not impede communion by hindering the recognition and reception of the universal apostolic faith, nor should the culture of a particular church be forced upon the universal church.

Pope John Paul II, who served as a participating member of the synod of bishops before being elected pope, enthusiastically affirmed in 1983 its importance in promoting collegiality.

> The synod of Bishops, which the Church received as a legacy from the Second Vatican Council, is indeed a great good. We are more convinced of this each day. Every session confirms us in this judgment.... The Synod of Bishops is a singularly excellent sign of episcopal collegiality to the Church—and is, in a peculiar way, its effective instrument. Perhaps this instrument could be made even better. Perhaps the collegial responsibility could be more clearly manifest in the Synod. Nevertheless it is fitting to observe that the Synod in that form in which it now exists and operates . . . offers the greatest service to the Church.[36]

One of John Paul II's statements about communion has particular relevance for the work of the synod of bishops:

> "[C]ommunion" is a living and dynamic reality; it is the "community" entering into reciprocal communication. This "communion" is, consequently, the communication of the goods of the Church among the faithful, and especially among the bishops. The Church makes its universality and its catholicity become real both in its unity and its diversity.[37]

Schotte draws the relevant conclusion for the synod of bishops: "as collegiality functions better among the bishops, so will communion within the entire Church be fostered. Moreover, the very unity of the Church will become ever more profound and assure an ever fuller expression of collegiality."[38]

John Paul II and Cardinal Schotte were certainly justified in their overall positive assessment of the synod of bishops at the level of doctrinal principle and pastoral significance. Beyond their general commendation, positive evaluations can be made of the concrete conversational dynamics introduced in both the preparatory phase of the synod and the actual synod assembly. In the preparatory phase, the *lineamenta* and the *instrumentum laborum* have been drafted in light of dialogical deliberations among various groups—the members of the General Secretariat and their council, episcopal conferences, and any conversations bishops engage in with theologians and with other sectors of the people of God. In particular, there is an extremely valuable dialogue-like dynamic that unfolds in the sequence of issued documents and responses. The release of the *lineamenta* invokes written responses by the delegates. Their responses contribute to the formation of the *instrumentum laboris*. This public document in turn elicits further written responses. These responses are incorporated into the summary report, prepared by the general synod relator, which initiates the formal dialogical procedures used during the synod assembly. At the level of principle and practice, there are valuable communicative dynamics at work here, not unlike the feedback loop that was used by the U.S. bishops in the preparation of their pastoral letters. Similar positive evaluations can be made of the small-group discussions, conversations in the drafting commissions, and formal deliberations in full assembly as themes, specific issues, and ultimately proposals are advanced and voted upon.

CONSTRAINTS

The positive evaluations by John Paul II and Cardinal Schotte must be weighed in relation to concerns and criticisms raised about the dialogical procedures used during these synods. As Archbishop Rembert Weakland observed:

> The Synod of Bishops was to be a way of bringing more awareness of the life of the local Churches into the discussion of the whole Church. For

> many reasons . . . it has never reached its full potential. The methodology is clumsy; real open dialogue and discourse on the deeper issues affecting the Church do not have a way of surfacing. . . . [T]he Synod of Bishops is a good idea, but has yet to be brought to its full potential.[39]

Thomas Reese has gone so far as to claim that when American bishops arrived in Rome in December 1997 for their special synod they became a part of "a synodal structure that has developed over the last 30 years into an episcopal torture chamber."[40] I will restrict my treatment to criticisms of constraints imposed on dialogical procedures.[41]

One wide-ranging criticism is that the authority of the synod of bishops, in their exercise of dialogical discernment and deliberation, has been unduly restricted insofar as it has been constituted as derivative of and in service to papal authority. Instead of establishing the synod of bishops as a means of exercising the collegial authority of bishops as full and proper sharers in their own universal pastoral ministry with the bishop of Rome, it has been formed with limited authority and with the sole mandate to assist the pope in his universal pastoral ministry.[42]

To clarify the issues involved in this complaint, it is helpful to recall that when the bishops at Vatican II were discussing ways to continue their involvement in governance in the church, Melkite patriarch Maximos IV recommended to the bishops at Vatican II the synod-of-bishops structure of the Eastern churches, "the supreme . . . executive and decision-making council of the worldwide church." In particular, he emphasized that "all the Roman departments must be subject to this."[43] Before the bishops at the council were given an opportunity to address openly and explore fully the options available to them concerning the establishment and nature of the synod of bishops, Pope Paul VI in his *motu proprio Apostolica Sollicitudo* established the synod of bishops as a permanent institution, but understood in a particular way.

By this act Paul VI narrowed the authority and structure of the synod of bishops relative to the suggestion advanced by Maximos IV and concentrated on its advisory, not decision-making, role, thus making clear that its authority comes from working with and at the discretion of the pope. This decision by Paul VI asserted the authority and power of papal primacy in the synodal structure, and by so doing the synod bishops are required to function more under Peter than with Peter.

In addition, the way Paul VI defined the synod enabled the Roman curia to function as an extension of the papacy in the synodal process unchecked by participating bishop delegates. Canon law established the synod of bishops as one of the advisory groups to the pope in the church alongside the college of cardinals and the curia. But the curia has exercised authority in the activities of synods above all through the work of the General Secretariat of the Synod of Bishops.

Some believe it would have been better for the bishops at Vatican II if they had been given the opportunity to define the synod of bishops first and foremost in terms of and as an expression of the college of bishops, and then in its abiding relation to the pope. One must keep in mind that the synod of bishops has not yet been recognized as an authoritative body representative of the entire college of bishops. The relation between the synod of bishops and the college of bishops has not been sufficiently addressed theologically, canonically, or in practice.[44]

One crucial issue is that the synod of bishops has been restrained by doctrine and canon law so that it can function only as a consultative body, advisory to the pope, and not by its nature decision-making. To say that the synod of bishops has functioned only as consultative since Vatican II is historically accurate. However, it was not restricted by canon law to be a consultative-only body, because a given pope could use his prerogative and make one, some, or all of the synods during his pontificate decision making and not simply advisory. However, if a pope were to give one, some, or all synods decision-making authority, this would still be an exceptional situation and the pope would be granting the synod this authority, and he would be required by canon law to ratify any decisions they made.[45] If this deliberative authority were granted to synods in this manner, it would be exceptional, not doctrinally and canonically normative.[46] This formulation of the role of the synod must be openly discussed at some future council and, some would argue, remedied.

A second, related critical issue concerns the unresolved issue of the collegial character of this body. Does the synod of bishops provide only an opportunity for the cultivation of affective collegiality among bishops or does it allow for genuine collegial acts of judgments and decisions to be made?[47] This topic also bears, in an analogous manner, upon the work of episcopal conferences, as has been previously indicated. It is widely agreed that synods of bishops have provided valuable occasions for the cultivation of collegial affections among bishops around the world. But to what extent, if any, can their collaborative process, and specifically the votes they give in support of a collective document or set of propositions, be considered official collegial acts of judgment and decision intended to serve the good of the universal church. Cardinal Schotte defended the work of the synod of bishops as a genuine expression of collegiality, while simultaneously strictly delimiting the synod's authority relative to the pope's.[48] The disputed issue raised here concerns the extent and limits of episcopal collegiality operative in the synod of bishops.

Although the synod of bishops is not in the canonical sense decision making but consultative, it has in the past approved official statements that were publicly released for the entire church. The most widely recognized document might be the statement "Justice in the World" from the Second General Assembly of the Synod of Bishops, issued in 1971.[49] But, as previously noted, in 1974 when the synod of bishops attempted to address the issues of evangelization, the bishops were unable to reach a consensus concerning their final document. They chose not to develop their own instrument of communication to the church universal, but instead chose to prepare propositions, recommendations, and proposals for the pope. This further accentuated their advisory role in relation to the pope. The pope used these propositions in the generation of the apostolic exhortation *Evangelii Nuntiandi*. Subsequently this practice became standard procedure. In 1977 the synod also prepared a Message to the People of God, which has likewise became standard practice. Reaching a final consensus at a synod by means of voting to approve a final report or a set of propositions does not constitute the exercise of a full episcopal act of judgment and decision making as occurs at an ecumenical council, but it must be viewed by its nature as some form of expression of a collegial action. Nevertheless, the shift from reaching an agreement on a complete final report to reaching an agreement about a set of propositions is a further diminishment of an already restricted collegial action, conceding greater authority to the pope rather than struggling to live up to the mandate of episcopal ordination to exercise their teaching and governing authority together with the bishop of Rome for the good of the universal church.

At a practical level, this transition to approving a set of propositions results in the relinquishment to the pope and curial officials, who are involved in the preparation of apostolic exhortation, the role of fashioning their own discrimination and deliberative interpretations of the most important results from the synodal process. In the end, the pope has chosen what advice from the synod of bishops to use and how to frame the issues. What this means is that the pope's particular theology and the dominant school (or schools) of theology operative among curial officials who are enlisted to help craft the apostolic exhortation shape the interpretation of the results of the synod of bishops. John Johnson, who has written an in-depth analysis of the new Code of Canon Law as it pertains to the synod of bishops, believes that "the less the participants saw themselves as engaged in preparing independent documents to issue to the world and the more they accepted their function of communicating information and advice to the pope, the more smoothly the assemblies have operated. . . . [T]he assemblies appear to have begun working best after 1974, after they abandoned the hope of drafting their own documents."[50]

Johnson may well be correct that the synod has been running more smoothly and working best with a curtailed assignment. It is no doubt easier to reach a two-thirds consensus about a set of propositions than to work through deeper, sometimes contested, issues in a document that is constructed to reflect collective judgments and decisions. But in fact this limitation can be viewed as a diminishment of the role of dialogical discernment and decision making exercised by the synod of bishops.

Beyond the pivotal issues raised about papal authority relative to the synods of bishops is the related criticism, repeatedly heard, concerning the role played by representatives of the Roman curia in the synod of bishops. One can acknowledge in principle that the synod of bishops has been established to bring together representative bishops from around the world to deliberate about important matters for the good of the universal church. In keeping with that objective, it is fitting to have the heads of the various departments of the curia as *ex officio*, nonvoting participants in the synod. The complaint, however, is that the Roman curia controls in numerous ways both the synod process and the results.

At the level of practice, the Roman curia has been accused of exercising influence and control over the synodal proceedings at every step of the process. Complaints are frequently made that the curia has stifled and steered the synodal discussions through the general secretary of the General Secretariat or the participation of curial officials from the General

Secretariat by their involvement in the drafting committees of the *lineamenta* and the *instrumentum laboris*, and other synod documents as well.[51] When these documents are criticized for not framing issues well and accused of forcing the topics into preconceived schemas, it is curial influence that is usually blamed.[52] It is often heard that certain topics, concerns, and recommendations included in written responses to the *lineamenta* have been ignored or filtered out in the original draft of the *instrumentum laboris* by the General Secretariat of the Synod or by the council as they edited the original draft.[53]

Cardinal Schotte maintained that these documents, strictly speaking, were the product not of the Roman curia but of the council of the General Secretariat of the Synod of Bishops chosen by the bishops themselves at the previous synod to guide this process. While this distinction may be valid in principle, in the concrete these documents have been drafted by staff members of the General Secretariat, a curial department, and the council of the General Secretariat often reflects or can be influenced by the concerns and mind-set of the curia. Moreover, the prefect of the Congregation for the Doctrine of the Faith, who has served as a member of the council of the General Secretariat and exercised oversight on doctrinal matters at issue in synod documents, has played "a key role" in the process, perhaps to the point of "overshadowing the general secretary and the council."[54]

The complaint of curial interference is also raised in terms of the small-group meetings during the synod assembly. As previously noted, small-group moderators are instructed to encourage everyone's participation, but to keep the discussion on topic. Still, certain kinds of issues germane to the synod topic raised in small groups have been squelched by curial officials participating in the groups. During the synod on the family in 1980, Archbishop John Quinn spoke in his small group of pastoral issues raised by Paul VI's encyclical *Humanae Vitae* banning the use of birth control in marriage. He was criticized by prominent curial cardinals for doing so, and several bishops from mission countries likewise reported that they were told by the Cardinal Prefect of the Propagation of the Faith not to raise these issues in the small-group discussions during the synod.[55] At that same synod, John Paul II said that controversial issues such as artificial contraception could be raised, but that there was no possibility of discussing changing the church's position on these issues.[56] In the synod of

Asian bishops, emphasis was given to the need for greater collegiality and decentralization, and in these contexts the word "subsidiarity" was invoked. The general secretary told the chairmen of the small language groups that they were not to use this term because it was a secular or sociological concept.[57] Likewise, during the 2001 Extraordinary Synod of Bishops on episcopacy, concerns were raised by a significant number of people about exaggerated centralization threatening collegiality throughout the synod, and these concerns were addressed by specific recommendations and propositions. But in the process of compiling and editing these proposals, these critical issues became invisible in the documents. Some reporters drew the conclusion that no serious concerns had been raised about centralization and collegiality during the synod.

By being satisfied with reaching agreement about a set of propositions, rather than a final report, the bishops have failed to move the conversation and the deliberative process forward as far as possible during the time allotted. Are contrasting points of view and conflicts in the church being avoided, excluded, and repressed in the preparation of synod documents and in the small-group discussions? The decision to vote on a set of propositions rather than prepare a final report suggests that the bishops are content to identify areas of general agreement, rather than attempt the harder task of sharpening contested issues, confronting conflicts, and negotiating agreements with representatives of different positions. At ecumenical councils, by contrast, bishops are required to work through, as far as time allows, the positions of diverse theological schools of thought, contrasting points of view, and unresolved issues. At ecumenical councils the process of dialogical disputation and deliberation has consequently been embedded in the agreed-upon documents as a reflection of the living tradition of the church at work. In the current practice of the synod of bishops, dialogue is impoverished by only requiring a two-thirds majority vote on a set of propositions. Even in this process of compiling and editing the propositions submitted by the small groups in the interest of maximizing affirmative votes, propositions often lose their strength, concreteness, and sharpness.[58] The comments of Edward Schillebeeckx are relevant here:

> Although it is not easy to devise another method of working, the procedure followed at the synod makes everything a matter of numbers. There is no discussion. Arguments are put on the table, but they are never discussed, nor

> is their strength tested. An argument which is advanced a great many times wins through in the end, no matter what its intrinsic value. An argument of high intrinsic value which is only presented once immediately gets discounted. The result of all this is that the editorial committee is given a position of virtual omnipotence. Although they are bound by the speeches in debate they can influence the final version quite fundamentally, above all depending on whether or not they take account of minority views.[59]

The problem is aptly described by Thomas Rausch: "the synod process resembles a funnel which filters the diversity of opinions expressed on the floor down to the acceptable common denominator. But it is the lowest common denominator which emerges. The problem is compounded when the editorial board doing the filtering is not composed of members of the synod itself, but of conservative advisors appointed by the Vatican. . . ."[60]

One further set of issues merits attention. Should not the advancement of the collegiality of the bishops at the synod of bishops be combined with an obligation to work collaboratively with theologians and consultatively with lay women and men representing the entire people of God during the various phases of the synod process?[61] In reality, collaboration and consultation take place frequently, if inconsistently. By doctrine and law they are freely permitted and not ruled out. Why, however, are these practices neither explicitly encouraged nor required? This gaping omission in *Apostolica Sollicitudo*, the *Ordo*, and the Code of Canon Law provides one more negative symbol of the conflict between a centralized hierarchical ecclesiology and a genuinely dialogical one.

During the preparatory phase, it would be advantageous for the good of the universal church if societies of Catholic theology around the world, and in the absence of such societies, distinguished theological faculties representing diverse cultures and theological traditions, were invited by the General Secretariat as a matter of course to hold congresses on the topic of the synod. Their charge would be to bring to the surface the important points of consensus, emerging trends, and disputed questions among the diverse schools and traditions of Catholic theology on the chosen topic, and to identify the relevant ecumenical and interreligious issues at stake. It would likewise be appropriate for delegate bishops and episcopal conferences to be required to invite the advisory councils of episcopal conferences and the diocesan pastoral councils and diocesan priests' councils to deliberate with them about the *lineamenta* and the *instrumentum laboris*.

There needs to be wider participation of theologians and lay women and men at the synod assemblies. Currently delegate bishops are not allowed to have theologians accompany them as collaborators and advisors during the month-long synodal process, as they can at ecumenical councils. This restriction runs contrary to the deepest impulses operative in the synodal practices of the church.[62]

Let me close this chapter with the classic phrase cited by Archbishop John Quinn in his discussion of the synod of bishops: *"Quod omnes tangit, ab omnibus tractari et approbari debet,"* which is translated, "What touches everyone should be discussed and approved by everyone."[63] Realizing the promise of the synod of bishops as an instrument for communion and catholicity requires not only that bishops work collegially with one another in concert with the bishop of Rome but also that this collegiality be combined with collaboration with theologians and broad consultation with representatives of the entire people of God during every phase of the synod process.

8

Differentiated Consensus, Imperfect Communion

Ecumenical Dialogues

It is impossible to imagine the number of ecumenical dialogues that have taken place over the last century. Such efforts have occurred during previous centuries. In fact, one could go back over the entire history of Christianity and discover countless attempts at such dialogue by individuals and groups who eventually removed themselves or were expelled from one community and forced to form another over matters of doctrine and practice. Imagine the discussions with Gnostics, Arians, and Pelagians. Yet, during the last century, there have been unprecedented concerted efforts to engage in dialogue in the interest of promoting unity by Roman Catholic, Orthodox, and Protestant Christians.

When people think about ecumenical dialogues, they often imagine a formal gathering of scholars and church leaders representing two or more Christian churches in a room around a large table.[1] These structured conversations have taught all the participating churches much about dialogue. As important as these are, they are but one form of dialogue associated with the ecumenical movement. Wider spheres of ecumenical dialogical interaction include times of prayer, fellowship, and collaborative action supporting the social mission of churches. These sites of ecumenical encounter are at least as important as scholarly exchanges, and one might argue that they have always been or are now becoming even more important.

Still, formal ecumenical dialogues have provided the most widespread object lesson in dialogue among all Christians, including Roman Catholics. What can be learned about the topic of dialogue in the church from those who have participated in ecumenical dialogues? Numerous statements have been prepared to offer guidelines and reflections on ecumenical dialogue. For historical reasons this chapter will begin with an analysis of three methods of ecumenical dialogue developed by the Faith and Order movement, which became a part of the World Council of Churches. These methods will be identified in statements from Faith and Order Conferences and from the Faith and Order Commission of the World Council of Churches. This will be followed by a consideration of certain documents issued by officials of the Roman Catholic Church alone or with other churches. It is important to note in passing that the World Council of Churches and its commissions, such as Faith and Order, bring together representatives of Orthodox and Protestant churches to discuss topics of mutual importance and to address collectively these topics, but any statements on which they reach consensus have the authoritative weight only of a recommendation to their respective churches, which may or may not be officially received. By contrast, statements from the Second Vatican Council or other councils, and different modes of teachings by popes and by Vatican curial offices, have varying degrees of authority for members of the Catholic Church. The different kinds of texts treated in this chapter testify collectively to the aims and methods of ecumenical dialogues as well as provide reflections on the animating desires and the obstacles and frustrations encountered in the process. They provide steps toward a phenomenology and hermeneutics of ecumenical dialogue.[2]

THE FAITH AND ORDER MOVEMENT AND THE WORLD COUNCIL OF CHURCHES

Those individuals who paved the way for the first Faith and Order Conference in the early twentieth century developed what has been called a comparative approach to ecumenical discussions about beliefs and practices of the churches. In 1910 the General Convention of the Protestant Episcopal Church in the United States adopted a proposal to form a commission that would plan a conference concerning questions pertaining to Faith and Order "and asked . . . all Christian Communions throughout the world which confess our Lord Jesus Christ as God and Savior . . . to unite with us in arranging for and conducting such a conference."[3] The following year's report on the plan and scope of a World Conference on Faith and Order specified the conference's basis, goal, method, and conditions: "The Conference is for the definite purpose of considering those things in which we differ, in the hope that a better understanding of divergent views of Faith and Order will result in a deepened desire for reunion and in official action on the part of separated Communions themselves. It is the business of the Conference, not to take such official action, but to inspire it and to prepare the way for it."[4] The working agenda for such a conference was further developed in the 1913 paper, "A First Preliminary Conference."[5]

Herbert Kelly, an Anglican priest from Kelham, England, founder of the Society of the Sacred Mission, who was familiar with the 1911 and 1913 reports, presented a paper in 1915 entitled "The Object and Method of Conference" on Faith and Order. He had been encouraged by Robert Gardiner, one of the original planners, to address the topic.[6] Kelly wrote:

> the ulterior object of Conferences, as of all sincere thought and discussion, is to ascertain the truth. . . . Our search should be directed not so much to discovery of agreements, as to an appreciation of differences. . . . A Conference will be helpful if its members honestly desire to receive as well as to give help. At least this far, that they desire to learn what others are thinking, i.e., what their ideas or convictions are, what exactly they mean by them, and how they apply them. . . . We must be prepared to face new questions, not only in regard to the views of others which we have not studied, but even in regard to our own, however carefully we may have thought them out.[7]

In order to reach these objectives, the discussion must be "more like a conversation than a debate, where, free from the rules of debate, questions can be asked and re-statements and explanations made. When a position has been stated, and criticisms have been offered, if any progress is to be made, we want opportunity to hear how far the original speaker will admit his position was affected."[8]

Kelly proposed that this kind of discussion is possible only if participants avoid hurling insulting descriptions at one another, such as heretical and orthodox, narrow-minded and latitudinarian, idolatrous, emotional, or dogmatic, for these only fuel controversy. On the other hand, he was convinced that one can be too polite. The ability to express criticism without sowing bitterness can be a sign and test of the mutual trust established in dialogue. One should aspire to unity, but not at the expense of one's convictions. One's views can nevertheless "undergo development in two ways:

(a) we may say that the convictions remain valid, but are less complete, less universally applicable and all-sufficient, than we supposed them to be; (b) on the other hand, we only express the same thing in a different way if we say that our convictions remain, but that our conscious realization of them was incomplete."[9]

In order for a conference devoted to bringing diverse Christian communions together to be effective, he suggested three guidelines: there must be leisurely discussions, abundant time for exchanges, and respites so that participants can develop and modify their views. He was convinced that the most valuable work at such a conference would go on in informal discussion, "in the lobbies and smoke-rooms rather than in full-dress debates." He proposed a small conference so that a genuine and honest discussion could take place and papers could, optimally, be circulated beforehand. He also showed a wise sense of the time needed for attaining agreement. "'What time should be allowed for the reconciliation of opposing convictions?' . . . We ought not to be unprepared for the real answer, 'Perhaps one, and possibly two, generations.' Few of those who go to Conferences holding firmly the convictions and habits of a lifetime can modify them very seriously."[10]

Kelly ended by offering a set of rules for the proposed conference. Since to change attitudes and opinions requires prolonged reflection, one must have more realistic objectives. Participants should explain their own positions and seek to understand the positions of the other to the best of their ability: "a better mutual understanding may allay a sense of irreconcilable opposition" and "may suggest . . . new ideas and possibilities for further consideration."[11] He suggested that such a conference should be composed of two parts. First, statements would be delivered by representatives of one church tradition followed by questions and discussions about the statements. Second, a chair would guide "a friendly conversation, so that a speaker may be at liberty to restate or amend explanations which have not fully expressed his meaning."[12] There should be a significant interval between the first and the second part for reflective thought. "In discussion the inquirers are at liberty to point out inconsistencies, difficulties, or objections, which seem to them involved in the views of another. But, in accordance with the courtesy of debate, it should be clear that these are put as inquiries with a view to learning how the representatives answer the difficulties: they should not be put as with an implied assumption that they cannot be answered."[13] If any reunion of the Christian churches is to take place, Kelly confessed that "we must recognize that we ourselves are powerless, and that God alone can give us grace to find and accept that unity which He desires. That can only be done by prayer. . . ."[14]

Kelly's lecture offered no formal policy statement on the upcoming inaugural ecumenical assembly. However, his commitment to a dialogical method, marked by a spirit of generosity and honesty in exploring the differences between Christian churches reflects the earliest phase of the Faith and Order movement.

The First World Conference of Faith and Order held in Lausanne, Switzerland, in 1927,[15] launched this comparative method of dialogue in terms of this aim: "to consider the things wherein we agree and the things wherein we disagree." "The Conference . . . is emphatically not attempting to define the conditions of future reunion. Its object is to register the apparent level of fundamental agreement within the Conference and the grave points of disagreement remaining; also to suggest certain lines of thought which may in the future tend to a fuller measure of agreement."[16] Seven topics were treated: (1) the call to unity; (2) the gospel as the church's message to the world; (3) the nature of the church; (4) the church's common confession of faith; (5) ministry; (6) sacraments; and (7) the unity of Christendom and the relation among existing churches.

A plenary session with all the members was devoted to each topic, and each topic was then discussed in sections with more than one hundred members. Some sections divided into subsections to discuss the assigned topic. A report was drawn up and voted on in the section meetings, and subsequently voted on twice in plenary sessions. Common statements of agreement were made—which some would later criticize as abstract and vague—about the call to unity and the church's proclamation of the gospel to the world. But when it came to reports about the nature of the church, the confession of faith, ministry, and the sacraments, differences prevailed.

The comparative approach to dialogue used in this conference created a safe zone for representatives of various churches to become acquainted with one another. Participants with antithetical confessional convictions met and witnessed to their own faith heritage with one another. The personal and social wounds inflicted during the originating disputes, which were made more severe by years of separated existence and mutual animosity, were spoken of again. Whatever its limitations, and many were subsequently expressed, this conference achieved a major breakthrough by allowing participants the opportunity to confront and openly discuss with new generosity, honesty, and humility conflicts that had been collectively handed on for generations. This afforded a sign of hope. The same comparative method was used ten years later at the Second World Conference on Faith and Order held in 1937 in Edinburgh, Scotland, and at the First Assembly of the World Council of Churches in 1948 in Amsterdam, where the effort was made to come to grips with the "deepest difference" among Christians—the contrast between Catholics and Protestants.

For all the hope unleashed by this new effort, there were those who complained that these dialogues offered nothing more than idle talk: "an international exchange of views organized at great expense, a noncommittal encounter between theologians from various countries, which may well stimulate and foster theological thinking, but leaves no traces in the lives of the various churches."[17] That there are no guarantees that conversations among theologians and church leaders will have any impact on the living dialogue of faith has been a concern voiced ever since. No less important was the growing anxiety about the heightened awareness of differences between the churches and the lack of movement toward genuine union.

At the Third World Conference on Faith and Order, held in Lund, Sweden, in 1952, now a part of the recently formed World Council of Churches, there was a concerted effort to change the method of dialogue by reorienting the aim.

> We have seen clearly that we can make no real advance toward unity if we only compare our several conceptions of the nature of the church and the traditions in which they are embodied. . . . We need to penetrate behind our divisions to a deeper and richer understanding of the mystery of the God-given union of Christ with his Church. We need increasingly to realize that the separate histories of our churches find their full meaning only if seen in the perspective of God's dealing with his *whole* people.[18]

"As we have come to know one another better our eyes have been opened to the depth and pain of our separation. . . . The measure of unity . . . must now find clearer manifestation." Lukas Vischer describes the difference in this way: "Whereas up till then the churches had stood confronting one another, now a common point of view had been achieved which gave the necessary direction to their conversation."[19] This new common point of view did not mean denying past divisions and offenses, but required searching for mutual obedience to God in order to form an ecumenical future through conversion, mutual forgiveness, and an enlarged vision of this broken past in light of the future opened up by God.

This second form has been called a christological method of dialogue. The final report from Lund provided a frame of reference to answer why "A faith in the one Church of Christ which is not implemented by acts of obedience is dead. There are truths about the nature of God and His Church which will remain forever closed to us unless we act together in obedience to the unity which is already ours. We would therefore earnestly request our Churches to consider whether they are doing all they ought to do to manifest the oneness of the people of God."[20] The new challenge was to respond in obedience to the one confession of Christ in ecumenical dialogues and to the church of Christ's mission to the world.

One could call this a shift to an obediential method of dialogue wherein each group and member was required to be more deeply receptive and responsive to the work of God in the common aspirations and movements of the group as it articulated a way into the future. One could also reasonably call it a theocentric approach to dialogue, or a trinitarian approach, but, reflective of the theological currency of mid-century, a christocentric orientation was emphasized. Whatever one calls it, this new approach fostered a common biblical and christological orientation that was more alert to the hermeneutical issues involved "in terms of the different 'language' and thought-forms concerning the subject under discussion."[21]

This new phase of dialogue was marked by a sense of penitence, of standing under the Lord's judgment for not being fully obedient. If the comparative method sought to create a space for the burdens of past divisions to be spoken about and come into clearer light so as to be understood, the new christological method demanded mutual obedience to God. Different groups had to listen and learn from one another through these dialogues and strive to articulate their common Christian beliefs and hopes for the future in ways that honored the pain and struggle of the past, while adumbrating a new, more catholic, more genuinely apostolic, and more purified, holier form of church unity. As the question clarified, it became posed this way: how could the communion of churches be promoted while recognizing the genuine diversity that exists? This marked a crucial transition in the dialogue.

One way of charting the effectiveness of the christological method of ecumenical dialogue is to examine the formal documents that have resulted from the use of this method in multilateral and bilateral dialogues. One of the most important examples is the multilateral statement of Orthodox, Protestant, and Roman Catholic churches on *Baptism, Eucharist, and Ministry* (BEM), the so-called Lima document, issued in 1982. Two bilateral statements also merit recognition: the *Final Report* in 1982 of the Anglican and Roman Catholic International Commission (ARCIC I) and *The Joint Declaration on Justification* in 1998 by the Lutheran World Federation and the Roman Catholic Church. These documents are the result of disciplined dialogue of church leaders and theologians who developed a new way of stating basic beliefs and practices in the service of the cause of Christian unity, without denying the past or undermining differences between traditions. No less important than the process of generating these three documents has been the corresponding effort to promote ongoing dialogue among wider circles within the churches about these joint statements. All sectors of the churches have been invited to react to these documents. Where did they recognize their own faith in the joint statements? Can these documents be received as a statement of their own faith? If problems surfaced, what were the obstacles to recognition and reception? In response to this formal process of enlarging the circles of dialogue to garner reactions to these joint statements, there have been efforts by the working groups that generated the original statements or their designated heirs to develop further "elucidations" or "responses" to specific criticisms raised, and in some cases revisions of the original documents, which initiated a new phase of the dialogue. All of this bears witness to the patience and organized exertion of energy required for genuine, fruitful dialogue.

A third, contextual approach to ecumenical dialogues can be traced all the way back to the Lund Conference held in 1952, though it was not until the 1960s, 1970s, and 1980s that those participating in ecumenical dialogues began to address these issues explicitly. This transition was influenced in part by the growing attention being given in biblical studies to the diversity of theologies, liturgies, and church polities in the New Testament churches. Simultaneously, more representatives from Latin America, Africa, and Asia, that is, people from the south and so-called third world regions, became active in the World Council of Churches and in particular in the work of the Faith and Order Commission, which had been initiated by people from the north and first world contexts. As a result, the aim of ecumenical dialogue shifted to give more attention to cultural and social factors that affect the reception of the gospel and to social justice issues pertaining to poverty, class, race, and gender. In comparison with the second method of dialogue, one could say that the third method invited a new kind of obedience to the voice of God in the culturally and politically marginalized, which required new commitments to advance the social missions of the churches and the inculturation of the gospel in non-Western contexts. Also noteworthy were the fuller representation of Eastern Orthodox churches at the World Council of Churches beginning in 1961 and the involvement of representatives of the Roman Catholic Church in the World Council of Churches after Vatican II as guests and speakers, and later in the formation of a joint working group. The Roman Catholic Church became a member of the Faith and Order Commission of the World Council of Churches in 1968.[22] A further, and central, catalyst for a contextual approach to ecumenical dialogue during this period of time was the increasing significance of the women's movement.

This third approach to dialogue came into sharper relief after the 1960s, but social and cultural dimensions of the ecumenical movement had always been a focal point within the Life and Works wing of the World Council of Churches, and as a result they were not far from the surface throughout the history of the Faith and Order wing and their collaborative work in the World Council of Churches. From the First Assembly of the World Council of Churches in 1948, cultural and social issues received considerable notice, beginning with the issues of women and Jews, the abuse of power and technology, and economics and politics. At the Third Faith and Order Conference, in 1952, contextual issues surfaced that were identified at the time as nontheological factors influencing ecumenical discussions of differences in the practice of worship: "In considering our differences . . . we have been constrained to ask whether they spring, wholly or in part, from social, cultural, and other factors." This led to the judgment that "a new line of approach . . . may help the Churches to see that many of the differences in ways of worship are not bound up, as has been thought, with irreconcilable dogmatic differences, but may co-exist in the one Church."[23] Cultural traditions can and do positively affect the expression of faith and spiritual traditions, but as people are sinners, corruption can also take place here.

> It must be emphasized that . . . political and social factors operate not merely to postpone re-union, but frequently contribute to hinder evangelism and to damage the internal life of individual Churches. Thus within the same Church there are often differences of idiom between congregations recruited from different social classes. . . . [O]ne cannot neglect the many unhappy examples within Churches of discrimination practiced on grounds of class, economic level, politics, and race. When these are continued to the present or actually introduced *de novo*, existing divisions are not only hardened, but Churches are split on occasion into additional fragments.[24]

In the Constitution on the Commission of Faith and Order accepted at Lund in 1952 one of the commission's functions is identified as follows: "to study questions of faith, order, and worship with the relevant social, cultural, political, racial and other factors in their bearing on the unity of the church."[25]

One could argue that the World Council of Churches from its inception in 1948 espoused and fostered a contextual approach to ecumenical dialogue responsive to the diversity of pressing social needs, while the Faith and Order Commission of the World Council of Churches and particular World Conferences on Faith and Order remained committed primarily to using the christological method of dialogue in an effort to reach greater areas of agreement among participating churches. Member churches were reaping the benefits of the christological method of dialogue in multilateral and bilateral dialogues; this method served well the enlargement of the circles of ecumenical dialogue to include more representatives of the Orthodox, the new participation of Roman Catholics, and over time the increasing involvement of Pentecostals and evangelicals in the dialogue. Simultaneously, over the next three decades, women, people from the Southern Hemisphere, especially those from poverty-stricken regions of the world and from situations of racial and ethnic conflict, and those affected by the cold war, the culture wars, and the burgeoning tensions between religious civilizations made their mark on the shape of ecumenical dialogues. What were first designated at Lund in 1952 as nontheological issues affecting worship throughout the rest of the century became increasingly considered in terms of their theological status and implications. The problems of racism and sexism became central ecclesiologically as members asked how the ecumenical circles of dialogue had to be enlarged to include participants from underrepresented groups, and as racial and sexual discrimination became a self-conscious topic that demanded its own contextual model of dialogue.[26]

THE ROMAN CATHOLIC CHURCH ON PROMOTING CHRISTIAN UNITY

Individual Catholics promoted ecumenical dialogue during the modern period, but they were viewed with suspicion, and in fact their efforts were condemned by Pope Leo XIII in 1896 and Pius XI in 1928.[27] The Decree on Ecumenism, *Unitatis Redintegratio*, issued in 1964 at the Second Vatican Council marked a major turning point for Catholics on the issue of ecumenical dialogue. The word *dialogue* came into currency at the council when the participants addressed the relations of Catholics to other Christians, members of non-Christian religions, those involved in nonreligious traditions, and those in the world.[28] Not unlike the comparative method of dialogue espoused at the inaugural World Conference on Faith and Order, the Decree on Ecumenism described ecumenical dialogue as an exchange between experts from different churches aimed at explaining "the teachings of their communion in greater depth and bring[ing] out clearly its distinctive features" (4) so that one can "become familiar with the outlook of separated churches and communities" (9). Also like the Conferences on Faith and Order and the Faith and Order Commission of the World Council of Churches, the decree said that the success of ecumenical dialogue required a thorough presentation of doctrine and the rejection of a false irenicism (11). A real, "though imperfect, communion" among Christians and Christian communities inspires the promotion of Christian unity through ecumenical dialogues (3, 4). Love of truth, charity, and humility are to be combined in this dialogue. The council advanced the doctrine that in such dialogues one must be mindful that there is "a hierarchy of truths," since doctrines "vary in their relation to the foundation of the Christian faith," which can open the way so that "friendly rivalry" among members of different traditions "will incite all to a deeper realization and a clearer expression of the unfathomable riches of Christ" (11). Especially noteworthy was the council's recognition that ecumenical dialogue has a bearing on the church's call to ongoing reformation and renewal in terms of addressing deficiencies in morality, church discipline, and how church teachings are formulated (6). As a result, it was acknowledged, ecumenism requires interior conversion, a confession of sins against unity, as a part of the ongoing purification that needs to take place in the church as a whole (7). These latter themes are consistent with the christological method of dialogue that was introduced at the Lund Conference, and so one may say that in the Decree on Ecumenism both comparative and christological methods of dialogue were affirmed.

The connections the decree made between dialogue, conversion, and church purification, reformation, and renewal have become increasingly important, especially with the teachings of Pope John Paul II, as will be explored in more detail below. The importance of penitence in ecumenical dialogues was a note sounded earlier at the First World Conference of Faith and Order in 1927: "God wills unity. Our presence in this Conference bears testimony to our desire to bend our wills to His. However we may justify the beginnings of disunion, we lament its continuance and henceforth must labour, in penitence and faith, to build up our broken walls."[29] The theme of penitence became especially pronounced at the Lund Conference:

> Penitence involves willingness to endure judgment—the judgment of the Lord to whom has been given the power to sift mankind and to gather into one the scattered children of God. We await His final triumph at the end of history. But, in God's mercy, tokens of judgment which are also calls to a new and active obedience come to us in our day also, here and now. Surely we cannot any longer remain blind to the signs of our times and deaf to His Word.[30]

Even against this larger backdrop it was still deeply moving that Pope Paul VI at the opening of the second session of the Second Vatican Council in September of 1963 spoke of the problem of the division among Christians in the following manner: "If among the causes of this division any fault can be imputed to us, we humbly beg God's forgiveness and we also ask pardon from the brethren who feel that they have been offended by us." This statement made a deep impression on Protestant observers (and on many Jews who longed for an apology from representatives of the Catholic Church too), and these new seeds of conversion took root in the Decree on Ecumenism.

It is important to recall that Paul VI, in the first encyclical of his papacy, *Ecclesiam Suam*, issued in the same year as the Decree on Ecumenism, further advanced the insight emerging at the council about the dialogical character of all of the church's relations both internally and externally. Dialogue, he states, has its origin "in the mind of God," who initiates prayer, revelation, the "dialogue of salvation" (70), and thereby establishes the universal character and significance of dialogue. He proposes dialogue as one important method, among others, for the church's apostolic relation to the world. He states more explicitly than the documents of Vatican II the dialogical character of the church's internal identity and relations with God (in terms of revelation, prayer, liturgy). However, like the council, Paul VI accentuates the church's external dialogue in the evangelical mission of the church, and in ecumenical, intercultural, and interreligious dialogues. In the words of the encyclical, "the Church must enter into dialogue with the world in which it lives. It has something to say, a message to give, a communication to make" (65).

Seeking to show a way between stubborn prejudice in holding on to older expressions and pursuing peace at the expense of risking the loss of differences, the encyclical urges that "we must adopt a way of life of the most humble people, if we wish to be listened to and understood. Then, before speaking, we must take great care to listen not only to what men say, but especially to what they have it in their hearts to say. Only then will we understand them and respect them, and even, as far as possible, agree with them" (87). Reminiscent of the statement made at Lund, the encyclical ends by speaking about obedience; but instead of emphasizing obedience to God among all those in the churches engaged in dialogue, the emphasis is on obedience to authorities in the internal dialogue in the Catholic Church. "This desire that the Church's internal relationships should take the form of a dialogue between members of a community founded upon love, does not mean that the virtue of obedience is no longer operative.... [T]he very exercise of authority becomes, in the context of this dialogue, an exercise of obedience, the obedient performance of a service, a ministry of truth and charity." The contrasting vices are "independence, bitter criticism, defiance, and arrogance." These "completely vitiate dialogue, turning it into argument, disagreement, and dissension—a sad state of affairs, but by no means uncommon. St. Paul warned us against this when he said: "Let there be no schisms among you" (115, citing 1 Cor. 1:10).

In the aftermath of Vatican II, Catholics began to initiate and actively participate in numerous bilateral dialogues. Because of the church's international and national institutional structures, they were able to sustain bilateral dialogues on many fronts simultaneously. In 1966 Paul VI met with Archbishop Michael Ramsey of Canterbury, initiating the Anglican–Roman Catholic dialogue, and in 1967 with the patriarch of Istanbul, inaugurating a new phase in Orthodox and Roman Catholic dialogue. Subsequently dialogues began with Lutheran, Methodist, and Reformed Churches and more recently with Baptist, Disciples of Christ, Pentecostal, evangelical, and Mennonite communities. In 1968 the Catholic Church joined the World Council of Church's Faith and Order Commission and in the United States, the National Conference of Catholic Bishops joined the National Council of Churches of Christ and the Faith and Order Commission.

During this period, two formal documents were written to address the topic of ecumenical dialogue. These merit special attention because of what they say about the aims, methods, and possible struggles of such dialogues. The "Working Paper on Ecumenical Dialogue" of the Joint Working Group between the World Council of Churches and the Roman Catholic Church was issued in 1967.[31] This document describes the aims in terms of discovering the truth, growing together in fellowship, and finding areas of convergence. Convergences are horizontal by being based on agreement about common formulas and vertical insofar as they are attained by commitment and service. Unity or full communion is not the aim of these dialogues, but an exchange that allows churches to cooperate, to bear joint witness, "to obey the Lord whose will it is that they should be one so that the world may believe." Anything can become important in these dialogues. One does not know beforehand what will be the most decisive or the most interesting; this is revealed in the course of the dialogue. Because dialogue is a spiritual endeavor and not an academic exercise, certain conditions are required: purification of heart, genuine love of others, loyalty to one's own church. These character traits should entail avoiding the two enemies of dialogue: "Monologue [which] does not pay due attention to the *other* person in his otherness. And false broad-mindedness, [which] is a failure to show oneself as one really is." Loyalty to one's own church must be combined with a concern for church renewal that rejects "theological rigidity, conservatism (clinging to unimportant forms), [and] a refusal to reconsider anything. . . ."[32] On the personal level, one must be open to other people and their reasons, trying to listen and understand and avoid the power dynamics of the group or individuals. On the spiritual level, one must be open to God's Spirit working in this process to bring conversion and repentance. On the practical level, one must be cooperative, neither competitive nor seeking converts. The document ends with advice about the practice of dialogue: be patient and trust in the efficacy of dialogue, experiment with language that will clarify disagreements and agreements, contextualize historically controversial points, give priority to what is held in common, especially the scriptures as means and source of knowledge.

The Secretariat for the Promotion of Christian Unity, established on Pentecost in 1960 by Pope John XXIII, issued "Reflections and Suggestions Concerning Ecumenical Dialogue" on August 15, 1970.[33] This text was prepared by the secretariat with broad consultation with members of other churches, and ecclesial communions not formally recognized by the Vatican as churches. Although no special juridical authority was granted to this statement, it was sent to episcopal conferences to guide them in their work. It addressed many of the topics treated in "Working Paper on Ecumenical Dialogue." The aims of ecumenical dialogue were identified: "discern the common elements in their different ways of approaching the revealed mystery of Christ and of his Church" (2); "give common witness" (3); respond to what the Lord expects of them in their mission to the world and in the internal life of the communion (4). In sum, "ecumenical dialogue is . . . striving for a more complete communion between the Christian communities, a common service of the Gospel and closer collaboration on the level of thought and action." The ultimate aim is "the fullness of unity that Christ wishes."

Like the 1967 "Working Paper on Ecumenical Dialogue," this document speaks of doctrinal bases of dialogue, but instead of concentrating on revelation, this statement speaks of the spiritual riches held in common by the baptized: Word of God, life of grace, faith, hope, and charity; the mystery of salvation mediated through their respective churches; the call to deeper fidelity. Six conditions for dialogue are enumerated: (1) attitude of sympathy and openness; (2) equality at one level is affirmed, without denying differences and inequalities, and the need for reciprocity and mutual commitment; (3) theological and practical competence of participants; (4) an ability to present doctrine in an informed manner (cf. loyalty in the previous document) without either overstating or minimizing, mindful that there is a hierarchy of truths, and with the critical hermeneutical skills needed to use language suitable to advance the dialogue; (5) cognizance of legitimate diversity within the church's unity; (6) willingness to follow practical procedures and have a genuine confidence in the efficacy of dialogue.

This statement differentiates various elements in the method of dialogue. At a general level dialogue includes the exchange of ideas, comparing divergent ideas, and research on shared positions, by which new aspects are brought to light. Ecumenical dialogue in particular requires identifying important tenets held by the other and articulating the position of one's own church "in a constructive manner, putting aside the tendency to define by opposition, which generally results in certain positions becoming overstressed or unduly hardened. This is a purifying process; the warping from which our respective theologies suffer can only be corrected at this price."[34] One's method must contribute to a constructive synthesis, deeper insight, and new perspectives. Although both the 1967 and the 1970 documents discuss various forms of ecumenical dialogue, the latter describes a far greater variety of settings and kinds.

In keeping with Vatican II, Pope John Paul II affirmed forcefully the importance of dialogue as a central category for understanding the church. Like the council and Paul VI, he concentrated on the church's external dialogues, that is, the church's dialogue with those outside the church (other Christians, other religions, other worldviews, "the world"), while giving limited attention to the importance of internal dialogue among members within the church. Arguably John Paul II's most important achievement on the topic of dialogue is the teaching he developed about the connections between dialogue, conversion, and repentance. Building on Paul VI's "method of dialogue" and drawing on the 1983 synod of bishops' discussion of penance, John Paul II proposed in his post-synodal apostolic exhortation that "the church in fact uses the method of dialogue in order to lead people . . . to conversion and repentance."[35] This line of argument was further developed in his 1994 apostolic letter paving the way for the jubilee year, *Tertio Millennio Adveniente*, and in his 1995 encyclical on ecumenism, *Ut Unum Sint*.[36] Both documents called the church, which, as Vatican II taught, "is at the same time holy and always in need of being purified" (*Lumen Gentium* 8), to repentance for past failings and affirmed that dialogue provides a means for conversion and reconciled unity.

Speaking of ecumenical relations, *Ut Unum Sint* teaches that "dialogue serves as an examination of conscience" not only for individuals but for communities. Thus, "not only personal sins must be forgiven and left behind, but also social sins, which is to say the sinful 'structures' themselves which have contributed and can still contribute to division and to the reinforcing of division" (34). The implication of this statement is not drawn out in this document but was developed by John Paul II in other public statements: ecumenical dialogue fosters repentance for personal and collective sins of the past that have contributed to division in the church and should foster statements of lament, pardon, forgiveness, and reconciliation. *Ut Unum Sint* goes on to say that ecumenical dialogue serves as "'a dialogue of conversion,' and thus, in the words of Pope Paul VI, an authentic 'dialogue of salvation'" (35). Thus, dialogue opens a possible way to find deeper levels of truth that can be held in common through comparing different points of view and disagreements, and in the process the prospect of fuller communion and reconciliation is opened up. This was the apex of John Paul II's reflection on ecumenical dialogue, which began with the personalist insight that "dialogue is an indispensable step along the path *toward human self-realization*, the self-realization both of *each individual* and *of every human community*" that ends with "the new task . . . of receiving the results already achieved" (28, 80).[37]

FAITH AND ORDER COMMISSION OF THE NATIONAL COUNCIL OF CHURCHES

One of the most thoughtful reflections on ecumenical dialogue was issued in 1989 by a bilateral study group formed by the Faith and Order Commission of the National Council of Churches, which included Roman Catholic, Protestant, and Orthodox participants. This group devoted three years (1984–1987) to an examination of the experience of national and international bilateral dialogues.[38] The result was a list of thirty-four findings on ecumenical dialogues grouped under several headings: aspects of conversion, the nature of unity, what constitutes the faith and order of the church, and future prospects. This document identifies two previous periods in the work of dialogue: the initial period of discussing the issues that divided the churches (recalling the comparative method), followed by a period of finding commonalities and consensus building (the christological method) that resulted in the multiplicity of bilateral statements and the Lima document. The group came to the conclusion that now is the time for a new agenda, "for proceeding to the reception of these results and for proposing common action based upon this new level of ecumenical agreement."[39] This text reflects the growing attention, since Lausanne in 1927 and Lund in 1952, given to the process of personal and ecclesial repentance and conversion that takes place through ecumenical dialogues.

> Like every conversion, ecumenism requires that we allow for the possibility that God may speak to us not only directly but also through others; we must be prepared to admit that the Word of God may come to us through our partners in dialogue. Ecumenical dialogue should be approached in the same way as we approach prayer: ready to have our hidden sins and blindnesses exposed, ready to be shown that God's truth and goodness are always greater than we had imagined. (no. 2)

This conversion results in an enlarged vision of faith, a deeper commitment to Christ, and a fuller appreciation of how the diverse traditions reflect the great Tradition, which is the saving message of the gospel.

Two aims of ecumenical dialogue, unity and consensus, receive special attention in these findings. Numerous issues are raised that bear upon them, for instance, the fact that doctrinal development has received limited treatment in terms of both the study of the original events that led to church division and in the generation of ecumenical statements. But one of the most "problematic and paradigmatic" topics concerns efforts to arrive at consensus statements through ecumenical dialogue. What constitutes such consensus? How does consensus allow for diverse interpretations and diversity in practices? And is compromise reached merely for the sake of unity? The final finding reads:

> The quest for Christian unity relies on a process where answers can be discovered only through the painstaking, and at times painful, process of dialogue. . . . Ecumenists have come to realize that ecumenical questions are shaped by a variety of social, cultural, geographical, and demographic factors; consequently, ecumenical questions are raised today in ways quite different from their classical dogmatic formulations. Thus, ecumenists have come to ask: Is the search for Christian unity, like Christianity itself, basically a pilgrimage?[40]

SEARCHING FOR UNITY, LEARNING FROM CONFLICT

The previous sections have analyzed some of the most important statements about ecumenical dialogues written during the twentieth century. In light of these documents, what are their intended aims?[41] There is general agreement that the one intended goal of ecumenical dialogues, their basic aim or motivation, has been to promote unity among Christian churches and, in areas where unity does not exist and seems beyond reach, to promote mutual understanding and respect of differences, even though there are disagreements about what kind of unity is intended and what kind of appreciation of differences is allowed.

Just what are the kinds of unity and differences intended by ecumenical dialogue and what are their limits? Initially the Faith and Order movement aimed at promoting unity in multiplicity among the Christian churches. It did not aim at visible church unity. Rather it promoted spiritual fellowship among Christians, sought mutual understanding of differences, and strove to identify areas of church convergence. At the Second World Conference of Faith and Order in Edinburgh in 1937 the decision was made to move beyond the goal of a spiritual union to promote a visible organic union, the "unity of a living body, and the diversity characteristic of the members of a healthy body."[42] In 1952, at the Third World Conference in Lund the intended goal was further clarified: "We need . . . to penetrate behind our divisions to a deeper and richer understanding of the mystery of the God-given union of Christ with His Church. We need increasingly to realize that the separate histories of our Churches find their full meaning only if seen in the perspective of God's dealings with His *whole* people. . . . The measure of unity which it has been given to the Churches to experience together must now find clearer manifestation."[43]

As a result of this newer formulation of the goal some sought visible church unions based on consensus in matters pertaining to the confession of faith, sacramental life, and church order.

In contrast to the Faith and Order movement, the Life and Work movement aimed at promoting unity through common action, and the International Missionary movement, which became a part of the World Council of Churches in 1961, brought to light the importance of promoting common witness. At the New Delhi assembly of the World Council of Churches in 1961 there developed what has become a landmark "formula of unity," which spoke of the intended goal as "one fully committed fellowship, holding the one apostolic faith, preaching the one Gospel, breaking the one bread, joining in common prayer, and having a corporate life reaching out in witness and service to all."[44] The orienting aims of Faith and Order, Life and Work, and Mission are here intertwined into a richer, denser, and more complex understanding of the one intended goal of ecumenical dialogue. At the assembly in Canberra in 1991 the union of all people of God, and of the church and world, became explicitly a part of the intended goal of ecumenical dialogue: "gather together in unity the scattered children of God." "The calling of the church," this document asserts, "is to proclaim reconciliation and provide healing, to overcome divisions based on race, gender, age, culture, color, and to bring all people into communion with God. Because of sin and the misunderstanding of diverse gifts of the Spirit, the churches are painfully divided among themselves and among each other."[45] The Canberra statement, "The Unity of the Church as Koinonia: Gift and Calling," summarizes the main goal of ecumenical dialogue.

> The unity of the church to which we are called is a *koinonia* given and expressed in the common confession of the apostolic faith; a common sacramental life entered by the one baptism and celebrated in one eucharistic fellowship; a common life in which members and ministries are mutually recognized and reconciled; and a common mission witnessing to the gospel of God's grace to all people and serving the whole of creation. The goal of the search for full communion is realized when all the churches are able to recognize in one another the one, holy, catholic and apostolic church in its fullness. This full communion will be expressed on the local and the universal levels through conciliar forms of life and action. In such communion churches are bound in all aspects of their life together at all levels in con-

fessing the one faith and engaging in worship and witness, deliberation and action.[46]

In their constant promotion of unity among previously contentious groups, ecumenical dialogues have provided an ongoing workshop on conflict and conflict resolution. There has been a collective realization of the need for sufficient time to cultivate informal personal relations so that bonds of mutual respect and even friendship can develop as the necessary condition for constructive, generous, and honest dialogue to take place. Equally important is the need for common prayer, in which personal and collective dialogue with God—in worship, petition, lamentation, and repentance—serves to build an ecumenical community. These personal and prayerful prerequisites have provided a framework for the harder work of identifying and rooting out pernicious personal and social dynamics that have damaged and destroyed these relationships.

Ecumenical dialogues have provided case studies of how people define themselves and their group identities in relationship to, and over against, other groups in ways that result in prejudiced and distorted views of the other and of the self.[47] This kind of behavior has been analyzed from a variety of perspectives: rhetorically in the study of polemical discourse; sociologically in terms of the formation of group identities, cultural and social borders, and ideologies; and psychologically in terms of what is described as splitting off where the ability to recognize ambiguity and complex motivations is lost in an oppositional, and even demonizing, thought pattern. The three methods of ecumenical dialogue advanced in the Faith and Order movement and utilized by Roman Catholics have provided resources for overcoming these destructive patterns of behavior through dialogue. The comparative method of dialogue has required that one must allow the other to describe one's own point of view in order to correct what has been perceived as a distorted representation of one's church's most cherished beliefs and practices. Utilizing the second method of dialogue, there has been a collaborative effort to find areas of consensus and common convictions about core beliefs. And in accordance with the third method, there has been a renewed appreciation of the social and psychological dynamics in ecumenical relations and the need to promote culturally sensitive and socially effective common witness and action in the world. Ecumenists' increasing exploration of the role of repentance, mutual forgiveness, conversion, and reconciliation in negotiating conflictual relations is one of their greatest achievements.[48] In this effort one of the most important lessons learned has been that conflict and contention are dynamics that should not be repressed, nor can they really be expelled, but rather they continue to provide challenges and opportunities for growth in church and ecumenical existence if they are addressed in the open through dialogue.

DEFENDING PAST DIFFERENCES, DISCERNING A SHARED FUTURE

Participants in ecumenical dialogues have made great efforts to move beyond destructive polemics. But some complain that this has been at too high a price, criticizing these dialogues for fostering indifferentism and false irenicism. The fear is that through the construction of joint statements, consensus documents, and the promotion of common actions and witness that the distinctive identities of churches will be lost or negotiated away through dialogue. This dispute about overcoming interconfessional polemics and maintaining confessional identity reflects contrasting assumptions about language. In this vein, two basic ecumenical orientations can be identified. Some ecumenists are especially devoted to using language to reach mutual understanding of the differences between positions in order to honor those differences and guarantee that any movement toward consensus in confession, action, and witness does not occur at the expense of distinctive pasts and perduring identities of the groups involved. Other ecumenists accentuate the need to develop a common language that can pave the way for a new ecumenical future, one that honors the past and present differences but also seeks to promote a common future of confession, worship, witness, and action.

Avery Dulles, SJ, who is widely recognized for his efforts to delineate distinctive, contrasting models in theology, is known for advancing a similar, model-oriented, approach to ecumenical dialogue. By so doing he represents the former approach, which stresses differences between confessional positions.[49] This tendency is highlighted when he says that "nearly all who have been involved in ecumenical dialogue could certify the difficulty of explaining to members of another confessional body the traditional formulations of one's own. . . . Through patient dialogue it is often possible to reinterpret such terms [like *transubstantiation* and *infallibility*] in ways that render them intelligible, tolerable, or even acceptable to communities that previously rejected them. In the course of the dialogue each community deepens and refines its own experience, reflection, and expression."[50] Catholics involved in ecumenical dialogues do "not restrict themselves to a confessionally neutral historical method."[51] Rather, "any given question [will] be approached, in the end, with all the tools that may be useful," recognizing the role of the Roman Catholic Church's magisterium as "a precious instrument in their quest for truth."[52] "Now that the easy agreements have been achieved, it becomes necessary to face the hard questions. . . . To an increasing extent the dialogues are running up against the hardcore differences on which the theologians of each side do not feel authorized or even inclined to change the established position of their churches."[53]

George Tavard, AA, represents the alternative approach that underscores the need to form a fresh language that can set up the conditions for a new ecumenical future through dialogue. This orientation is evident in his own description of two phases in ecumenism, which correspond to the comparative and christological approaches previously analyzed.

> [T]he phase of mutual understanding leads to a phase of common discovery and elaboration. . . . There emerges the possibility of a common language, which, compared to all the languages previously in use, will be new. Ultimately, this second phase of the dialogue should arrive at a new formulation of faith, in which all the partners in dialogue, through the *renovatio ecclesiae,* the *interior conversio,* the *novitas mentis* asked for in . . . the decree *Unitatis redintegratio,* will be able to recognize not only their unity with the other, but also the proper development of their specific tradition. The ultimate end of dialogue is the formulation of a semiotic that will be new in relation to all older symbolic systems, for Catholicism and Orthodoxy as well as for Protestantism, yet in which continuity with the past will be recognizable by all.[54]

Tavard is critical of Dulles's approach because he believes it will lead to an impasse.

> Among those with whom Roman Catholics have been in dialogue since 1965 in the wake of Vatican Council II, there are those who, however they may appreciate the intellectual wealth and the spiritual depth of the

> Catholic Church, cannot regard the magisterium with the confidence of Avery Dulles. There are even those who see the magisterium as at times acting without warrant from Scripture and the tradition, and possibly also against the witness of Scripture and of the patristic tradition. And there are also those in the Catholic Church who honestly believe that the magisterium and some of its decisions have been in the past and can still be in the future obstacles to the fulfillment of the purpose of God for the Church. . . . In keeping with the limits that he has thus imposed on ecumenical dialogue, Dulles judges that the agreed [upon] statements issued by several ecumenical commissions conceal deep divergences under a veneer of agreement. "The agreements are frail, and are in danger of coming unraveled when the contentious questions are raised." It does not seem to occur to him that for at least some of the authors of those agreed upon statements, the contentious questions were raised, and then the agreement was reached.[55]

Tavard testifies that this was his experience in the process used in the first phase of the Anglican–Roman Catholic International Commission. "Models can indeed be compared. Comparison may well suggest further models that will be more comprehensive and more satisfactory. But there is bound to come a time in an ecumenical conversation among Christians, when dialogue partners, leaving their old models behind, must attempt to go forward by doing theology together." In order to arrive at a reunion, the patrimony of various traditions will not be renounced, "but the moment of such a reunion can be arrived at only if the two sides, working together as one, develop an understanding of themselves and of their mutual relationship. . . . We cannot rest content with staying indefinitely on the positions that have been responsible for our separations."[56]

The difference between the approaches to ecumenical dialogue represented by Dulles and Tavard needs to be respected. Even though Dulles has worked hard to formulate statements of ecumenical agreement, he seems to be an apologist for the magisterium, undertaking a form of border patrol in these dialogues. Tavard, on the other hand, aspires to collaboratively and creatively envision and articulate deeply shared ecumenical convictions so as to create a new future that does not repudiate the past but is willing to acknowledge its limits. Regardless of how one judges the approaches to ecumenical dialogue espoused by these two figures, the challenge they represent is to hold together a certain allegiance to how a community has described its own identity in the past, while being willing to explore ways to articulate that identity in new and more inclusive ways for the future. If this combination is lost in the interest of innovative formulations, there is the risk of fueling new forms of confessionalism and fundamentalism that threaten to make ecumenical dialogue obsolete. On the other hand, an unchecked disregard of past traditions of belief and practices can foster a concern that ecumenism is paving the way for a post-denominational situation in which particular churches maintain no distinctive identities.

A NEW PARADIGM SHIFT IN ECUMENICAL DIALOGUES?

Further unresolved issues in ecumenical dialogue have surfaced in the heated debates surrounding Konrad Raiser's 1989 book, *Ecumenism in Transition: A Paradigm Shift in the Ecumenical Movement?*[57] In this book, Raiser, who served as the general secretary of the World Council of Churches from 1993 to 2003, concurred with the diagnosis of others that there is a destabilizing uncertainty about the ecumenical movement: about the intended goals (doctrinal and spiritual more than practical and prophetic), about the christological method of dialogue focusing on consensus statements of beliefs rather than common prophetic witness, and about the role of the active professional agents of ecumenism combined with the difficult efforts at reception and local ecumenism.

He argued that these uncertainties have deeper roots in four governing theological convictions that fund the older approach to ecumenism, all of which have limitations. The first is a christocentric theology. The second is a christological universalism in which Christianity embraces the whole world and motivates the evangelization of the whole world. The third coordinated conviction is a vision of salvation history that offers meaning to world history as an alternative to a secularizing view of history. The fourth claim concentrates on the church's role in the world and its unity as reflecting the universal significance of the Christ event. The uncertainties and limitations in these theological underpinnings of the older approach to ecumenism reveal for Raiser its instability and insufficiency.

Because this older approach to ecumenical dialogue is limited and flawed, Raiser argued that there is a need for a paradigm shift in ecumenical dialogues. There is a need to rethink *oikoumenē* as one household of life. This means changing topics. Instead of focusing on the central role of

Christ in the world, attention should be given to the problems of religious pluralism in relation to the role of the Spirit and in light of a trinitarian approach to the relationship of God, the world, and humankind. Rather than concentrating on salvation history as the solution to secularization, attention should shift to the ecological crisis as revealing life as "a web of reciprocal relationships." And as an alternative to overcoming the diversity of the churches by means of the strategies of consensus, he proposes reconceiving "the one church" as that which is "in each place and in all places as a fellowship in the sense of a community of those who are different from one another."[58] Dialogue still characterizes ecumenical relations, but not as a method or a means to an end called consensus, which in turn provides the conditions for communion, but rather as the most basic expression of the relationship among members.[59] "Dialogue *is* living communion."[60]

A number of respected figures in the ecumenical community have been highly critical of Raiser's argument, most notably Lesslie Newbigin.[61] Two central issues concerning the nature of dialogue are evident in the criticisms offered. On one level, the concern is that Raiser's agenda threatens to undermine the complex and hybrid aims of the ecumenical dialogues espoused by the coalition formed in the World Council of Churches among the four subgroups: Faith and Order, Life and Work, the International Missionary Council, and the World Council of Christian Education. Raiser's position is judged as reflecting a Life and Work agenda—far more concerned with promoting concerted action for justice and peace in the world than in doctrinal agreements, spiritual formation, and evangelization. On another level, it appears that Raiser's agenda is consistent with a contextual approach to dialogue, but instead of being integrated into christological and comparative approaches to dialogue, it is in fact being set up in opposition to them. In other words, older fault lines that have been addressed before and, some would say, mended are now resurfacing, and some believe they are widening, because of Raiser's kind of argument.

In the wake of these debates, a new investigation of "The Nature and Purpose of Ecumenical Dialogue" for the Joint Working Group Between the Roman Catholic Church and the World Council of Churches was formally initiated in 2000 and approved in 2004. The task was to reflect on the achievements, lessons, and problems encountered since the 1967 report of the Joint Working Group, "Ecumenical Dialogues." Konrad Raiser, as general secretary of the World Council of Churches, and Bishop

Walter Kasper (appointed cardinal in 2001), as president of the Pontifical Council for Promoting Christian Unity, initiated this effort by offering their own agenda items and, together with the Joint Working Group, generated a list of topics for further study.[62]

The joint document issued in 2005 begins by celebrating the emergence of a culture of dialogue as a gift to the churches. Simultaneously, it grieves the ascendance of an antidialogical counterculture that is "fueled by fundamentalism, new experiences of vulnerability, new political realities , . . . globalization, . . . [and an] increased awareness of ethnic and national identities" (1).[63] In this complex and contentious context, this document "charts the impact of the culture of dialogue on the churches, offers a theological reflection on the nature of dialogue, and suggests a spirituality which can guide Christians and their communities in their approach to one another" (1). In concluding this chapter, I will focus on this document's treatment of the aims of ecumenical dialogue and its analysis of the obstacles and frustrations involved, passing over its valuable description of ecumenical dialogues and their achievements over the past thirty years.

To enunciate the overriding goal of ecumenical dialogue, this text cites a passage from the Canberra statement, which was quoted above in its entirety. The goal is identified in terms of unity (*koinōnia*, *communio*) expressed in myriad ways—in the profession of the apostolic faith, sacramental life, witness, conciliar methods of deliberation, and actions. This aim is achieved not only by striving for "agreement on doctrine, but also [for] the healing of memories through repentance and mutual forgiveness" (31). This implies that addressing conflicts, if not their resolution, is one of the aims of ecumenical dialogue. "Not all doctrinal conflicts can be resolved. Therefore a careful consideration of the positions—how far they are complementary, and where and how they diverge—can be useful in furthering churches' growth in ecumenical relationships" (55).

This document identifies current obstacles and frustrations facing ecumenical dialogues. Three major obstacles or frustrations are raised. The perceived growth and influence of confessionalism is the first and an overriding concern: "a renewed allegiance to confessional identity has . . . developed, leading possibly to exclusivist confessionalism" (16). This obstacle is clarified by means of an analysis of a difficulty long recognized: "Dialogue with Christians from whom we are divided requires examining how our identity has been constructed in opposition to the other, i.e., how we have identified ourselves by what we are not" (40). Consequently, confessional identity as a positive expression of the profession of faith must be distinguished from confessionalism that is "an ideology constructed in enmity to the other" (40). Later in the report it is stated that while there has been a growth in communion, there has been at the same time, "greater fragmentation and fracture between and within churches. There are those who assert strongly that dialogue is inimical to the Christian tradition, and who wish to assert claims of absoluteness and uniqueness" (81). Confessionalism fuels an antidialogical culture. To address this obstacle, the study recommends a rededication to the basic goals of ecumenical dialogue and the cultivation of a spirituality of ecumenical dialogues to resist this destructive dynamic.

A second major obstacle or frustration concerns the "difficulty of achieving wider consensus within the different churches. Difficulties in reception have sometimes led to division *within* churches" (16). There have been numerous consensus or convergence documents agreed upon by official representatives of participating churches since the previous report of 1967. This document identifies five difficulties in receiving these texts. They may be the result of churches operating with "different modes and processes of reception" (61). A lack of consistency and coherence among the results of one church's dialogues with different churches can adversely affect reception (62). There can be doubts about the relevance of a document generated from Europe or North America for those in other contexts (63). International dialogues may not address existential, pastoral, or theological priorities of the local churches in diverse contexts (64). The final difficulty concerns the lack of reception among the whole community, not just the officially designated agents and leaders involved in the generation and acceptance of consensus documents, but among various sectors, including "dissenting groups and divisions *within* churches" (65). To address these problems, this study commends greater attention to the diverse experiences of ecumenical reception, both the struggles and achievements.

Given the diverse kinds of reception in the aftermath of the development of major ecumenical consensus documents, such as the *Joint Declaration on Justification* by Lutherans and Roman Catholics, many ecumenists made efforts to articulate the combination of consensus and dissensus at work in the generation and reception of these documents, what has been called, in the words of Harding Meyer, "differentiated consensus."[64] These emerging insights into ecumenical reception need to be situated and understood within the larger context of the development of ecumenical hermeneutics. Ecumenical hermeneutics of scriptures, creeds, doctrines, liturgies, and theologies, which has been developed over the years by those engaged in comparative, christological, and contextual methods of dialogue, has been advanced explicitly only more recently.[65]

A third major obstacle raised in this document is that "under the influence of post-modern culture authority structures and authority in all aspects of life have been called into question. This raises challenges within the churches to doctrinal statements and to structures of governance as well. Some question whether it is at all possible for any one group to represent a community" (81). This awareness suggests why, in recent ecumenical discussions, increased attention has been given to the exercise of authority.[66]

This document of the Joint Working Group, celebrating the development of a culture of dialogue and grieving the obstacles to ecumenical dialogue that remain, offers an apt closing for this chapter. However, the clarity of its analysis of the challenges facing ecumenical dialogues should be juxtaposed with the intensity and complexity involved in the concrete life of the church, as is illustrated by the recent debates surrounding homosexuality. The issues of hermeneutics, reception, and the exercise of authority have figured prominently in recent ecumenical discussions concerning the dialogical discernment and decisions made by particular synodal structures of the Anglican Communion to consent to the election of a practicing homosexual man as bishop and the decision to authorize a public rite of blessing for same-sex unions. Proposals for ordaining publicly acknowledged and practicing homosexuals and for blessing same-sex unions in Lutheran, Methodist, and Reformed traditions are also being debated in various adjudicatory bodies. These decisions and deliberative processes have become the occasion for much debate within specific churches and between churches engaged in ongoing ecumenical dialogues. In some cases these heated disputes have retarded and stopped the progress of ecumenical dialogues. Undoubtedly, such developments will affect not only the future of ecumenical dialogues and how one understands their obstacles and frustrations but also patterns of migration of practicing church members between churches based on the stances the churches take on these and other contested issues.

9

Rethinking the Oldest Divisions in the Interests of Larger Truths and Lasting Peace

Interreligious Dialogue

The dialogue between Christians and people of other living faiths is in certain respects the most challenging and most important frontier in the church's dialogue. It is most challenging because the differences between religious traditions are so basic and influence personal and social identity and behavior in untold ways. It is most important because interreligious relationships have often been marked by hostility. Religious differences have been the source of profound misunderstanding and cruelty, and a decisive factor fanning the flames of racial, ethnic, and nationalist hatred and violence. Religions, celebrated as vehicles of life, healing, renewal, and communion, are among the most lethal agents of harm and destruction in the history of the world.

As long as religions have coexisted, there have been important dialogical exchanges between members of diverse faith communities. Sometimes these conversations have left lasting marks on religious traditions and practices, but more often they have been fleeting, undermined, and quickly forgotten.

During the twentieth century new opportunities for interreligious dialogue emerged. A potent symbol of the dawning of a new age of interreligious dialogue was provided by the World Parliament of Religions, held in Chicago in 1893.[1] This assembly brought together representatives of religions from around the world to converse about the changing world in relation to their own most cherished beliefs and practices and so "to unite all religion against irreligion." But it was a complex and fleeting moment. During the second half of the twentieth century, in the aftermath of the atrocities of the *Shoah*, there was a new sense of urgency to enter into ongoing conversations between Jews and Christians. Some were initiated by individuals and groups in Europe, others by the Faith and Order Commission of the World Council of Churches, and still others by the Catholic Church. Subsequently, the World Council of Churches and the Catholic Church became active proponents of interreligious dialogue with Muslims, Hindus, Buddhists, and traditional indigenous religions in Africa, Asia, and Latin America. The advancement of interreligious dialogue by the World Council of Churches and the Roman Catholic Church is examined in this chapter.

THE WORLD COUNCIL OF CHURCHES AND THE DIALOGUE OF LIVING FAITHS

The World Council of Churches has been one of the primary institutional agencies promoting experiments in interreligious dialogue. From its inception, the World Council of Churches sought to promote better relations between Christians and Jews. The Committee on the Christian Approach to the Jews was established in 1928 by the International Missionary Council and became incorporated into the World Council of Churches in 1961 and renamed the Committee on the Church and the Jewish People. The relation of Christianity to other religious traditions took center stage at the assembly of the International Missionary Council held in Tambaram, Madras, South India, in 1938. Discussions centered on Hendrik Kraemer's book *The Christian Message in a Non-Christian World*, which espoused a neo-orthodox approach to world religions that emphasized the uniqueness of the revelation in Jesus Christ, the necessity of the Christian church in mediating salvation, and the obligation of the church to proclaim the gospel to the whole world. Kraemer shared Karl Barth's negative view of all religions: religion is "a fundamental 'being in error'; a field in which we can trace God's own footmarks; [a source of] noble aspirations and tremendous capacity for creative action; and in the light of Jesus Christ humiliating aberration."[2] Everyone agreed that God sought to reveal the divine identity and purpose to humankind, but consensus could not be reached about whether God was working in and through other religions. In 1955 a consultation in Davos, Switzerland, revisited the topic of the relation of Christianity and non-Christian religions as it had surfaced at the 1938 Tambaram meeting. To address these issues the participants proposed a new research project entitled "The Word of God and the Living Faiths of Men," which was approved in 1956 by the Central Committee of the World Council of Churches. The International Missionary Council also initiated what were called Study Centers in those parts of the world where Christianity was a minority tradition, beginning in Asia. These Study Centers had the objective of promoting the study of other religions in the interests of missionary work, and over time they became a central catalyst for interreligious dialogues.

Between 1955 and 1969 numerous consultations among Christians about the prospect of bilateral interreligious dialogues took place at the invitation of the World Council of Churches. During 1960–1961 discussions were held in Jerusalem among Christians concerning their relations with Muslims; in Nagpur, India, with Hindus; in Hong Kong with Buddhists from countries where the Mahayana tradition is dominant; and in Rangoon, Burma (Myanmar), with Buddhists from countries where the Theravada tradition prevailed.

At the Third Assembly of the World Council of Churches in New Delhi, India, in 1961, increasing attention was given to interreligious issues, and the Study Centers were charged with taking on the task of sponsoring and hosting dialogues of Christians with believers of other religions. This agenda was reaffirmed at the 1963 assembly of the Commission on World Mission and Evangelism of the World Council of Churches held in Mexico City: "dialogue with adherents of other faiths was urged as part of the Christian witness. It was hoped that through the work of the Study Centers and through actual dialogue with men of other faiths fresh insights might be gained which would enable the Study of the Living Faiths to enter a new phase breaking through the stalemate of the debate which had been carried on in rather abstract terms since Tambaram."[3]

The momentum promoting interfaith dialogue increased. Muslim–Christian dialogues were advocated at a consultation held in Broumana, Lebanon, in 1966, with thirty Christian scholars in attendance—Protestant, Orthodox, and Roman Catholic—from seventeen countries with significant Muslim populations in Africa, the Middle East, Southeast Asia, and the West.[4] Dialogues with people of diverse faiths were endorsed at the consultation held in Kandy, Ceylon, in 1967, with Protestant, Orthodox, and Roman Catholic representatives in attendance.[5]

Because disputed theological issues remained unresolved, interreligious relations were not addressed in the plenary sessions at the Fourth Assembly of the World Council of Churches in Uppsala, Sweden, in 1968. However, the topic could not be avoided in section meetings devoted to missionary work, the Study Centers, and the Living Faiths series.[6]

Formal interreligious dialogues between Jews and Christians sponsored by the World Council of Churches began in 1965. They were the first interfaith dialogues initiated by the World Council of Churches under the leadership of the Faith and Order Commission. The World Council of Churches and the Synagogue Council of America cosponsored a bilateral meeting in Bossey, Switzerland, in August 1965, with nine Jewish leaders and eleven Christian leaders, with papers read and discussed. In 1967 the Faith and Order Secretariat in concert with a World Council of Churches subcommittee advanced the need for further dialogue in the document entitled "The Church and the Jewish People."[7] Subsequently a series of six Jewish–Christian dialogues took place between 1968 and 1972 with twenty-five to fifty participants in attendance.

Interfaith dialogues between Christians and Muslims, Hindus, and Buddhists began in 1969. Twenty-two Christians and Muslims gathered in March 1969 in Cartigny, Switzerland, to consider the necessity and challenges of bilateral dialogues, with papers read and discussed.[8] In December 1969, for the first time, a Hindu, a Buddhist, and a Muslim participated in a committee meeting of the World Council of Churches to discuss the study project on dialogue between persons of living faiths. It is striking that no Jewish participant was involved in this meeting, leaving aside for the moment the larger question of representatives of traditional religions in Africa and other parts of the world.

A historic multilateral interreligious dialogue took place for nine days in 1970 in the city of Ajaltoun, Lebanon. The World Council of Churches brought together thirty-eight participants: three Hindus, four Buddhists, four Muslims, and twenty-seven participants from various Christian denominations. Again, the absence of Jewish participation is noteworthy. The meeting was planned by Christians and devoted to the topic "dialogue between men of living faiths: present discussions and future possibilities." The aim was "to gather together the experience of bilateral conversations between Christians and men of the major faiths of Asia [no doubt a key reason for the lack of Jewish participants], with the full participation of members of these faiths, to experiment with a multi-lateral meeting and to see what could be learned for future relations between people of living faiths."[9]

At the Ajaltoun gathering the days began and ended with worship, and papers were read and discussed by representatives from the four religious groups—two sessions in the morning, a long break for lunch, a late afternoon session, followed by dinner, and an evening session. For the first four days the entire group worked together examining actual interreligious dialogues, what helped and what hindered these efforts, and the problem of understanding other religions and the importance of the spiritual sources of religions. Days 5 and 6 were spent in small-group bilateral discussions on specific topics: Hindu–Christian, Buddhist–Christian, and Muslim–Christian. After a free day, the final two days were devoted to open-ended group discussions.

The Ajaltoun Memorandum, prepared by the participants, asserted that "a full and loyal commitment to one's own faith did not stand in the way of dialogue" but rather this faith "was the very basis of, and driving force to, intensification of dialogue and a search for common action between members of different faiths" (108). The importance and even urgency of pursuing interreligious dialogue were evident in the document. Such dialogues can address the incompleteness and mutual need experienced by members of all faiths and respond to their great tensions, conflicts, and differences. The memorandum began and closed with a joint declaration and included statements by a representative from each of the four religious groups. It ended by acknowledging the need for future dialogues, including with Jewish participants and representatives of the religions of Africa, stating that these dialogues must have an impact on future religious education and theological training. Specific topics meriting further attention were identified: more reflection on the nature, purpose, and contexts of such dialogues; the relation of dialogue to mission and proselytism; the phenomenon of secularization; and spiritual practices and experiences.

Two months later, twenty-three Protestant, Orthodox, and Roman Catholic theologians met in Zurich, Switzerland, to evaluate the Ajaltoun meeting. Their assessment was insightful and honest: it promoted interfaith dialogue, but was devoid of enthusiastic expectations. Still there was a sense of urgency: interreligious dialogue must be fostered, motivated by the desire for common action in a complex and rapidly changing world.

The framing issue for these theologians was how to articulate the Christian churches' charge to witness to the gospel in terms of proclamation and missionary work in relation to this call to interreligious dialogue. Proclamation and dialogue are both means of communication that "are open to abuse and ineffectiveness."[10] Proclamation has been practiced at the expense of other faiths, while dialogue can "degenerate into sophistic intellectualism or the dilution of all conviction for the sake of a false harmony" (34). The quest for "superficial consensus" and the "greatest common denominator" pose real dangers to dialogue. Dialogue demands honesty, risk, and vulnerability, and it opens up the possibility of individuals and communities being changed by the encounter with the other in a mutual transformation that can be progressive and cumulative.

These theologians identified a twofold fear in the area of missionary work: dialogue can be a betrayal of mission and it can become a new tool for mission.[11] Christian missionaries are frequently characterized by the very qualities that make interfaith dialogue impossible or at least difficult: dominance, arrogance, and insensitivity. There must be a way of understanding the Christian church's mission in relation to other religions, which have their own sense of divinely bestowed mission, in terms of a larger framework that considers the place of the church's mission within God's mission to the world. At the same time there is a need for sober realism about the threats of sin and the demonic in these matters, threats that openness will not overcome. "[N]o true dialogue which is part of true mission can be free from suffering and judgment.... Sometimes living in dialogue with other men will not even be possible or advisable and contestation or refusal of dialogue may in some instances be the only means for initiating communication at a deeper level" (39). On the other hand, the fear of syncretism, as real as the danger is, can jeopardize the formation of creative and life-giving relationships within a Christian community in a given place, for instance, in the area of worship. The theologians ended their meeting by raising numerous questions about the witnessing and universal character of the church in diverse cultures ("Indigenization"). Their closing paragraph reads:

> Clearly we are only at the beginning of exploring a new dimension and possibility in the Church's life and mission in the world. We must seek to be as realistic about the dangers as about the promises. Nothing in the Christian

> faith suggests that there is creativity without risk or newness without suffering. Our hope lies in the continuing work of the Holy Spirit in judgement, mercy, and new creation. Christians must surely show great boldness in exploring ways forward to community, communication and communion between men at both the local and the world level. All the circumstances of human life on the globe at this present stage force upon us the search for a world community in which men can share and act together. Dialogue between Christians and men of other commitments, in the sense of a talking together, which is a sharing together concerned with finding a way forward to living together, is an inevitable, urgent and promising manner of discovering how to bring together God's offer of communion in Christ and our diverse ways of common human living.[12]

The Central Committee of the World Council of Churches met at Addis Ababa, Ethiopia, in January 1971. The Orthodox metropolitan George Khodr of Mount Lebanon and Stanley J. Samartha, associate secretary of the Secretariat on Studies in Mission and Evangelism, presented papers on interfaith dialogue.[13] After much discussion, it was clear that there was no consensus among the member churches about how this kind of dialogue was to be understood or evaluated. Following the initiative of Samaratha, a new subunit on dialogue with people of living faiths and ideologies (henceforth identified as subunit on dialogue) under the general program unit called Faith and Witness was established to foster and engage in such dialogue, to promote reflection upon it, and to document fully the results. Subsequently, a dialogue working group was established and regularly met to plan and evaluate the work of the subunit on dialogue.[14]

An interim policy statement and guidelines were approved at this time and a secretariat was established in Geneva to proceed with interfaith dialogues, especially bilateral conversations, under the leadership of Stanley Samartha. This interim policy made five basic points. First, different occasions for dialogue with other faiths and secular ideologies are rooted in a belief in a common humanity and the christological vision of redemption, which unites the spiritual and the material. Second, dialogue is aimed at breaking down fears and building confidence. Third, dialogue includes the promise of discovering new dimensions of one's own faith and of new relations with people of other faiths. Fourth, dialogue takes on different forms (bilateral and multilateral; local, regional, and international) with distinct aims: common action in service of people in pluralistic societies, mutual understanding, and indigenization. Fifth, the religious freedom "to be committed, to be open, to witness, to change and to be changed" is a pivotal basis for interreligious dialogue.

With an ambitious agenda set by Samartha and the subunit on dialogue, an increasing number of bilateral interreligious dialogues took place. Dialogues took place with Muslims in Broumana, Lebanon, in July 1972; in Legon, Ghana, in July 1974; in Hong Kong in January 1975; in Cartigny, Switzerland, in June 1976.[15] Dialogues with indigenous religious traditions in Africa were considered in Ibadan, Nigeria, September 1973. Because of the influence of indigenous African religions on African Christians, a distinction was introduced between an outer dialogue between people of different faiths and an inner dialogue within oneself, with the traditions that have left an inheritance in one's memory and upon one's sense of identity.[16] The thematic concerns of nature, science, and technology were raised in a series of consultations with Muslims, Buddhists, and representatives of "primal religions."[17]

Four years after the multilateral dialogue in Ajaltoun, a second major World Council of Churches experiment in multilateral dialogue took place in Colombo, Sri Lanka, in April 1975 with fifty-four participants: eight Hindus, eight Buddhists, four Jews, ten Muslims, and seventeen Christians, with seven World Council of Churches staff members. The efforts to raise the number of participants from the non-Christian traditions, add representatives of Judaism, and lower the number of Christian participants reflected a major adjustment after Ajaltoun. In addition, although the effort was initiated by the World Council of Churches, the planning group was composed of a Hindu, a Buddhist, a Jew, a Muslim, and a Christian.[18] The title of the memorandum indicates the predominantly practical orientation shaping these dialogues: "Towards World Community: Resources and Responsibilities for Living Together." Major social and political concerns, it was acknowledged, framed the discussion and motivated the interest in promoting world community. Religious traditions and communities often work against the development of world community. The memorandum offered a list of seven common beliefs in support of promoting this world community: the present human condition not exhausting reality; oneness of humankind; person in community being prior to the individual; dignity of person; loving-kindness and forgiveness; promotion of peace and social and economic justice; spiritual disciplines of worship and meditation sustaining humans. Dialogue was identified as a fundamentally transforming process that might contribute to the formation of a world community as a "larger community of communities."[19]

After this first intensified wave of interfaith dialogues, there was an attempt to step back and reflect on their significance at the General Assembly of the World Council of Churches in Nairobi in November 1975. The emerging position about the need to develop a world community, advanced by the subunit on dialogue and articulated in the memorandum prepared at the Colombo multilateral dialogue, and in the various statements from bilateral dialogues found expression at Nairobi in the statement from section 3 devoted to "Seeking Community: The Common Search of Peoples of Various Faiths, Cultures, and Ideologies." However, this document raised serious concerns and unleashed a storm of criticism that reflected worries in many sectors of the ecumenical community about the purpose of interreligious dialogue, especially among those committed to the work of the Faith and Order Commission and in particular evangelical Christian groups.[20] The ensuing conflict has proven to be productive and not easily resolved.

The statement described dialogue as "both a matter of hearing and understanding the faith of others, and also of witnessing to the gospel of Jesus Christ" (par. 3). Syncretism and mission are mentioned, but what was stated raised suspicions. The document spoke of "seeking a community beyond our own" especially driven by the human concerns for peace and justice (which will later be expanded to the goods of creation and ecology). It argued that Christians should search for and promote with people of other faiths "the community of all humanity," and that we all participate in a "world community" (par. 15). Interfaith dialogue provides the "means" in this search for community, though "not . . . as an alternative to mission and it should not compromise our faith" (par. 20). This dialogue has different contexts and diverse partners. Some aim to address problems in society; others concentrate on theological matters, and often both are treated. But certain questions persisted. What does it mean to speak of a world community? Does this vision of world community undermine the identities and missions of individual communities? Does this kind of dialogue foster syncretism? In short, what is the precise purpose of dialogue with people of other faiths, and how can it support and not undermine particular religious faiths?

The subunit on dialogue felt it necessary to address the disputes and confusion surrounding the Nairobi statement on interreligious dialogue. In April 1997 in Chiang Mai, Thailand, an ecumenical consultation of Protestants, Orthodox, and Roman Catholics, eighty-five persons from thirty-six countries, took place on the topic "Dialogue in Community." The deliberations and joint statement prepared there were characterized by Stanley Samartha as a significant step beyond the setbacks of Nairobi. The closing statement was devoted to a discussion, first, of communities and the community of humankind, and the Christian community as a communion of churches, and second, of the reason for dialogue in community, the theological significance of peoples of other faiths and ideologies, and the question of syncretism. The document sought to resolve issues raised at Nairobi by offering a more contextualized and concrete treatment of the nature of dialogue within religious communities and between them for the sake of a wider community of justice and peace, and of the need to promote a community (*koinōnia*) of communities. Two particular problems arose about the use of the phrase "world community." "On the one hand, people in Asia, Africa and Latin America were suspicious of it because they felt that this was perhaps the notion of a 'secular Christendom' being imposed on them by the West with dialogue as a tool in this not too subtle a game. On the other hand, people in the West, despite all evidence to the contrary, saw in the talk of 'world community' a creeping syncretism that might lead to one religion for one world. . . ."[21]

Four group reports on specific dialogues were prepared at Chiang Mai, without being approved as such. The first one on Christian–Jewish–Muslim relations was divided into a report on bilateral relations between Jews and Christians, followed by Muslims and Christians, with each concentrating on the present situation in light of a chronicle of past encounters, describing the specific nature of the relation, and offering recommendations for issues to be discussed in the future. This was followed by a proposal of issues for a trilateral dialogue between Jews, Christians, and Muslims. The second report was devoted to Christian–Hindu–Buddhist relations. In the third, traditional religions and cultures were mentioned, with Africa serving as the primary example. The fourth category was ideologies; Christian–Marxist dialogue was the key example.

Out of the Chiang Mai Consultation came the "Guidelines on Dialogue with People of Living Faiths and Ideologies," which was subsequently revised and approved by the Central Committee of the World Council of Churches in 1979. The document advanced beyond the provisional statement of 1971 and drew on eight years of experience of bilateral and multilateral dialogues sponsored by the World Council of Churches. The debates surrounding the General Assembly at Nairobi provided the proximate context for the Chiang Mai gathering as well as some of the impulses in these Guidelines. "Religions and ideologies," the document begins, "contribute to the disruption of communities and the suffering of those whose community life is broken" (intro). Communities provide the context for dialogue, and Christians should "feel themselves called to share with others in the community of humankind in the search for new experiences in the evolution of communities, where people may affirm their interdependence as much as respect for their distinctive identities" (par. 8). This vision for "community in a pluralistic world [is] not one of homogeneous unity or totalitarian uniformity, nor does it envisage self-contained communities simply co-existing" (par. 8). Rather the individual faith communities have a role to play in developing a community of humankind, as a reflection of the Christian belief in the fuller realization of the kingly reign of God over all human communities. Although it is acknowledged that the terms mission and evangelism are not often used in this text, it is stressed that "we understand our calling as Christians to be that of participating fully in the mission of God (*missio Dei*) with the courage of conviction to enable us to be adventurous and take risks" (par. 15).

In a particularly powerful formulation, the Guidelines claimed that "dialogue can be recognized as a welcome way of obedience to the commandment of the Decalogue: 'You shall not bear false witness against your neighbor.' Dialogue helps us not to disfigure the image of our neighbours of different faiths and ideologies" (par. 17). Stated positively, dialogue is identified as a *diakonia*, a service within community, as a means for advancing human communities. *Martyria*, witness, is also an ingredient in the work of service. Dialogue and witness are not to be antithetical, whereas dialogue and bearing false witness are. In fact, "time and again the relationship of dialogue gives opportunity for authentic witness" (par. 19).

"The aim of dialogue," the Guidelines maintains, "is not the reduction of living faiths and ideologies to a lowest common denominator, not only a comparison and discussion of symbols and concepts, but the enabling of a true encounter between those spiritual insights and experiences which are only found at the deepest levels of human life" (par. 22). Responding to the controversy about syncretism raised by the Nairobi statement, the Guidelines stated that interreligious dialogue should not "compromise the authenticity of the Christian faith and life" (par. 27), nor should it promote interpreting a living faith in terms of another faith or ideology and not on its own terms. In this regard, two of the document's twelve recommendations merit attention. One confirms a basic tenet learned in ecumenical dialogues: "Partners in dialogue should be free to 'define themselves'" (par. 4). Creating a space for the partners in dialogue to define their own identity provides the means to address the history of prejudice, stereotyping, and condescension. In a second, related point, listening and obeying are set up over against false witness: "Listening carefully to the neighbours' self-understanding enables Christians better to obey the commandment not to bear false witness against their neighbours . . ." (par. 4).

The international experiments in interreligious dialogue that were initiated through the World Council of Churches, beginning with Jewish–Christian dialogues and then Muslim–Christian dialogues in the 1960s, on through the multilateral international dialogues at Ajaltoun in 1970 and Colombo in 1974, increased during the last two decades of the twentieth century and in turn fostered and were enriched by increasing interreligious dialogues at national, regional, and local levels. The topics for these dialogues varied greatly. Dialogues with Jews, Muslims, Hindus, and Buddhists were now taking on lives of their own. New attention was devoted to initiating dialogues about tribal and indigenous religious traditions in Africa, Asia, and North and South America. The Reports of the Central Committee to the General Assemblies of the World Council of Churches at Vancouver (1983), Canberra (1990), and Harare (1998), each chronicled the international bilateral interfaith dialogues and multilateral interfaith dialogues sponsored by the subunit on dialogue.[22] The Consultation on the Church and Jewish People initiated a process in 1975 that resulted in the preparation of a draft statement on the Ecumenical Considerations on Jewish–Christian Dialogue, which was approved in 1982.[23] The multilateral dialogues of Ajaltoun (1970) and Colombo (1974) were followed by a third held in January 1983 in Mauritius devoted to the topic of life, which was the focus of the upcoming General Assembly.[24] Bilateral and multilateral dialogues were sometimes devoted to special topics (e.g., new religious movements, "fundamentalism," humanity's relation to nature, religious resources for promoting a just society, and the role of religion in conflict situations), while other subgroups were formed to give more attention to the topic of spirituality (Vancouver 1983) and to address the issue of women (Canada 1988). By the 1990s the concerns about interreligious relations and religious pluralism were as a matter of policy being integrated into all the subunits of the World Council of Churches, and the vigorous promotion of bilateral and multilateral interreligious dialogues at international, national, and local levels has continued into the new millennium.[25] But these developments by no means meant that the critical theological issues raised by these dialogues had been resolved.

The relation between interfaith dialogue and the mission of the Christian church has remained openly contentious since the General Assemblies of the World Council of Churches held in Nairobi in 1975 and Vancouver in 1983. The Vancouver section on "Witness in a Divided World" led to a heated discussion about how God was present and active in the lives of our neighbors who are not Christians. As a result the proposed formulation, "we recognize God's creative work in the religious experience of people of other faiths," was replaced by the statement "we recognize God's creative work in the seeking for religious truth among people of other faiths."[26] In the years that followed Vancouver a study program was initiated in 1987 on "My Neighbor's Faith—and Mine: Theological Discoveries through Interfaith Dialogue," and a consultation on the theology of religions to wrestle with these issues was conducted at Baar, Switzerland, in January 1990. In 1989 the World Council of Churches' world mission conference commended a dialogue of life alongside of witness or proclamation. Dialogue provides the opportunity "to listen in openness to the possibility that the God we know in Jesus Christ may encounter us also in the lives of our neighbours of other faiths."[27] Controversy surrounding interreligious issues, mission, and specifically syncretism were center stage at the Seventh General Assembly in Canberra 1991, in no small measure because of the keynote address by Professor Chung Hyun Kyung of the Presbyterian Church in South Korea, who gave an "electrifying" presentation drawing on indigenous Korean symbols, music, and rituals to address her topic, "Come, Holy Spirit—Renew the Whole Creation."[28] Orthodox participants and representatives of evangelical and Pentecostal churches were especially unsettled by the issues raised by Hyun Kyung's presentation, precisely at a time when the World Council of Churches was attempting to promote closer bonds with Orthodox and Pentecostal churches.

The question can be raised whether the methods and aims of the World Council of Churches on interreligious dialogue are analogous to their approaches to ecumenical dialogue: comparative, christological, and contextual. The aim has often been to promote mutual understanding and closer bonds in the interest of common action for justice and peace and the restoration of the earth, locally, nationally, and internationally. In interreligious dialogues, the attempts to find points of consensus around basic convictions are in the interest of concerted action in the face of violence and the promotion of justice and the goods of creation. These do share certain impulses with the christological and contextual approaches in ecumenical dialogues. However, the ongoing debates surrounding mission and the theology of religious pluralism reflect the need for a comparative approach to interreligious dialogue that is as honest about the distinctiveness of individual religious traditions as it is generous in terms of seeking to promote mutual understanding and common action. Like the recent efforts of the World Council of Churches to promote ecumenism through local dialogues, theological education, and grassroots receptions of consensus statements noted in the previous chapter, there is heightened attention to these issues in the interreligious arena as well. Also similar is the increased discussion of the problems associated with the threat of confessionalism and fundamentalism. In the aftermath of traumatic acts of terrorism and governmental abuse in the name of religion, the World Council of Churches has dedicated itself in the new millennium to addressing the issues of religious extremism and violence. Moreover, there have been attempts to reconsider the most basic guidelines and aspirations of interreligious dialogues in light of a clear assessment of the criticisms leveled against them, their limitations, and the lack of impact of these dialogues in local communities.[29]

THE ROMAN CATHOLIC CHURCH AND INTERRELIGIOUS DIALOGUE

The Second Vatican Council marks a profound turning point in the Catholic Church's self-understanding of its relation to non-Christian religions and has served as the framework and catalyst for a new era of interreligious dialogue. The council teaches that God desires to draw all women and men together to God's self and to make of them a people of God, and that those who do not accept the gospel of Jesus Christ are still related to this people of God (*Lumen Gentium* 9, 16). Every individual should be free, not forced, to believe and their religious quest for truth aided by instruction and dialogue (*Dignitatis Humanae* 3). Just as Jesus Christ touches the human heart through dialogue, so too Christian disciples, empowered by the Spirit of Christ, should pursue "sincere and patient dialogue" with people among the nations, fraternal and sororal dialogue with those who search for peace, and friendly dialogue with non-Christians (*Ad Gentes* 11, 12, 16). Of all the documents from the council, the Declaration on the Relation of the Church to Non-Christian Religions (*Nostra Aetate*) is recognized as the watershed in interreligious relations that paved the way for future developments.

The genesis of this declaration can be traced back to Pope John XXIII's request in 1960 to Cardinal Augustin Bea, the head of the newly established Secretariat for Promoting Christian Unity, to consider how the topic of the Jewish people could be incorporated into the draft document being prepared on ecumenism for the upcoming ecumenical council. There were no formal dialogue procedures established between Jews and those charged with preparing this document. There were, however, numerous memoranda by Jewish leaders and organizations to Cardinal Bea and informal meetings urging that some of the grievances about anti-Semitism be addressed, specifically concerning how Jews and Judaism were depicted in Catholic doctrines and liturgy. Although there was no official Vatican policy allowing observers at the council, in June 1962 the World Jewish Council announced that a prominent Israeli Jew had been selected as an unofficial observer and representative to attend the council. The announcement was met with significant protests by Muslims, and nine Arab nations requested Muslim representation at the council.[30] In the midst of this turmoil, the decision was made to postpone consideration of the document on the Jews from the first session of the council held in the fall of 1962. The death of John XXIII on June 3, 1963, and the election of Giovanni Montini, the new Pope Paul VI, further contributed to the changing dynamics surrounding this document. The revised text on the Jews, expanded to include Catholic attitudes toward non-Christians, was introduced at the second session of the council in the fall of 1963 as a chapter of the Decree on Ecumenism. No discussion or vote on this material took place at the time. In February and March of 1964, the Secretariat for the Promotion of Christian Unity prepared a stronger document on the Jews, to be included now as an appendix, with added material on Muslims.

As the council proceeded, Paul VI underscored the growing importance of dialogue in his first encyclical, *Ecclesiam Suam*. It endorsed the church's external dialogue in relation to the world in terms of a series of concentric circles, in which were included those who worship the one God, and mention was made of Jews, Muslims, and followers of Afro-Asiatic religions, but there were no references to Hinduism, Buddhism, and others.

By the time of the third session of the council in the fall of 1964, the document on Jews and non-Christians was treated as a separate document and approved in October 1965. It acknowledged the religious aspirations of the human heart. It spoke of the spiritual depth of Hinduism and Buddhism and claimed that "the Catholic Church rejects nothing of what is true and holy in these religions. . . . The church . . . urges its sons and daughters to enter with prudence and charity into discussion (*colloquia*) and collaboration with members of other religions" (2). The document goes on to address the particular issues of Muslims (it does not speak of Islam) and of Jews (not Judaism), and friendly dialogue (*fraternis colloquiis*) is encouraged to promote deeper mutual understanding (4). It is noteworthy that the Latin term *dialogus* was not used in speaking of relations with people of other religions, whereas it was used when speaking of ecumenical dialogue, missionary work, the dialogue between the church and the world, and when speaking of the social nature of the human person in the context of religious freedom.[31]

Before and during the council there were numerous informal conversations between representatives of various religious traditions and representatives of the Catholic Church, but it was only in the midst and in the immediate aftermath of the council that formal dialogues began to take place. Each bilateral dialogue is unique. However, the encounter between Jews and Catholics has been especially momentous, distinctive in certain respects but also pioneering for other interreligious dialogues.

The first formal dialogues between Jews and Catholics started before the final session of the council in January 1965 and May 1965. There was a mixed reaction among members of Jewish communities to what *Nostra Aetate* said about Jews and the Jewish tradition. They wanted a stronger condemnation of anti-Semitism, an explicit repudiation of the teaching that the Jews were guilty of deicide, and the removal of an unsettling statement about conversion, implicitly of the Jews. In the years following the council, Jews continued to raise criticism about how Judaism was portrayed in Catholic liturgies, catechesis, and in church teachings, and about Catholic depictions of the role of Jews in the death of Jesus. The year after the council, Paul VI established the Office for Catholic–Jewish Relations in the Secretariat for Promoting Christian Unity and in 1974 the Vatican Commission for Religious Relations with the Jews.[32] Ongoing Jewish–Catholic dialogues, with the U.S. Bishops' Conference taking on a lead role, resulted in the revision and reform of Catholic traditions on Judaism and Jewish people. Jews involved in the dialogues continued to press for acknowledgment of the role of Christianity and Catholicism in the horrors of the *Shoah*.[33] But on this topic there was for a long time no official response.

The Secretariat for Non-Christians was established on Pentecost Sunday in 1964 by Pope Paul VI. The office was renamed in 1988 the Pontifical Council for Interreligious Dialogue. This office has promoted interreligious dialogues since the council.[34] However, Jewish–Catholic dialogues have remained under the auspices of the Secretariat for Promoting Christian Unity. During the first period of the Secretariat under Cardinal Paolo Marella as president (1964–1973) sponsoring interreligious dialogues was not on the agenda. However, guidelines for interreligious dialogue and studies of non-Christian religions were published. Selected multifaith dialogues sponsored by other groups were attended by representatives of the Secretariat. In 1973, Cardinal Sergio Pignedoli became the second president of the Secretariat, and a shift to sponsoring bilateral and to a lesser degree multilateral dialogues took place. Closer ecumenical collaboration with the World Council of Churches and especially the subunit on dialogue on interfaith matters began, after an initial period of reservation about the viability of such cooperation because of contrasting theological assumptions about non-Christian religions. In 1974, the same year as the Vatican Commission for the Religious Relations with the Jews was formed under the auspices of the Secretariat for Promoting Christian Unity, a Vatican Commission for the Religious Relations with Muslims was also established in the Secretariat for Non-Christian Religions. Various Vatican offices endorsed additional institutional efforts to promote and sponsor dialogue between Christians and Muslims.[35]

The Secretariat promoted improved relations with Muslims. International Muslim–Catholic dialogues began to take place in the mid–1970s initiated or cosponsored by the Secretariat while Cardinal Pignedoli was president.[36] Muslim–Catholic dialogues in local settings became a priority during the presidency of Archbishop Jean Jadot (1980–1984), who encouraged the involvement of national episcopal conferences. During the years Cardinal Francis Arinze served as head of the Secretariat (1984–2002), and under the current president, Archbishop Michael L. Fitzgerald, Muslim–Catholic dialogues and relations on international and national levels have continued to develop.[37] Regional dialogues with Muslims from northern, western, and eastern Africa as well as with Muslims in Southeast Asia were initiated in the 1980s and 1990s.[38]

The Secretariat organized a dialogue between Catholics and Theravada Buddhists in Bangkok, Thailand (1974), and with Japanese adherents of Buddhism and Shintoism in Nemi, near Rome (1976). The Secretariat cosponsored a series of Buddhist–Catholic dialogues beginning in the 1990s.[39] The Federation of Asian Bishops' Conferences, which held its first plenary assembly in 1974, has from its inception been a tireless advocate of dialogue with Eastern religious traditions—in particular, Hinduism and Buddhism, as well as Islam.[40] Catholic–Buddhist dialogues were also cosponsored by U.S. diocesan ecumenical and interreligious offices.[41] The Secretariat for Non-Christian Religions also initiated discussions with indigenous religious traditions in Africa with western African French-speaking participants in Abidjan, Ivory Coast (1974), with English-speaking people from eastern and southern Africa in Kampala, Uganda (1974), in Yaoundé, Cameroon (1976), and in Kinshasa, Zaire (1978).

The Secretariat for Non-Christians published a series of short guidelines to interreligious dialogue. The first installment appeared in 1967 and offered a general theological framework and some general suggestions for dialogue. In 1969 and 1970 numerous installments came out describing the basic beliefs of Muslims, Buddhists, Hindus, and African Religions. The final volume, *Religions: Fundamental Themes for a Dialogistic Understanding,* employed a phenomenological approach to the anthropological basis of religion, the quest for salvation, views of the Absolute, and good and evil.[42] These documents reflect scholarly research on the nature of interreligious dialogue more than scholarly reflection on practices of dialogue. There is a certain clarity, honesty, and coherence of vision of the aims and theology of interreligious dialogue, but some working assumptions (e.g., about the distinction of a natural dialogue and religious dialogue proper) became problematic as experiments in dialogue continue.

The first volume in this series appeared a year before the document "Reflection and Suggestions Concerning Ecumenical Dialogue" was issued by the Secretariat for the Promotion of Christian Unity in August 1970. The documents are significantly different in structure and content. Yet there is a comparable appreciation of the multiple contexts of dialogue: the one speaks of the "domains" of interreligious dialogue, and the other of the "forms" of ecumenical dialogue. The domains of dialogue include the human or secular form of interfaith dialogue that takes place in ordinary social life, in families, shops, offices, between citizens, and in cultural contacts, where on occasion religious convictions intersect with certain common practical problems that need to be addressed in society. The second is religious dialogue "properly so-called" where there is discussion of beliefs and practices usually in formal and structured meetings of experts. In both kinds of dialogue emphasis should be on personal encounter between participants, rather than a meeting of systems of beliefs. But these persons are called in these encounters to witness to the faith and beliefs of their religious communities. The effort of the Secretariat to concentrate on religious dialogue proper in distinction from natural or secular dialogue was crucial during the first period, but the working assumptions about the effort to distinguish supernatural and natural kinds of dialogues were viewed as overdrawn and problematic in light of subsequent experience in dialogues.

One of the most important topics treated in these documents, similar to the World Council of Churches discussions, is the relation of dialogue, mission, and witness. The first treatise begins by describing the path of dialogue as one of faith and of charity—charity aims at communion, faith insists upon distinctions, and both are needed and are complementary, not contradictory. Dialogue is viewed as distinct from missionary activity and evangelization, but it can pave the way for both. Through interfaith dialogue Catholics cannot help but bear witness to the gospel as they represent the church. Bearing witness to the gospel includes not only witnessing to the truths of faith but also living a truly Christian life through moral conduct. This entails cultivating certain habits of mind: a versatile and frank spirit, a spirit of humility, appreciation and esteem, right discernment, patience, and a docility of spirit to the divine.

This booklet speaks of the purpose of Christian faith in the world: salvation and proclamation and witness of the gospel to lead non-Christians to salvation. This is why the document envisions the aim of dialogue in relation to the divine aims of proclamation and evangelization. On the other hand, interreligious dialogue aims "on the human level . . . to promote in common the good of the entire community in accordance with the Gospel, also to seek the values inherent in the various religions, and finally to engage in religious dialogue properly so-called." In other words, interreligious dialogue aims at collaboration for the common good of humankind. One aims at a growth in mutual familiarity and enrichment in the process. The document insists that all of this will lead to the evangelization of non-Christians. But there will also result among the members of the church a deeper knowledge and appreciation of "God's relations with the world and the relations of revelation and grace with human nature," "the riches and the variety of God's work in the world," which can in turn lead to proclamation.[43] In the document especially devoted to Hindu–Christian dialogue, it is recognized that the dialogue partners "do not merely search for some 'common denominator' between their religious convictions; they wish to enrich, deepen, broaden their own religious life by listening to God as He has spoken to men of other faiths, as He is speaking now to each dialogue partner, through the other's experience and realization."[44] There may thus be dimensions of the truth of one's own religious tradition that have not been perceived or have been disregarded.

In treating African religions an inner dialogue with indigenous traditions is discussed, and the aim of indigenization of the gospel, subsequently called inculturation, comes into focus.

Later in the first document, separated from the discussion of the divine aims of proclamation and witness, and the human aims of dialogue, it is recognized that participants in interreligious dialogue must face the history of hostility, prejudice, and abuse between religions and seek to overcome misunderstandings and hostilities. "Each man, each nation comes to us with certain traumatisms either ancient or recent, due to historical wounds which we must recognize and to which healing balm must be applied before we go any further." The "rancor" and "bitterness" between Christians and Muslims are mentioned. "Humiliating or mercenary colonialism" is associated with the religious affiliations of rulers. Such conflicts have at times resulted in "the falsification of history and the propagation of prejudices through textbooks used in schools." These past conflict situations demand historical scrutiny, new methods of relating, and examination of consequences. The aim of interfaith exchanges at this point is "to heal the wounds of the past by a silent example of true Christianity, by selfless charity, deep and sincere piety and an easy, humble and courteous approach."[45] It should be recalled that *Nostra Aetate* called on Christians and Muslims to "forget the past" when considering quarrels and dissensions over the centuries (3).

As has been noted, between 1970 and 1984 the Secretariat for Non-Christian Religions engaged in numerous interreligious dialogues and ongoing collaboration with the World Council of Churches subunit on dialogue in these endeavors. These practices of dialogue contributed to the Secretariat's vision as articulated in the document *The Attitude of the Catholic Church Toward the Followers of Other Religious Traditions: Reflections on Dialogue and Mission*, issued in June 1984, twenty years after the publication of Paul VI's *Ecclesiam Suam*.[46] The document concentrates on the relationship between mission and interreligious dialogue. The first part of the document discusses the constitutive dimensions of mission: the living witness of Christian life, service, liturgical life and prayer, interreligious dialogue, and proclamation and catechesis. It is here that this document marks a momentous change in the Secretariat's position, subtle but important, beyond the teaching of Pope Paul VI and the council: interreligious dialogue is no longer described as distinct from, but is now related to, the evangelizing mission of the church to proclaim the gospel. It is described as pre-evangelical, a preparation, but it is viewed as a constitutive ingredient of the church's mission, "in order to walk together toward truth and to work together in projects of common concern."[47] In short, interreligious dialogue is one facet of the evangelical mission, which includes proclamation and witness.

The second part of the document is devoted to interreligious dialogue. What is said in this section reflects an accumulation of wisdom learned by practices of interreligious dialogues.

> One experiences one's own limitations as well as the possibility of overcoming them. A person discovers that he does not possess the truth in a perfect and total way but can walk together with others towards that goal. Mutual affirmation, reciprocal correction, and fraternal exchange lead the partners in dialogue to an ever greater maturity which in turn generates interpersonal communion. Religious experiences and outlooks can themselves be purified and enriched in this process of encounter. The dynamic of human encounter should lead us Christians to listen to and strive to understand what other believers communicate to us in order to profit from the gifts which God bestows so generously.[48]

This text makes no distinction between natural or secular dialogue and religious dialogue properly so-called. Consequently, all forms of interreligious dialogue are recognized: a dialogue of life, action, theological exchange, and religious experience.

The third part of the document explores the relationship between dialogue and mission in terms of conversion and building up God's reign. "In dialogue . . . the Christian normally nourishes in his heart the desire of sharing his experience of Christ with his brother of another religion. On the other hand, it is natural that another believer would similarly desire to share his faith" (40).

In 1991 two major documents were issued from Rome that addressed the issue of interreligious dialogue. Commemorating the twenty-fifth anniversary of Vatican II's Degree *Ad Gentes*, John Paul II issued *Redemptoris Missio: An Encyclical Letter on the Permanent Validity of the Church's Missionary Mandate*. The second document, *Dialogue and Proclamation: Reflections and Orientations on Interreligious Dialogue and the Proclamation of the Gospel of Jesus Christ,* commemorated the twenty-fifth anniversary of

Nostra Aetate and was prepared by the Pontifical Council for Inter-Religious Dialogue and the Congregation for the Evangelization of Peoples. The purposes of these two documents are different: the papal encyclical is offered as a larger defense of the church's missionary activity, while the latter is focused on the narrower topic of the relationship of dialogue and proclamation.[49] The encyclical touches upon the topic of interreligious dialogue late in the text (in the chapter entitled "The Paths of Mission").

Both documents speak of interreligious dialogue and proclamation of the gospel as two aspects of the evangelical mission of the church. However, *Redemptoris Missio* defends the importance and "permanent priority" (44) of proclamation as "missionary activity proper" (34), whereas *Dialogue and Proclamation* stresses that interreligious dialogue should not be undervalued, even though "interreligious dialogue and proclamation . . . [are] not at the same level" (82). Dialogue "remains oriented toward proclamation insofar as the dynamic process of the Church's evangelizing mission reaches in it its climax and fullness" (82).

John Paul II's encyclical is written to address "the difficulties both internal and external [that] have weakened the church's missionary thrust toward non-Christians . . ." (2). Is missionary work among non-Christians still relevant? "Has it not been replaced by interreligious dialogue" (4)? Or has missionary work been reduced to work for human development and social justice? The encyclical advances a theological argument criticizing various alternative approaches to non-Christian religions for undermining missionary zeal. The universal activity and efficacy of the Word of God in the world cannot be separated from Jesus Christ as the Word made flesh mediated by the church. The kingdom of God is active outside the church, but it can only be properly understood in relation to Jesus Christ and the church. Any (theocentric) approaches to the power of God or creation in the diversity of cultures and beliefs that make no mention of the particular mystery of redemption are inadequate. The universal activity and efficacy of the Spirit cannot be separated from the Spirit's particular activity in the body of Christ.

The threats to missionary activities include compromises by the people of God that lead to de-christianization within Christian countries. "But one of the most serious reasons for the lack of interest in the missionary task is a widespread indifferentism, which, sad to say, is found also among

Christians. It is based on incorrect theological perspectives and is characterized by a religious relativism which leads to the belief that 'one religion is as good as another'" (36). Another difficulty is that diverse cultures are overvalued: "there is a risk of passing uncritically from a form of alienation from cultures to an overestimation of culture. Since culture is a human creation and is therefore marked by sin, it too needs to be 'healed, enobled and perfected.' (*Lumen Gentium* 17)" (54). These arguments establish the frame of reference for the pope's claim that interreligious dialogue is an ingredient in the evangelizing mission of the church, but it must be seen in relation to the other dimensions, especially proclamation and witness, which take precedence.

As strong as John Paul II has been in his defense of the role of proclamation and witness in the evangelizing mission of the church and in his criticism of those factors which undermine it, he also recognized that interreligious dialogue has an important part to play in this mission. Even as he claimed that culture is a human creation in need of being purified and perfected (54), he also advanced beyond *Nostra Aetate* and postconciliar statements by claiming that "the Spirit's presence and activity affect not only individuals but also society and history, peoples, cultures and religions" (28). This helps him explain the importance of the new cultural sectors and modes of communication that "promote dialogue" (37) as comparable to the Areopagus, where Paul proclaimed the gospel of Christ in dialogue with other religions and cultures. "Interreligious dialogue is a part of the Church's evangelizing mission," which is not in conflict with proclaiming Christ (55), but in fact must be linked to it. "These two elements [dialogue and proclamation] must maintain both their intimate connection and their distinctiveness; therefore they should not be confused, manipulated or regarded as identical, as though they were interchangeable" (55). One of the purposes of interreligious dialogue is to help the church "to uncover 'the seeds of the Word' (*Ad Gentes* 11, 15), a 'ray of truth which enlightens all men' (*Nostra Aetate* 2); these are found in individuals and in the religious traditions of mankind" (56). The church aims "to discover and acknowledge the signs of Christ's presence and the working of the Spirit" in non-Christian individuals and traditions through dialogue. And through interreligious dialogue, the church aims "to examine more deeply her own identity and to bear witness to the fullness of Revelation which she has received for the good of all." The net effect is that through dialogue Christians and non-Christians can be enriched and can honor the agency of God at work in their respective traditions, but they also come to a clearer understanding of their own identity and witness in the process. Simultaneously, the understanding of one's religious traditions can be purified in the dialogical process without the participants relinquishing those traditions (56). The agency of the divine Spirit can be operative in other religious traditions and not just in non-Christian individuals, but there are human elements that limit and can adversely, even perniciously, affect these traditions. The same is true for Christians, including Catholics.

The document *Dialogue and Proclamation*, developing the position advanced by Paul VI in *Ecclesiam Suam*, finds the foundation for the church's commitment to dialogue not only in anthropology but in claims about the identity and mission of God: "God, in an age-long dialogue, has offered and continues to offer salvation to humankind. In faithfulness to the divine initiative, the Church too must enter into a dialogue of salvation with all men and women" (38). The intended aim of such dialogue is not "merely mutual understanding and friendly relations," but at a much deeper level of spirit, "where exchange and sharing consists in a mutual witness to one's beliefs and a common exploration of one's respective religious convictions" (40).

In an unprecedented way *Dialogue and Proclamation* enumerates some of the most important obstacles to interreligious dialogue as well as to the proclamation of the gospel. Eleven are identified (52).

1. Insufficient grounding in one's own faith.
2. Insufficient knowledge and understanding of the beliefs and practices of other religions leading to a lack of appreciation for their significance and even at time misrepresentation.
3. Cultural differences, arising from different levels of instruction, or from the use of different languages.
4. Sociological factors or some burdens of the past.
5. Wrong understanding of the meaning of terms such as *conversion, baptism, dialogue,* and so on.
6. Self-sufficiency, lack of openness leading to defensiveness or aggressive attitudes.

7. A lack of conviction with regard to the value of interreligious dialogues, which some may see as a task reserved to specialists, and others as a sign of weakness or even a betrayal of the faith.
8. Suspicion about the other's motivation for dialogue.
9. A polemical spirit when expressing religious convictions.
10. Intolerance, which is often aggravated by association with political, economic, racial and ethnic factors, a lack of reciprocity in dialogue, which can lead to frustration.
11. Certain features of the present religious climate, e.g., growing materialism, religious indifference, and the multiplication of religious sects, which create confusion and raise new problems.

This list acknowledges historical, social, and cultural factors and dynamics that offer difficulties, while it accentuates the limitations of those involved in dialogue—their deficient or faulty knowledge and understandings of their own traditions, as well as their defective, one might say sinful, habits of mind, self sufficiency (pride), polemical spirit, intolerance, and aggressiveness toward other religious traditions and members from those traditions. These problems are attributed to individuals, but they can likewise be operative in groups.

The list of obstacles to proclaiming the gospel also have a bearing on interreligious dialogue. Some obstacles are attributed to Christians: (1) "Christian witness does not correspond to belief, there is a gap between word and deed," (2) "negligence, human respect, or shame, . . . or because of false ideas about God's plan of salvation . . . ," (3) "lack of appreciation and respect for other believers and their traditions," and (4) "an attitude of superiority" (73). Other difficulties come from outside factors: (1) "the weight of history," such as when "the fear and suspicion . . . of the followers of other religions" is a result of "certain methods of evangelization in the past," (2) members of other religions fear that Christians seek "the destruction of their religion and culture," (3) "lack of religious freedom," (4) "persecution of Christians," (5) "the identification of a particular religion with the national culture or with a political system [which] can create a climate of intolerance," (6) "conversion . . . forbidden by law," (7) "in pluralistic contexts, the danger of indifferentism, relativism, or of religious syncretism" (74).

This new level of forthrightness and comprehensiveness in official

Catholic doctrine about obstacles confronting interreligious dialogue was subsequently made concrete and its consequences manifest in the church's effort to address the issue of the *Shoah*. As previously mentioned, one recurring issue raised in the dialogues between Catholics and Jews during and since the council has been this: can and should the Catholic Church officially apologize for its actions or lack of action in the long history of Jewish–Christian relations, and especially in the events surrounding the *Shoah*? Over the last several decades the church has examined and in some cases reformulated its teachings, but in none of its documents, prior to 1998, has there been a public apology for the church's offenses. Repentance was never expressed, either for the acts of individuals or for the acts of the institutional church. During the 1990s John Paul II made an unprecedented appeal to the church, calling for an examination of conscience (in the Jewish tradition *heshbon hanefesh*, reconsideration of the soul) and repentance or conversion (*teshuvà*) to usher in the new millennium, outlined in his apostolic letter *Tertio Millennio Adveniente* (1994).[50] During this period the pope apologized to various groups, but Jews were not the recipients of a public apology until 1998.[51] Jews had repeatedly requested a public statement from the Catholic Church on the *Shoah*. In 1987 it was decided that the Vatican Commission for Religious Relations with the Jews would prepare such a statement.[52]

In response to the request by Jewish dialogue partners and after considerable in-house reflection,[53] the Commission for Religious Relations with the Jews, under the prefect of the Pontifical Council for Promoting Christian Unity and the Commission on Religious Relations with the Jews, Cardinal Edward Cassidy, issued *We Remember: A Reflection on the Shoah* in March 1998.[54] This document was introduced by a letter from John Paul II, which began,

> on numerous occasions during my pontificate I have recalled with a sense of deep sorrow the sufferings of the Jewish people during the Second World War. As we prepare for the beginning of the Third Millennium of Christianity, the Church is aware that the joy of a Jubilee is above all the joy that is based on the forgiveness of sins and reconciliation with God and neighbor. Therefore she encourages her sons and daughters to purify their hearts, through repentance of past errors and infidelities. . . .

We Remember addressed the central question: What gave rise to the *Shoah*? "The fact that the *Shoah* took place in Europe, that is, in countries of long-standing Christian civilization, raises the question of the relation between the Nazi persecution and the attitudes down the centuries of Christians toward the Jews" (II). This document acknowledges that "certain interpretations of the New Testament regarding the Jewish people as a whole" influenced anti-Jewish beliefs and attitudes (III). Anti-Semitism, identified in this document with racial theories, is distinguished and indeed separated from anti-Judaism, "of which, unfortunately, Christians also have been guilty," without exploring any possible connections between the two. The verdict of this document is that the *Shoah* was the work of the neo-pagan anti-Semitism of Nazi ideology. To its credit, the document does not stop there but further asks "whether the Nazi persecution of the Jews was not made easier by the anti-Jewish prejudices imbedded in some Christian minds and hearts. Did anti-Jewish sentiment among Christians make them less sensitive, or even indifferent, to the persecutions launched against the Jews by National Socialism when it reached power?" "Did Christians give every possible assistance to those being persecuted, and in particular to the persecuted Jews? Many did, but others did not." In this context the unprecedented confession is made: "We deeply regret the errors and failures of the sons and daughters of the Church" (IV). This solemn apology is offered as "an act of repentance (*teshuvà*), since, as members of the Church, we are linked to the sins as well as the merits of all her children. . . ." "We pray that our sorrow for the tragedy which the Jewish people has suffered in our century will lead to a new relationship with the Jewish people" (V).

The teaching of *We Remember* was given liturgical form on the first Sunday of Lent in the new millennium (March 12, 2000), which was designated a special Day of Pardon. The day's liturgy included a prayer offered by the pope and certain cardinals as a "confession of sins and asking for forgiveness." Cardinal Cassidy said: "Let us pray that, in recalling the sufferings endured by the people of Israel throughout history, Christians will acknowledge the sins committed by not a few of their number against the people of the Covenant and the blessings, and in this way will purify their hearts." The pope continued "we are deeply saddened by the behavior of those who in the course of history have caused these children of yours to suffer, and asking your forgiveness we wish to commit ourselves to genuine brotherhood with the people of the Covenant."

The response by Jews and Catholic theologians to *We Remember* and this liturgical confession has been mixed. On the one hand, some Jewish scholars have recognized these as a part of a larger sincere effort on the part of Catholics and Protestants that merits a comparable response.[55] On the other hand, many have been critical of the church's reticence to speak of the responsibility of the entire church as a collectivity and an institution, and not just some of its individual members, for anti-Jewish attitudes and actions, and for the reticence to explore and admit a deeper connection between Christian anti-Judaism and the various manifestations of anti-Semitism, including Nazi ideology.[56] The church has articulated and continues to defend the distinction between the objective holiness of the church, the sinless church, as mediation of salvation, and the sinfulness of individual church members.[57]

The question can also be raised: Is there room for a comparable examination of conscience and repentance in the case of Muslims? It should be recalled that in *Nostra Aetate* there was a public acknowledgment that "many quarrels and dissensions have arisen between Christians and Muslims." But instead of inviting an examination of conscience, the document "pleads with all to forget the past and urges that a sincere effort be made to achieve mutual understanding" (3). Forgetting is not so easy. More recently, some Muslims mentioned the Crusades when they turned down an invitation to meet with John Paul II in Nigeria in February 1982 and in Kenya in September 1995. Some Arab Muslims described the African Synod convoked by the pope in Rome in 1994 as "a Crusade against Islam."[58] In 1985 John Paul II initiated a different approach in a meeting with a crowd of young Muslims: "Christians and Muslims, in general we have badly understood each other, and sometimes, in the past, we have opposed and even exhausted each other in polemics and wars. I believe that, today, God invites us to change our old practices. We must respect each other, and also we must stimulate each other in good works on the path of God."[59] In the spirit of John Paul II's efforts, Cardinal Francis Arinze, in commemorating the end of Ramadan in 1996, sent to Muslims in the name of the pope a message entitled "Christians and Muslims: Beyond Tolerance." The message reads in part: "To reach beyond tolerance to reconciliation and love there is still a long way to go. As we prepare for the future we cannot afford to forget the past or neglect the present." This last line must be intended to convey that the advice of *Nostra Aetate* to forget the past is rejected. Arinze goes on:

> The time has come to free our memories of the negative consequences of the past, however painful they may be, and look resolutely toward the future. The one who has given offense must repent and ask for pardon. We need mutual pardon. Without true reconciliation we cannot commit ourselves together on behalf of our fellow believers and for the good of the whole world. Muslims and Christians can become, in today's world, examples of reconciliation and instruments of peace.[60]

This message lays out a choice for the future of Muslim–Christian relations: one of ongoing confrontation, of mere coexistence, or one of growth in mutual understanding, respect, and fruitful collaboration. "Is this [latter] not what God wants of us? But this supposes, as I have said already, mutual forgiveness from the bottom of the heart, true reconciliation and a common commitment to building a better world for future generations."[61]

These efforts by Catholic officials to address obstacles to relations with Jews and Muslims caused by the sons and daughters of the Catholic Church as a matter of personal sin, and possibly a matter of social sin as well, by calling for conversion, forgiveness, and reconciliation are important dramatic developments in the teachings and practices of the Catholic Church that may have applicability in relation to people from other religious traditions.

Of all the obstacles to both interreligious dialogue and the proclamation of the gospel identified in *Dialogue and Proclamation*, and amid the attempts to address particular grievances with Jews and Muslims by promoting reconciliation through acts of mutual repentance, it is the problem of relativism that was given special attention by Cardinal Joseph Ratzinger in 2000 in the Declaration of the Congregation for the Doctrine of the Faith, "Dominus Iesus." Relativism is identified as a growing problem that risks undermining the uniqueness and universality of Jesus Christ and the evangelical mission of the church. Here Ratzinger advances the argument made by John Paul II's encyclical *Redemptoris Missio*. "The church's constant missionary proclamation is endangered today by relativistic theories which seek to justify religious pluralism."[62] The importance of interreligious dialogue and its role in the evangelical mission of the church is not denied in "Dominus Iesus," but clearly relativism has been identified as "the central problem for faith today."[63] This assessment issued by Ratzinger received widespread critical reaction. Even though this document did not repudiate the promise of interreligious dialogue, it seemed to offer little room for development, only reestablishing and defending older boundaries. The controversy surrounding this document illustrates the larger debate going on not only among Catholics but also among the various participants in the World Council of Churches about the aims and obstacles of interreligious dialogue. This declaration has not stopped the conversation on this topic, but has surely refocused the debate and placed the future of dialogue in the church and between the church and other Christians and people of other faiths in question.

10

Lessons and Laments and the Unfinished Agenda of a Dialogical Church

What conclusions can be drawn from these various efforts at dialogue in the church? Do these studies simply chronicle so many frustrating and sad episodes in a tragic story of the Catholic Church since Vatican II, one in which the prospect of reforming the church by cultivating such practices has been thwarted by the deficiencies of the practitioners and the reassertion of a muscular hierarchical vision of the church? Or is there a different kind of story unfolding here about communal conversion to a dialogical vision of the church, about diverse forms of resistance to implementing these reforms, and about the difficulties involved in learning new ways of being in relationship and collaboration? In short, do these episodes amount to a tragedy, or to the narration of a difficult pedagogical pilgrimage involved in identity formation, which is associated with the genre called *Bildungsroman*? I believe it is the latter, but one in which there is a full measure of tragedy involved.

In this unfolding drama there are no guarantees that the lessons will be learned and a mature character will emerge. "History can come to grief," as Edward Schillbeeckx has reminded us.[1] The economy of salvation is always intertwined with and threatened by economies of suffering, betrayal, and destruction, with the outcome of the interaction between divine and human freedom held in the balance. Consequently, eyes of faith are needed to see these episodes aright in their deepest meaning for the larger plot unfolding. But even eyes of faith require spectacles of charity and hope to see through the suffering and ruin caused by human finitude and sin so as to perceive more accurately a fuller reality, both cross-marked and glorious, that is coming into view.

In order to assess whether this is a tragedy or a pedagogical odyssey, the question needs to be addressed: What lessons and laments have arisen over the course of this investigation? Below I describe those that I consider the most important. I begin with lamentations, invoking a genre comparable in pathos and wisdom born of suffering to those derived from the apocalyptic imagination. I will seek to articulate the laments of both critics and advocates of dialogue in the church. If one were to stop there, one would conclude that the grand narrative linking these various episodes is tragedy. However, once the laments have been voiced, I will identify what I believe are some of the most important lessons revealed by these practices. These are promising lessons at work amidst the travail of dialogue. This will lead to some closing reflections on the unfinished theological agenda for a dialogical church.

LAMENTATIONS

The Cry of the Critics: Dialogue Undermines Tradition and Authority

There has been a litany of laments expressed about internal dialogical practices among members of the Catholic Church studied here. Each practice had its critics: Call To Action was criticized by numerous U.S. bishops and Roman curial officials; Catholic Common Ground Initiative by U.S. Cardinals Bernard Law, Anthony Bevilacqua, Adam Maida, James Hickey, Avery Dulles, and by David Schindler; the dialogical method developed by the U.S. Episcopal Conference for generating teaching documents by Cardinal Joseph Ratzinger; the work of the Adrian Dominicans by curial officers at the Congregation of Institute of Consecrated Life and Societies of Apostolic Life; synods of bishops met resistance from representatives of various curial dicasteries. The reasons vary—at various times theological, historical, philosophical, or canonical—but the core issue raised by these critics is the same: dialogue can undermine traditional authority.

The concerns raised by the critics are not simply in the interest of defending ecclesiastical authority. Their deeper suspicion and fear are that these practices are pulling people away from the most basic perduring convictions and practices of faith by the attraction and influence of popular modern Western culture. They worry that an ecclesial culture of dialogue fosters an illiterate church culture because such dialogue will eventually be dominated by endless trivial conversations about individual, narcissistic experiences, and the latest social fads and movements.

These critics ask, Where do people learn this approach to dialogue? According to some, these Catholics have been educated into what is called a "liberal approach to democracy," where self-interest politics means not being governed by principles, lasting values, and abiding norms, but reflects a relativistic and ultimately individualistic approach to human goods that rejects classical norms and authorities. Those who espouse deliberative approaches to dialogue in the church, so the argument goes, are beguiled and captivated by popular culture, the world of TV talk shows and movies filled with mindless dialogues that entertain, mesmerize, and stupefy. Often a wasteland of sexual immorality and materialism devoid of genuine love and transcendence, popular culture feeds the deepest hungers of the human heart with cotton-candy conversation.

Creating an ecclesial culture of dialogue of this liberal variety will result in the ongoing formation of cafeteria Catholics who pick and choose which beliefs and practices to embrace based on their own individual needs and lifestyle preferences. In the end, on this reading, the dialogical church is the dissenters' church, which is sacramentalized at the meetings of Call To Action. The working assumption is that in the calls for dialogue at all levels of the church one hears the voices of Beelzebub speaking in different dialects that jeopardize the unity, apostolicity, catholic fullness, and holiness of the Catholic Church.

This leads the harshest critics, so-called extreme traditionalists, to call for an abandonment of any practices of dialogue in the church, because dialogue threatens the proclamation of the faith and faithful assent. Instead, these extremists call for a return to the pre–Vatican II form of communication that transmits and defends the apostolic faith. The people who make this kind of argument have not been treated here because they are not known for engaging and criticizing dialogical practices in the post-conciliar church. Rather, they attack what they believe is the source of the problem: Vatican II. One thinks here of Archbishop Marcel Lefebvre, who argued that the council capitulated to the French Revolution: "Liberty is the religious liberty . . . which gives error rights. Equality is collegiality with its destruction of personal authority, of the authority of God, the pope, the bishops; it is the law of numbers. Fraternity, finally, is represented by ecumenism. Through these three words the revolutionary ideology of 1789 has become the Law and the Prophets. The Modernists have achieved what they wanted."[2] Lefebvre gathered like-minded bishops, the "Coetus Internationalis Patrum," who followed him in repudiating all internal and external church dialogue in the forms of collegiality, ecumenism, and religious freedom.

The most outspoken critics of dialogical practices, such as Cardinals Dulles and Ratzinger, and David Schindler, do not call for the abandonment of dialogue in the church, but rather they reject what they call a liberal, procedural approach to dialogue, which they set up in opposition to a classical, theologically articulated approach to dialogue. They argue that major efforts at dialogue in the church in the United States, for instance, the Catholic Common Ground Initiative, have been influenced, if unwittingly, by this procedural approach. By contrast, their classical approach to dialogue is said to be informed by the Platonic dialogues, by Augustine, and by the Christian personalists, who were so important for Hans Urs von Balthasar and Pope John Paul II. Their belief is that this classical approach to dialogue works in the service of truth whereas the modern liberal approach is a game of power dynamics, fads, and whims.

The Outrage of the Advocates: Dialogical Practices Are Being Restricted and Subverted

Advocates of dialogue are as concerned as the critics with the deleterious effects on believers of the dominant Western, especially U.S. culture of individualism, materialism, sexual exploitation, and violence that results in the insufficient transmission of basic beliefs and practices of Catholic Christians and among all religious communities. This Western problem is now being exported wholesale through processes of globalization. Like the critics of dialogue, advocates also complain about the shallowness of dialogue presented in popular culture. But unlike the critics, advocates emphasize the important role of dialogue in building individuals and communities with a strong sense of identity and mission, with a sense of conviction that can resist and fight against destructive cultural trends, but also with an ability to be open to God's Wisdom and Spirit at work in these cultural trends as well.

What distinguishes the advocates' lament is their complaint that the cultivation of dialogical practices is being jeopardized and frustrated by traditionalist critics and by the reassertion of centralized, paternalistic, and clerical authority. In its extreme form, there is a deep fear among some advocates that proponents of an older hierarchical and clerical ecclesiology are set on repudiating dialogical reforms. There is a suspicion and fear that nondialogical approaches to teaching, governance, and liturgy are eroding dialogical inroads. In keeping with this line of thinking, advocates complain that the church promotes dialogue with other churches, other religions, and people who profess no religious convictions, and even promotes dialogue in situations of social and political strife, but not dialogue within the Catholic Church. Advocates view the dismissal of dialogue on grounds that the church is not a democracy as a cheap rhetorical ploy, neither theologically probing nor fair. The claim that what the church needs instead is clear and unwavering episcopal and clerical leadership in line with the pope and received tradition and faithful obedience on the part of the laity is viewed as deeply unresponsive to the real questions and concerns about the content and credibility of the church.

This kind of lament was ignited in a momentous way in the aftermath of Call To Action by the limited and cautious response and disengagement of the U.S. bishops from the dialogical process they initiated. The profound disappointment of Archbishop Dearden at the reaction of his fellow U.S. bishops was matched by a growing sense of betrayal among many participants. This lament was further fanned by the curial criticisms of the approach to pastoral teaching developed by the U.S. bishops, especially during the failed women's pastoral process. The lament increased again during the initial waves of criticism leveled against the Catholic Common Ground Initiative. There are many people who have left the Catholic Church because of the restrictions and subversions of meaningful dialogue about the pressing apostolic mission of the church in the world, about the pastoral priorities of the parochial and local church, and about contested disciplinary and moral issues: women and homosexuality, birth control and divorce.

Additional factors contribute to the escalation of the advocates' laments. The priests selected to be bishops and many of the men attracted to being priests seem largely committed to a pre–Vatican II clerical and hierarchical ecclesiology, not one attuned to dialogical reforms. Likewise, certain communities of women religious, which have defined themselves over against those congregations that cultivated dialogical models of discernment and decision making, have received strong and vocal support among some members of the hierarchy. Moreover, certain conservative secular institutes that have gained ascendance since the council, such as Opus Dei, Communio e liberatione, Legionaries of Christ, and the Neo-Cathecumenate, do not appear to advocate dialogue in the church as a priority or as an important ingredient in their view of church. Also noteworthy is the mixed episcopal reaction to various efforts to promote dialogue in the wake of the sex abuse crisis in the U.S. church surrounding the cases of pedophilia by priests and the way bishops have handled them. When the U.S. bishops finally reached the collective conclusion that they should establish review boards composed primarily of laypeople with special expertise and commissioned with real deliberative authority to advise the bishops, the Roman curia made sure that these boards were understood by all to be consultative-only and in no way decision making and that the bishops' authority remained inviolate. When the national review board sought to exercise its authority by requesting further information and holding the bishops accountable for what was transpiring in specific dioceses, there were strong pockets of resistance among some U.S. bishops. The Voice of the Faithful and the Survivors' Network of those Abused by Priests have repeatedly called for greater dialogue with bishops aimed at collaborative decision making and have not been satisfied with the responses given.

The suspicion and fear among the advocates of dialogue are that these forces and movements are coalescing to repudiate once and for all the role of dialogue within the church. The conclusion being drawn is that dialogue with those outside the church is acceptable, but dialogue has no place in the internal mechanisms of the church.

What is an advocate of dialogical practices to do? After being disappointed, frustrated, and angered long enough by the retrenchment of non-dialogical forms of leadership and church life, some people change parishes in search of more dialogical leadership styles and practices at the level of everyday church life. A considerable number of people, however, end up migrating to Christian communities where more synodal and conciliar forms of involvement and leadership operate in the daily lives of communities, and where mutual participation, responsibility, and accountability are living realities, or at least valued ideals. At other times, people opt for communities that are voluntary associations of the like-minded, where membership bespeaks shared convictions and commitments, without practices for collective deliberation specified or operative.

Other advocates of a dialogical vision of the church choose to stay in the Catholic Church because they believe that the church is still in the early phases of a long period of revisioning the church and reforming its practices based on the dyad of *ressourcement* and *aggiornamento*. The seeds sown at Vatican II have come to life in the early phase of germination, witnessed in these studies. The advocates place their trust in the communicative power of God that this new life can survive the pernicious forces working against these ecclesial visions and reforms, but probably not without more crises, scandal, and ruin, which will bring into clearer relief the hard lessons that have not yet been learned, and the habits of dialogue not yet cultivated.

Are the first and second laments overly harsh? Possibly. Do they include distortions? Most likely they do. But lamentation is the genre of those who find themselves struggling in darkness and who are seeking to name the fears and narrate the sinister powers that threaten the very vitality of the group and individuals within it. Even if harsh and perhaps distorting, the lamentations offered by both critics and advocates should be respected and generously interpreted. Otherwise, there is little hope for the church's ongoing purification and growth. What this means is that the intentions behind the laments must be respected and understood. If these intentions are discredited and maligned, there has most likely been a failure to comprehend the deepest aspirations, desires, and convictions that animate the lamenters' cries of the heart. To respect and seek to understand the intentions expressed by lamentations, and the deeper fears and suspicions they represent, is not to stop at intentions. Rather it is to acknowledge that there are complex and often unconscious dimensions working at the borders of intentionality. In the regions of consciousness between twilight and pitch darkness lurk deeper desires and dynamics. There are voices in these regions that ought not be denied or ignored. Just as one dares not demonize the intentionality of the critics and advocates of dialogue, one ought not trivialize or totalize the darkness that dwells within them. Here too God is at work. Where intentionality and the unconscious intersect, where vision discovers blind spots and love faces the abject, there lies the possibility of the purification not only of intentions but of deeper desires as well. This personal and collective process of purification, which leads to purity of heart, takes place at the levels of intentionality and the unconscious and requires confronting these conflicting lamentations.

Excluded People, Taboo Topics

The voices of certain individuals or groups have been excluded from the dialogue. This lament is heard most frequently when discussing internal dialogical practices in parishes and dioceses, nationally and internationally. At times individuals in the group silence or drown out other voices simply by the force of their personalities, their loquaciousness, their dominating agendas, or the way those in authority exercise their power. Many different groups of people have been excluded or have felt excluded in different ways, by not being welcomed, by being ignored, by being overlooked: members of racial or ethnic groups, outspoken critics of church teachings and practices in one area or another (birth control, divorce and remarriage, married and women clergy, homosexuality), women, laity, traditionalists, youth, and young adults. Some have been discredited as radical feminists, dissenters, neoconservatives, or reactionaries. Still others are not invited because they are viewed to be obstructionists preventing the conditions for dialogue, or because they are so preoccupied with one set of issues that they seem to be unable to discuss wider topics concerning the identity and mission of the church. Even though every group examined here has sought to be inclusive to a certain degree, the question of who is or may feel excluded must be raised perennially and addressed.

There is a category of the excluded that I believe merits special consideration: theologians. Call this special pleading, if you wish, but there is significant evidence that theologians, and certain schools of theology in particular, have too often been excluded from dialogical practices with bishops, the curia, and other sectors of the church. There is no doubt that theologians have frequently been involved in dialogues, such as Call To Action and the Catholic Common Ground Initiative. However, synods of bishops, diocesan synods, and diocesan pastoral councils offer important examples where the contributions of theologians have been minimal or nil. It is remarkable that of all the groups in the church described in the documents of Vatican II, not one word was written about the role of theologians in the life of the church, about their constructive collaborative relationships with bishops, or about the importance of the relationship of theologians with wider circles of the faithful, in parish and diocesan pastoral settings, in ecumenism, in interfaith relations, and in social and political engagement. Moreover, and equally telling, the synod of bishops has addressed every group in the church except theologians. It has been left to the Congregation for the Doctrine of the Faith to describe, and actually prescribe, the vocation of the theologian. The exclusion of theologians from the doctrine and the daily practice of the church is more than a diminishment—it is a defect.

Theologians, on the other hand, must be held accountable for the ways they have excluded bishops and various sectors of the people of God from the circles of relationships that habitually affect their theology. Rather than cultivating the mythic lifestyle of university professors, aloof academics remote from their students and broader communities, theologians have an obligation to develop methods and styles of doing theology that incorporate dialogical collaboration with the people of God and bishops. This takes on added importance now because of the increasing number of lay women and men who are becoming theologians. In the past, theologians were almost always clerics and occasionally bishops. The bonds between bishops and theologians were consequently closer, as were the relationships of theologians with various groups of people in the church through their pastoral obligations to preach, celebrate liturgy, teach in parish settings, and make pastoral judgments and decisions. Lay theologians often suffer on both accounts: they have little or no opportunity to develop close relationships with bishops and are often restricted from preaching, and they do not pursue or are not asked to serve in pastoral matters in the parish or diocese. These situations must be remedied.

Laments about exclusion are usually accompanied by laments about taboo topics. Aversion to conflict about matters of deep conviction and strong emotion is one reason why controversial topics are avoided. An ability to work through conflicts about doctrine and moral issues, or about pastoral priorities and practices, is thus not cultivated at most levels of the church. The lack of authority to address specific disputed topics beyond reasserting the traditional position is often given as a decisive reason to stay away from doctrinal and even disciplinary topics. As a result, at times official or self-designated guardians make sure that these topics are not broached or are quickly squelched. The synod of bishops offers one of the most telling examples. Individual bishops have complained that they were unable to discuss certain topics (for example, married clergy, women's ordination, birth control, subsidiarity in the church) in the small-group discussions because curial officials sometimes policed the sessions and told bishops to stay on topic. Another key example is Call To Action. The U.S. bishops who initiated the project wanted issues of justice in the world discussed, but participants wanted to expand the topic to include issues of justice in the church and grievances in various areas being treated: family, neighborhood, and so on. There are other kinds of topics at the parochial and local levels that are often avoided. For example, are race relations discussed in the parish or diocesan pastoral councils? Are there church forums to discuss controversial social and political issues? Are there public forums for the formation of public opinion on difficult issues facing the church?

In point of fact, diocesan synods and the synods of bishops have allowed for some controversial topics to be raised, and have voted upon them and included them in public documents conveyed to the local bishops and Roman offices. However, in these settings certain controversial topics have been raised, but not really publicly discussed or addressed. The dialogical process has been cut short. And this has evoked a widespread sense of frustrated expectations and cynicism. The often-excoriated cafeteria Catholics, otherwise known as those who exercise selective reception of magisterial doctrine, can be understood as the collective reaction to the breakdown of dialogical discernment and decision making. The other response, which is also widespread, is the migration out of the church into other churches that do talk about these issues in meaningful ways and act in ways more responsive to the voices of the faithful.

Abuse of Power, Loss of Leadership

There are many reasons for lament concerning how power and status have been exercised in dialogical practices. At one end of the spectrum is the concern that dialogue is being undermined by paternalism, clericalism, and the exercise of personal hierarchical authority by superiors. At the other end is the concern that dialogical practices of decision making are hindering the development of individual leadership skills and the exercise of authority. Let me identify several specific reasons for this lament that have arisen in our studies.

Roman curia. Many of the practices we have examined have opened a window on the use of power by the curia. This has been seen in the cases of Call To Action, the U.S. bishops' conference, women religious institutes, synods of bishops, as well as in ecumenical and interreligious dialogues. When it comes to internal practices of dialogue, representatives of the curia have been suspicious and critical of the role of dialogue in matters of pastoral planning, church teaching, and governance. It must be acknowledged that the curia has been instrumental in the development of national episcopal conferences and synods of bishops, the main vehicles for collegial dialogue among bishops. Moreover, curial officials are recognized as a source of communal memory and collective wisdom of the universal church, especially when there is a need to examine and evaluate texts and practices of local and national church bodies and religious institutes. What has been repeatedly lamented, however, is that the curia has restricted open dialogue among the bishops at synods of bishops and has called into question the results of collegial deliberations of the U.S. Conference of Catholic Bishops. Moreover, the curia has raised doubts about the legitimacy and fecundity of wider dialogue in the church pertaining to pastoral teaching and administration among laity, religious, clergy, theologians, and bishops. The inference seems clear: the curia fears that the hierarchical authority of the papal and curial magisterium will be undermined by the collegial decision making of the bishops, and likewise the authority of local bishops will be jeopardized by wider practices of dialogue in the local church. On the other hand, ecumenical and interreligious dialogues, following the logic of Vatican II and official teaching since then, have been consistently advanced by curial offices. Concerning the work of ecumenical and interreligious dialogues, however, it would be acknowledged by some that the curia has been regularly cautious and occasionally too confining.

Curial officials no doubt lament that their critical interventions in the practices of dialogue, which have simply been in fidelity to the highest mandate of their office—to guard and protect the communal memory and collective wisdom of the faith of the Catholic Church and hierarchical authorities—have been repeatedly maligned. Nevertheless, advocates of dialogical discernment and decision making counter that these processes are being restricted, questioned, and dismissed by curial representatives.

The consultative-only clause in the new Code of Canon Law. This clause proves a second reason for a lament about power differences. One of the major advances of Vatican II was its encouragement of active participation of all the baptized in the life and mission of the church at the parish and diocesan levels and beyond. One of the ways the new code allowed for laypeople, religious, clergy, and bishops to participate in the mission of the church was by means of consultation in parish and diocesan pastoral councils and in diocesan synods and synods of bishops. However, consultation in these contexts has been contrasted with deliberation and decision making, which have been reserved for the proper hierarchical authorities in parishes with pastors, in dioceses with bishops, and among the bishops with the pope. Synods of bishops are to serve as a consultative body for the pope, although there could be an exception for decision making if the pope so chooses, which up to this point he has not. It has been lamented at a basic level that parishes and dioceses are only encouraged and not required by the new code to implement pastoral councils and that many parishes and dioceses have not done so. Likewise, diocesan synods have in many cases not been used or have been used only very infrequently. When dialogical procedures have been implemented, people have still complained that they are only consultative. The lament is that the consultative-only clause limits the baptismal responsibility and mandate of all sectors of the church to participate and share in its mission. Moreover, the consultative-only clause provides no regular means for those in authority to be held accountable for following through on the discernment and deliberation of councils or synods. This is no doubt a complex issue with many theological, canonical, and pastoral aspects involved, yet the lament has not subsided since the council, but has increased.

Leadership. The third area of lament concerning the use of power in dialogue pertains to leadership. This has surfaced in studies of religious institutes of women and men. Consensual processes and team leadership can lead to "mediocre management, representing the least common denominator within an organization. Uninformed implementation about consensual methods often paralyzes visionary leadership."[3] The question can be posed this way: Is the prophetic character of leadership, which implies not only the responsibility to be a guardian of communal memory and collective wisdom, but also the ability to be a visionary and to act decisively on behalf of the community, necessarily undermined by dialogical procedures of discernment and decision making? The critics of dialogue would no doubt argue in the affirmative and contend that this lament simply proves the genuine limitation of dialogical practices of governance. The advocates, however, would claim that the church is still in the process of cultivating leaders and communities able to exercise dialogical discernment and decision making that draw on communal memory and collective wisdom and fund vision and decisiveness on the part of leaders in the service of specific communities.

Costly Consensus, Reception Deferred

Sometimes in an effort to attain a wider consensus, councils or synods omit difficult and controversial topics rather than attempt to address them at different, sometimes deeper levels. This can be seen in the work of drafting committees. If conflict avoidance is the operative motive, the community is not being well served in the dialogical process. On occasion this strategy of seeking a wider consensus by filtering out controversial topics seems to be the only realistic option under the restricted conditions of time. Still, people lament that there is not a way for minority positions to have their voices honored and recorded as a part of the traditioning process at work so that the next time people revisit these topics the wider conversation can be considered. This means that dialogue can be productive without achieving full consensus. Sometimes the community must agree to disagree.

A frequent complaint about the formal dialogical practices examined in this study is that the collective judgments reached and the decisions made are not acted upon or received either by those in positions of authority or by people in the local churches. The results are either disregarded or explicitly rejected. Call To Action offers a clear example of judgments and decisions being reached by a group but rejected by higher levels of authority in the church. Ecumenical dialogues have frequently discussed the issue of reception. The phenomenon of nonreception can offer important information for those engaged in dialogical processes, but it can also be the source of frustration and anger when limited efforts have been made to foster widespread dissemination of deliberative practices so that the process of nonreception and reception can take place.

LESSONS LEARNED FROM THE PRACTITIONERS OF DIALOGUE IN THE CHURCH

Of the many lessons learned, I will concentrate on only a few. I will not discuss important, often-mentioned lessons about the need for sufficient time, the importance of having focused goals and realistic agendas, and the challenge of balancing the need to stay on topic with being open to the introduction of unexpected relevant topics.

Requisite Habits

Fostering productive dialogue is the objective of all the groups studied here and in a number of cases ground rules or strategies to reach this end have been generated and agreed upon. The Catholic Common Ground Initiative and ecumenical dialogues offer the best examples. Whether stated or implied, the conviction is the same: to advance effective practices of dialogue requires that people cultivate certain habits, we can call them the virtues of dialogue, which correspond to the two basic movements of all dialogue, the reciprocal back and forth dynamic of speaking and listening. For dialogue to flourish individuals must develop the abilities to speak well and listen well. This twofold habit is the heartbeat of dialogue. In the distinctive kinds of dialogical practices examined here, this combined habit is further differentiated by the objective or goal of moving the conversation toward collective judgments and decisions, which I will treat as the second lesson.

These character traits of speaking well and listening well may seem vague and trivial, but in fact they are the most fundamental specific qualities required for human flourishing as well as for facing and confronting situations of conflict and suffering. These qualities are skills that are learned. One learns by watching others engage in dialogue, by being invited into dialogue, by making initial efforts to enter a conversation, by practicing and refining one's skills as one goes along, by being self-correcting in light of personal or collective difficulties and failures, by making adjustments in one's practical judgments, and by being vigilant to further information along the way.

Speaking well is the mean found between two extremes. On the one hand, it is opposed to being withdrawn from the conversation out of shyness or fear of having one's contribution ignored or criticized; on the other hand, it is contrary to offering an endless self-absorbed description of one's stream of consciousness or opinions. Speaking is one of the central ways that one gives of oneself to others and so enters into relation. Speaking well requires that individuals are self-reflective and have a willingness to offer a considered opinion on a topic, even though it might be criticized or not shared by others. Speaking well presupposes that one has a sense of one's own dignity and self-confidence, which are the conditions of the exercise of freedom of speech, and that one has a genuine contribution to make to the conversation, which is contrary to being self-deprecating and unduly reticent, as well as contrary to being self-promoting and prone to dominating the conversation. One must exercise practical wisdom in deciding when to speak, when not to speak, and when to stop speaking. Simply because one has a relevant thought does not mean it should be spoken. It is not enough to stay on the topic; one must also determine what is the proper way to address the topic, what personal contribution is relevant and helpful to advance the discussion. But it is also important to style one's remarks in terms of vocabulary, kinds of examples, and information given in ways best suited to the members of the group.

Listening well begins by conveying hospitality to another individual or a group, welcoming and encouraging others to speak. One of the most important lessons learned, which we find most dramatically illustrated in ecumenical and interreligious dialogues, but also in the Catholic Common Ground Initiative, is that in order to listen well one may need to admit to oneself that one has preconceived judgments about the other, but to hold them in check in order to give others a chance to name and narrate their own identity and offer their own contribution without being dismissed out of hand. Active listening is certainly aided by eye contact and attentive posture, but even more important it is helped by the skill of knowing what questions might be asked of the speaker to clarify the other's contribution and in the process to help others understand themselves and to state their own convictions better, and how to convey that the message has been understood and received.

Learning a New (Old) Way to Be Church: Dialogical Discernment and Decision Making

There are many different kinds of conversations with different aims and objectives and subject matters. Many occur in the daily rituals of commerce, work, and education, where conveying information is crucial. Other kinds are concerned with building and maintaining relations of friendship, love, and family life, where one gives and receives support, encouragement, and even challenges. In these settings one learns to speak the language of compassion, appreciation, and affection. In the practices of dialogue we have explored, conveying information and building relationships are two indispensable ingredients, but what distinguishes the practices examined here is that all of them aim, in some way or another, at advancing collective discernment and decision making.

In these diverse kinds of ecclesial conversations, speaking well and listening well are not sufficient for the cultivated habit of dialogue. Rather one must develop the ability to engage the subject matter of the conversation fully, to give oneself to the oscillating movement of the treatment of the topic at hand, and so to be led by and contribute to the movement of the conversation. When one attains this level of skill, one can still find dialogue hard work, even difficult and frustrating at times, but there are times when there is a flow, a dynamic movement, even occasionally an ecstatic quality to the dialogical process. This is not unlike the mystical experience in meditation where one is caught up in one's imagination into the dialogue between the characters in a biblical narrative, drawn into colloquy with God, and even absorbed by the wordless gaze of contemplation. In dialogical discernment, participants freely and creatively enter into the conversation, but each person can be taken over by the subject matter transfixed in the movement of the dialogue. In the process deeper dimensions of the topic can be revealed and new courses of action and mission opened, and the very transfiguration of self, community, and God can occur.

In our study, the specific version of this habit of keeping one's attention on the subject matter that is unfolding through the conversation has been identified in terms of collective discernment and decision making. In these cases, in order to enter into the flow members must have prepared for the conversation by gathering relevant information, studying reports and pertinent literature, talking to people with special knowledge as well as with the people who are affected by the topic being discerned, and praying to be disposed to the movement of God's Spirit in the conversation and to be able to resist distractions and destructive dynamics.

The development of the skills of dialogical discernment and decision making is one of the defining lessons of this postconciliar period. The clearest example of these skills would be found in congregations of women religious, in our case, the Adrian Dominicans. Women religious in the United States have dedicated themselves over the last forty years to cultivating these practices and experimenting with strategies for acquiring these habits as a way of life. Their expertise in this has been shared in many of the other settings we have explored: parishes, dioceses, Call To Action, Common Ground Initiative, and the U.S. Episcopal Conference.

Dialogical discernment and decision making are arguably the most important lesson learned over the last forty years in all of these practices. This is not entirely a new lesson; it is also simultaneously the recovery of ancient conciliar, synodal, collegial, and chapter practices of the church. While many would agree that this is the most important new lesson and retrieval of ancient wisdom, there is a fault line and conflict of interpretation about this lesson that will ultimately need to be further explored and addressed. On the one hand, some would limit this lesson about dialogical discernment and decision making only to the extent that it is consistent with the formulation of the consultative-only clause in the Code of Canon Law, which adheres to a traditional understanding of personal papal, episcopal, and priestly authority in matters of teaching and governing. On the other hand, a wide variety of people would argue that these various practices are the firstfruits of the deeper reformation called for by Vatican II, which should invite mutual responsibility, participation, and accountability among all members at all levels of the church in realizing its identity and fulfilling its mission.

The cultivation of practices of communal discernment and decision making has entailed a rethinking of the understanding of power in the exercise of authority. Many of the experiments, from parish and diocesan councils to the U.S. bishops' experience in developing their pastoral letters, have brought new insights and new experiences of mutual listening and witnessing, where mutual learning and teaching take place. Before Vatican II, the conceptions of hierarchy and group identity relative to other groups resulted in the exercise of authority and the understanding of boundaries that promoted an us-versus-them—really an us-over-them—conception of internal and external power relations. These various exercises of dialogue explored in this study have served to promote, if not always realize, the possibility of mutual listening and learning, mutual witnessing and teaching. We will return to this contested topic below.

Because of the specifically collective nature of these practices, the process is a matter of giving of oneself and receiving from another, and of growing in understanding and appreciation of oneself and others. More importantly, participants in dialogue are asked to speak as representatives of communities and are called upon to speak intelligently and wisely about the world of the community. This requires gathering relevant information sometimes about the history and traditions of the community, and at other times by listening to people with special knowledge about the matters under discussion, or often consulting members of the community and rendering one's own judgment about this material in the group. In light of various kinds of information the group is called upon to offer its own judgments and decisions about the community. If an expert is consulted or relevant materials are made available, but the fuller deliberating body does not take the time to comprehend the issues involved, they have not deliberated well. A procedural democracy, where everyone has a voice and the voice of the majority rules, is not the same as a discerning, deliberating, decision-making community of the wise. The quality of judgments and decisions made in the dialogical procedure will be commensurate with the ability of individuals and the group to speak well, listen well, and deliberate well about the community.

Discerning Identity and Mission

Practices of genuine dialogue in families, with friends, and in religious communities play a crucial role in the lifelong process of discerning and making decisions about one's identity and mission. One comes to know and become oneself in and through dialogue. This book has concentrated on the practices of Catholic Christians, but there are similar kinds of experience for people of diverse faiths: dialogue, especially in parochial and local settings, serves as the primary place where one's identity is discovered and evolves. One learns over time to witness to the truth of one's identity as a Catholic Christian, and one gains some sense of direction and orientation in personal mission and vocation. These are basic ingredients in faith sharing at every level of the church. One's faith and one's *sensus fidei* (sense of the faith) are personally engaged and activated through dialogue in small groups, in worship, and in catechesis, that is, by participating in the communal *sensus fidelium* (sense of the faithful).

What has been said about the role of dialogue in personal identity and mission formation is analogously true of groups, and in this case, the Catholic Church as a collectivity. The *sensus fidelium* is engaged and activated in collective discernment and decision making in the church. The identity and mission of the church come into clearer focus through dialogue. This is why synods and councils are central to the life of the church. Synods and councils allow for the identity of the church to be named, narrated, and professed. On one level this takes the shape of forming and reforming doctrine about the identity of the church. On another level there is the ongoing effort to articulate and realize practically the pastoral mission of the church at particular times and in particular places.

Many of these dialogical practices have generated new experiences of collaboration that have resulted in joint decisions and joint declarations. It is not that these experiences of collaboration are entirely unprecedented in the church. Here one must recall the long history of conciliar and synodal practices and chapters. However, there has been an unprecedented effort to foster greater involvement of members of the church in these collaborative efforts of discernment, generating official documents, and forging collective action. The authority of the church, and the personal authority of individual leaders in the church, is increased and enhanced to the degree that a dialogical process of collective discernment and deliberation has been involved in developing teachings and designing strategic pastoral plans. This is a lesson claimed by advocates of dialogue in the church.

In order to participate effectively in any of these dialogues, it is presumed that one has cultivated the practices of dialogue with scripture and tradition by being mentored in the intellectual, imaginative, and affective practices of personal prayer, meditating on the scriptures, and liturgical worship. These provide personal and collective ways of realizing one's identity and mission and how one participates in the dialogical character of the identity and mission of the trinitarian God.

Harder Lessons: On Self-Examination, Conversion, Reform

What will long be hailed as a watershed lesson learned during the second half of the twentieth century concerns how some of these practices of dialogue have drawn individuals and groups into a process of conversion leading to personal and ecclesial repentance and reform. Ecumenical and interreligious dialogues offer the most dramatic examples, but no less important are Call To Action and the Catholic Common Ground Initiative. Discussion of "consciousness-raising" at Call To Action pertaining to women's role in the church, race relations, and homosexuality provide important examples. The Catholic Common Ground Initiative has struggled from the beginning to move their participants beyond polarized thinking and speaking in the church. Interreligious and ecumenical dialogues have also urged the renunciation of polemical modes of discourse—communicative acts that have been espoused in the interest of promoting one's own clear sense of identity, boundaries, and mission through contrastive self-definition—as acts of bearing false witness against one's neighbor. A central impetus in the dialogical process that results in self-examination and repentance has been provided by insisting that others name and narrate their own experiences and that all are to honor these self-descriptions. New ways are being forged to bear mutual witness to the truth of the distinctive identities of participating groups.

One aspect of dialogue that has received considerable attention over the last decade in various social, political, and religious settings is its role in fostering repentance, forgiveness, and reconciliation. The example that has received the most attention in the second half of the twentieth century is Jewish–Christian dialogue.[4] The deeper lesson here concerns how a false sense of self, community, and even God has influenced, clouded, and poisoned one's sense of identity and mission. Dialogue here plays a purifying role in the process of moving beyond the remnants of idolatry, projection, and introjection.

The Goal of a Dialogical Way of Being Church: Communion among the People of God

Dialogue provides the most important means for promoting communion in the church: *communion in relations* by advancing bonds of mutual trust and goodwill; *communion in convictions* by the effort to reach a consensus in judgments and decisions, even if a differentiated consensus, so as to foster a mutual commitment and witness to the truth; *communion in mission*, promoting collaboration in action in fostering the common good. The fruits of dialogue can be spoken of in terms of communion, common good, consensus. Dialogue provides the most important means to promote genuine communion among the catholic diversity of members in the church, even among members who disagree on important issues. Moreover, dialogue offers a social process to foster the conceptualization of and work toward advancing beyond personal goods to more inclusive goods, the common good, even when not everyone's subjectively perceived good is attained.

Are there any other means besides dialogue for advancing communion in relations, in convictions, and in action? The Eucharist is recognized as the sacrament through which Catholics are transformed into a living communion of faith and love. One also may consider the communion in convictions and actions realized by following the proclamation and programs of ordained and nonordained leaders. Sometimes one may get the impression that it is only through the official church administration of the sacraments, teaching, and governing and the adherence of the faithful that communion can be realized. Here a hierarchical model of authority, a unilateral model of communication, and a descending model of power provide the officially recognized means of creating and really imposing communion. The practices we have considered imply that even in the mediation of the sacraments and in the exercise of teaching and governing, dialogue plays a constitutive role in the realization of communion: the dialogical self-donation and reception about common loves, common convictions, and common actions cannot be filtered out of the process of realizing the church's identity and mission as a communion of persons. There is a necessary place for nondialogical modes of communicative actions involved in teaching, sacraments, and governance, but these are to be situated and normatively evaluated in terms of the one exercising authority being and acting in dialogical communion with all relevant sectors of the church.

CRITICAL THEOLOGICAL REFLECTIONS ON PRACTICES: THE UNFINISHED AGENDA

The work of Cardinal Avery Dulles, the most widely respected North American ecclesiologist, shows why there is a need for a theoretical and theological approach to the practices of dialogue.[5] Dulles has defended a model of dialogue that draws on classical Platonic, Augustinian, and personalist theories of dialogue as representative of Catholic doctrine and thus most suitable for it, while repudiating what he characterizes as the widespread alternative, which he describes as a modern liberal approach. A similar kind of argument has been espoused by Cardinal Joseph Ratzinger and David Schindler, as mentioned in previous chapters. An initial response on my part to Dulles's argument will demonstrate the need for more sustained theoretical and theological attention to this issue.

The chapter on the Catholic Common Ground Initiative examined Dulles's concerns about the theoretical underpinnings for contemporary approaches to dialogue in the church. Dialogue is acceptable, he asserts, if it is based on classical Platonic, Augustinian, and personalist theories, which are able to guarantee and safeguard the weight of truth in dialogue in contrast to a liberal approach, which is open to fads and mob rule and risks placing the truth of tradition in jeopardy.

In my judgment the current situation is more complex theoretically and practically than Dulles's analysis indicates. In order to be fair to Dulles's claims, one would need time to work through his theoretical arguments methodically, but also through counterarguments. As I envision it, such an endeavor would strive to appreciate and affirm the strengths of the philosophical and theological theories Dulles invokes, but also offer an assessment of the limitations and deficiencies of those same theories. Two issues merit closer scrutiny.

First, the approach to dialogue that draws on Platonic, Augustinian, and personalist theories defended by Dulles, Ratzinger, and Schindler is offered in defense of the hierarchical, centralized authority in the Catholic Church as the medium for transmitting and conveying the truth of tradition already established rather than in the interest of advancing an approach to dialogue interested not only in handing on but also in generating, developing, or revising the truth of the living tradition of the Catholic faith. Within this context, it would be important to investigate and reflect on the Platonic dialogues. These treatises are not intended to chronicle real practices of dialogue as much as they are using a philosophical and aesthetic genre for conveying the philosopher's truth already known, or as an imaginative device for the philosopher to explore dimensions of his or her own position in order to deepen it. This Platonic version certainly provides a richer exercise of dialogue than the questions and answers of the *Baltimore Catechism,* but it is not a genuine dialogue with real actors. As invoked by Dulles, the Platonic approach to dialogue serves to commend a hierarchical arrangement that may consult with theologians, representatives of the clergy, women religious, and the laity but is not required to do so, and certainly not mandated to discern and deliberate with broader circles of the Catholic community.

Second, we need to consider whether Bernard Lonergan's critique of a classicist approach to Christian culture and doctrine is relevant.[6] Lonergan faulted a normative view of Christian culture for failing to account sufficiently for the rise of historical consciousness and the emergence of empirical approaches to cultures. This critique can be raised again with respect to Dulles's as well as Ratzinger's and Schindler's defense of classical theories of dialogue and even personalist variations on classical theories. Does Dulles's approach give sufficient attention to the importance of changing historical circumstances and the differences of cultures, even what is distinctive about U.S. culture, for shedding light on new, forgotten, or obfuscated dimensions of the truth of the faith? Can dialogue not only affirm the truth that has already been articulated by the magisterium and received by all the faithful but also draw the church, often through conflict, into new insights into the tradition? Can dialogue over contentious matters in full synodal assemblies help the church to discover and recognize deeper dimensions of truths that may be in some way discontinuous with formally recognized teachings and disciplinary practices but are supported by deep bonds of continuity of beliefs and practices in the church and thus foster the future of the church's apostolic mission in history?

The precise issue concerns whether and, if so, to what extent the classical views on dialogue drawn upon by Dulles and others are genuinely dialogical with real actors in real social and ecclesial settings. I would judge that they are not. More recent theorists advance approaches to dialogue that promote concrete practices of dialogue rather than idealist models of how dialogue communicates truths already held, and consequently they account for real historical individuals and communities and their struggles and failures.

Dulles joins others who are suspicious of practices of dialogue in the church because those who advance them subscribe to a modern, liberal, democratic approach to dialogue, which is judged to be contrary to the classical model. This is a substantive claim. In order to engage it sufficiently, one would need to analyze the issues involved. First of all, one needs to understand what is being posited as a democratic proceduralist approach to dialogue and its relation to philosophical theories and concrete practices of dialogue. Second, advancing a concrete and historical approach to the practices of dialogue in the church is not, in principle, the same agenda as that of classical, liberal democratic theory. In fact, besides the wealth of practical wisdom gained by experience and experimentation in numerous church contexts, there is a wide variety of modern and postmodern approaches to dialogue that have been used as resources for contemporary ecclesial practices.

To begin with, one would need to devote far more energy to exploring three trajectories of dialogical thought: first, the modern personalist approach to dialogue associated with Martin Buber and Christian personalists such as Gabriel Marcel and Ferdinand Ebner; second, the hermeneutical approach that concentrates on the dialogue-like relationship between readers and texts as espoused by Hans-Georg Gadamer; and, third, the range of social theoretical approaches to communication, including the influential work of Jürgen Habermas and the longer tradition of George Herbert Mead and Josiah Royce.[7] I would argue that the personalists (like Buber), and the hermeneutical theorists (like Gadamer), and the social theorists (like Habermas) are self-consciously attempting to attend to the concrete historical practices of dialogue, often by means of a phenomenological analysis of various regions of dialogue. The idealist character of Platonic and Augustinian dialogue is concretized by the personalist theorists, hermeneutic theorists, and social theorists by means of more detailed phenomenological analysis of dialogue, often informed by the longer phenomenological tradition that is indebted to Immanuel

Kant, Friedrich Schleiermacher, and G. W. F. Hegel and more immediately to the work of Edmund Husserl, Martin Heidegger, Max Scheler, and Alfred Schutz.

Equally important, each one of the modern schools of dialogical theory (personalist, hermeneutical, social) has been criticized by other theorists for not giving sufficient attention to specific challenges and difficulties in concrete historical practices of dialogue. As a result, their particular theories have been augmented and revised by those who have dared to burrow into various quagmires and to report on their findings. Let me appeal to a chorus of postmodern critics of dialogue. Emmanuel Levinas repudiates Buber's dialogical I–Thou because it privileges responsible reciprocity, equality, intimacy, friendship—even friendship with God—rather than giving deference to the asymmetrical, higher, exterior invocation and moral demands of the other, especially God, when one confronts the face of the other. Mikhail Bakhtin raises troubling questions about whether an authoritarian monologue plagues Gadamer's reverence for the classic in his approach to the dialogue between reader and text, while Bakhtin tries instead to open eyes to the disorienting and contentious plurivocity of dialogues (the "heteroglossia") in novels and in everyday life, where voices clash in conflicts of ideologies, vested interests, and demands for decision.[8] Hans Robert Jauss insists that we confront the provocation of the multiplicity of dialogues in the history of receptions as a corrective to Gadamer's valorizing of the fusion of horizons in the history of effective consciousness. François Lyotard summons readers to question every effort of Habermas to reach an agreement, or a consensus, because of the unresolved dissensus in every community that witnesses the horrors of suffering, while Jodi Dean challenges her readers to take seriously all those concrete individuals and groups who are excluded from Habermas's theory of communicative competence. To this chorus of literary and social theorists must be added psychological theories about the unconscious, complexes, blind spots, and bias, and the critical social theories about distorted modes of communication, false consciousness, and ideologies in the consciousness collective. In order to do justice to Dulles's critique and to offer a sufficient rejoinder, one would need a far more detailed theoretical topography to clarify the approaches to the concrete practices of dialogue in the church that are alternatives to the hybrid model (Platonic, Augustinian, and personalist) like the one Dulles offers.

As these studies have amply demonstrated, it is not only or even primarily philosophers or social theorists who have informed dialogical practitioners. Above all, practitioners learned about dialogue through experimentation and self-correction based on what has worked and what has not worked in their own experience. It is likewise true that the practitioners learned and sometimes had to unlearn what was taught by *Robert's Rules of Order*, psychological and sociological programs of sensitivity training, group dynamics, various schools of depth psychology, community organizing workshops, and management programs.

By examining this larger field of dialogical practices and theories, which requires a slower, more patient, and more attentive process, I believe one would be able to affirm the prime importance of truth in dialogue and be able to discern the truth in the voice of authority whether it is expressed by a leader, or in the Christian scriptures, creeds, liturgies, or practices of meditation. However, one would also be able to recognize—and this is the corrective judgment—that it is not only established traditional authority that affirms, defends, and articulates the truth in the process of its development, but that there are people in every sector of the church who contribute to the handing on and development of tradition. People at every level of the church have authority and gain credibility, by baptism and among those ordained, by being receptive and responsive to the gift of the truth that is recognized and received in and through a dialogical process. All members of the church thus have a divinely bestowed interest through the gift of faith in guarding the saving truth of the gospel that is mediated through tradition; all witness to this truth, which is still coming into view, by participating in the dialogical identity and mission of the church.

To take the argument one step further, it is precisely the historical character of the process involved in receiving the gift of truth that is at issue in Dulles's critique. Dulles's classical approach to dialogue, and here I can only propose and not demonstrate, does not really help us to address unresolved issues of conflict and polarization in the church. Dulles is unable to allow for the fact that sometimes those who disagree with magisterial teachings or prescribed practices could be carriers, guardians, and defenders of a truth that has not been fully articulated or a moral order that has not yet fully come into view and been realized. In fact, Dulles's approach to dialogue reflects the traditional approach to the authority of the magisterium, which would allow only a consultative role, not some wider participation of all sectors of the church in a deliberative process of discerning the identity, mission, and pastoral priorities of the church in parochial, local, regional, national, and international settings. This offers a sufficient justification for why further theoretical reflection on this range of practices is greatly needed.

Let me close by raising the most important matters that need to be addressed. The issues raised by the critics of dialogue and the defenders of an older hierarchical model of authority and tradition—and here Dulles offers the most fully developed U.S. Catholic example—must be matched by an alternative theology of the church's identity and mission equal in scope and depth and spiritual richness to his own. Such an alternative theology, I would argue, does not need to deny the crucial roles of papal, episcopal, and clerical authority. However, the theology of ordination and of offices and their exercise must be reformulated within a larger field of vision associated with the dialogical understanding of the church and world that has come more clearly into view during and since Vatican II. This will require that the theology and exercise of officeholders in the church be repositioned and more fully articulated in terms of a set of relations with all of the baptized faithful, who have received a mandate to participate fully and actively in the life and mission of the church, and in terms of the larger network of relations among all of God's people in the world.

Avery Dulles's position serves as a reasonable but ultimately unpersuasive defense of the consultative-only clause of the new Code of Canon Law. It justifies the asymmetrical dominance of the hierarchy and clergy in relation to all the faithful in the life and mission of the church. An alternative approach would need to build on a theology of revelation, liturgy, and the church that capitalizes on the communicative and dialogical character of God's identity and economic mission in the world. Such a theology would not deny the most profound aspects of Dulles's classical symbolic and dialogical theology, but it would affirm them within a vision of the whole church as mandated to engage in collective discernment and decision making. Only by addressing these deeper theological issues will a theology of the church develop that combines coresponsibility among all the church's members with mutual accountability. The choice is not, as Dulles suggests, between a classical view of dialogue and a liberal proceduralist approach. Rather the decision is about whether to affirm an older paternalistic, hierarchical model of authority or develop a richer collegial, conciliar, and synodal vision of the church that can be worked out in practices at every level of the church. Such a dialogical ecclesiology would bolster the authority of the church's teachings and its credibility in the world, cultivate strategic pastoral planning at the parochial and diocesan levels, and foster a dialogical apologetics and missiology that does not undermine ecumenism and interreligious dialogue but promotes a collective witness to the truth of the distinctive ways God is at work in the world. Developing this larger dialogical ecclesiology will serve and advance structures and practices that can help address more openly and honestly deep-seated conflicts and unresolved matters about pastoral strategies and church teachings.

Ultimately, an alternative theology of the church that advocates dialogical discernment and decision making will be based on a more comprehensive understanding of the communicative character of revelation, liturgy, and the church; on a revised understanding of all of the baptized faithful, and the ministries and offices of the laity and ordained; and on a theology of the communion of the Catholic Church in relation to other Christian communions and a theology of the people of God that can illuminate the relations between all God's people in the world. Most importantly, the identity and mission of the church draw their inspiration and justification from Christian convictions about the identity and mission of the Triune God. This has always been the case. The immense amount of work in the fields of christology, pneumatology, and trinitarian theology that has taken place over the last century is still in the process of being received and integrated into a trinitarian ecclesiology. The issues raised about dialogue in the church will be adequately worked out and addressed only within the fuller development of a trinitarian ecclesiology and spirituality, one in which the obstacles and frustrations involved in the practices of dialogue will be illuminated through the trinitarian drama of the paschal mystery and Pentecost. The *Bildungsroman* that has been described in these chapters is at its most profound level the narration of *Itinerarium mentis in Deum.*[9] The identity and mission of the church will be enlarged and purified as the church continues on its journey into the reality of God.

CONCLUSION

This study has followed a pathway from a phenomenology of intentionality and a hermeneutics of texts, through a postmodern approach to cultural anthropology that searches for the interconnections of intentions and aspirations evident in the aims and frustrations of those engaged in practices of dialogue in the church. We have witnessed passages from light to darkness, revealing in fragments along the way what lies beneath and beyond in deeper desires and fears. This journey into darkness is a necessary and recurring one, but need not lead to simply subverting texts out of frustration and anger or relinquishing intentions out of cynicism and despair. Instead, members of the church need to return to the level of intentionality along this pilgrimage in order to purify intentions and the deepest desires of the human heart. When one faces the breakdowns and failures of dialogue, one confronts the limitations of intentionality, and one must search in the twilight and darkness for the false sense of self, false view of community, and the residue of idols in our vision of God. This collective passage through the dark night leads to a more profound vision of God, community, and self as a communion of persons formed in and through dialogue.

Notes

INTRODUCTION

1. "Dialogue within the church" was given explicit, though limited, treatment in the pastoral instruction issued by the Pontifical Commission for the Means of Social Communication, *Communio et progressio,* January 29, 1971, in *Vatican Council II, the Conciliar and Post-Conciliar Documents,* ed. Austin Flannery (Northport, N.Y.: Costello, 1986, 1987), nos. 115–21, pp. 330–32.

2. Although John Paul II acknowledged in principle the value of diocesan and parish pastoral councils for providing the means for collaboration and dialogue, following the widespread opinion at the 1987 synod of bishops on the laity, this pope was not an activist in promoting participatory forms of governance. See the scattered and undeveloped statements on dialogue in Pope John Paul II's discussion of the laity in the apostolic exhortation *Christifideles Laici* (Boston: St. Paul Books & Media, 1988), 25, 35, 37, 42, 46, 54, 57, 61. He acknowledged the necessity of "structures of participation" for advancing ecclesial communion at every level of the church's life by calling for greater listening by pastors. See John Paul II, *Novo Millennio Ineunte* (apostolic letter, January 6, 2001), 45. But such participation is understood to be consultative, not deliberative. This distinction between consultation and deliberation is intelligible and perhaps even practical, yet it implies a restriction of the roles of theologians and of the entire people of God in matters of teaching and governance, and eschews a fuller exploration of the dynamic interrelationships between them in a way that expresses the shared responsibility of all those involved in the teaching and learning processes, in governance and communal discernment. In John Paul's address during the *ad limina* meeting with bishops of Pennsylvania and New Jersey on September 12, 2004, he quoted from his 2003 postsynodal apostolic exhortation, *Pastores Gregis* (44), which states the need for each bishop to develop "a pastoral style which is ever more open to greater collaboration with all." But with the bishops he offered this telling caveat: "Within a sound ecclesiology of communion, a commitment to creating better structures of participation, consultation and shared responsibility should not be misunderstood as a concession to a secular 'democratic' model of governance, but as an intrinsic requirement of the exercise of episcopal authority and a necessary means of strengthening that authority."

3. My use of the term *reception* is informed by the research into the reception of church doctrine by the faithful since Vatican II pioneered by Yves Congar and Aloysius Grillmeier. For a helpful overview of the subject and valuable development drawing on the literary theory of Hans Robert Jauss, see Ormond Rush, *The Reception of Doctrine: An Appropriation of Hans Robert Jauss' Reception Aesthetics and Literary Hermeneutics* (Rome: Pontificia Università Gregoriana, 1997).

4. Hans Georg Gadamer, *Truth and Method,* 2nd rev. ed., revised translation by Joel Weinsheimer and Donald G. Marshall (New York: Crossroad, 1989). David Tracy treats in some detail the contribution of Gadamer in *Analogical Imagination* (New York: Crossroad, 1981) and *Plurality and Ambiguity: Hermeneutics, Religion, and Hope* (San Francisco: Harper & Row, 1987).

5. See Paul Ricoeur's critique of the use of dialogue to describe the act of reading texts in *From Text to Action: Essays in Hermeneutics, II,* trans. Kathleen Blamey and John B. Thompson (Evanston, Ill.: Northwestern University Press, 1991), 107.

6. Psychoanalyist Ruth C. Cohn has advanced this point, which has been drawn upon by Matthias Scharer and Bernd Jochen Hilberath in their *Kommunikative Theologie: Eine Grundlegung* (Mainz: Matthias-Grünewald-Verlag, 2002, 2003), 156.

7. C. G. Jung, "A Review of Complex Theory," in *The Collected Works of C. G. Jung,* trans. R. F. C. Hall (London: Routledge & Kegan Paul, 1960), 92–104, at 100; also see Murray Stein, "The Populated Interior," in *Jung's Map of the Soul: An Introduction* (Chicago: Open Court, 1998).

8. Vilém Flusser, *Kommunikologie* (Mannheim: Bollmann, 1996); idem, *Writings*, ed. Andreas Ströhl; trans. Erik Eisel (Minneapolis: University of Minnesota Press, 2002). For a discussion of Flusser's contribution in relation to communication in the church, see Scharer and Hilberath, *Kommunikative Theologie*, 96–122.

9. Here Gutiérrez invokes the work of Catholic philosopher Maurice Blondel: "This reflection attempts to understand the internal logic of an action through which persons seek fulfillment by constantly transcending themselves" (Gustavo Gutiérrez, *A Theology of Liberation* [Maryknoll, N.Y.: Orbis Books, 1988], 7–8). Gutiérrez combines this Blondelian anthropological approach to action with a Marxist insight into the social and political character of historical praxis bent on transforming the world.

10. Hermeneutics denotes an approach to interpreting the meaning of a text or a tradition. In ancient Christianity, interpretative strategies were learned from Jewish scribes and rabbis and from Greco-Roman grammar and rhetoric. My characterization here of classical and modern approaches to theology in terms of a hermeneutics of application and a hermeneutics of correlation is indebted to discussions with Matthias Scharer and Jochen Hilberath. As they point out in their work, this more praxis-oriented approach does not deny the importance and value of a hermeneutics of correlation, but complements it with a hermeneutics of difference, which gives greater attention to disruptions and conflict in discourse and praxis.

11. Alasdair MacIntyre, *After Virtue,* 2nd ed. (Notre Dame, Ind.: University of Notre Dame Press, 1984), 187.

12. Ibid., 191.
13. Ibid., 222.
14. Ibid.
15. In addition to the work of Pierre Bourdieu, which will be discussed below, the contributions of Emmanuel Levinas and Mikhail Bakhtin, especially in relation to the dialogical personalism of Martin Buber, have influenced my approach to these issues.
16. Pierre Bourdieu, *Outline of a Theory of Practice*, trans. Richard Nice (Cambridge: Cambridge University Press, 1977), 83, 80–81; also see John B. Thompson's introduction to Pierre Bourdieu, *Language and Symbolic Power*, trans. Gino Raymond and Matthew Adamson (Cambridge: Polity Press and Basil Blackwell, 1991), 12.
17. Bourdieu, *Outline of a Theory of Practice*, 168–69.
18. Pierre Bourdieu, *The Logic of Practice*, trans. Richard Nice (Stanford: Stanford University Press, 1990), 86.
19. Alfred Schutz, *The Phenomenology of the Social World*, trans. George Walsh and Frederick Lehnert (Evanston, Ill.: Northwestern University Press, 1967); see in particular Schutz's effort to think through and beyond Max Weber's approach to meaningful understanding by way of a closer analysis of the concept of action in terms of project and protention, and motivational context as the meaning context for social action.
20. Edward Farley, *Ecclesial Man: A Social Phenomenology of Faith and Reality* (Philadelphia: Fortress Press, 1975); Bernard Lonergan, *Insight: A Study of Human Understanding* (New York: Harper & Row, 1978); and *Method in Theology* (Minneapolis, Minn.: Seabury Press, 1979).
21. See, e.g., Paul Ricoeur, *From Text to Action*; idem, *Interpretation Theory: Discourse and the Surplus of Meaning* (Fort Worth: Texas Christian University Press, 1976); Martin Heidegger, *Being and Time*, trans. John Macquarrie and Edward Robinson (London: SCM Press, 1976). See also the texts by David Tracy and Hans Georg Gadamer previously cited.
22. E. D. Hirsch, Jr., *The Aims of Interpretation* (Chicago: University of Chicago Press, 1976); idem, *Validity in Interpretation* (New Haven: Yale University Press, 1967).
23. M. Shawn Copeland, "Self-Identity in a Multi-Cultural Church in a Multi-Cultural Context," in *The Multicultural Church: A New Landscape in U.S. Theologies*, ed. William Cenkner (New York: Paulist Press, 1996), idem, "Toward a Critical Christian Feminist Theology of Solidarity," in *Women and Theology*, ed. Mary Ann Hinsdale and Phyllis H. Kaminski (Maryknoll, N.Y.: Orbis Books, 1995); Mary McClintock Fulkerson, "Finding Place through Practices" a chapter from a forthcoming book with the working title *Traces of Redemption: Theology for a Worldly Church;* idem, "Practice," in *Handbook of Postmodern Biblical Interpretation*, ed. A. K. M. Adam (St. Louis: Chalice Press, 2000), 189–98; Kathryn Tanner, *Theories of Culture: A New Agenda for Theology* (Minneapolis, Minn.: Fortress Press, 1997); idem, "Theological Reflection and Christian Practices," in *Practicing Theology: Beliefs and Practices in Christian Life*, ed. Miroslav Volf and Dorothy C. Bass (Grand Rapids: Eerdmanns, 2002), 228–44.
24. Kathyrn Tanner offers a most helpful discussion of the shift from modern to postmodern approaches to culture in her book *Theories of Culture*.

1. THE MATRIX OF DIALOGUE IN THE CHURCH

1. Thomas P. Sweetser, *Successful Parishes: How They Meet the Challenges of Change* (Minneapolis, Minn.: Winston Press, 1983); Paul Wilkes, *Excellent Catholic Parishes: The Guide to the Best Places and Practices* (Mahwah, N.J.: Paulist, 2001).

2. I call these "hybrid" forms because in these acts communication often includes handing on a message or information by means of what may appear to be a one-way relation of speaker to many listeners, but in which one can detect dialogical dynamics and presuppositions at work between the ostensive speaker and listener.

3. The new Rite of Christian Initiation, called for by the Constitution on Sacred Liturgy (*Sacrosanctum Concilium* 64), offers an important example of a hybrid liturgical form that includes dialogical components.

4. This distinction of the threefold dialogue of preaching is my own; for relevant literature, see Robert P. Waznak, *An Introduction to the Homily* (Collegeville, Minn.: Liturgical Press, 1998), 23–25; Mary Catherine Hilkert, *Naming Grace: Preaching and the Sacramental Imagination* (New York: Continuum, 1997), esp. 89–107; (Bishop) Ken Untener, *Preaching Better: Practical Suggestions for Homilists* (New York: Paulist, 1999), esp. 67–72.

5. Luis Erdozain, "The Evolution of Catechetics: A Survey of Six International Study Weeks on Catechetics," *Lumen Vitae* 25 (1970): 7–31, at 10. The kerygmatic approach highlights salvation history as a grand narrative schema operative in the scriptures, liturgy, and catechesis. See, e.g., Josef Jungmann, "Theology and Kerygmatic Teaching," *Lumen Vitae* 5 (1950): 258–63. Drawing on a personalist version of existentialism, one is urged to "encounter," as if in a personal dialogue, the living God in the gospel message conveyed through the biblical and liturgical traditions.

A second, anthropological approach emerged during the 1960s and reflected the new brands of neo-Thomism associated with Karl Rahner, Bernard Lonergan, and Edward Schillebeeckx (see Erdozain, "Evolution of Catechetics," 15–22). This approach incorporated the basic tenets of the kerygmatic approach, but often fostered an experience-centered model of religious education that sought to surface basic questions and concerns that animated the lives of believers. Dialogue between educators and students and among students about the religious dimensions of human life was a basic ingredient in this approach to catechesis, but often it focused more on giving expression to life's questions and was unable to explore these issues in terms of the patterns of the scriptures and liturgy.

A third, praxis-based approach developed after the council, which gave special attention to social and political issues and promoted dialogue about Christian praxis in a world of suffering (Erdozain, "Evolution of Catechetics," 22–31). The model of see, judge, and act associated with Catholic Action groups that emerged in the 1920s in Europe gave way to the primacy of praxis in political theology in post-Shoah Germany and in Latin American liberation theology. Brazilian educator Paulo Freire was especially influential among pastoral ministers and theologians in Latin America, and his work eventually became well known to educators around the world, including religious educators. He criticized an information-oriented approach, which he called a banking concept of education, where teachers are the authorities who control discourse and transmit knowledge. His alternative was to develop a problem-solving approach to education that fostered critical consciousness, conscientization through dialogue about the contradictions and conflicts in social, political, and economic reality (Paulo Freire, *Pedagogy of the Oppressed*, trans. Myra Bergman Ramos [New York: Seabury Press, 1970]). For Freire's impact on religious education, see Mary C. Boys, *Educating in Faith: Maps and Visions* (San Francisco: Harper & Row, 1989), 124–26. The influential shared-praxis approach to religious education of Thomas Groome draws on Freire's work. Groome describes this approach as "a group of Christians sharing in dialogue their critical reflection on present action in light of the Christian story and its vision toward the end of lived Christian faith." Thomas H. Groome, *Christian Religious Education: Sharing Our Story and Vision* (San Francisco: Harper & Row, 1980), 184–232, at 184; cf. idem, *Sharing Faith: A Comprehensive Approach to Religious Education and Ministry: The Way of Shared Praxis* (San Francisco: HarperCollins, 1991), 135–54. See also the work of Matthias Scharer, *Begegnungen Raum geben: Kommunikatives Lernen als Dienst in Gemeinde, Schule und Erwachsenenbildung* (Mainz: Grünewald, 1995); and Matthias Scharer and Bernd Jochen Hilberath, *Kommunikative Theologie: Eine Grundlegung* (Mainz: Grünewald, 2002).

6. The cumulative advances in catechesis are reflected in the official Catholic documents the *General Catechetical Directory*, released in 1971, the new *Catechism of the Catholic Church* in 1994, and the revised *General Directory for Catechesis* in 1997. As these various catechetical methods were being criticized, the new *Catechism* emerged as a codification of certain achievements of Vatican II. At the same time, it offers a moment frozen in time governed by a distinctive official theology associated with Roman curial offices. The *Catechism* can foster the threefold pedagogical conversations with the saving mystery of faith conveyed through the scriptures and liturgy, with the dialogue of everyday life, and with the shared praxis of Christians in the world, but it can also cut short these conversations.

7. On small Christian communities, see Thomas A. Kleissler, Margo A. LeBert, Mary C. McGuinness *Small Christian Communities: A Vision of Hope for the 21st Century* (New York: Paulist, 1997); e.g., Renew, see http://www.renewintl.org/SmallChristianComm/index.htm (accessed August 22, 2005); see also Bernard J. Lee, William V. D'Antonio, and Virgilio Elizondo, *The Catholic Experience of Small Christian Communities* (New York: Paulist, 2000). On base Christian communities, see Leonardo Boff, *Ecclesiogenesis: The Basic Communities Reinvent the Church*, trans. Robert R. Barr (1977; Maryknoll, N.Y.: Orbis Books, 1986). Alvaro Barreiro, *Basic Ecclesial Communities: The Evangelization of the Poor*, trans. John Drury (Maryknoll, N.Y.: Orbis Books, 1982).

8. Susan K. Hedahl, *Listening Ministry: Rethinking Pastoral Leadership* (Minneapolis: Fortress, 2001).

9. The Decree on the Pastoral Office of Bishops in the Church (*Christus Dominus*) called for pastoral councils at the diocesan level presided over by the bishop, with clergy, religious, and laity chosen to participate with the aim "to investigate and consider matters relating to pastoral matters and to formulate practical conclusions concerning them" (27). The Decree on the Apostolate of Lay People (*Apostolicam actuositatem*) reiterated the desirability of such councils not only at the diocesan level but also at the parochial level, to foster the

apostolic work of evangelization, sanctification, and charity and social mission, and to coordinate "the various lay associations and undertakings, the autonomy and particular nature of each remaining intact" (26). The new Code of Canon Law requires that each parish have a finance council to help the priest administer the goods of the parish (canon 537). Parish pastoral councils are not required; however, the bishop can mandate parish pastoral councils after consulting with his priest council to determine whether it is opportune that a pastoral council be established in each parish of the diocese (canon 536). Almost two-thirds of the bishops in the United States have required parish pastoral councils.

10. Mark F. Fischer reported on the findings of previous studies by Charles A. Fecher for the National Council of Catholic Men in 1970, Robert G. Howes in 1976, and the Notre Dame Study of Catholic Parish Life in 1986. In 1994 Fischer developed a questionnaire about parish pastoral councils, which he sent to officials in every diocese in the United States. His own findings confirm this trajectory of growth: based on statistical percentages, Fischer concluded that of the 18,764 parishes in the United States according to the *Official Catholic Directory* of 1994, almost 79 percent of parishes and missions had councils, roughly 17,000 councils. See Mark Fischer, *Pastoral Councils in Today's Catholic Church* (Mystic, Conn.: Twenty-Third Publications, 2001), 11–16.

11. United States Catholic Conference of Bishops Committee on the Laity, "Report on Diocesan and Parish Pastoral Councils," March 12, 2004, http://www.usccb.org/laity/summary.htm (accessed November 19, 2004); an earlier survey was conducted in 1997 by the Center for Applied Research in the Apostolate (CARA) at the request of the National Conference of Catholic Bishops' (the earlier name of the USCCB) Committees on the Laity and on Pastoral Practices, http://www.usccb.org/laity/dpc.htm (accessed November 25, 2004).

12. The Decree on Bishops speaks of the collaboration of pastoral councils with the bishop concerning his pastoral work by investigating and considering pastoral activities and formulating practical conclusions (27). Interestingly, the same document speaks of the collaboration of bishops in episcopal conferences, such as synods, provincial councils, and plenary councils, so that by "sharing their wisdom and experience and exchanging views they may jointly formulate a program for the common good of the church" (37). Comparing these passages, the first text (27) states that pastoral councils collaborate by investigating and considering, while the latter (37) says that bishops do it by sharing and exchanging, with both groups aiming at formulating responses to pastoral issues. These texts may betray an assumption that only equals, in this case bishops, can share and exchange, whereas investigating and considering imply an inequality between the work of the pastoral councillors handed on to priests or bishops. However, even if this assumption is suggested, the sets of operations are combined in the dialogical work of councils, synods, and conferences.

13. Pope John Paul II in *Christifideles Laici*, described diocesan councils in terms of collaboration, dialogue, and discernment, and "in certain instances also in decision-making" (25), and parish councils in particular in terms of "general discussion," echoing the Decree on Lay People, as the means for examining and solving pastoral problems (10).

14. Fischer, *Pastoral Councils*, 57–64, 130–38. Fischer provided the results of his 1990

and 1995 surveys of pastoral council guidelines prepared by dioceses in the United States. The vast majority hold elections, but many also allow for appointed members either by the pastor or by committees as a supplement for elected members. There are instances of *ex officio* members, including associate priests, past parish council presidents, trustees, and representatives of the finance committee.

15. A process of group discernment is developed by Mary Benet McKinney, OSB, *Sharing Wisdom: A Process of Group Decision Making* (Allen, Tex.: Tabor, 1987; repr., Chicago: Thomas More Press, 1998). Fischer commends this kind of approach in *Pastoral Councils*, 214–15. Also see the proposals by William J. Rademacher and Marliss Rogers based on the process advanced by the Archdiocese of Milwaukee in *The New Practical Guide for Parish Councils* (Mystic, Conn.: Twenty-Third Publications, 1988), 221, 235.

16. Dennis O'Leary, "Parish Pastoral Councils: Instrument of Visioning and Planning," in *Developing a Vibrant Parish Pastoral Council*, ed. Arthur X. Deegan II (New York/Mahwah, N.J.: Paulist, 1995), 19–35, at 25.

17. McKinney pioneered this approach in *Sharing Wisdom*; also see Rademacher and Rogers, *New Practical Guide*, 140–46; and Fischer, *Pastoral Councils*, 43–44, 111, 115–26.

18. Fischer, *Pastoral Councils*, 124.

19. Ibid., 179; also see 144–46. Fischer sent questionnaires in 1994 and 1995. Of the 174 U.S. dioceses he received 98 responses, and he examined pastoral council guidelines from each of the thirteen regions.

20. Fischer, *Pastoral Councils*, 145.

21. The same Decree on Lay People recommended that the laity cooperate with parish priests in the apostolic mission of the church by examining the problems of the ecclesial community in the world and proposing solutions through general discussion, but not in the context of the parish council (10). No mention is made of a diocesan or parochial council in this text, but the agenda corresponds to the pastoral model of council introduced in the Decree on the Bishops.

22. USCCB Committee on the Laity, "Report on Diocesan and Parish Pastoral Councils." A comprehensive list of additional activities was provided in the report.

23. Fischer, *Pastoral Councils*, 24–32; also see the work of William Rademacher and Marliss Rogers, Loughlan Sofield, and the Parish Evaluation Project of Thomas Sweetser.

24. John T. McGreevy, *Parish Boundaries: The Catholic Encounter with Race in the Twentieth Century Urban North* (Chicago: University of Chicago Press, 1998).

25. Various U.S. canon lawyers have written on shared responsibility and consultation. Robert T. Kennedy ("Shared Responsibility in Ecclesial Decision Making," *Studia Canonica* 14 [1980]: 5–23) identifies a variety of steps in the process of decision making: "gathering the factual data, producing creative ideas or options, making a choice, implementing a choice, evaluating the results." Kennedy's article is often cited against the tendency to dichotomize consultation and decision making, but the question whether Kennedy's argument simply lends support to canon 536 and other instances where only consultation is allowed, or whether it dilutes the canon's binding force, merits further consideration. Also see James Provost, "Canon Law and the Role of Consultation," *Origins* 18 (May 4, 1989): 793, 795–99; James A. Coriden, "Lay Persons and the Power of Governance," *The Jurist* 59

(1999): 335–47; John Beal, "The Exercise of the Power of Governance by Lay People: State of the Question," *The Jurist* 55 (1999): 1–92; John Huels, "The Power of Governance and Its Exercise by Lay Persons," *Studia Canonica* 35 (2001): 59–96.

26. In the apostolic letter *Novo Millennio Ineunte* (45) (2001), and in the apostolic exhortation *Pastores Gregis* (44) (2003), John Paul II commended participatory structures of collaboration at the parish level, while reaffirming their consultative, not deliberative, nature. This position, which some regard as restrictive and repressive, was reiterated in the document signed by the prefects of numerous curial dicasteries entitled "The Instruction on Certain Questions Regarding the Collaboration of the Non-ordained Faithful in the Sacred Ministry of Priests" (August 15, 1997), *Acta Apostolicae Sedis* 89 (1997): 852–77, especially article 4, "The Parish Priest and the Parish," and article 5, "The Structures of Collaboration in the Particular Church." It is noteworthy that the report on the 2004 survey of U.S. bishops on diocesan and parish pastoral councils offers no information about the mode of decision making for these councils as recommended by the bishops, as stated in diocesan pastoral council guidelines, or as utilized by bishops and priests in their dioceses.

27. Fischer, *Pastoral Councils*, 39–47, at 42; see also 184–96.

28. Ibid., 45.

29. On this debate, see Rademacher and Rogers, *New Practical Guide*, 31–61; Thomas P. Sweetser and Patricia M. Forster, *Transforming the Parish: Models for the Future* (Lanham, Md.: Sheed & Ward, 1993; rev. ed., 1999), 83–103; Sweetser, *Parish as Covenant*, 23–42. Rademacher's critique can be found with a number of responses, including Mark Fischer's, in *The Role of the Council Today: Consultative Only?* which originally appeared in *Today's Parish* (March 2000) and was reprinted in the *Parish Ministry in Practice* series (Mystic, Conn.: Twenty-Third Publications, 2001).

30. Forster and Sweetser, *Transforming the Parish*, 92–103, at 93.

31. Ibid., 101; see also Sweetser, *Parish as Covenant*, 32–34.

2. DISCERNING THE MISSION OF THE LOCAL CHURCH

1. On the need to develop new structures of conversation and collaboration between theologians and bishops, see "In Service to the Gospel: A Consensus Statement of the Joint Committee" of the Catholic Theological Society of America and the Canon Law Society of America, *Cooperation between Theologians and the Ecclesiological Magisterium*, ed. Leo J. O'Donovan (Washington, D.C.: Canon Law Society, Catholic University of America, 1982), 175–89, esp. 183–85. Based on this work, the United States Conference of Catholic Bishops approved the statement *Doctrinal Responsibilities: Approaches to Promoting Cooperation and Resolving Misunderstandings between Bishops and Theologians* (Washington, D.C.: United States Catholic Conference, 1989). The Archdiocese of Milwaukee has experimented with a council of theologians designated the Archbishop's Consultation on Theological Issues.

2. Dennis J. O'Leary, "An Integrated Approach to Shared Responsibility: Where

Does the Diocesen/Eparchial Pastoral Council Fit?" (2004), http://www.usccb.org/laity/oleary.htm (accessed December 17, 2004).

3. Of the 166 surveys sent out, 137 responses were received. See the United States Catholic Conference, *A Survey of Diocesan Pastoral Councils in the U.S.A.* prepared by the steering committee of the USCC Advisory Council (Washington, D.C.: United States Catholic Conference, 1972). In conjunction with that USCC project, see *The CARA Symposium on Diocesan Pastoral Councils*, published in May 1971. For further information on diocesan pastoral councils, see Mark F. Fischer, *Pastoral Councils in Today's Catholic Parish* (Mystic, Conn.: Twenty-Third Publications, 2001), 19–20, 79–86.

4. United States Conference of Catholic Bishops, Committee on the Laity, *Building the Local Church: Shared Responsibility in Diocesan Pastoral Councils*, ed. Mary P. Burke and Eugene F. Hemrick (Washington, D.C.: United States Catholic Conference, 1974), 65–66. The National Conference of Catholic Bishops Secretariat for the Laity published *Journeying Together: Proceedings of Three Regional Convocations on Shared Responsibility in America*, ed. Dolores R. Leckey and Caroline Chastain (Washington, D.C.: United States Catholic Conference, 1985).

5. Bryan T. Froehle, *Diocesan and Eparchial Pastoral Councils: A National Profile,* A Study Commissioned by the U.S. Bishops' Committees on the Laity and Pastoral Practices, undertaken by the Center for Applied Research in the Apostolate (CARA) (Washington, D.C.: United States Catholic Conference, 1998), 7–8.

6. USCCB Committee on the Laity, "Report on Diocesan and Parish Pastoral Councils" (March 12, 2004).

7. Froehle, *Diocesan and Eparchial Pastoral Councils*, 11.

8. Ibid., 21.

9. John R. Vaughan, "A Canonical Analysis of the Second Synod of the Diocese of Owensboro [Kentucky] compared to the Recent Synods of the Dioceses of Helena [Montana], La Crosse [Wisconsin], New York [New York], and St. Louis [Missouri]" (Ph.D. diss., Pontificia Università Gregoriana, Rome, 1995), 7.

10. Lay participation was permitted in the eighteenth century as an exception for "grave and urgent" reasons. See Vaughan, "Canonical Analysis," 75–76, drawing on the work of Giuseppe Spinelli, "Il rapporto di collaborazione dei fedeli della Chiesa particolare con l'assemblea sinodale," in *La Synodalité: La participation au gouvernement dans l'Église; Acts of the 7th International Congress of Canon Law* (Paris: Faculté de Droit Canonique de L'Institut Catholique de Paris, 1992), 685–88; Giorgio Corbellini, "Il Sinodo Diocesano nel Nuovo Codex Iuris Canonici" (Diss., Pontificia Università Lateranense, Rome, 1986); David Ross, "Participation in the Synod," *Monitor Ecclesiasticus* 116 (1989): 462–82.

11. Vaughan, "Canonical Analysis," 15–16, 74–78.

12. This contrast is made by Seamus O'Connor, "The Structure of a Post-Conciliar Diocesan Synod in the United States of America" (J.C.D. diss., Catholic University of America, 1970), 136–49. See also David M. Ross, "Diocesan Synods: The Application of the Law in Three Dioceses in the United States of America [Boston, New Orleans, Toledo]" (J.C.D. diss, University of Ottawa, 1992), 27–28, 205–6.

13. Congregations for Bishops and for the Evangelization of Peoples, "Instruction on Diocesan Synods," *Origins* 27 (October 23, 1997): 324–31, at 328.

14. James A. Coriden, "The Diocesan Synod: An Instrument of Renewal for the Local Church," *Jurist* 34 (1974): 68–93; see also Francis Bernard Donnelly, *The Diocesan Synod: An Historical Conspectus and Commentary*, Canon Law Studies 74 (Washington, D.C.: Catholic University of America Press, 1932).

15. Synod of Bishops, "Final Report," *Origins* 15 (December 19, 1985): 446.

16. The 1973 *Directory on the Pastoral Mission of Bishops* issued by the Congregation for Bishops specified the following purposes: "adapting the laws and norms of the universal Church to local conditions, resolving problems encountered in the apostolate and administration, giving impetus to projects and undertakings, and correcting errors in doctrine and morals if they have crept in." More recently attention has been focused on diocesan synods as a source of spiritual renewal and *aggiornamento* through pastoral planning aimed at advancing the pastoral mission of the diocese (*Directory*, 163, as cited in Vaughan, "Canonical Analysis," 17–18).

17. "Instruction on Diocesan Synods," 325. The same document identifies certain circumstances that suggest the need for a synod: "lack of an overall diocesan pastoral plan; the need to apply at the local level norms and other directives; acute pastoral problems requiring pastoral solutions; a need to further a more intense ecclesial communion, etc." (325).

18. There were 141 dioceses in existence in the United States at the start of Vatican II, and there have been 35 established since the end of the council in 1965.

19. I have developed a chronicle of diocesan synods that have taken place in the United States since Vatican II that I have correlated with records of existing diocesan pastoral councils from surveys taken in 1972, 1984, and 1998. Many of the diocesan synods that took place between Vatican II and 1990 were noted in the essay by James Provost, "Ecclesiological Nature and Function of the Diocesan Synod," 540 n. 7. Additional information was provided by Msgr. Daniel J. Murray, Diocese of Orange County; Paul Philibert, OP, Aquinas Institute; and Siobahn Verbeeck, associate director of the USCCB Secretariat for Doctrine and Pastoral Practices. Barbara Anne Cusack, chancellor of the Archdiocese of Milwaukee, posted on my behalf on the listserv of the Canon Law Society a request for information about diocesan synods that took place since Vatican II in the United States. Bryan Froehle also offered several pieces of information and recommendations. Additional post-Vatican II synods may yet be discovered, but the numbers presented here are based on the most complete listing available at this time.

20. This correlative judgment is based on the findings from the 1984 USCC Committee on the Laity survey and 1998 CARA survey of dioceses with active diocesan pastoral councils and my own collection of data on diocesan synods. The correlation pertains to dioceses that have diocesan pastoral councils during approximately the same time period of the synod or subsequently. There are several dioceses that have had synods but did not indicate an active diocesan pastoral council in 1984 or 1998: Steubenville synod held in 1983; Toledo, Peoria, 1984; El Paso, 1988; La Crosse, 1986; St. Louis, 1989; Philadelphia, 2002.

21. Archdiocese of Detroit Diocesan Synod Planning Booklet, 4 (emphasis in original).

22. The Milwaukee synod provides an important example because Archbishop Weak-

land was an outspoken proponent of broad-based consultation among those in the U.S. hierarchy. Moreover, several years after the synod Donald H. Thimm, a priest of the archdiocese and chair of the Synod Coordinating Committee, wrote a description and analysis of the synod entitled "Synod 1987: 'Walking Together' Archdiocese of Milwaukee 1984–1987" (D. Min. diss., St. Mary of the Lake, Mundelein, Ill., 1991). Additional documents were obtained from the archdiocesan archives.

23. The code does not discuss the role of prayer and liturgy in diocesan synods. Some synods were preceded by a spiritual renewal program, such as RENEW or Christ Renews His Parish. Others viewed the synod itself as promoting spiritual renewal. Ross, "Diocesan Synods," 28.

24. The methodology of the commissions had three components: (1) State needs and experiences of the church at present and into the probable future. (2) Analyze those needs and experience. Foster social analysis by asking: Why are things the way they are? Promote theological analysis and reflection by asking: What do the gospel, our tradition, the documents of Vatican II, and other church documents or writings have to say about our needs and experiences? (3) Develop recommendations for what should be done to meet needs. Specify who should do what and why. See Thimm, "Synod 1987," 44–45. This method drew from Joe Holland and Peter Henriot, SJ, *Social Analysis: Linking Faith and Justice* (Maryknoll, N.Y.: Orbis Books, in collaboration with the Center for Concern, 1983). The code requires that all participants make a creedal profession of faith as approved by the Congregation for the Doctrine of the Faith in the context of the synod (canon 833).

25. Thimm, "Synod 1987," 103.

26. Ibid., 73.

27. Ibid., 76.

28. Ibid., 40.

29. The 1984–1987 Milwaukee synod numbers were as follows: 55,000 people returned surveys; 66,000 participated in parish/community synods; 4,000 participated in regional synods; 2,000 at the general synod. The number of people involved in leadership roles: 1,000 were involved in parish/community synod teams; 150 were involved in the various synod committees and commissions; 150 people were small-group leaders.

30. Thimm, "Synod 1987," 56.

31. Ross, "Diocesan Synods," 207.

32. "Instructions on Diocesan Synods," 327.

33. Domenico Mogavero in his essay "Il Sinodo Diocesano" (in *Chiesa Particolare e Strutture di Communione* [Bologna: Edizioni Dehoniane, 1985], 53–70, at 61–64) raises these concerns. Vaughan discusses Mogavero's cautions but concludes, based on his own analysis of five U.S. synods: "Indeed there is no evidence that any of these notions was a particular problem in the synods we have studied" ("Canonical Analysis," 162).

34. Weakland drew attention to three passages from the Acts of the Apostles: the election of Matthias (Acts 1:15–26); the care of the Greek-speaking Christians who were being neglected (6:2–6); and the first council of Jerusalem (chap. 15). He located in these and other New Testament passages three "democratic" seeds.

35. Thimm, "Synod 1987," 130–34.

36. David Ross discusses two means of discovering popular opinions among the people of God: listening sessions ("town hall" meetings) and surveys ("Diocesan Synods," 111–18).

37. Ibid., 30.

38. Ibid., 30–31.

39. "Instruction on Diocesan Synods," 328, citing *Christus Dominus* 8 and canon 381.

40. Ross, "Diocesan Synods," 67.

41. The quotations from Alesandro and Green are taken from Ross, "Diocesan Synods," 162–63; J. Alesandro in *The Code of Canon Law: A Text and Commentary*, ed. J. Coriden, T. Green, and D. Heintschel (New York/Mahwah, N.J.: Paulist, 1985), 381; T. Green, "The Diocesan Bishop in the Revised Code: Some Introductory Reflections," *The Jurist* 41 (1982): 337.

3. AN OVERWHELMING RESPONSE TO A U.S. BISHOPS' INVITATION

1. Several dialogical consultations took place during this period. The 1975 pastoral letter "This Land Is Home to Me: Powerlessness in Appalachia," prepared by the Catholic bishops in the region, began in May 1973 with extensive dialogue sessions in the Appalachian region. See Regional Pastoral Letter, "Powerless in Appalachia," *Origins* 4 (February 13, 1975): 529, 531–43; "A Regional Ministry for Appalachia," *Origins* 5 (February 12, 1976): 540–47. The U.S. bishops also engaged in broad consultation in the preparation of the *National Catechetical Directory* in 1979 and the pastoral letter on moral values in 1976.

2. My treatment of Call To Action draws on an unpublished book manuscript by David O'Brien describing the history of the bicentennial program and a few of the debates surrounding it, which was written within six months after the national convention. Also invaluable were exchanges with Francis J. Butler, the chair of the bicentennial justice subcommittee, and Maria Riley, OP, who designed the national CTA process. Important too is Anthony J. Pogorelc, "Social Movements within Organizations: The Case of Call to Action and U.S. Catholic Bishops" (Ph.D. diss., Purdue University, West Lafayette, Indiana, 2002). Pogorelc offers a valuable analysis of the CTA as a social movement organization within an institutional organization (the Roman Catholic Church) oscillating between phases of cooperation and opposition.

3. A similar model was used by the Austrian Bishops' Conference on October 23–26, 1998, when they convened a national assembly, Dialog für Osterreich, to discuss and vote on church policies. This work related to the 1995 Kirchenvolks-Begehren, the petition drive calling for five church reforms: full equality of all the people of God; equal rights to women; lifting mandatory celibacy; encouraging a more positive understanding of sexuality; teaching the gospel as a message of joy, which led to the development of the We Are Church movement in Austria, Europe, and, through the Web, around the world.

4. "NCCB/USCC Mission Statement," *Pastoral Letters of the United States Catholic Bishops*, ed. Hugh J. Nolan (Washington, D.C.: USCC, 1984) vol. 4, *1975–1983*, 486.

5. Marie Augusta Neal, SNDdeN, was a member of the advisory council to the U.S. bishops, which was initiated in 1970 by the NCCB president, Cardinal John Dearden. This advisory committee is composed of bishops, priests, women religious, and laypersons selected from each region of the country and meets regularly before the NCCB meetings to reflect on its agenda in light of Catholic opinion. Neal explored the idea of a National Pastoral Council with church leaders and scholars, but decided against it because of the uneven experience of the new implementation of parish and diocesan pastoral councils. More experience with structures of consultation was needed (O'Brien, manuscript, 68–69).

6. Bishop James Rausch persuaded Cardinal Dearden and Archbishop Bernardin to get involved in the project.

7. Women religious were promoting consideration of the theme of justice in the church as well as outside the church, following up on the 1971 synod statement on *Justice in the World.*

8. I am indebted to Francis Butler for drawing my attention to the influence of Msgr. Jack Egan on the parish phase of the bicentennial program. Also see John J. Egan, Peggy Roach, and Philip J. Murnion, "Catholic Committee on Urban Ministry: Ministry to the Ministers," *Review of Religious Research* 20 (Summer 1979): 279–90.

9. See Saul Alinsky, *Reveille for Radicals* (Chicago: University of Chicago Press, 1946); idem, *Rules for Radicals* (New York: Vintage Books, 1971). For background, see David P. Finks, *The Radical Vision of Saul Alinsky* (Ramsey, N.J.: Paulist Press, 1984); Standford E. Horwitt, *Let Them Call Me Rebel: Saul Alinsky, His Life and Legacy* (New York: Vintage Books, 1989). On the training centers and their relation to Alinsky, see Gary Delgado, *The Roots of Acorn* (Philadelphia: Temple University Press, 1986); on the Industrial Area Foundation, the oldest center started by Alinsky, in 1940, see Cynthia Perry: *IAF: 50 Years Organizing for Change* (Franklin Square, N.Y.: Industrial Area Foundation, 1990).

10. David Hollenbach has criticized the limited role given to conflict and confrontation in Catholic social thought in *Claims in Conflict: Retrieving and Renewing the Catholic Human Rights Tradition* (New York: Paulist, 1979), esp. 161–66.

11. See Robert McClory, *Turning Point: The Inside Story of the Papal Birth Control Commission, and How Humanae Vitae Changed the Life of Patty Crowley and the Future of the Church* (New York: Crossroad, 1997).

12. O'Brien, manuscript, 103.

13. Cardinal John Dearden, letter on inside cover of *Liberty and Justice for All: A Discussion Guide*, prepared by the Institute for Continuing Education Archdiocese of Detroit (1975).

14. O'Brien, manuscript, 119.

15. Ibid., 123.

16. Anthony Pogorelc has listed the speakers at all of the Justice Hearings in his Appendix H, with the exception of the special session devoted to international issues.

17. O'Brien, manuscript, 124.

18. Mark R. Warren, *Dry Bones Rattling: Community Building to Revitalize American Democracy* (Princeton, N.J.: Princeton University Press, 2001), 51. On the shift from

Alinsky's approach to that of Communities Organized for Public Service (COPS), see pp. 40–71.

19. O'Brien, manuscript, 149.

20. The seven volumes called "The Justice Hearings" can be found in the USCCB library and in the archives at the University of Notre Dame. A few volumes are also available in the archives in the Detroit archdiocese from the Dearden years.

21. Maria Riley, OP, "Religious Life and Women's Issues," in *Journey in Faith & Fidelity: Women Shaping Religious Life for a Renewed Church*, ed. Nadine Foley, OP (New York: Continuum, 1999), 242–59, at 250.

22. The seven final reports can be found in the archives of the USCCB in the archives at The Catholic University of America (Box 226, File Folders 26–33).

23. O'Brien, manuscript, 142.

24. A modified version of *Robert's Rules of Order* was used. After amendments were presented in the various section groups and in plenary sessions, people were asked, "Shall this amendment be considered?" A voice vote could be taken. The moderator could ask for counting if the outcome was in doubt. Many amendments were rejected in this manner.

25. O'Brien, manuscript 169–72, at 171; also text on http://www.justpeace.org/NCCB 101976.htm.

26. O'Brien, manuscript, 176.

27. The approved resolutions can be found in *Origins* 6 (November 4, 1976): 309, 311–23.

28. According to Pogorelc, only 14 (or 8 percent) of the 182 resolutions passed at the Call To Action conference were controversial; 92 percent were not ("Social Movements within Organizations," 121).

29. There are certain lacunae in the documents: for example, the role of media and culture in promoting domestic and urban violence, materialism, and various forms of sexual abuse were not addressed (rape is mentioned in the resolution on personhood, no. 5). The experience and vocation of singles were not substantively addressed.

30. There may be more to Greeley's animus toward the U.S. bishops' bicentennial program than meets the eye. Greeley had done confidential research on the American priesthood for the NCCB two years before the bicentennial program that had not been well received by the bishops. Moreover, he was not invited to become a member of one of the bicentennial committees.

31. Andrew Greeley, "Catholic Social Activism—real or rad/chic?" *National Catholic Reporter*, Microfilm 11 (February 7, 1975): 7–8, 10–11; Letters to the editor in response 11 (February 28, 1975) 10–11; David J. O'Brien, "Greeley's Scenario Features Straw Men," and additional letters to the editor, 11 (March 7, 1975): 10–11; Greeley's response, "Greeley Defends Critique of Bishops' Booklet," 11 (March 14, 1975): 14.

32. John A. Ryan (1869–1945) taught moral theology at St. Paul Seminary in Minnesota and at The Catholic University of America and was the author of *A Living Wage* (New York: Macmillan, 1906), which discussed in moral and economic terms the challenges facing wage workers.

33. The Center for Concern was established in Washington, D.C., at the request of

Father Pedro Arrupe, SJ, by two Jesuits, Bill Ryan and Phil Land, who were present at the1971 Rome Synod, which framed the statement entitled "Justice in the World" on work for justice as a constitutive dimension of the gospel. The Center played a leadership role in the NCCB bicentennial program.

34. O'Brien manuscript, 97–100, at 100.

35. Andrew Greeley, "Catholic Social Activism–real or rad/chic?" 11.

36. Quoted in O'Brien, manuscript, 187.

37. Msgr. George G. Higgins, "Comments on Father Andrew Greeley's Views," in "The Yardstick," his syndicated column for the week of April 14, 1975, from the archives at The Catholic University of America.

38. Msgr. George G. Higgins, "Comments on Father Andrew Greeley's Views." He goes on to commend the bishops for being "attentive listeners," "superbly good listeners," which made a favorable impression on Catholics and some of the visiting experts as well. He also notes that "the San Antonio meeting invalidated Father Greeley's repeated allegation that the subcommittee is not interested in hearing from the ethnic groups in American society. Articulate spokesmen for several ethnic groups made very effective presentations to the panels."

39. On issues of birth control, married clergy, and divorce and remarriage, one could argue that there would be no difference between the delegates who attended the Call To Action convention and the overall Catholic populace. This is confirmed by none other than Andrew M. Greeley's survey, *The American Catholic: A Social Portrait* (New York: Basic Books, 1977). According to his study: 83 percent of Catholics approved of artificial contraception, 73 percent of remarriage after divorce, 80 percent would accept and 62 percent were in favor of married clergy; 29 percent approved of women's ordination.

40. Pogorelc's dissertation examines the horizontal relationships between the bishops, the community, and the broader culture and the vertical relationships of the bishops to the pope and Roman curial offices. He provides many details based on interviews and archival work. One of the most interesting is a letter from the Vatican secretary of state, Cardinal Villot, dated May 31, 1977, to Archbishop Bernardin, commending him for his leadership in having the U.S. bishops not pursue recommendations at variance with church teaching and discipline: women's ordination, celibacy, contraception. "I have brought the entire matter and all your observations to the personal attention of the Holy Father [Pope Paul VI]. His Holiness now directs me to commend you in his name for all that you have done. . . . He is deeply pleased with your desire to maintain close ecclesial communion with the See of Peter and with the universal Church. In particular he thanks you for your vigilance on behalf of the Catholic and apostolic faith . . ." ("Social Movements within Organizations," 141).

41. Bernardin and other critics who spoke of special interest groups rarely indicated which groups they meant (O'Brien, manuscript, 228).

42. Marginal note, *Origins* 6 (May 19, 1977): 761.

43. *Origins* 7 (September 29, 1977): 230–31.

44. "U.S. Bishops Meet: A Response to the Call To Action," *Origins* (May 19, 1977): 757–64, at 759.

45. Ibid., quoting *Lumen Gentium* 25.

46. "U.S. Bishops Meet: A Response to the Call To Action," 759–60.

47. Ibid., 763.

48. "Progress Report of the Call To Action Committee," *Origins* 7 (September 29, 1977): 230–31.

49. Donald Cozzens, *Sacred Silence: Denial and the Crisis in the Church* (Collegeville, Minn.: Liturgical Press, 2003), 29.

50. NCCB, "To Do the Work of Justice: A Plan of Action of the Catholic Community in the U.S.," approved May 4, 1978; for document, see A Call To Action, "Five-Year Plan of Action," *Origins* 8 (May 25, 1978): 12–16.

51. Each of the appropriate committees at the USCC/NCCB did have to reckon with the Call To Action recommendations and in numerous cases one can find traces of their work carrying on. In fact, in an indirect way the advisory process that was initiated by the bicentennial program did reach its intended goal by offering each of the committees of the USCC/NCCB concrete recommendations concerning problems that were to be worked on for years to come.

52. The subsequent appointment of Bernardin as archbishop in Chicago eventually improved relations with the social activists in the area. Cardinal Bernardin met with the Chicago Call To Action staff when he first arrived in Chicago in the early 1980s, acknowledging that there were issues about which they disagreed, but expressing his hope of establishing good working relationships. Toward the end of his life Bernardin met on two occasions with several members of the Chicago Call To Action staff. He wanted to talk with them about his desire to attend a future Call To Action Conference. He died before this could take place. But his actions suggested an awareness on his part that broken bridges that he himself had contributed to by his public response to Call To Action were in need of repair.

53. Bernard J. Cooke describes the work of the Chicago Call To Action in his essay "Call To Action: Engine of Lay Ministry," in *What's Left? Liberal American Catholics*, ed. Mary Jo Weaver (Bloomington/Indianapolis, Ind.: Indiana University Press, 1999), 135–46.

54. *Commonweal* devoted a special supplement in 1986 to commemorating CTA's tenth anniversary: "A Call To Action: An Unfinished Experiment," with essays by David O'Brien, John Cardinal Dearden, Francis J. Butler, Dolores L. Curran, James Finn, Dennis McCann, Kenneth Briggs, and John Tracy Ellis.

55. O'Brien, manuscript, 253; for Dearden text, see *Origins* 6 (November 18, 1976): 345–48, at 347 (italics in original).

4. A NEW WAY OF TEACHING WITH AUTHORITY

1. On the college of bishops and the character and structure of collegiality, see *Lumen Gentium*, nos. 18–23; *Christus Dominus*, nos. 3–6; 36–38.

2. For a brief description of regional councils, provincial councils, and plenary councils, see Francis A. Sullivan, "The Teaching Authority of Episcopal Conferences," *Theological Studies* 63 (2002): 472–93, at 472–73.

3. *Christus Dominus*, no. 37. On episcopal conferences, see Thomas J. Reese, ed., *Episcopal Conferences: Historical, Canonical and Theological Studies* (Washington, D.C.: Georgetown University Press, 1989); H. Legrand, J. Manzanares, and A. García Y García, eds., *Les Conférences épiscopales: Théologie, statut canonique, avenir* (Paris: Éditions du Cerf, 1988).

4. The Latin American Episcopal Conference (CELAM) launched a new period in the exercise of episcopal teaching authority at the second general conference in Medellín, Colombia, in 1968 and at the third general conference in Puebla, Mexico, in 1979. These documents received wide attention for being prophetic statements addressing the dire economic and social situation in Latin America. But what is equally important is the changed method of teaching used to generate these documents. The bishops paid special heed to the lived experience and harsh realities of the people of Latin America. The Medellín documents have a definite structure: first, attention is given to pertinent facts about the contemporary situation in Latin America; second, relevant church doctrines are reflected upon; and third, pastoral plans are developed applying the doctrines to the situations. As important as these formal declarations were and as innovative as they were in terms of their data gathering and social analysis, they still reflect the common practices of generating such documents: bishops working with selected theologians and consulting with other experts in the relevant fields as needed, and revisions made by bishops working collegially. But the effort of the bishops to learn about the everyday struggles of the members of their community offered a major step in advancing a dialogical procedure for generating teaching. Roberto Oliveros reports that "the various meetings that had been held in preparation for the [Medellín] Conference allowed our peoples to make their voices heard and bring their situation to expression." "History of the Theology of Liberation," in *Mysterium Liberationis: Fundamental Concepts of Liberation Theology*, ed. Ignacio Ellacuria, SJ, and Jon Sobrino, SJ (Maryknoll, N.Y.: Orbis Books; New York: Collins Dove, 1993), 3–32, at 15.

5. For the longer history of pastoral letters by the U.S. bishops, see Camilla J. Kari, *Public Witness: The Pastoral Letters of the American Catholic Bishops* (Collegeville, Minn.: [Michael Glazier] Liturgical Press, 2004).

6. Peter Guilday, *A History of the Councils of Baltimore (1791–1884)* (New York: Macmillan, 1932); idem, *The National Pastorals of the American Hierarchy (1792–1919)* (Washington, D.C.: National Catholic Welfare Council, 1923).

7. On Bishop John England, see Patrick Carey, *An Immigrant Bishop: John England's Adaptation of Irish Catholicism to American Republicanism* (Yonkers, N.Y.: U.S. Catholic Historical Society, 1982), 141–47.

8. On the formation of the National Catholic War Council in 1917 and the National Catholic Welfare Council in 1919, see Elizabeth K. McKeown, "The 'National Idea' in the History of the American Episcopal Conference," and Gerald P. Fogerty, "The Authority of the National Catholic Welfare Conference," in *Episcopal Conferences: Historical, Canonical and Theological Studies*, 59–84 (at 68) and 85–103.

9. See Vatican II's Decree on the Pastoral Office of the Bishops in the Church (*Christus Dominus*), 36–38.

10. "NCCB/USCC Mission Statement," in *Pastoral Letters of the United States Catholic Bishops*, vol. 4, *1975–1983*, ed. Hugh J. Nolan (Washington, D.C.: USCC, 1984), 486.

11. As of July 1, 2001, the USCC and the NCCB combined as the United States Conference of Catholic Bishops (USCCB).

12. I am not considering here formal policy statements drafted by committees of either the NCCB or the USCC.

13. "The Challenge of Peace: Second Draft," *Origins* 12 (October 28, 1982): 326.

14. Kari, *Public Witness*, 132. Although personal testimonies from poor people were not included in the pastoral letter, they were heard at regional hearings.

15. "Partners in the Mystery of Redemption: A Pastoral Response to Women's Concerns for Church and Society," *Origins* 17 (April 21, 1988): 759. See also "On File," *Origins* 14 (December 27, 1984): 460.

16. Jim Castelli attributes the so-called leak to Bishop Thomas Gumbleton of Detroit. See Kari, *Public Witness*, 74–75.

17. See, e.g., Archbishop Joseph Bernardin, "Bishops Delay Peace Pastoral," *Origins* 12 (April 26, 1982): 170–71.

18. The dissemination and approval of the final documents are as follows. Peace pastoral: committee began July 1981; first confidential draft released June 11, 1982; second draft published October 28, 1982; third draft published April 14, 1983, and approved on May 3, 1983 (238 in favor, 9 against). Economic pastoral: committee began meeting in 1981; first draft released November 11, 1984; second draft released October 5, 1985; third draft released June 2, 1986, and approved November 13, 1986 (225 in favor, 9 against). Women's pastoral: committee began March 1984; first draft released, April 21, 1988; second draft released April 5, 1990; third draft published April 23, 1992; fourth draft published September 10, 1992, and rejected on November 18–19, 1992 (137 in favor, 110 against, 190 needed for two-thirds majority for approval). The U.S. Catholic bishops created an ad hoc committee on the role of women in society and the church in 1972; in November 1978 the bishops decided women's concerns needed further attention; in November 1982 the committee proposed that the bishops address women's concerns through pastoral actions. In 1983 the bishops unanimously approved a proposal to write a pastoral addressing these concerns.

19. Jim Castelli reports that John Cardinal O'Connor spoke of the "spontaneous" character of these changes in procedure (*The Bishops and the Bomb: Waging Peace in a Nuclear Age* [Garden City, N.Y.: Image Books, 1983], 81).

20. "Prayer, reflection and discernment are as much needed as computer printouts. Listening, praying, reflecting, take time and a certain distance." Archbishop Rembert Weakland, "The Issues: Between Drafts of the Pastoral," *Origins* 15 (May 1985): 9.

21. The call for greater consultation with the laity is found in the 1967 doctrinal pastoral of the U.S. bishops, "The Church in Our Day," see Kari, *Public Witness*, 62–64.

22. Paul Joseph Fitzgerald, *L'Église comme lieu de formation d'une conscience de la concitoyenneté: Étude sur la rédaction en public de la lettre pastorale 'Economic Justice for All' (1986)*

(Villeneuve d'Ascq Cédex, France: Presses Universitaires du Septentrion, 1992), esp. 170–216, 217–87, 373–402; David O'Brien, *Public Catholicism*, 243–45, 249–52.

23. The first meeting of the Ad Hoc Committee on War and Peace took place on July 26, 1981. What was to be an initial set of four to six meetings grew into a much longer process of consultation because of the high level of interest in addressing the committee. The first draft was finished during the committee's fourteenth meeting in May 1982. When the committee reconvened to discuss reaction to the draft on July 28–30, they were overwhelmed with written responses, and because of the bulk of material to work through they had to prolong the process. By the time the second draft was ready to be released in October of 1982, there was much anticipation and an eager audience. Archbishop Roach and Cardinal Bernardin made a public statement on April 10, 1983: "In the final analysis . . . the third draft is far more the product of reflection and dialogue within the Catholic community than of dialogue between the drafting committee and the administration." Quoted in Jim Castelli, *Bishops and the Bomb*, 151.

24. *Origins* 15 (November 20, 1986): 395; also see his comments at the meeting a year before, "Collegiality, the Council and the Synod," *Origins* 15 (November 21, 1985): 388–91.

25. Thomas J. Reese, *Inside the Vatican: The Politics and Organization of the Catholic Church* (Cambridge, Mass.: Harvard University Press, 1996), 34.

26. *Origins* 12 (February 3, 1983): 545.

27. *Origins* 12 (April 7, 1983): 690–96, at 692–93.

28. *Origins* 12 (1983): 693.

29. For the various statements from the meeting, see *Origins* 18 (March 23, 1989): 677–86.

30. "The Bishop as Teacher of the Faith," *Origins* 18 (March 23, 1989): 681.

31. For the quoted comments by Ratzinger, see ibid., 681–82. Ratzinger is reflecting in this text on the scholarship of Jean Colson, Adalbert Hamman, and Hans Küng on the early exercise of episcopacy. Also see the comments by Cardinal John O'Connor about "the emergence of consensus theology," but also his defense of the approach of the U.S. bishops (682–86, esp. 685–86).

32. *Origins* 18 (March 30, 1989): 726.

33. Mozambique, Ireland, Canada, Brazil, Mexico, Italy, France, Germany, the Philippines, Poland, England, and Australia.

34. *Origins* 21 (June 13, 1991): 73.

35. *Origins* 21 (June 13, 1991): marginal note on p. 76.

36. The Vatican Congregation for Bishops in its draft document "Theological and Juridical Status of Episcopal Conferences" contrasted sharply *actio collegialis* (*effectus collegialis*) and *affectus collegialis* (sometimes translated as "collegial spirit"), which is found in *Lumen Gentium* at the ends of nos. 22 and 23 respectively (II. 2, *Origins*, 117 [April 7, 1988], 733). This distinction is used in the document on episcopal conferences as the basis for arguing that a collegial spirit and action are strictly speaking possible in the full sense only by the entire college of bishops, whereas episcopal conferences foster a collegial spirit among bishops, but as a group are not capable of a collegial action (and do not have a *munus magisterii* [*mandatum docendi*]) (ibid., sections IV–V, 734–35). This distinction, in my judg-

ment, is being too sharply drawn here and is hard to justify historically and conceptually as a basis for denying to episcopal conferences the ability to achieve a collegial action in teaching. John Paul II in his *motu proprio* on the episcopal conference neither explicitly denies nor affirms it has a *mandatum docendi* as a manifestation of a collegial act, but the net effect may be its denial. See John Paul II, *motu proprio Apostolos Suos, On the Theological and Juridical Nature of Episcopal Conferences* (May 21, 1998); Joseph Komonchak, "The Roman Working Paper on Episcopal Conferences," in *Episcopal Conferences: Historical, Canonical and Theological Studies*, 188–95; idem, "Authority and Its Exercise," in *Church Authority in American Culture: The Second Cardinal Bernardin Conference* (New York: Crossroad, 1999), 29–46, at 34–35; Francis A. Sullivan, "The Teaching Authority of Episcopal Conferences," *Theological Studies* 63 (2002): 472–93.

37. My own views on the triadic relationships between the entire people of God, the magisterium (bishops and pope), and theologians, which I will return to below, have been developed in conversation with the work of Bernd Jochen Hilberath who distinguishes and relates three levels of communication in the church and three groups that participate in this communication: (1) everyday communication of faith—the process of tradition—by all the people of God, (2) doctrinal discourse stated by the magisterium, and (3) theological discourse by theologians. *Communio* and consensus are realized only when the magisterium and theology are in active dialogue with the entire people of God. See Bernd Jochen Hilberath, "Vom Heiligen Geist des Dialogs: Das dialogische Prinzip in Gotteslehre und Heilsgeschehen," in *Dialog als Selbsvollzug der Kirche?* Quaestiones Disputatae series, ed., Gebhard Fürst (Freiburg: Herder, 1997), 93–116, at 110–11; idem, "Welche Theologie brauchen wir in der Fortbildung," in *Im Ursprung ist Beziehung: Theologisches Lernen als themenzenrierte Interaktion,* ed. Karl Joseph Ludwig (Mainz: Matthias Grünewald, 1997), 67–70; idem, "Der Wahrheit des Glaubens: Anmerkungen zum Prozeß der Glaubenskommunikation," in *Dimensionen der Wahrheit: Hans Küngs Anfrage im Disput*, ed. Bernd Jochen Hilberath (Tübingen: Francke Verlag, 1999), 51–80; idem, "Vorgaben für die Ausarbeitung der Communio-Ekklesiologie," in *Communio—Ideal oder Zerrbild von Kommunikation?* Quaestiones Disputatae series, ed., Bernd Jochen Hilberath (Freiburg: Herder, 1999), 277–97, at 291–97.

38. Dolores Leckey speaks of collaboration and consultation between the laity and the bishops, "Becoming a Collaborative Church," *Origins* 27 (August 27, 1987): 171–74; canonical issues are explored by James Provost, "Canon Law and the Role of Consultation," *Origins* 18 (May 4, 1989): 793–99.

39. See Kari's discussion of conservative Catholic reactions to the peace and economic pastorals, *Public Witness*, 80–86, 105–13.

40. Ibid., 130–31, 136–37.

41. Ibid., 144–45.

42. The passage from Bishop Joseph Imesch is cited by Dolores Leckey in "Crossing the Bridge: Women in the Church," *Church* 17 (2001): 11–17, at 11, emphasis mine.

43. The U.S. bishops address the issue of collaboration of bishops and theologians in two documents: "Doctrinal Responsibilities: Approaches to Promoting Cooperation and Resolving Misunderstandings between Bishops and Theologians," which was originally

drafted by the Catholic Theological Society of America and the Canon Law Society of America, and subsequently revised and approved by the bishops in June 1989 (Washington, D.C.: United States Catholic Conference, 1989); and "The Teaching Ministry of the Diocesan Bishop: A Pastoral Reflection," which is a statement of the NCCB issued in November 1991, *Pastoral Letters and Statements of the United States Catholic Bishops*, vol. 6, *1989–1997*, ed. Patrick W. Carey (Washington, D.C.: National Conference of Catholic Bishops/United States Catholic Conference, 1998), 321–65.

44. This is likewise reflected in the joint pastoral statement on migration and globalization by the Mexican and U.S. bishops' conferences, *Strangers No Longer: Together on the Journey of Hope*, issued January 22, 2003.

45. The review boards in the original draft were described as advisory, but with the implication that they have a measure of deliberative authority. A commission of four representatives of the Roman curia and four U.S. bishops was formed to address problems with the draft Charter for the Protection of Children and Young People, and the Norms for Diocesan/Eparchial Policies Dealing with Allegations of Sexual Abuse of Minors by Clergy or Other Church Personnel. As Bishop Wilton Gregory, the president of the USCCB at the time, said, "the Holy See wants to look at some of the provisions for actions that we have called for in the documents, because as they are currently described they 'are difficult to reconcile with the universal law of the church' and therefore 'can be the source of confusion and ambiguity.' An example would be the proper role of the review boards. . . ." This quotation is from Bishop Wilton Gregory, "Vatican-U.S. Bishops Commission to Address Points in Sexual Abuse of Minors Policy," *Origins* 32 (October 31, 2002): 341, 343, at 343. For the draft document and norms, see *Origins* 32 (June 13, 2002): 65, 67–72; and *Origins* 32 (June 27, 2002): 107–10. The revised document underscored the consultative character of the review boards, see *Origins* 32 (November 28, 2002): 409, 411–18, e.g., Article 2, p. 412; Norms 4, p. 417.

5. PLACATING POLARIZATIONS OR MAKING THEM PRODUCTIVE?

1. The statement drafted between 1995 and 1996 by the original discussion group appealed for reflection on this pastoral situation and invited readers "to consider whether the criteria for authentic and effective dialogue proposed in the document spoke to the church." They also offered a practical response to their own appeal: "an effort to conduct dialogue in the church that would both illumine a particular issue and identify methods and models of dialogue that could enhance discussion of issues in any form." A committee of twenty-five members was formed by the cardinal, which included about half of the original discussion group. Cardinal Joseph Bernardin and Archbishop Oscar H. Lipscomb, *Catholic Common Ground Initiative: Foundational Documents*, introduction by Philip J. Murnion (New York: Crossroad, 1997).

2. *CCGI: Foundational Documents*, 11.

3. Ibid., 40.

4. Ibid., 42–44.

5. Cardinal Bernard Law, "Response to 'Called to Be Catholic,'" *Origins* 21 (August 29, 1996): 170–71.

6. "Reaction to the Common Ground Project," *Origins* 26 (September 12, 1996): 197, 199–206, at 199.

7. Ibid., 197.

8. Ibid., 200.

9. Ibid., 202.

10. *CCGI: Foundational Documents*, 54.

11. Ibid., 52.

12. Ibid., 53.

13. Ibid., 64.

14. Ibid., 72.

15. James R. Kelly in his article on Cardinal Bernardin in the newsletter of the Catholic Common Ground Initiative, *Initiative Report* ([Hereafter cited as IR], vol. 1, no. 3), highlights his contribution to the Initiative model of dialogue.

16. Avery Dulles, "The Travails of Dialogue," Laurence J. McGinley Lecture delivered at Fordham University on November 19, 1996, printed manuscript, 10–13.

17. Ibid., 16.

18. Ibid., 14. Cardinal Avery Dulles delivered the Third Annual Catholic Common Ground Initiative Lecture, *Dialogue, Truth, and Communion* (New York: National Pastoral Life Center, 2001). There he accentuated again the positive features of dialogue that he finds in the classical heritage of Plato, Augustine, and the personalists—building relationships, communities, and friendships based on consensus about the good and the true. And he reiterated the flaws and deficiencies in the modern, liberal paradigm that foster procedural dialogues with no end in sight, which thus undermine the universal authority of the pope and the curia. "The problem," Dulles concluded, "is not whether dialogue should take place on the various levels [of the church], but what kind of dialogue is appropriate" (11).

19. David L. Schindler, "Editorial: On the Catholic Common Ground Project: The Christological Foundations of Dialogue," *Communio: International Catholic Review* 23 (1996): 823–51, at 826 (emphasis in original text).

20. Ibid., 830–31.

21. Ibid., 839.

22. Ibid., 841. Robert Imbelli has offered a critique of the christocentric character of Schindler's position for its limitations in addressing the pneumatological character of the church. I treat Imbelli's analysis in Bradford E. Hinze, "Ecclesial Repentance and the Demands of Dialogue," *Theological Studies* 61 (2000): 207–38. Robert P. Imbelli, "The Unknown Beyond the Word: The Pneumatological Foundations of Dialogue," *Communio* 24 (1997): 326–35. For the response, see David Schindler, "The Pneumatological Foundations of Dialogue: Response to Imbelli, Tekippe, and Culpepper," *Communio* 25 (1998): 366–76, at 367–68; and idem, "Institution and Charism: The Missions of the Son and the Spirit in Church and World," *Communio* 25 (1998): 253–73.

23. Oscar H. Lipscomb, "Dialogue: A Labor of Love," in *CCGI: Foundational Documents,* 79–96, at 93–94.

24. The conferences had the following titles: "Church Authority in American Culture" (1998), "The Celebration of the Eucharist" (1999), "Catholics in the Public Arena: Opportunities, Obstacles, Obligations for the Church's Mission of Evangelization" (2000), "Young Adults in the Church, For the World" (2001), "Participation in the Church as Envisioned by Vatican II" (2002), "The Priest in the Church" (2003), "The Wisdom of Catholic Teaching on Sexuality That Young People Desire and Our Culture Needs" (2004), "Religion, Law, and Politics" (2005).

25. *CCGI: Foundational Documents,* 14.

26. IR, vol. 1, no. 2.

27. Ibid., vol. 2, no. 1.

28. Ibid., vol. 2, no. 2.

29. Ibid., vol. 4, no. 2.

30. During one session there was a group of observers who were to serve as a "Greek chorus" and so to listen and present what they had heard at the end of the conference. The participants were asked whether it concurred with their own sense of what had transpired, which it had (IR, vol. 3, no. 2).

31. Three symposia were offshoots of earlier conferences: the first was a two-year, four-part symposium on "What Kind of Church Are American Catholic Women Looking Towards in the 21st Century?" (1999–2001), published as *The Church Women Want: Catholic Women in Dialogue,* ed. Elizabeth A. Johnson (New York: Crossroad, 2002); the second was a two-part dialogue on liturgy and church architecture entitled "How Do We Seek Common Ground about Holy Ground?" (2000–2001); and the third was a two-day dialogue devoted to the clergy sexual abuse scandal, "Restoring the Moral Integrity of the Church: Response of Catholic Higher Education to the Current Crisis in the Church" (2003).

32. Characteristics of the Initiative, its aims, outcomes, tasks, and a checklist for fostering effective dialogue are found in *Voices of the Catholic Common Ground,* Participant's Workbook and Facilitator's Manual, developed by Mary Jo Klase with Catherine Patten, Catholic Common Ground Initiative Publications, 1998.

33. Leonard Swidler, "The Dialogue Decalogue: Ground Rules for Interreligious Dialogue," cited in *Voices of the Catholic Common Ground,* Facilitator's Manual, 7; and in IR, vol. 2, no. 1, p. 2. Patten derived other practical considerations about the nature of dialogue from Swidler's work: "1. It is a structured conversation. . . . 2. Who is at the table with a voice? . . . 3. Participants also agree to speak honestly, truthfully and to listen openly. . . . 4. Participants must be willing to be self-critical and open to their own conversion. 5. The aim of dialogue must be clear. . . . Mutual understanding; gathering of information; coming to common action; negotiation; conflict resolution. . . . 6. The locus of authority must be clear . . ." (IR, vol. 2, no. 1, p. 2).

34. *Voices of the Catholic Common Ground,* Facilitator's Manual, 25. Passage taken from David Tracy, *Plurality and Ambiguity* (San Francisco: Harper & Row, 1987), 19. Klase and Patten offered "Characteristics of Effective Common Ground Dialogue," on p. 7.

35. See the statements by Katarina Schuth (vol. 1, no. 1), Eugene Fischer (vol. 1, no. 1),

Leonard Swidler (vol 2, no.1), Richard K. Taylor with LaVonne France (vol. 4, no. 3), Frank Hartmann (vol. 4, no. 4), Robert Schreiter (vol. 5, no. 1).

36. Cardinal Basil Hume, OSB, *One in Christ: Unity and Diversity in the Church Today,* the First Annual Catholic Common Ground Initiative Lecture (New York: National Pastoral Life Center, 2000). R. Scott Appleby, *The Substance of Things Hoped For: Common Ground and the Source of Our Disputes,* the Second Catholic Common Ground Initiative Lecture (New York: National Pastoral Life Center, 2000). Cardinal Avery Dulles, SJ, *Dialogue, Truth, and Communion,* the Third Annual Catholic Common Ground Initiative Lecture (New York: National Pastoral Life Center, 2001). John L. Allen, Jr., *Common Ground in a Global Key: International Lessons in Catholic Dialogue,* the Sixth Annual Catholic Common Ground Initiative Lecture (New York: National Pastoral Life Center, 2004). Archbishop James Weisgerber, *Building a Church of Communion,* the Seventh Annual Catholic Common Ground Initiative Lecture (New York: National Pastoral Life Center, 2005).

37. Cardinal Walter Kasper, *The Church and Contemporary Pluralism,* the Fourth Annual Catholic Common Ground Initiative Lecture (New York: National Pastoral Life Center, 2002), 23.

38. Joseph A. Komonchak, *Dealing with Diversity and Disagreement: Vatican II and Beyond,* the Fifth Annual Catholic Common Ground Initiative Lecture (New York: National Pastoral Life Center, 2003), 18.

39. *Voices of the Catholic Common Ground,* Facilitator's Manual, 8. The manual also states that a dialogue "will be successful if: we agree to abide by the principles of dialogue; we clarify the expectations of the participants; we clarify the function of the group (mutual understanding, gathering information, common pastoral action); we include a variety of viewpoints and all participants are willing to listen carefully to the other and to be self-critical; we are clear whether authority to decide on an action resides in the group or elsewhere; we have a facilitator to help with the discussion and keep it on track." (7).

40. Avery Dulles delivered the lecture "*Humanae Vitae* and *Ordinatio Sacerdotalis:* Problems of Reception," at the second conference of the Initiative, followed by lectures by Joseph Komonchak, James Coriden, Philip Selznick. The essays and discussion with panelists and participants, including with the Honorable John T. Noonan, Jr., U.S. Circuit Court Judge, Berkeley, California, were published as *Catholic Common Ground Initiative: Church Authority in American Culture* (New York: Crossroad, 1999).

41. *CCGI: Church Authority in American Culture*, on Noonan and Dulles, 102–4; on Dulles and Komonchak, 86–90; on Dulles and Coriden, 94–96.

42. Allen, *Common Ground in a Global Key*, 7.

43. Ibid., 7–8.

44. Ibid., 9.

45. Ibid.

46. John Paul II, *Novo Millennio Ineunte*, no. 45.

47. IR, vol. 7, no. 3, pp. 7–8.

6. THE CHURCH WOMEN WANT

1. Certain events before and after Vatican II bear directly on the subject matter of this chapter, but cannot be explored in any detail. In 1950, during the same year Pius XII published the apostolic constitution *Sponsa Christi*, he convoked an assembly of major superiors of religious orders of men and women to discuss the adaptation of religious institutes. In 1951 he convened the first International Congress of Teaching Sisters, which resulted in major superiors mandating the improvement of the education of teaching sisters and adaption to modern society. Subsequently three organizations of women religious were formed in response to the pope's initiative in the interests of advancing reform of religious life. In 1953 the Institute of Spirituality for Sister Superiors, also called Spirituality Institute for Sisters (SIS) was formed to promote spiritual guidance for sisters. In 1954 the Sisters Formation Conference (SFC) was established to promote religious, cultural, and professional formation of sisters, including the uses of social sciences, which provided a major channel of information about interpersonal communication and group dynamics. In 1956 the Conference of Major Superiors of Women (CMSW) was founded by 235 women religious superiors in response to a request by Pius XII, thereby overturning entrenched patterns of concentration on one's own congregation and suspicion of others and initiating a new phase of cooperation among American sisters. The CMSW, which in 1972 was renamed the Leadership Conference of Women Religious (LCWR), played a pivotal role in advancing dialogical discernment and decision making among women religious. A group of more conservative women religious broke off from LCWR and formed initially the consortium *Perfectae Caritatis.* Ultimately the women religious associated with the consortium petitioned the Congregation for Religious to approve of a new Council of Major Superiors of Women Religious (CMSWR), which was granted in June 1992. This group represents eighty-six congregations at this writing, in comparison to 422 congregations in the LCWR. On the origins of the consortium and CMSWR, see Anne Carey, *Sisters in Crisis: The Tragic Unraveling of Women's Religious Communities* (Huntington, Ind.: Our Sunday Visitor, 1997), 268–69. Carey treats important archival materials, but her polemical narrative is deeply flawed insofar as it fails to provide a judicious rendering and assessment of the conflicts as they emerged and the efforts to address them throughout the period.

2. For background, see Elizabeth McDonough, "General Chapters: Historical Background," *Review for Religious* 55 (1996): 320–25; Catherine M. Harmer, MMS, "Chapters Present and Past," *Review for Religious* 53 (1994): 120–29. The practice of holding chapters can be traced back to the sixth century following chapter 3 of the Rule of Benedict. General chapters came into prominence in the twelfth-century monastic reforms, especially with the Norbertines (Canons Regular of Prémontré, established by St. Norbert). Lateran Council IV in 1215 required general chapters to be part of the governing structures of religious groups. The Dominicans, for example, established in 1216, welcomed the chapter idea and, following Dominic's lead, developed chapters at the general, provincial, and priory levels.

3. House chapters is an ambiguous term. In the past it referred to the weekly chapter of faults, where the house members gathered to discuss their own and other house members' shortcomings. After Vatican II the chapter of faults came to be replaced with more open-ended conversations among community members. In her address to the general chapter on August 12, 1970, Adrian Dominican prioress Rosemary Ferguson spoke eloquently of the revival of the local house chapter, which by nature and function "establish[es] goals and objectives, discusses collegially matters pertaining to the good order and harmony of the community, arrives at certain determinations to which each member is held accountable, and holds each member co-responsible for good order in communal life. It is the basic governing body of the community." This quotation is from Patricia Walter, OP, "Religious Authority: A Conflict of Interpretations" (Ph.D. diss., Graduate Theological Union, Berkeley, 1991), 303–4.

4. *Perfectae Caritatis* must be set within a larger frame of reference. Especially important were the 1971 apostolic exhortation of Pope Paul VI, *Evangelica Testificatio*, the 1983 statement by the Sacred Congregation for Religious and Secular Institutes (CRIS), *Essential Elements in the Church's Teaching on Religious Life as Applied to Institutes Dedicated to Works of the Apostolate*, and the 1996 apostolic exhortation by Pope John Paul II, *Vita Consecrata*.

5. Canon law identifies various forms of religious life. Institute is the genus of all forms of religious organizations. Most formed before the Council of Trent are called orders (e.g., Augustinians, Dominicans, Franciscans, Jesuits). Those institutes of women religious dedicated to apostolic work are designated congregations.

6. Valuable resources include Judith Sutera, *True Daughters: Monastic Identity and American Benedictine Women's History* (Atchison, Kans.: Mount St. Scholastica, 1987); Ann Lynn Koehlinger, "'For the Renewal of Power Structures': Sociological Influences in the Transformation of American Women Religious, 1950–1980" (master's thesis, University of Oregon, 1996); Helen Sanders, *More Than a Renewal: Loretto Before and After Vatican II: 1952–1977* (Nerinx, Ky.: Sisters of Loretto, 1982); Lucy Ruth Rawe, "Decision-Making in Religious Communities of Women: A Case Study of the Sisters of Loretto" (doctor of management dissertation, Webster University, St. Louis, Mo., 1991).

7. Marie Augusta Neal, SNDdeN, reported that some sisters learned methods of group decision making and empowerment in their work with the poor and struggling, with one example being Paulo Freire's dialogical pedagogy in Latin America. These sisters in turn witnessed to the effectiveness of these methods at their chapters where they served as a basis for further development of participatory forms of decision making (Marie Augusta Neal, SNDdeN, *From Nuns to Sisters* [Mystic, Conn.: Twenty-Third Publications, 1990], 99–100).

8. My description of the Adrian Dominicans draws especially from the detailed work of Patricia Walter, an Adrian Dominican and former prioress herself, who has narrated and analyzed the chapter of renewal and the revision of the constitution of her congregation (Walter, "Religious Authority"). On the origins of the Adrian congregation, see Walter, "Religious Authority," 97–98. See also Sister Mary Philip Ryan, *Amid the Alien Corn*, vol. 1, *The Early Years of the Sisters of St. Dominic, Adrian, Michigan* (St. Charles, Ill.: Jones Wood, 1967).

9. Besides the work of Walter, see the work of Virginia O'Reilly, OP, "For the Sake of the Gospel," in *Journey in Faith and Fidelity: Women Shaping Religious Life for a Renewed Church*, ed. Nadine Foley, OP (New York: Continuum, 1999), 170–98.

10. My views on the subject of obedience have been influenced by the work of Judith Katherine Schaefer, OP, *The Vow of Obedience as Decision-Making in Communion: Contributions from Ecclesiology and Psychology* (Ph.D. diss., Marquette University, Milwaukee, Wis., 2004).

11. Walter, "Religious Authority," 104.

12. Koehlinger, "'For the Renewal of Power Structures,'" 45.

13. See Daniel Bell, "Notes on Authoritarian and Democratic Leadership," in *Studies in Leadership: Leadership and Democratic Action*, ed. Alvin Gouldner (New York: Harper & Brothers, 1950), 395–408; Erving Goffman, *Asylums: Essays on the Social Situation of Mental Patients and Other Inmates* (Chicago: Aldine Publishing, 1962). Goffman's theories were applied to the experience of women religious by Sr. Aloysius Schaldenbrand, "Asylums: Total Societies and Religious Life," in Sr. Charles Borromeo, ed., *The New Nuns* (New York: New American Library, 1967), 115–27. Sr. Lillanna Kopp recalls the impact of Goffman's ideas on women religious: "the damage effected by such initiative-suppressing, personality-deforming structures as TOTAL INSTITUTION, faced the devastating realization that TOTAL INSTITUTION was their own religious pattern of organization." Passage taken from *Sudden Spring: Sixth Stage Sisters. Trends of Change in Catholic Sisterhood, a Sociological Analysis* (Walport, Ore.: Sunspot Publications, 1983), 21; cited in Koehlinger, "'For the Renewal of Power Structures,'" 50.

14. A document from the prechapter commission, "Guidelines for Pre-Chapter Dialogue," 25–27, dated 1967, is included in Jeanne Lefebvre, "A Decade of Change" (Adrian Dominican Congregation Archives, typed manuscript, 1986), 36. Suggestions about possible ways of proceeding in these dialogue sessions were included in the one-page document.

15. O'Reilly, "For the Sake of the Gospel," 181; Walter, "Religious Authority," 104–9.

16. At the first session the chair was appointed; at the second, delegates wanted to elect the chair, and by the third session in 1970 it was decided to hire an outside chair, a Sister of Mercy, who facilitated the discussion and the deliberation process. At subsequent general chapters the Adrian congregation decided to elect chairs from among their own ranks.

17. This formulation of the meanings of collegiality and subsidiarity is derived from the working definitions offered in Appendix A of the *Enactments of the General Chapter of 1982*.

18. Walter, "Religious Authority," 118.

19. The Nelson Associates' "Works Questionnaire" was sent out on March 6, 1969. Several years earlier the Conference of Major Superiors of Women (CMSW) developed a congregational questionnaire, which was distributed to administrators of religious congregations in 1966, and the *Sisters' Survey*, with 649 questions was constructed in 1966 and sent out in 1967 to all 157,000 women religious represented in the CMSW in the United States, of which 139,691 responded. Marie Augusta Neal, SNDdeN, together with a committee, designed the questionnaire. The information gathered from the 1966 report was not published, but each congregation's results were compared with the national totals, and

mimeographed for distribution to the congregations alone. Neal again conducted the survey in 1982 for a longitudinal study. Her report and the surveys were published in *Catholic Sisters in Transition: From the 1960s to the 1980s*, Consecrated Life Series, vol. 2 (Wilmington, Del.: Michael Glazier, 1984). Neal's previous publications on the survey are noted on pp. 16–17. She further comments on these studies and her findings in *From Nuns to Sisters*.

20. O'Reilly, "For the Sake of the Gospel," 183.

21. Ashley's remarks are quoted in Walter, "Religious Authority," 122.

22. Citation from chapter decisions in ibid., 123.

23. Ibid.

24. Walter's comment and citation from ibid., 129–30.

25. Cited in ibid., 129.

26. O'Reilly, "For the Sake of the Gospel," 191.

27. During this transitional period after the council there was a considerable decline in the number of women entering religious congregations and an increasing number of women leaving. Marie Augusta Neal described these trends in her analysis of data from surveys administered to women religious in the United States in 1966 and 1982 . The numbers of women entering dropped precipitously from the highpoint of 32,433 reached in the period of 1958–1962, to the low point of 2,590 in 1971–1975. The total number of women religious leaving, both before and after final vows, slowly increased during the 1950s, then spiked in the 1960s and 1970s before returning to the level of the early 1960s. These trends were also reflected in the Adrian congregation. During the period of 1968 to 1973, the number of newer members making first profession dropped dramatically (from 28 in 1968 to 1 in 1972 and 1973) while the number of those who dispensed from final vows spiked between 1970 and 1972 (with 67 leaving in 1970, 81 in 1971, 77 in 1972) (Neal, *Catholic Sisters in Transition*, 20–21, 81–82).

28. The Adrian Dominicans' experience of the chapter of renewal was similar to many other women religious during this period. As documented by the Sisters' Survey Project, which studied closely the documents resulting from the chapters of 278 congregations, religious congregations of women across the United States, as around the world, made efforts to comply with the conciliar mandates with mixed results. But they fulfilled the mandate: they read and reflected on the conciliar documents, returned to the sources of their own communities, and, at their chapters, gathered to converse about their past as they attempted to find their way, their orienting missions, on into the future. Marie Augusta Neal, as a part of the Sisters' Survey Project, collected and analyzed 278 new chapter decrees to see how U.S. women religious were implementing Vatican II's *Perfectae Caritatis*. These materials are in the Notre Dame archives CNEA 20–32. We read in the archive description, "A team of three sisters coded the documents according to 49 pre-established categories of style and content." The final report is in CNEA 40/13, and reports for individual orders are often in the orders' decrees in CNEA 20–32.

29. The survey taken in 1968 was recorded in 1969 (98% return) and was administered again during the following years: in 1972 (89%), 1977 (89%), and 1981 (88%). Sr. Mary Beth Beres compiled the results from the Adrian Synthesis questionnaire during these years and slightly revised the questionnaire as needed by changing circumstances.

30. These questions are taken from the original seventy-four-question Adrian Synthesis submitted in 1968 and from Walter, "Religious Authority," on the 1968 Adrian Synthesis, 118–20; on the 1972 version, see 132–35, on the 1977 version, 137–39; no comments on the 1981 version.

31. Following the practice that emerged during the chapter of renewal, discussion groups provided the major means for preparation for the general chapters held in 1974, 1978, 1982, 1986, 1992, 1998, 2004.

32. Nadine Foley, OP, "Women Religious and the Mission of the Church Today," in *New Visions, New Roles: Women in the Church*, ed. Lora Ann Quiñonez, CDP (Washington, D.C.: Leadership Conference of Women Religious in the United States, 1975), 54–77, at 61.

33. Ibid., 61.

34. Ibid., 62.

35. The approval of the new "Adrian Dominican Congregation Government Plan" and the directive to implement this new plan is recorded in the Enactments of the General Chapter of 1978. Appendix A, "Government Document" in the Enactments of the General Chapter of 1982 (pp. 17–21) provides a full description of the reorganized structure of governance.

36. Jeanne Lefebvre, "A Decade of Change" (typed manuscript, over 165 pages), 141, quoted in Walter, "Religious Authority," 142. Carol Jean McDonnell, OP, was the architect of the revised governance structure.

37. Following the report of Neal, the results from the 1982 Sisters' Survey distributed to six thousand sisters, with 3,720 completed and returned (62%), indicated the diversity of the governance structures at that time: "[1] the major superior should make the decisions with the advice of her council . . . (9%); [2] council should act as a team making the decisions (7%); [3] there should be consultation with the members of the congregation with the council making the decisions (22%); [4] committee or delegated group should research the issue and report to the council and the council make the decision (12%); [5] the council should administer decisions made by an assembly and be accountable to that assembly for all policy decisions (38%), [6] other (11%)." In the same survey, when asked which model of leadership and decision making the sister preferred, 10 percent chose the older model, where chosen superiors are ultimately responsible and to whom members are accountable, but this was being superseded by two collaborative models. The remaining votes were given to two options. One approach "places decision making ultimately in an assembly of the whole which then delegates authority to administrators who are ultimately accountable to the members in assembly—which assembly is ultimately responsible for the outcomes" (45%). And a second approach "places decision making in the hands of lawfully chosen delegates who in turn lawfully choose administrators to whom they delegate responsibility and who are ultimately accountable to them" (45%). Neal, *From Nuns to Sisters*, 100–102. Also see part 6 devoted to governance and chapters comparing the 1966 and 1982 surveys, *Catholic Sisters in Transition*, 53–61.

38. Marie Augusta Neal began in 1974 "a systematic analysis of constitutions being revised in 280 different religious congregations in the U.S. In 1983, she examined in greater

detail the interim constitutions of twenty congregations" (*From Nuns to Sisters*, 5). The findings from her study were not published. However, some of this information is provided in chapter 3, "Constitutions and Mission," in *From Nuns to Sisters*, 52–113. The archival report at the University of Notre Dame indicates that "Sr. Neal continued to collect the chapter decrees, rules and constitutions of religious orders. She undertook a further study of chapter decrees in 1977 and a comparison of 20 constitutions with these decrees in 1983. These studies are mentioned in Neal, "Who They Are and What They Do: Current Forms of Religious Life in the U.S. Church," in *Religious Life in the U.S. Church*, ed. Robert J. Daley et al. (New York: Paulist Press, 1984), 152–71.

39. Besides the work of Patricia Walter already mentioned, this section draws on the following materials from Nadine Foley, "Constitution Chronology: Adrian Dominican Sisters" (manuscript, 2003); idem, "Negotiations with Rome: A Reflection on Possibility," LCWR Occasional Papers (Spring 2001): 21–28; idem, "Locus of Authority in the Religious Congregation," in *Journey in Faith and Fidelity*, 124–38.

40. The other CRIS members were Miriam Celetti, SDS, Father Terence Carey, OCD, and Francis X. Gokey, SSE.

41. During their time in Rome, Johannes and Foley also met with Cardinal Pironio, the prefect of CRIS, and Archbishop Meyer, the secretary. They also met with the master of the Order of Preachers, Damien Byrne, and discussed with him the concerns raised about the constitution's depiction of authority residing in the congregation, which he endorsed as consistent with the Dominican tradition.

42. Walter, "Religious Authority," 146–47.

43. The new Code of Canon Law, promulgated in January 1983, and the text on "Essential Elements" of religious life issued by CRIS in May 1983 accentuated a theology of consecration rather than mission and advanced a more traditional theology of obedience. On April 3, 1983, John Paul II sent a letter to the U.S. bishops establishing the Quinn Commission, composed of Archbishop John R. Quinn from San Francisco as pontifical delegate, Archbishop Thomas C. Kelly, OP, from Louisville, and Bishop Raymond W. Lessard of Savannah, "to facilitate the pastoral work of their brother Bishops in the United States in helping the religious of your country whose Institutes are engaged in apostolic works to live their ecclesial vocation to the full." This commission was to consult with members of religious communities. In 1984, the officers of the LCWR began a second phase of monitoring numerous instances where approbation by CRIS was being delayed over what seemed like incidental matters. The first phase of the LCWR effort began in 1976 and ended in 1980 with the publication of *Starting Points: Six Essays Based on the Experience of U.S. Women Religious*, ed. Lora Ann Quiñonez, CDP (Washington, D.C.: Leadership Conference of Women Religious in the United States, 1980). This project included sending questionnaires to a random sample of 520 women religious. The responses confirmed the increasing importance among those sampled of a communal, collaborative method of learning. See Jeanne O'Laughlin, OP, "Learnings about the Learnings of U.S. Women Religious," *Starting Points*, 132–37. One issue became increasingly clear during this second phase of data collection: "the concept of shared authority or government by a team seemed to be rejected uniformly by CRIS. Many congregations found

their negotiations with CRIS demoralizing and debated the merits of such strategies as the renunciation of canonical status, noncompliance, expedient compliance, and continued dialogue" (Walter, "Religious Authority," 150).

44. Texts from proposed constitution and from Hamer letter and commentary are from Walter, "Religious Authority," 151.

45. Ibid., 152. As Walter points out, the letter requested more explicit acknowledgment of the authority of the hierarchy by adding to a list of activities done by community members "all in accord with the directives of the Church" and in matters of ministry adding "in collaboration with the local bishop." The CRIS intervention, in short, "reflected a belief that all religious authority comes from God through the mediation of the hierarchical Church and that it is exercised in a fundamentally hierarchical fashion in religious life. The document attempted to resolve any potential conflicts by underlining subordination to ecclesiastical authority, by emphasizing the personal authority of superiors at every level of the Congregation, and by drawing attention to the limitations of collegial authority exercised by the General Chapter and the General Council" (153).

46. On April 21, 1985, over five thousand representatives of five Midwestern pontifical congregations, the Adrian Dominicans, the Sinsinawan Dominicans, Servants of the Immaculate Heart of Mary (Monroe, Michigan), Sisters of St. Joseph (Nazareth, Michigan), and the School Sisters of St. Francis (Milwaukee, Wisconsin) met to discuss the difficulties facing them during the approbation process. Among the common issues of concern were governance, authority, obedience to the pope, the object of the vows, the use of classical terminology, and the Holy See as the authentic interpreter of documents (Walter, "Religious Authority," 349 n. 75).

47. Ibid., 157.

48. Ibid., 158. There was also a sense that the dialogues between the bishops and women religious made possible through the Quinn commission and the U.S. bishops' tensions with Rome over their own exercise of dialogical discernment and decision making in the pastoral letters on war and peace, economics, and women, had set up a new sense of solidarity among some of the U.S. bishops and women religious.

49. Ibid., 159; See Mary Linscott, "The Service of Religious Authority: Reflection on Government in the Revision of Constitutions," *Review for Religious* 42 (1983): 197–217. Linscott offers a substantive defense of a traditional approach to hierarchical (personal) authority drawing on a christocentric ecclesiology, while exploring some of the issues raised by collegial and communal forms of authority and decision making. She argues that religious authority in the Catholic Church "to direct, judge and teach" is "an authority that cannot come from her members and which she cannot take upon herself but which is the authority of Christ whose presence she is" (200–201). She seriously wondered, "can it be said that the authority," not religious authority in the strict sense, "is in the members of the institute or in the communion of its members" (215)?

50. See Margaret Brennan's essay, "The Experience of the Essential Elements in the Lives of the U.S. Religious, " in *Religious Life in the U.S. Church: The New Dialogue*, ed. Robert J. Daley et al. (New York: Paulist Press, 1984), 134–39.

51. Walter, "Religious Authority," 160–61.

52. Ibid., 168.
53. Ibid., 169.
54. Ibid., 170.
55. In May 1986, LCWR organized a meeting of a group of approximately sixty women from various religious congregations to discuss the experiences of tension with CRIS while going through the approbation process. In August 1986 representatives of LCWR met with Mary Linscott to discuss these issues.
56. Walter, "Religious Authority," 171.
57. Ibid., 173.
58. Foley letter cited in ibid., 173.
59. Foley letter cited in ibid.
60. Foley letter cited in ibid., 173–74.
61. The rationales can be found in appendix B of Walter, "Religious Authority," 323–32.
62. The LCWR project, which investigated major themes present in selected chapter and governance documents from a random sample of 20 percent of the superiors in the United States with membership in the LCWR, corroborated the conclusions about their own sense of identity being reached by the Adrian congregation: "Women modeling co-responsible, accountable and collegial governance process." Anne Munley, IHM, "An Exploratory Content Analysis of Major Themes Present in Selected Documents of United States Women Religious," in *Claiming Our Truth: Reflections on Identity by United States Women Religious*, ed. Nadine Foley (Washington, D.C.: Leadership Conference of Women Religious, 1988), 183–91, at 191.
63. Nadine Foley, "Introduction," in *Claiming Our Truth*, 1; see also Anne Munley, IHM, "Some Learnings about a Collaborative Process of Learning," in *Claiming Our Truth*, 5–7.
64. Nadine Foley, "Locus of Authority in the Religious Congregation: Implications of Religious Life as Charism," in *Journey in Faith and Fidelity*, 124–38, at 129.
65. Ibid., 137.
66. Ibid.
67. Foley, "Religious Life as Charism," in *Journey in Faith and Fidelity*, 66–79, at 78.
68. David J. Nygren, CM, and Miriam D. Ukeritis, CSJ, *The Future of Religious Orders in the United States: Transformation and Commitment* (Westport, Conn./London: Praeger, 1993). This work was based on personal interviews, questionnaires, and other forms of information gathered from over ten thousand religious priests, brothers, and sisters.
69. David Nygren, CM, and Miriam Ukeritis, CSJ, "Future of Religious Orders in the United States," Research Executive Summary, *Origins* 22 (September 24, 1992): 257, 259–72, at 266.
70. Further research is needed into the exercise of chapters and governance patterns among the women religious who broke away from the LCWR and the individual sisters who left certain congregations because of the reforms that were taking place. While it may seem fair to assume that traditional hierarchical models of authority have been utilized and emphasized among women religious and institutes associated with the consortium *Perfec-*

tae Caritatis and the Council of Major Superiors of Women Religious, it cannot be taken for granted. The extent to which collegial, dialogical models have been combined with traditional forms of chapters and governance for women in these religious institutes, creating hybrid models of discernment and authority, must be scrutinized and should not be underestimated or dismissed at the outset. It is also the case that the ongoing effort to promote dialogue among the communities associated with the LCWR and the CMSWR should continue to be a priority. As Benedict Ashley stated at the Adrian Dominican chapter of renewal in 1969, the future of the catholicity of the church and the Dominican order depends on keeping these groups talking with each other. In that vein the church needs to find ways to narrate what has transpired during the postconciliar period among women religious that avoid valorizing one group and demonizing another group. In fact, what has occurred is a complex process of differentiation among women religious. The vast majority came to a new realization of their identity and mission, while others came to confirm what had been received previously. The insights, gifts, and witnesses of these various groups ought not be pitted against one another, but it will be to the advantage of the larger network of religious institutes if they can continue to stay in relation and talk through common areas of concern, common convictions, and within that to address contested issues. Discussions among women religious about the aims and hurdles of the practices of chapters and governance will remain a high priority in these conversations.

71. Nygren and Ukeritis, "Future of Religious Orders," 267.

72. Mary Linscott defended the need for a clear distinction between a major superior's personal authority and that of the council. "The advisory nature of the council is respected and, if there is a deliberative vote, it is understood that the superior may not act against it, but is not obliged to act in accordance with it. . . . She is free not to act at all. . . . If the major superior and council are not distinguished from each other, the voting on matters which constitutionally require a vote may be more decisive than deliberative. In that case, the major superior may be required to act in accordance with the numerical majority whether she is in agreement with it or not" ("Service of Religious Authority," 213–14). See Linscott's later essay, "Leadership, Authority, and Religious Government," *Review for Religious* 52 (1993): 166–93.

73. Donna J. Markham, *Spiritlinking Leadership: Working Through Resistance to Organizational Change* (New York: Paulist Press, 1999), 124.

7. COLLEGIALITY AND CONSTRAINT

1. See, for example, the discussions of ancient synodal practices by Michael Fahey, "Eastern Synodal Traditions: Pertinence for Western Collegial Institutions," in *Episcopal Conferences: Historical, Canonical & Theologies Studies*, ed. Thomas J. Reese (Washington, D.C.: Georgetown University Press, 1989), 253–66.

2. Pope Paul VI, *motu proprio Apostolica Sollicitudo* (September 15, 1965), *Acta Apolostolicae Sedis* 57 (1965): 775–80, trans. *Canon Law Digest* 6:388–93; Vatican II, *Christus Dominus*, nos. 36–38; *Ordo Synodi Episcoporum celebrandae* (December 8,1966), *Acta Apostolicae Sedis* 59 (1967): 91–103, trans. "Norms for the Synod of Bishops," *The Jurist* 17 (1967): 232–43; second revision, June 24, 1969, *Acta Apostolicae Sedis* 61 (1969): 525–39;

trans. "Order of the Celebration of the Synod of Bishops," *Canon Law Digest* 7:323–37; the third revision *Acta Apostolicae Sedis* 63 (1971): 702–4, trans. "Changes in the Revised Order of Its Celebration," *Canon Law Digest* 7:338–41.

3. *New Commentary on the Code of Canon Law*, ed. John P. Beal, James A. Coriden, and Thomas J. Green (New York: Paulist, 2000).

4. My description of the practices of synods of bishops draws especially on the work of Thomas J. Reese, *Inside the Vatican: The Politics and Organization of the Catholic Church* (Cambridge, Mass.: Harvard University Press, 1996), 42–65; and John G. Johnson, "The Synod of Bishops: An Analysis of Its Legal Development" (J.C.D. dissertation, Catholic University of America, Washington, D.C., 1986). Also see "Synodal Information," provided in the Preface for the Secretariat for the Synod of Bishops: http://www.vatican.va/roman_curia/synod/index.htm (accessed August 12, 2005).

5. The topics for ordinary synods are as follows: 1967: challenges to faith, revisions to the Code of Canon Law, seminaries, mixed marriages; liturgy; 1971: ministerial priesthood and justice in the world; 1974: evangelization in the modern world; 1977: catechesis; 1980: the Christian family; 1983: penance and reconciliation in the mission of the church; 1987: the vocation and mission of the lay faithful in the church and world; 1990: the formation of priests; 1994: The consecrated life and its role in the church and the world. The 2005 synod devoted to the Eucharist lies outside the scope of this study.

6. The *Explicationes* are revised before every synod and are not, strictly speaking, laws since they have not been promulgated in *Acta Apostolicae Sedis*, but rather are practical decisions that are made to fill in the gaps of the *Ordo*. Consequently they adapt it without requiring a revision of the *Ordo* (see Johnson, "Synod of Bishops," 372–73).

7. The representatives of the Eastern Catholic Churches (Copt, Melkite, Maronite, Syrian, Chaldean, Armenian, Ukrainian, and Syro-Malabar churches) include patriarchs, major archbishops, and metropolitans aside from the patriarchates.

8. The designated representatives of the episcopal conferences are chosen following this formula: one for each national episcopal conference that has not more than twenty-five members, two for more than forty, three for not more than one hundred, four for conferences with more than one hundred members.

9. In the case of an extraordinary synod, the presidents of episcopal conferences take the place of elected representatives of episcopal conferences specified in categories (2) and (3), and there are three instead of ten representatives of religious institutes of men. In the case of the special synods held in the 1990s there was a special formula developed for electing representatives from episcopal conferences. The formula stated that "for the first 20 members, one for every 5 members or fraction thereof, for the following 30 members, one for every 10 or fraction thereof, for the following 50 members, one for every 20 or fraction thereof, for those members numbering over 100, one for every 40 or fraction thereof." See Thomas J. Reese, "The Experience of Special Synods," *CLSA Proceedings* 59 (1997): 26–46, at 29, citing Jan P. Schotte, CICM, "Report by the Secretary General," *Bulletin: Synod of Bishops Special Assembly for America*, Holy See Press Office, no. 4, November 17, 1997, 10. This formula gave smaller conferences a higher percentage of numerical representatives relative to larger ones.

10. Titular bishops are auxiliary bishops and bishops with diplomatic and administrative posts assigned to historically founded, yet now extinct diocesan cities. Thus they are given the honorary "titles" of these dioceses.

11. These figures are taken from *Annuarium Statisticum Ecclesiae/ Statistical Yearbook of the Church 1994* (Vatican City: Liberia Editrice Vaticana, 1994), 105.

12. The total number of bishops per continent in 1994 follows: Africa, 392 diocesan bishops and 121 titular bishops; America, 913 diocesan bishops and 688 titular bishops (in the U.S. alone there were 255 diocesan bishops and 274 titular bishops); Asia, 394 diocesan bishops and 197 titular bishops; Europe, 643 diocesan bishops and 797 titular bishops; Oceania, 73 diocesan bishops and 39 titular bishops.

13. Giuseppe Ferraro, *Il Sinodo Dei Vescovi 1994* (Rome: Edizioni La Civiltà Cattolica, 1998), 641–58.

14. Joseph Cardinal Bernardin was repeatedly elected by the U.S. Bishops' Conference as a delegate. Archbishop Rembert Weakland, OSB, attended five synods (1969, 1971, 1974, 1987, and 1997). Archbishop John Quinn attended three (1974, 1980, 1994).

15. The *Ordo* treats the establishment of study commissions in articles 8 and 9.

16. See the documents from various stages of the special Asian synod of bishops in their chronological sequence, *The Asian Synod: Texts and Commentaries*, compiled and edited by Peter C. Phan (Maryknoll, N.Y.: Orbis Books, 2002). The most detailed documentation of each synod and its history is provided by the Italian series begun by Giovanni Caprile, SJ, *Il Sinodo dei Vescovi* (Rome: La Civiltà, 1968–1990).

17. Reese lists the four criteria given to the bishops when making a recommendation distributed by the General Secretariat of the Synod of Bishops (*Inside the Vatican*, 289 n. 18); Schotte speaks of the basic criteria for selecting a topic as universality, pastoral character, and urgency ("The World Synod of Bishops: Media Event or Pastoral Powerhouse?" *CLSA Proceedings* 50 [1988]: 52–69, at 65; also idem, "The Consecrated Life in Church and World: Toward the Synod," *Review for Religious* 53 [1994]: 29–42, at 35–36).

18. Reese, *Inside the Vatican*, 51.

19. Once the English and French translations of the *lineamenta* were received, it took another three months to produce a Japanese translation in preparation for the special Asian synod (*Asian Synod*, 27).

20. Reese, *Inside the Vatican*, 54.

21. The president-delegate of the synod chairs the various sessions of the plenary sessions of the synod and grants time to individual bishops to speak. He can also establish a study commission composed of members of the synod, to be approved by the pope. But these commissions have rarely been utilized, with the exception of those established for preparing the final reports.

22. Archbishop John Quinn has written, "These speeches go on for five and a half hours six days a week for two weeks. One speech follows another without any reaction or interaction from the assembly, no comments, no questions, no debate. Many bishops prepare their speeches before they leave home, in other words, before they hear what the other bishops will say. This reinforces the disconnected quality of the speeches. While there is simultaneous translation it is not professional and not uniformly effective. Two weeks are

thus given to a passive and deadening experience" ("A Permanent Synod? Reflections on Collegiality," *Origins* 31 [April 18, 2002]: 730–36, at 734). Archbishop Daniel Pilarczyk, who has participated in four synods, "suggests that the bishops be given all the speeches [in written form] on the first day of the synod and then be told to spend the next three days at home reading them" (Reese, "Experience of Special Synods," 38).

23. "Synodal Information," D. "Certain explanations on the order of the Synod of Bishops; Re: Article 23: The Manner of Seeking an Opinion," 22.

24. Reese, *Inside the Vatican*, 56.

25. In preparation for the October 2–23, 2005, synod on "The Eucharist: Source and Summit of the Life and Mission of the Church," several changes were announced by Archbishop Nikola Eterovic, general secretary of the General Secretariat of the Synod of Bishops. The synod would last for three weeks, not an entire month as John Paul II first planned. Pope Benedict XVI made this decision to honor the bishops' primary commitment to their own sees and to promote "greater concentration" during the synod conversations. The second change is that each bishop delegate will be allowed, but not required, to give a six-minute address to the entire assembly, not eight minutes as in the past. According to Archbishop Eterovic, "The main reason for this reduction is the introduction of free addresses by participants for one hour, from 6–7 P.M. every day at the end of the general congregation."

26. There is considerable evidence that the speeches by the bishops are a major obstacle in promoting dialogical deliberations among the bishops. I am of the opinion that there should be experiments with dropping these speeches entirely from the synod assembly. It is understandable that a participant wants to be able to have the position of his episcopal conference or his own personal opinion made available to the entire assembly. A couple of possible alternatives to the speeches would be that the written responses to the *instrumentum laboris* by all the bishop-delegates and a three- or four-page statement (comparable in length to the one they would have made orally) of anyone could be mailed to all participants before the synod assembly. Each bishop (preferably with his collaborating theologians and laypeople) would be expected to go through these written responses before the gathering and begin to identify emerging trends, areas of consensus, and disputed issues. Following the general *relatio* at the beginning of the full assembly, the bishops could then be invited to start their discussions of these documents in small groups and in full assembly.

27. Reese, *Inside the Vatican*, 56.

28. Concerning the involvement of the prefects in the small groups, John Quinn comments, "some interpret this as a mechanism to guide and control the discussion along certain lines" ("Permanent Synod?" 734).

29. Quinn gives an example of the many recommendations made at the synod of bishops held in October 2001 about exaggerated centralization and the need for greater collegiality, which never made it into the final proposals (propositions) given to the pope ("Permanent Synod?" 734).

30. Reese, "Experience of Special Synods,"42.

31. Reese, *Inside the Vatican*, 59.

32. Paul VI's allocution of September 14, 1965, cited by Jan P. Schotte, "The Synod of Bishops: A Permanent Yet Adaptable Church Institution," *Studia canonica* 26 (1992): 289–306, at 292.

33. Paul VI, *Apostolica Sollicitudo*, *Acta Apostolicae Sedis* 57 (1965): 775–80, at 776–77. *Canon Law Digest* 6:388–93.

34. Schotte, "World Synod of Bishops," 53.

35. Ibid., 66, 67.

36. John Paul II, allocution "In fide huius Synodi," October 29, 1983, *Acta Apostolicae Sedis* 76 (1984): 287, cited in Johnson, "Synod of Bishops," 237. Pope Paul VI raised at the beginning of the first Extraordinary Synod of Bishops in 1969 the task of clarifying the meaning of the collegiality of bishops and how it can grow, and he expressed his own mystical understanding of collegiality in terms of communion. See Paul VI, allocution "Quemadmodum nostris," October 11, 1969, *Acta Apostolicae Sedis* 61 (1969): 717–18, cited by Johnson, "Synod of Bishops," 54.

37. John Paul II's "Letter to the Faithful of the Church in the Netherlands," January 6, 1980, from *L'Osservatore Romano*, January 14–15, 1980, cited in Schotte, "World Synod of Bishops," 56; Schotte goes on to offer a quotation on catholicity in no. 13 in *Lumen Gentium*, which was presented above.

38. Schotte, "World Synod of Bishops," 56.

39. Rembert G. Weakland, OSB, "Structuring *Communio* in a Church Formed of Many Cultures," *CLSA Proceedings* 60 (1998): 19–30, at 23.

40. Thomas J. Reese, "Synod for America," *America* 177 (December 13, 1997): 3–5, at 3; also idem, "The Synod Points Out Needs," *America* 178 (January 3–10, 1998): 3–5.

41. Many have criticized the demands for secrecy at every level of the synod process; see, e.g., Thomas P. Rausch, "The Synod of Bishops: Improving the Synod Process," *The Jurist* 49 (1989): 248–57, at 253. The problems associated with time constraints were encountered during every phase of the process. The 1974 council discussed the procedures and made certain recommendations, some of which related to time constraints (Johnson, "Synod of Bishops," 142–43).

42. I am indebted to Richard Gaillardetz for this particular formulation of the issue.

43. Cited by Brian E. Daley, "Structures of Charity: Bishops' Gatherings and the See of Rome in the Early Church," in *Episcopal Conferences: Historical, Canonical, and Theological Studies*, 29; and in Reese, *Inside the Vatican*, 42.

44. One question raised concerns whom the bishops represent in what they say and in their voting: the entire college of bishops, the episcopal conference, or their local churches? *Apostolica Sollicitudo* specifies that bishops from around the world represent the complete Catholic episcopate. See the discussion of this norm in Johnson, "Synod of Bishops," 288–327.

45. Canon 343. For an initial exploration of the topic of consultation and deliberation as it bears upon the synod of bishops, see Johnson, "Synod of Bishops," 327–56.

46. John Johnson is of the opinion that the architects of the new code "did not want to enhance the authority of the Synod," and "its view of the decision-making capacity of the Synod is expressed in more restrictive language" than even the language of the *motu proprio*

Apostolica Sollicitudo, which was already limited. Moreover, the code did not want to identify the synod of bishops with the college of bishops, but with one of the ways that bishops offer assistance to the pope ("Synod of Bishops," 487, 488).

47. See the distinction between *collegial affectus* and *collegial effectus* as it emerged in discussions surrounding episcopal conferences, but which also has a bearing on the work of synods of bishops. Jan Grootaers, "The Collegiality of the Synod of Bishops: An Unresolved Problem," in *Collegiality Put to the Test, Concilium,* ed. James Provost and Knut Walf (London: SCM; Philadelphia: Trinity Press International, 1990), 18–30, at 19, 24, and 29 n. 10 on Cardinal J. Hamer's introduction of the distinction before the 1975 Extraordinary Synod of Bishops. The nature and operations of the synod were addressed at the meeting held April 26–30, 1983 (Johnson, "Synod of Bishops," 225–27).

48. An interview with Cardinal Jan Schotte, "Is the Roman Curia 'Uncollegial'?" *Inside the Vatican* 4 (August-September 1996): 52–54; Schotte, "World Synod of Bishops," 54. The quotation is from *Karol Wojtyla e il Sinodo dei Vescovi* (Vatican City: Editrice Vaticana, 1980), 161–62, as cited in Schotte, "World Synod of Bishops," 57.

49. Synod of Bishops, "Justice in the World," in *Catholic Social Thought: The Documentary Heritage,* ed. David J. O'Brien and Thomas A. Shannon (Maryknoll, N.Y.: Orbis Books 1992), 287–300.

50. Johnson, "Synod of Bishops," 495, 496.

51. Reese, *Inside the Vatican*, 51.

52. During the special synod for Asian bishops, the Indonesian bishops, for example, believed that the *lineamenta* for the special Asian synod implied a criticism of Asian Catholic bishops' advancement of dialogue with cultures, religions, and the poor as developed by the Federation of Asian Bishops' Conferences, while Japanese bishops rejected the same *lineamenta* for being too Eurocentric and failing to address adequately the concerns raised in the Asian context. See Jonathan Y. Tan, "The Responses of the Indonesian and Japanese Bishops to the Lineamenta," in *Asian Synod*, 59–72, at 60, 62.

53. The drafting committee from the General Secretariat and the editing role played by the council have been regularly commended for the work they have done, specifically for preparing an *instrumentum laboris* that is markedly better than the *lineamenta*, which reflects the input of the written responses from episcopal conferences and individual delegates. Yet consistent questions are raised about the adverse influence of the curia on these documents and on the dialogue that takes place during the synod assembly.

54. Reese, *Inside the Vatican*, 52.

55. Quinn, "Permanent Synod?" 733.

56. The quotation is from Johnson, "Synod of Bishops," 182, referring to John Paul's final homily at the synod on the family in 1980.

57. "A Memo to Cardinal Schotte," *The Tablet*, June 6, 1998; Quinn, "Permanent Synod?" 734. For a longer discussion of subsidiarity, see John G. Johnson, "Subsidiarity and the Synod of Bishops," *The Jurist* 50 (1990): 488–523.

58. Ludwig Kaufmann, "Synods of Bishops: Neither concilium nor synodos: Fragments of a Criticism from the Perspective of the 'Synodical Movement,'" in *Collegiality Put to the Test*, 67–78, at 75.

59. Edward Schillebeeckx, *Ministry: Leadership in the Community of Jesus Christ* (New York: Crossroad, 1971), 129, as cited in Rausch, "Synod of Bishops," 254.

60. Rausch, "Synod of Bishops," 254.

61. This issue has been raised by a number of people; see, e.g., Rausch, "Synod of Bishops," 256.

62. Cardinal Schotte pointed out that nonmembers with expertise on the synod topics have become more common contributors to the plenary synod sessions. These are called *auditiones*, "listening meetings," and experts "are given the opportunity to make presentations to the entire Session for the benefit of the Synod Fathers and their discussion" (Schotte, "Synod of Bishops," at 302–3). The 1971 synod on justice and priesthood was the first one in which laypeople and priests addressed the assembly of bishops. This practice developed further during the synod on the laity (1987) and the European synod.

63. Quinn, "Permanent Synod?" 734, and 736 n. 41; Yves Congar, "Quod omnes tangit, ab omnibus tractari et approbari debet," *Revue historique du droit français et etranger* 36 (1958): 210–59.

8. DIFFERENTIATED CONSENSUS, IMPERFECT COMMUNION

1. For example, see Nils Ehrenstrom and Günther Gassmann, eds., *Confessions in Dialogue: A Survey of Bilateral Conversations among World Confessional Families 1959–1974*, 3rd ed. (Geneva: WCC, 1975), 130–31, 137–41.

2. Joseph Famerée develops a brief phenomenology of ecumenical dialogues in terms of (1) prerequisites; (2) the conception and spirit of dialogue; (3) the "decisive importance of factors that are not strictly theological" in "De l'affrontement à la reconnaissance: Petite «phénoménologie» du dialogue œcuménique," in *Ephermerides theologicae Lovanienses* 74 (December 1998): 344–63.

3. The 1910 statement is cited in n. 1 of the 1911 "Report on Plan and Scope," in *A Documentary History of the Faith and Order Movement 1927–1963*, ed. Lukas Vischer (St. Louis: Bethany Press, 1963), 199.

4. "Report of the Committee on Plan and Scope" (April 20, 1911), in Vischer, *Documentary History*, 199–201, at 200.

5. "A First Preliminary Conference," Faith and Order Pamphlet no. 24 (1913), 46f.

6. Tom Best brought to my attention correspondence in the World Council of Churches archives between Herbert Kelly and Robert Gardiner and Ralph Brown, founding figures of the Faith and Order movement; Brown served as General Secretary of the Faith and Order Conference. Paul Crow, Jr., discussed with me the 1911 and 1913 sketches for the first conference in relation to Kelly's essay.

7. Herbert Kelly, "The Object and Method of Conference," in *The World Conference for the Consideration of Questions Touching Faith and Order* (Gardiner, Me.: Protestant Episcopal Church, 1915), 9, 10, 11.

8. Ibid., 12.

9. Ibid., 25.
10. Ibid., 27.
11. Ibid., 29.
12. Ibid., 30
13. Ibid., 31.
14. Ibid., 33.
15. The Faith and Order Conferences took place in Lausanne in 1927, Edinburgh in 1937, Lund in 1952, Montreal in 1963, and thirty years afterwards in Santiago de Compostela, Spain, in 1993.
16. Lausanne, pars. 1 and 2, cited in Vischer, *Documentary History*, 27.
17. Lukas Vischer, "Introduction: Faith and Order Reports: Their Nature and Significance," in *Documentary History*, 12.
18. Final Report of the Third Conference of Faith and Order held in Lund in August 1952, cited in *Documentary History*, 85–86. This conference is also known for establishing what has been called the "Lund principle: whether they [the churches] should not act together in all matters except those in which deep differences of conviction compel them to act separately?" (p. 86).
19. Vischer, "Introduction," in *Documentary History*, 14.
20. Final Lund Report, in Vischer, *Documentary History*, 86.
21. *Baptism, Eucharist & Ministry 1982–1990: Report on the Process and the Progress*, Faith and Order Paper no. 149 (Geneva: WCC Publications, 1990), 7.
22. See Jeffrey Gros, FSC, "Toward Full Communion: Faith and Order and Catholic Ecumenism," *Theological Studies* 65 (2004): 23–43, at 25.
23. Final Lund Report, in Vischer, *Documentary History*, 111. See "Non-theological Factors that May Hinder or Accelerate the Church's Unity," discussed in preparation for the Lund Conference, Faith and Order Paper no. 10 (Geneva: WCC, 1952), 26–32; reprinted in *The Ecumenical Movement: An Anthology of Key Texts and Voices*, ed. Michael Kinnamon and Brian E. Cope (Geneva: WCC, 1997), 212–16.
24. Final Lund Report, in Vischer, *Documentary History*, 113.
25. "The Constitution of the Commission of Faith and Order," in Vischer, *Documentary History*, 203.
26. In 1969 the Faith and Order Commission initiated a study that resulted in *Unity in Today's World: The Faith and Order Studies on "Unity of the Church–Unity of Humankind,"* Faith and Order Paper no. 88 (Geneva: WCC, 1978); see especially "Toward Unity in Tension" (pp. 89–93). There followed a six-year study, *Church and World: The Unity of the Church and the Renewal of the Human Community*, Faith and Order Paper no. 151 (Geneva: WCC, 1990). These documents established a broader frame of reference for the subsequent treatment of racism and sexism. The World Council of Churches central committee developed a "Plan for an Ecumenical Programme to Combat Racism" in 1969, included in *Ecumenical Movement*, ed. Kinnamon and Cope, 218–20. The joint consultation of the World Council of Churches central committee and Faith and Order Commission on "Racism in Theology—Theology against Racism" (1975) is included in *Documentary History of Faith and Order, 1963–1993,* ed. Günther Gassmann (Geneva: WCC, 1993), 148–52. Women's

ordination was treated in 1979, and the issues surrounding sexism and ecclesiology were treated in the Sheffield Report, 1981. See *Ordination of Women in Ecumenical Perspective: Workbook for the Church's Future*, ed. Constance F. Parvey, Faith and Order Paper no. 105 (Geneva: WCC, 1980); *The Community of Women and Men in the Church: The Sheffield Report*, ed. Constance F. Parvey (Geneva: WCC, 1983).

27. See the encyclicals *Satis Cognitum* (1896) by Pope Leo XIII and *Mortalium Animos* (1928) by Pope Pius XI. The latter document "On the Promotion of True Religious Unity" "criticized the ecumenical movement and forbade Catholics to participate in it as it was founded on error and illusion. He accused it of seeking to reach unity by too easy compromise and by focusing too exclusively on service" (Jeffrey Gros, Eamon MacManus, Ann Riggs, *Introduction to Ecumenism* [Mahwah, N.J.: Paulist Press, 1998], 29). Similar issues were raised in *Satis Cogitum,* "On the Unity of the Church" in 1896. Indifferentism about the distinctive identity and nature of the church and false irenicism toward boundaries were decisive issues.

28. Forms of the Latin term *dialogus* are found in the following texts from Vatican II: *Unitatis Redintegratio* nos. 4, 9, 14, 18, 19, 21, 22, 23; *Gaudium et Spes* nos. 40, 43, 56, 92; *Ad Gentes* nos. 11, 12, 16, 20, 34, 41; *Dignitatis Humanae* 3. The Latin term *colloquium*, often translated "discussion," is used more widely.

29. Vischer, *Documentary History*, 28.

30. Ibid., 86.

31. "Ecumenical Dialogue," *Information Service* 1 (1967): 33–36.

32. Ibid., 35.

33. "Reflections and Suggestions Concerning Ecumenical Dialogue," in *Vatican Council II: The Conciliar and Post Conciliar Documents*, ed. Austin Flannery, rev. ed. (Northrop, N.Y.: Costello; Dublin: Dominican, 1992); also in *Ecumenical Documents I: Doing the Truth in Charity* (1964–1980), ed. Thomas F. Stranksy, CSP, and John B. Sheerin, CSP (New York: Paulist Press, 1982), 75–88.

34. "Reflections and Suggestions Concerning Dialogue," V.2.b.

35. John Paul II, *Reconciliatio et Paenitentia* (1984), 25. He affirmed that ecumenical and interreligious dialogue by Catholics and "dialogue within the church" take place in pursuit of reconciliation "in the midst of many conflicts." He insisted that the necessary positive characteristics of these dialogues for promoting reconciliation would not be present "if the magisterium were not heeded and accepted."

36. John Paul II, "Tertio Millennio Adveniente," *Origins* 24 (November 24, 1994): 401–16; idem, *Ut Unum Sint* (Boston: St. Paul Books & Media, 1995).

37. The Pontifical Council for Promoting Christian Unity issued "The Ecumenical Formation of Pastoral Workers" in 1998. This document elaborates in part 1 key elements for the ecumenical dimension of each theological discipline, an ecumenical methodology, and practical advice, and in part 2 proposes certain teachings in ecumenism. On training in dialogue, it directs attention to *Ut Unum Sint* (28–39) and *Directory* (nos. 172–82; see n. 40 below).

38. "Ecumenical Documents: A Report of the Bilateral Study Group of the Faith and Order Commission of the National Council of Churches," ed. John Ford, *Mid-Stream* 28 (1989): 115–36.

39. Ibid., 115.

40. Ibid., no. 34. The Pontifical Council for Promoting Christian Unity issued the revised *Directory for the Application of Principles and Norms on Ecumenism* in 1993. The original *Directory* was issued in two installments in 1967 and 1969, but the "Reflections and Suggestions Concerning Ecumenical Dialogue" were not included as part 3 as was originally proposed. The revised text has incorporated a short discussion on dialogue (nos. 172–82) treating many themes that have previously been discussed. The Joint Working Group between the Roman Catholic Church and the World Council of Churches issued a study document on ecumenical formation in 1993, which described the ecumenical imperative, what is meant by ecumenical formation, and how it can be realized.

41. A range of aims was identified in Ehrenstrom and Gassmann, *Confessions in Dialogue*, 124–26. The Institute for Ecumenical Research in Strasbourg, France, discussed multiple dimensions of the one goal of unity in the church in *Crisis and Challenge of the Ecumenical Movement: Integrity and Indivisibility* (Geneva: WCC, 1994), 23–34. Harding Meyer distinguishes the aim of the ecumenical movement in terms of the unity of Christians and the perception of the aim in terms of various models of union, in *That All May Be One: Perceptions and Models of Ecumenicity* (Grand Rapids, Mich.: Eerdmans, 1999), 3–5.

42. *The Second World Conference of Faith and Order* (Edinburgh: Lothian, 1937), 231–32, cited in *Ecumenical Movement*, 465–68.

43. Vischer, *Documentary History*, 85–86.

44. Section 3 on Unity (par. 2) from *The New Delhi Report: The Third Assembly of the World Council of Churches, 1961*, ed. W. A. Visser 't Hooft (London: SCM, 1962), 116, cited in *Documentary History*, Gassmann, 3.

45. Faith and Order Commission, "The Unity of the Church as Koinonia: Gift and Calling," in World Council of Churches, *Signs of the Spirit: Official Report Seventh Assembly* (Canberra), ed. Michael Kinnamon (Geneva: WCC; Grand Rapids: Eerdmans, 1991), no. 1.2, p. 172. For a discussion of these various levels of union, see Gros, MacManus, and Riggs, *Introduction to Ecumenism*, 123–24.

46. "Unity of the Church as Koinonia," no. 2.1, p. 173.

47. At the first meeting of the ad hoc Forum on Bilateral Conversations of the Faith and Order Secretariat, the first condition for advancing conciliar fellowship was identified as "ending prejudices and hostilities and lifting condemnations" (*Three Reports of the Forum on Bilateral Conversations*, Faith and Order Paper no. 107 [Geneva: WCC, 1981], 9).

48. The Groupe des Dombes, which includes Catholics and Protestants in France, has emphasized the importance of ongoing conversion. See Groupe des Dombes, *For the Conversion of the Churches* (Geneva: WCC, 1993).

49. Avery Dulles has developed a particular theological method for identifying distinctive models of theology over the course of his theological career. Examples of this approach are best represented in his works *Models of the Church* (Garden City, N.Y.: Doubleday, 1974), and *Models of Revelation* (Garden City, N.Y.: Doubleday, 1983), but they are also in evidence in *The Assurance of Things Hoped For: A Theology of Christian Faith* (New York: Oxford University Press, 1994), and *The Craft of Theology: From Symbol to System* (New York: Crossroad, 1992), 46–52.

50. Avery Dulles, "Paths to Doctrinal Agreement: Ten Theses," *Theological Studies* 47 (1986): 32–47, at 43–44. Other statements by Dulles move in a different direction, for

example, his tenth thesis: "For the sake of doctrinal agreement, the binding formulations of each tradition must be carefully scrutinized and jointly affirmed with whatever modifications, explanations, or reservations are required in order to appease the legitimate misgivings of the partner churches. This may require a measure of reformation" (p. 46).

51. Avery Dulles, "Method in Ecumenical Theology," in *Craft of Theology*, 179–95, at 183, 187.

52. Ibid., 187.

53. Ibid., 190. For Dulles the first phase of ecumenical dialogue was devoted to ecumenists surfacing "hidden agreements in their previous disagreements," whereas during the second phase ecumenists "are exposing hidden disagreements in their previous agreements. . . . After working for a generation to build up mutual confidence and friendship, the dialogues have matured to the point at which divisive issues may now be squarely faced. The theologians are today eager to explore the most neuralgic issues with a frank recognition that the prospects of full agreement are minimal" (pp. 191–92).

54. George Tavard, "The Bi-lateral Dialogues: Searching for Language," and "The Bi-lateral Dialogues: Speaking Together," in *One in Christ* 16 (1980): 19–30, 30–42; idem, "Lessons of Ecumenism for Catholic Theology," *One in Christ* 27 (1991): 346–51. I am leaving aside the larger methodological framework developed by Tavard in these essays, which is further elaborated in his book *La théologie parmi les sciences humaines: De la méthode en théologie* (Paris: Beauchesne, 1975).

55. George Tavard, review of *The Craft of Theology: From Symbol to System*, in *Dialogue & Alliance* 7 (1993): 142–46.

56. Tavard, review of *Craft of Theology*, 146.

57. Konrad Raiser, *Ecumenism in Transition: A Paradigm Shift in the Ecumenical Movement?* (Geneva: WCC, 1991), 79. The original German edition, *Ökumene im Übergang*, appeared in 1989.

58. Raiser, *Ecumenism in Transition*, 79.

59. Ibid., 106.

60. Here Raiser quotes from J. Brosseder, "Gemeinschaft zuerst leben, dann darüber reden!" in *Ökumenische am Ort* 9 (1984): 5ff., in Raiser, *Ecumenism in Transition*, 106.

61. See the critique of Lesslie Newbigin, former general secretary of the International Missionary Council, "Ecumenical Amnesia," *International Bulletin of Missionary Research* 18, no. 1 (January 1994): 2–5; Konrad Raiser, "Is Ecumenical Apologetics Sufficient? A Response to Lesslie Newbigin's 'Ecumenical Amnesia'" and Lesslie Newbigin, "Reply to Konrad Raiser," in *International Bulletin of Missionary Research*, 18, no. 2 (April 1994): 50–52. The statement by the Institute for Ecumenical Research in Strasbourg, *Crisis and Challenge of the Ecumenical Movement*, did not solely target Raiser's book, but the central argument does strike at the heart of his position. "To guard against th[e] splintering of the ecumenical movement [according to diverse dimensions of the one goal], we do not need a new, but rather *a more integrated vision of the ecumenical endeavor*. As the unity of the church is multidimensional, inclusive, and catholic so must ecumenical effort itself be multidimensional, inclusive, and catholic, if it is to correspond to and realize the unity it seeks" (p. 38).

62. See Konrad Raiser, "The Nature and Purpose of Ecumenical Dialogue: Proposal for a Study," *Ecumenical Review* 52 (2000): 287–92; and Walter Kasper, "The Nature and Purpose of Ecumenical Dialogue," *Ecumenical Review* 52 (2000): 293–99.

63. "The Nature and Purpose of Ecumenical Dialogue: A JWG Study," in *Joint Working Group Between the Roman Catholic Church and the World Council of Churches: Eighth Report 1999–2005* (Geneva: WCC, 2005), 73–89. In the body of the text I will cite the paragraph numbers.

64. Ehrenstrom and Gassmann indicated in *Confessions in Dialogue* that "the meaning of consensus and dissensus has not been clarified in ecumenical dialogues (p. 133). The Strasbourg Institute report, *Crisis and Challenge of the Ecumenical Movement*, discusses problems of reception of consensus documents (10–11) and hardening differences (15–18). A taxonomy of levels of agreement has emerged: convergence, substantial agreement, internally differentiated consensus, full consensus, and sufficient agreement that the issue is no longer seen as church dividing. One often finds that convergence has been found, but differences remain. A basic consensus (*Grundkonsensus*) has taken place, but without a reconciliation of remaining differences. It has become increasingly evident that somehow individuals and churches must be able to affirm consensus and differences (dissensus) at the same time. In response, the Lutheran ecumenist Harding Meyer proposed the formula: "differentiated consensus." See Harding Meyer, "Grundkonsensus und Kirchegemeinschaft: Eine lutherische Perspektive," in *Grundkonsens–Grunddifferenz: Studie des Straßburger Instituts für Ökumenische Forschung Ergebnisse und Dokumente*, ed. André Birmelé and Harding Meyer (Frankfurt am Main: Verlag Otto Lembeck, 1992), 126, cf. 43, 48; see also *Einheit–aber wie? Zur Tragfähigkeit der ökumenischen Formel vom "differenzierten Konsens,"* ed. Harald Wagner, Quaestiones Disputatae 184 (Freiburg/Basel/Vienna: Herder, 2000).

65. Hermeneutical issues in ecumenical dialogues have received considerable attention since the Fifth Faith and Order Conference in Santiago de Compostela in 1993, which initiated a five-year study on these issues that was approved in 1998, "A Treasure in Earthen Vessels: An Instrument for an Ecumenical Reflection on Hermeneutics," in *Interpreting Together: Essays in Hermeneutics*, ed. Peter Bouteneff and Dagmar Heller (Geneva: WCC, 2001), 134–60.

66. Two of the more recent documents which address the issue of authority can be found in *The Nature and Purpose of the Church*, Faith and Order Paper no. 181 (Geneva: WCC/Faith and Order, 1998), and *The Gift of Authority: Authority in the Church III* (New York: Church Publishing; London: Anglican–Roman Catholic International Commission, Catholic Truth Society; Toronto: Anglican Book Centre, 1999).

9. RETHINKING THE OLDEST DIVISIONS IN THE INTERESTS OF LARGER TRUTHS AND LASTING PEACE

1. See the work of Richard Hughes Seager, *The Dawn of Religious Pluralism: Voices from the World's Parliament of Religions, 1893* (La Salle, Ill.: Open Court, 1993); idem, *The World's Parliament of Religions: The East/West Encounter, Chicago, 1893* (Bloomington, Ind.: Indiana University Press, 1995).

2. Hendrik Kraemer, *Why Christianity of All Religions?* (London: Lutterworth Press, 1962), 104, cited by Stanley J. Samartha, "Mission in a Religiously Plural World: Looking Beyond Tambaram 1938," *International Review of Mission* 77 (1988): 311–24, at 312. The proceedings from a consultation commemorating the fiftieth anniversary of Tambaram in 1988 are located in volume 77 of the *International Review of Mission.* In addition, see Carl F. Hallencreutz, "A Long-Standing Concern: Dialogue in Ecumenical History 1910–1971," in *Living Faiths and the Ecumenical Movement,* ed. S. J. Samartha (Geneva: WCC, 1971), 57–71, at 59–60.

3. Gérard Vallée, "The World of God and the Living Faiths of Men: Chronology and Bibliography of a Study-Process," in *Living Faiths and the Ecumenical Movement,* ed. S. J. Samartha (Geneva: WCC, 1971), 165–82, at 174.

4. Victor E. W. Hayward, "Consultation among Christians from the Muslim World: Broumana, Lebanon, June 1966," in *Christians Meeting Muslims: WCC Papers on Ten Years of Christian-Muslim Dialogue* (Geneva: WCC, 1977), 13.

5. The Kandy Declaration, "Christians in Dialogue with Men of Other Faiths," can be found in *Study Encounter* 3, no. 2 (1967): 52–56.

6. See "Renewal in Mission," in section 2 of the Fourth Assembly, Uppsala, par. 6, reprinted in *Ecumenical Review* 21 (1969): 368. During this time Stanley J. Samartha was appointed associate secretary in the Department on Studies in Mission and Evangelism and took charge of Living Faith project.

7. *Jewish–Christian Dialogue: Six Years of Christian Jewish Consultations* (Geneva: WCC, 1975); "The Church and the Jewish People," in *Faith and Order Studies 1964–1967* (Geneva: WCC, 1968), 69–80.

8. "Christian/Muslim Conversations organized by the Commission of Faith and Order, World Council of Churches, Summary of Results, Cartigny, March 2–6, 1969," in *Christians Meeting Muslims,* 67–70.

9. "Dialogue Between Men of Living Faiths: The Ajaltoun Memorandum" (1970), in *Dialogue Between Men of Living Faiths*; Papers presented at a Consultation held at Ajaltoun, Lebanon, March 1970, ed. S. J. Samartha (Geneva: WCC, 1971), 107–17, at 107; also in *Living Faiths and the Ecumenical Movement,* 15–32, at 16.

10. "Christians in Dialogue with Men of Other Faiths," in *Living Faiths and the Ecumenical Movement,* 33–45, at 34.

11. Ibid., 36.

12. Ibid., 43.

13. Metropolitan George Khodr, "Christianity in a Pluralist World–the Economy of the Holy Spirit," and S. J. Samaratha, "Dialogue as a Continuing Christian Concern," found in *Living Faiths and the Ecumenical Movement,* 131–42, 143–58.

14. The Dialogue Working Group met for the first time March 19–24, 1973, in Pendeli, near Athens. For the work of this group, see Robert B. Sheard, *Interreligious Dialogue in the Catholic Church Since Vatican II: An Historical and Theological Study* (Lewiston, N.Y.: Edwin Mellon Press, 1987), 197–99, 211–15, 257–62.

15. The dialogues between Jews and Christians associated with the World Council of Churches had been taking place under the aegis of the Faith and Order Secretariat, and

initially they had sponsored dialogues with Muslims. This was subsequently taken over by the subunit on dialogue with peoples of living faiths. See the Joint Memorandum "In Search of Understanding and Cooperation: Christian and Muslim Contributions, Broumana, Lebanon, July 1972," *Meeting in Faith: Twenty Years of Christian–Muslim Conversations Sponsored by the World Council of Churches*, compiled by Stuart E. Brown (Geneva: WCC, 1989), 21–29.

16. See the Ibadan Memorandum, "The Wholeness of Human Life: Christian Involvement in Mankind's Inner Dialogue with Primal World-Views," *Study Encounter* 9/4 (1973): 1–20, at 2, cited in Sheard, *Interreligious Dialogue in the Catholic Church*, 202. Klaus Klostermaier, in the very first paper delivered at the Ajaltoun Consultation in 1971, spoke of an "inner dialogue" that must precede and prepare the way for "outward dialogue."

17. Christian–Muslim in Beirut, Lebanon, November 1977; Christian–Buddhist in Colombo, Sri Lanka, February 1978; and on primal worldviews among Christians in Yaoundé, Cameroon, in September 1978.

18. *Towards World Community: The Colombo Papers*, ed. S. J. Samartha (Geneva: WCC, 1975). A major bilateral dialogue between forty-six Christians and Muslims took place in Broumana, Lebanon, in 1972; see *Christian–Muslim Dialogue* (Geneva: WCC, 1973).

19. *Towards World Community*, 120.

20. See "Section III: Seeking Community: The Common Search of People of Various Faiths, Cultures, and Ideologies," in *Breaking Barriers: Nairobi, 1975: The Fifth Assembly of the World Council of Churches*, ed. David M. Paton (London: SPCK; Grand Rapids: Eerdmans, 1976), 70–85; also *Nairobi to Vancouver: 1975–1983 Report of the Central Committee to the Sixth Assembly of the World Council of Churches* (Geneva: WCC, 1983), 107–15.

21. S. J. Samartha, "Dialogue in Community: A Step Forward, An Interpretation of the Chiang Mai Consultation," in *Faith in the Midst of Faiths: Reflections on Dialogue in Community*, ed. S. J. Samartha (Geneva: WCC, 1977), 183–90, at 187.

22. *Nairobi to Vancouver*, 107–15; *Vancouver to Canberra: 1983–1990, Report of the Central Committee to the Seventh Assembly of the World Council of Churches* (Geneva: WCC, 1990), 130–40; *From Canberra to Harare: An Illustrated Account of the Life of the World Council of Churches, 1991–1998* (Geneva: WCC, 1998), 47–48.

23. "Ecumenical Considerations on Jewish-Christian Dialogue," *Ecumenical Review* 35 (1983): 297–302.

24. *The Meaning of Life: A Multifaith Consultation* (Geneva: WCC, 1983).

25. Marlin VanElderen, *From Canberra to Harare*, 47, cited by Douglas Pratt, "The Dance of Dialogue: Ecumenical Inter-religious Engagement," in *Ecumenical Review* 51 (1999): 274–87, at 284.

26. *Gathered for Life: Official Report VI Assembly World Council of Churches*, ed. David Gill (Geneva: WCC; Grand Rapids: Eerdmans, 1983), 31–42, at 40 (par. 41 b).

27. Quotation from Jan Hendrik Pranger, *Dialogue in Discussion: The World Council of Churches and the Challenge of Religious Plurality between 1967 and 1979* (Leiden: IIMO Research Publication, 1994), 164; cited in Pratt, "Dance of Dialogue," 284.

28. World Council of Churches, *Signs of the Spirit: Official Report Seventh Assembly*, ed. Michael Kinnamoon (Geneva: WCC; Grand Rapids: Eerdmans, 1991); the *International*

Review of Mission devoted one issue to examining the mission implications at the seventh assembly in vol. 80 in 1991.

29. Obstacles in interreligious dialogue were addressed at the consultation on "International and Global Inter-religious Initiatives" held in Tao Fong Shan, Hong Kong, with Buddhist, Christian, Hindu, Jewish, Muslim, and Sikh participants in April 2002, and at the international multilateral assembly devoted to the topic "Critical Moment in Interreligious Dialogue in Geneva" in June 2005. See above all the document of the World Council of Churches, *Ecumenical Considerations for Dialogue and Relations with People of Other Religions: Taking Stock of 30 Years of Dialogue and Revisiting the 1979 Guidelines* (Geneva: WCC, 2003).

30. See Arthur Gilbert, *The Vatican Council and the Jews* (Cleveland/New York: World Publishing Company, 1968).

31. To repeat what was noted in the previous chapter, the Latin term *dialogus* was used in the following texts from Vatican II, *Unitatis Redintegratio*, nos. 4, 9, 11, 14, 18, 19, 21, 22, 23; *Ad Gentes*, nos. 11, 12, 16, 20, 34, 41; *Dignitatis Humanae*, no. 3; *Gaudium et spes*, nos. 40, 43, 56, 92. The Latin term *colloquium*, often translated "discussion," is used more widely.

32. In 1970 the International Jewish Committee on Interreligious Consultations (IJCIC) was founded, which included representatives from the American Jewish Committee, the Anti-Defamation League of the B'nai B'rith, the Jewish Council of Israel on Interreligious Consultations, the Synagogue Council of America, and the World Jewish Congress. This committee met with representatives of various curial offices in December 1970 and composed the "Memorandum of Understanding," which established a framework for the International Catholic–Jewish Liaison Committee. The Catholic members of this liaison committee have been selected by the president of the Secretariat for Promoting Christian Unity and approved by the pope. This group has met almost yearly. In 1979 a formal dialogue between the Synagogue Council of America and the U.S. Conference of Catholic Bishops was started and has met twice yearly for over two decades. For the "Memorandum of Understanding," see International Catholic–Jewish Committee, *Fifteen Years of Catholic–Jewish Dialogue 1970–1985: Selected Papers* (Rome: Liberia Editrice Vaticana, Pontificia Università Lateranense, 1988).

33. For an overview of Catholic–Jewish dialogues, see Eugene J. Fisher and Leon Klenicki, *In Our Time: The Flowering of Jewish–Catholic Dialogue* (New York: Paulist Press, 1990); and Eugene J. Fisher, "Christian–Jewish Relations: An Historical Overview and Prognosis," in *Peace, in Deed: Essays in Honor of Harry James Cargas*, ed. Zev Garber and Richard Libowitz, South Florida Studies in the History of Judaism 162 (Atlanta: Scholars Press, 1998), 163–77.

34. For reports on interreligious dialogues and the work of the Pontifical Council for Interreligious Dialogue, see the report *Pro Dialogo*, formerly *Bulletin Pontificium Consilium Pro Dialogo Inter Religiones*.

35. The Pontifical Institute of Arabic and Islamic Studies was established during this period and sponsored the publication of the journals *Islamochristiana* (established in 1975), *Encounter* (1974), and *Etudes Arabes* (on Islamic religion and society).

36. International Muslim–Catholic dialogues initiated or cosponsored by the Secre-

tariat: in Cairo (1970, 1974, 1978); Luxembourg (1974); Vienna (1976); Rome (1974, 1985); Bamako, Mali (1974). A special dialogue took place with 350 Muslims and 150 Christians in Tripoli, Libya, in February 1976.

37. In 1981 a significantly revised edition of the *Guidelines for Dialogue between Christians and Muslims*, which was originally published in 1970, was written by Maurice Borrmans for the Pontifical Council for Interreligious Dialogue and includes an annotated list of Muslim–Christian dialogues that took place between 1969 and 1989 organized by various institutions, translated from the French by R. Marston Speight (Mahwah, N.J.: Paulist Press, 1990). Also see Pontifical Council for Interreligious Dialogue, *Recognize the Spiritual Bonds Which Unite Us: 16 Years of Christian–Muslim Dialogue* (Vatican City: Pontifical Council for Interreligious Dialogue, 1994).

38. The Pontifical Council for Interreligious Dialogue sponsored regional dialogues in Assisi, Italy, in 1988 with participants from six North African nations: Mauritania, Morocco, Algeria, Tunisia, Libya, and Egypt; a second was held in Ibadan, Nigeria, in 1991 with representatives from Gambia, Ghana, Nigeria, and Sierra Leone; and a third was held in Pattaya, Southeast Asia, in 1994 with Muslims from Brunei, Indonesia, Malaysia, Philippines, Singapore, and Thailand. The Pontifical Council for Interreligious Dialogue has jointly organized a series of seminars with the Royal Academy for Islamic Civilization Research of Amman, Jordan, 1989–1994.

39. There were Buddhist–Christian Colloquia cosponsored by the Secretariat in Kaohsiung, Taiwan (1995), Bangalore, India (1998), and Tokyo, Japan (2002).

40. The contribution of the Federation of Asian Bishops' Conferences (FABC) to interreligious dialogue merits its own investigation. They have been recognized especially for advocating a triple dialogue with Asian religions, cultures, and people, especially the poor. They sponsored the Bishops' Institute for Interreligious Dialogue, which met about every year to discuss one religious tradition during the 1980s, and they conducted nine meetings to develop a theology of dialogue between 1984 and 1991, which is recorded in *For All the Peoples of Asia: Federation of Asian Bishops' Conferences, Documents from 1970 to 1991*, ed. Gaudencio B. Rosales and C. G. Arévalo (Maryknoll, N.Y.: Orbis Books; Diliman, Quezon City, Philippines: Claretian, 1992). Also see "Theses on Interreligious Dialogue," in FABC Paper no. 48, cited in *Dialogue? Resource Manual for Catholics in Asia*, ed. Edmund Chia (Bangkok, Thailand: Federation of Asian Bishops' Conferences, Office of Ecumenical and Interreligious Affairs, 2001), 85–97. Also an invaluable resource on this topic is *The Asian Synod: Texts and Commentaries*, ed. Peter C. Phan (Maryknoll, N.Y.: Orbis Books, 2002).

41. Catholic–Buddhist dialogues in the United States were cosponsored by the National (Catholic) Association of Diocesan Ecumenical Officers in Malibu, California (1998), and in Graymoor, Garrison, New York (2003).

42. Secretariat for Non-Christian Religions, *Towards the Meeting of Religions: Suggestions for Dialogue: General Section* (Washington, D.C.: United States Catholic Conference, 1967); *Guidelines for a Dialogue between Muslims and Christians* (Rome: Ancora, 1969); *Meeting the African Religions* (Rome: Ancora, 1969); *Toward the Meeting with Buddhism*, 2 vols. (Rome: Ancora, 1970); *For a Dialogue with Hinduism* (Rome: Ancora, 1970); *Reli-*

gions: Fundamental Themes for a Dialogistic Understanding (Rome: Ancora, 1970). My analysis draws on the first installment and Sheard's discussion in *Interreligious Dialogue in the Catholic Church*, 54–80.

43. *Towards the Meeting of Religions*, 10.

44. *For a Dialogue with Hinduism*, 109, as quoted in Sheard, *Interreligious Dialogue in the Catholic Church*, 61.

45. *Towards the Meeting of Religions*, 46–47.

46. Secretariat for Non-Christian Religions, "The Church and Other Religions: Reflections and Orientations on Dialogue and Mission," in *The Pope Speaks* 29 (1984): 253–64. For the original Italian text, see *Acta Apostolicae Sedis* 76 (1984): 816–28.

47. "The Church and Other Religions," 256.

48. Ibid., 258 (no. 21).

49. *Redemptoris Missio* and *Dialogue and Proclamation* are published with a set of commentaries as *Redemption and Dialogue*, ed. William R. Burrows (Maryknoll, N.Y.: Orbis Books, 1993); see, in particular, the comparative analysis of the two documents offered by Jacques Dupuis, "A Theological Commentary: *Dialogue and Proclamation*," 119–58.

50. Pope John Paul II, "Tertio Millennio Adveniente," *Origins* 24 (November 24, 1994): 401–16, at no. 18, makes an indirect allusion to the *Shoah* and the corresponding need for *the world* to be purified and pursue conversion. No explicit mention of the Jews is made in this document, although there is reference to the counter witness and scandal of members of the church, past errors, instances of infidelity, inconsistency, and slowness to act (nos. 32, 33, 34).

51. The pope stated in a 1987 letter to the president of the U.S. Conference of Bishops that "there is no doubt that the sufferings inflicted upon the Jews are also for the Catholic Church a reason for deep sorrow." See Luigi Accattoli, *When a Pope Asks Forgiveness: The Mea Culpa's of John Paul II* (Boston: Pauline Books & Media, 1998), 118; Pope John Paul II, *Spiritual Pilgrimage: Texts on Jews and Judaism 1979–1995,* ed. Eugene J. Fischer and Leon Klenicki (New York: Crossroad, 1995), 100–101.

52. Cardinal Edward Idris Cassidy, "The Vatican Document on the Holocaust: Reflections Toward a New Millennium," in *Ethics in the Shadow of the Holocaust: Christian and Jewish Perspectives,* ed. Judith H. Banki and John T. Pawlikowski (Franklin, Wis.: Sheed & Ward, 2001), 7.

53. The Historical-Theological Commission of the Committee for the Great Jubilee of the Year 2000 sponsored a three-day international symposium on "The Roots of Anti-Judaism in the Christian Milieu" (October 30, 31, November 1, 1997), which was attended by more than sixty Catholic bishops, theologians, and experts, with representatives from Protestant and Orthodox communions. There is no indication of Jewish observers or participants. The International Catholic–Jewish Historical Commission composed of three Catholic scholars and three Jewish scholars was established to examine the eleven volumes of archival materials published by the Holy See's Secretariat of State between 1965 and 1981. In October of 2000 their preliminary report raised questions about the document and a request for further documents and information from the archives. A dissatisfying response to this request resulted in the decision to suspend its research. Walter Kasper, the

prefect of the Pontifical Council for Promoting Christian Unity and the Commission for Religious Relations with the Jews issued a communiqué on this suspension on August 24, 2001.

54. Statements surrounding the fiftieth anniversary of the *Shoah* were made by episcopal conferences in Europe (Hungarian, German, Polish, Dutch, Swiss, French, and Italian), in the United States, and from the Holy See; see Secretariat for Ecumenical and Interreligious Affairs, National Conference of Catholic Bishops, *Catholics Remember the Holocaust* (Washington, D.C.: United States Catholic Conference, 1998).

55. See the statement by the National Jewish Scholars Project, "Dabru Emet: A Jewish Statement on Christians and Christianity," available in *Origins* 30 (September 21, 2000): 225–28.

56. The International Council of Christians and Jews issued a statement in response to the papal apology on March 15, 2000, in which they judged that "the content did not go as far as past statements of the Church, national Bishops' Conferences and Pope John Paul II himself" and lacked "an unambiguous reference to the church's guilt in relation to individual groups of victims in this liturgical language of admission of guilt." These are acts not only of individuals, nor of Christians in general, but the Church has "institutional historic guilt and responsibility."

57. Cardinal Cassidy and the International Theological Commission's statement "Memory and Reconciliation: The Church and the Faults of the Past" (December 1999) have reaffirmed this position, although Cassidy has acknowledged that the claim that the institutional church is not responsible for anti-Judaism is an ongoing point of contention between Jews and Catholics.

58. Accattoli, *When a Pope Asks Forgiveness*, 85.

59. Cited in ibid., 186.

60. Cited in ibid., 187–88.

61. Cited in ibid., 188.

62. "Dominus Iesus": On the Unicity and Salvific Universality of Jesus Christ and the Church," *Origins* 30 (September 14, 2000): 209–19, at 212.

63. Cardinal Joseph Ratzinger, "Relativism: The Central Problem for Faith Today," *Origins* 26 (October 31, 1996): 309–17.

10. LESSONS AND LAMENTS AND THE UNFINISHED AGENDA OF A DIALOGICAL CHURCH

1. Edward Schillebeeckx, *Church: The Human Story of God*, trans. John Bowden (New York: Crossroad, 1990), 5.

2. Michel Lefebvre, *Lettre ouverte aux catholiques perplexes* (Parish: Michel, 1985), 132, cited by Joseph Komonchak in "Interpreting the Council: Catholic Attitudes toward Vatican II," in *Being Right: Conservative Catholics in America*, ed. Mary Jo Weaver and R. Scott Appleby (Bloomington/Indianapolis: Indiana University Press, 1995), 17–36, at 25; see also Komonchak, "Modernity and the Construction of Roman Catholicism," *Cristianesimo*

nella storia 18 (1997): 353–85; and Daniele Menozzi, "Opposition to the Council (1966–1984)," in *The Reception of Vatican II* (Washington, D.C.: Catholic University of America Press, 1987), 325–48; for another representative of this position, see Anne Roche Muggeridge, *The Desolate City: Revolution in the Catholic Church* (San Francisco: Harper-SanFrancisco, 1990).

3. David Nygren, CM, and Miriam Ukeritis, CSJ, "Future of Religious Orders in the United States," Research Executive Summary, *Origins* (September 24, 1992): 267.

4. There are analogous cases in political situations. The work of the Truth and Reconciliation Commission in South Africa offers a moving example. See Desmond Tutu, *No Future Without Forgiveness* (New York: Doubleday, 1999).

5. I have analyzed Dulles's position in chapter 5 on the Catholic Common Ground Initiative. See his essays "The Travails of Dialogue," the Laurence J. McGinley Lecture (Fordham University, November 19, 1996), manuscript, pp. 1–20; idem, "Dialogue, Truth, and Communion," The Third Annual Catholic Common Ground Initiative lecture (June 22, 2001).

6. Bernard Lonergan, "Transition from a Classicist World View to Historical Mindedness," in *Law for Liberty: The Role of Law in the Church Today*, ed. James E. Biechler (Baltimore: Helicon, 1967), 126–33; reprinted in Bernard Lonergan, *A Second Collection*, ed. William F. J. Ryan and Bernard Tyrrell (Philadelphia: Westminster Press, 1975), 1–9.

7. There is a range of influential North American philosophers and social theorists who contribute to this topic: Richard Rorty, Calvin Schrag, Charles Taylor, and Iris Marion Young, just to mention a few.

8. Mikhail Bakhtin, "Discourse in the Novel," in *The Dialogic Imagination*, ed. Michael Holquist, trans. Caryl Emerson and Michael Holquist (Austin: University of Texas Press, 1981), 259–422; see glossary, 426–27.

9. This is a reference to Bonaventure's classic work "The Journey of the Mind to God," sometimes translated "The Soul's Journey to God." See Bonaventure, *Itinerarium mentis in Deum*: Latin text from the Quaracchi ed., English trans. Zachary Hayes, introduction and commentary by Philotheus Boehner (St. Bonaventure, N.Y.: Franciscan Institute, Saint Bonaventure University, 2002).

Index